365
Days of
Gardening

365

Days of

Gardening

A Day-by-Day Book of More Than 1000

Terrific Facts, Tips, and Reminders

CHRISTINE ALLISON

📖 HarperCollins*Publishers*

A JOHN BOSWELL ASSOCIATES BOOK

This book is dedicated
to my grandmother, Yasuyo Kawamura,
in whose garden I first trampled

HarperCollins books may be purchased for educational, business, or sales
promotional use. For information please write: Special Markets Department,
HarperCollins Publishers, Inc., 10 East 53rd Street, New York, NY 10022.

FIRST EDITION

Design: Barbara Cohen Aronica
Illustrations: Madeline Sorel
Index: Maro Riofrancos

ISBN 0-06-017032-8

95 96 97 98 99   10 9 8 7 6 5 4 3 2 1

❧ Contents ❧

❦ *A c k n o w l e d g m e n t s* ❦

The list of contributors to this book is a long one but my editor Larry Ashmead should be thanked first. Larry came up with the idea of a book of days filled with gardening tips and advice. It is impossible to describe the care with which he nurtured me and the book during its two years in the making. If this is how he treats authors, I would love to see his garden.

In researching 365 *Days of Gardening,* Tom Peterson of Louisville, Colorado, was responsible for the core of the book, not only culling libraries and botanical gardens for data but helping to form the book's structure. His research and fact-checking were first-rate. Working with Tom was pure pleasure and, to put it plainly, there would be no 365 *Days of Gardening* without him.

I worked closely with the New York Botanical Garden, which has a wonderful library where I spent many winter afternoons, nosing around and double-checking my own experiences against those of other gardeners. I am grateful to the librarians there and also to the staff at the Larchmont Public Library who helped me to chase down numerous odd pieces of data; the Larchmont library has helped me to make many books and I am in its debt.

Michael Stanton of Nabel's Nurseries Inc. in White Plains, New York, was a fount of information, much of which circuitously ended up in this book. Over the years I have called him with the strangest and no doubt stupidest questions about plants, and he has always been always extremely knowledgeable and generous with his answers and advice.

Copyediting this book was no easy matter but editors Delores Simon and Amy Handy added to the project enormously. Both are gardeners, which made a big difference, and I am grateful for their contributions.

Jason Kaufman walked into this project just as it was about to bloom and took over the production and marketing of the book with a rare intensity. I hope to work with him again.

I am particularly indebted to Barbara Aronica. Barbara's intelligence and exuberance are reflected in the design, and she did a sensational job. Her design is a neat fit with Madeline Sorel's warm and pleasing illustrations.

Patty Brown put the entire project together and it was not easy. But Patty made it look easy, and she always does. After working with her for ten years, I am still in awe. Thanks also to Ward Calhoun for consistent good cheer and to John Boswell for being my friend.

Ginny Bauer and Karen Goodwin gave me enormous personal support (picture me a broken delphinium without them). Deborah Trumpet maintained serenity and order in our home. My mother-in-law, Jenny Lea Allison, sent me books and news clippings and her own advice from Texas, always underlined and exclamation-pointed.

My mother, Marie Peterson, has grown plants and children all her life. She gives her plants the same devotion she gives her children, tending us with love and appreciating us even when we are a little brown around the edges. I would hope that her attitude permeates this book.

My father, John Peterson, actually edited 365 *Days of Gardening*. Sitting at a desk near mine, he reviewed and questioned every page. The smart-aleck remarks were plentiful. I bore them only because his queries were so thoughtful. He is not only a natural father, but a natural editor. Thank you, Dad.

My gratitude to all named and unnamed, and not least to my husband, Wick, and my daughters, Gillea, Maisie, Chrissie, and Loddie, whom I love even more than my garden.

❧ *I n t r o d u c t i o n* ❧

This book comes to you through the generosity of hundreds of gardeners who shared their secrets and hard-earned tips over many seasons. I collected their successes and failures as a hobby, much as some gardeners collect antique roses, daylilies, heirloom seeds, or slugs. The gardeners ranged from neighbors to strangers to famous garden writers to Amish farmers to rhododendron breeders, and my 98-year-old Japanese grandmother. I tested all but a handful of the suggestions in this book and, as you can imagine, I came across some pretty weird tips. You would be amazed at what some people will do to grow a perfect tomato.

365 Days of Gardening covers a broad range of subjects in brief passages, to remind you of what needs to be done in the garden, to inspire you to experiment with a new technique, to entertain you with a piece of trivia, and to educate you on ways to use home remedies in the garden. The ambition of this book is to be your friend, a light-hearted, knowledgeable companion throughout the gardening year. Assuming it's your copy, I hope you will write in the margins and take notes, underline, sketch—do whatever you can to make this a working companion. It's a book to be read not straight through but bits at a time, year after year. I like the idea that you and I would spend every January together, in front of a fireplace, with our catalogues and our dreams.

WHAT IF YOU DON'T HAVE A FIREPLACE? • This book was written from a Northeastern perspective. It was unavoidable: I live in a village on the Long Island Sound, outside of New York City. I do have several zones under my belt, having gardened in Louisville, Ann Arbor, Key West, Dallas, on a New York City terrace, and near a trout stream in the Catskill Mountains. I know firsthand that there is no such thing as "April" from one zone to the next, or even within my own state.

I also know that we should be faithful to where we live. After three failed seasons of trying to grow Texas bluebonnets in the Catskill Mountains, I asked Lady Bird Johnson, patron saint of wildflowers, for some advice. "Don't," she said, her expression revealing amazement that anyone would even try.

Regardless of where we live, I wanted this book to be a book of days because we are gardeners all year long, not just when the tulips are blooming or when the tomatoes are ripe. And despite the different climates among us, all journeys in the garden are cyclical. I simply hope that in reading through *my* journey there will be information and advice of value, even if we prune our spring-flowering trees two months apart. I didn't time the entries in this book to correspond precisely to any one zone but to give a sense of movement and change throughout the gardening year. If you experience four separate and distinct seasons, we will be more or less in sync, though I realize there will be many gaps in our experiences.

Gardening is a spiritual undertaking for me; not a crutch or an obsession, but the very air I breathe. I have to garden just as I have to cook. It feeds my soul, and in the spring, summer, and fall, it feeds my family of six. (By the way, you'll find some favorite family recipes in this book, and I hope you like them.) My garden surrounds our 100-year-old Victorian house, and includes a handful of just about everything: herbs, cutting flowers, and vegetables in the large sunny bed; a perennial border; two shade borders; and a rhododendron and bulb display. The cat has a catmint patch. It is a modest arrangement but it is, to bend a phrase, a room of my own. I love taking care of it and I spend about 10 to 15 hours a week, puttering and sometimes just staring in awe.

I don't use a lot of luxurious gadgets in the garden. I am a big believer in using what you have on hand, so a lot of the tips in this book incorporate the use of household materials like toilet paper rolls (they make great faux peat pots), milk cartons, chopsticks, fishing line, and household detergent. Your medicine cabinet has a lot to offer the garden, too. Epsom salts grow big tomatoes, and crushed expired vitamins make a good tea for ailing houseplants. You can save money using household recyclables, and from all of my interviewing and observing, I can tell you the very best gardeners do not rely on pricey items to make their gardens work. They'd rather spend $200 on a couple of rare hostas than a fancy teak planter.

Before we get ready for spring planting, I'd like to make a few suggestions, especially for gardeners who are just now getting their feet wet, or muddy, as the case may be. These are thoughts for the emerging gardener, who has just discovered that gardening is his passion.

MAKE FRIENDS WITH OTHER GARDENERS • Your best source for gardening information is other gardeners, and I have never met a gardener I didn't like. Gardeners are preoccupied with life and beauty, and because they are at the mercy of drought, sudden downpours, and insects, they also understand loss. This gives them wisdom, a certain good humor, and a remarkable generosity. Make friends with the gardeners in your community. They will show you their gardens and share their seeds and transplants. Never be afraid to knock on the door of someone whose garden you admire; they will show you wonders you never knew existed. Go to flower shows, and talk to growers at greenmarkets. You will find most gardeners are happy to share all they know.

READING IS GOOD BUT THE GARDEN IS THE BEST TEACHER • I read catalogues and gardening books all year long. I owe a lot of what I know and how I see the world to the best of them. But there is no substitute for just getting out there and trying it. Experiment with any color combination you like, push the limits of your zone if you want to give a tender plant a try. Read what you will, but do what you want. Don't get caught up in trends or garden snobberies. After all, it's your garden.

DON'T SKIMP ON BASIC GARDEN EQUIPMENT • It doesn't take a lot of money or specialized equipment to create a magnificent garden. The list of what you need to start is a short one, but when it comes to the basics you should always buy the best quality you can afford.

Being a product of parents who have actually used hot dog stock as a basis for soup, I have tended to skimp on things whenever possible, and with gardening it's a mistake. Seeds are a case in point. Seeds cost, what? a little more than a dollar a packet. There is no need to go for bargain brands. I know, I have purchased them, and they are often mismarked and their germination rates are laughable.

Clay pots are another example. In Texas I would often frequent Mexican border towns for something fun to do. Once I found dozens of amazingly cheap clay pots on sale and decided to buy them. They were sun-cured, not kilned, and after a certain amount of watering, they fell apart. (I will not mention the cost of shipping them all the way back to Dallas because my father might read this.) In gardening, you get what you pay for.

TAKE YOUR TIME FILLING OUT THE GARDEN • Most errors in garden design are made because a gardener acted precipitously—he either ignored his designs or didn't have any in the first place. With vegetable and herb gardening this is deadly because you end up with no room, plus clutter and confusion. With flowers it's more a matter of grating combinations or overcrowding, so that plants eventually have to be given away. The best advice is to move slowly, take your time, and leisurely fill out your garden. Of course, I have yet to meet a gardener who operated that way.

NEVER APOLOGIZE FOR YOUR GARDEN • I have a hunch that if a hundred gardeners went in for a group evaluation, psychologists would find one hundred Type A's. Who else would create so much work for themselves? Gardeners can get overwrought about bad judgments, or weeds, or borers, but that's not the point of gardening. You didn't create the nematode problem—and you didn't create moonflowers, either. You're just the gardener. Step back and view the whole, listen to the birds, lean on your hoe. Whatever your garden is, it is beautiful.

—Christine Allison

Spring

❦ *March* ❦

Flower of the Month: Daffodil

❦ MARCH 1

It's a good practice to mark your seed packets with the date and their life expectancy the minute you receive them. Invariably, I've ordered much more than I can use, so these inscriptions are extremely useful, not only for knowing how long to save each packet but also for knowing when to throw the packet out.

As a rule, most flower seeds are good for 2 to 3 years. (Yes, you can toss out that 1983 packet of sweet alyssum.) Fruit and vegetable seeds vary. While an onion seed might be good for this season only, most lettuce seeds will last for at least 5 years. Even within plant categories, there are considerable differences. For example, while *most* okra seeds are good for 2 years, the Wyoming No. 4 will germinate at a 50 percent rate 258 years later. If you decide to use some old-timers, sow on the generous side.

THE COLOR OF SOIL • If your ground is dry enough, dig down about a foot and take a look at your soil. Brown and dark reds indicate good drainage. If your soil is black, you're to be congratulated; it's wonderfully rich in organic matter. On the other hand, yellowish or red colors mixed with gray suggest you have a drainage problem.

A light or pale color of soil means the news is not good: your soil is weak and depleted, and you've got to add substantial amounts of organic matter.

FIRST-TIME GARDENERS • *Always work peat moss deeply into the soil, not just to prevent it from blowing away but to assure that it does not mat down and block needed moisture to the soil.*

TOUGH NUT • The oldest seed in the world is believed to be the arctic lupine (*Lupinus arcticus*), which germinated in 1966 and according to radiocarbon tests, dates back 10,000 to 15,000 years. It was discovered in Yukon, Canada, in 1954 by Harold Schmidt.

THE LIFE EXPECTANCY OF SEEDS

ONE YR	TWO YRS	THREE YRS	FOUR YRS	FIVE YRS +
Onion	Leek	Lima bean	Beet	Cucumber
Parsley	Okra	Snap bean	Broccoli	Endive
Parsnip	Pepper	Carrot	Brussels sprout	Lettuce
	Sweet corn	Celery	Cabbage	
		Chinese	Cauliflower	
		cabbage	Swiss chard	
		Pea	Eggplant	
		Spinach	Pumpkin	
			Radish	
			Squash	
			Tomato	
			Turnip	
			Watermelon	

Spring is sooner recognized by plants than men.
—Chinese saying

MARCH 2

"April is the cruelest month."
—*T. S. Eliot*

I really would like to know what zone T. S. Eliot lived in. March, without question, is the cruelest month, and it's only just begun. My mother-in-law, the Southerner, just called to let me know how splendid the daffodils are this week, and I am happy for her, I really am, but that doesn't make the snow shoveling any easier. In early March, my outdoor gardening consists mainly of pruning diseased or dead branches when we get a heat wave (40 degrees). Just one snowdrop would make such a difference.

MILK AND JUICE CARTON GARDENING • Of course, my basement now is seedling-o-rama, mainly perennials and hardy vegetables, a few slow-going annuals. I haven't started my tender annuals yet, but when I do, a good number of them will be planted in old milk and juice cartons.

You can save a step in the transplanting process by planting tomato, pepper, eggplant, and other vegetable seeds in clean half-gallon cartons cut down to 3 or 4 inches. Instead of sowing lots of seeds in flats and then transferring them to little pots, you sow a few seeds in each carton and let the fittest survive. When you are ready to put the plants in the garden, just slice off the bottom and leave a few inches of the carton above the soil line to serve as a collar. You can't get as many plants under the grow lights this way but you save lots of stress on the plants—and it's easier on you, too.

PLANTING REMINDER • *Very hardy* vegetables can be planted 4 to 6 weeks before the average frost-free date in your area. You can plant seeds of cabbage, kale, lettuce, peas, rutabaga, salsify, spinach, and turnips provided your soil is ready. Onion sets or seeds can be planted, and transplants of broccoli, cabbage, cauliflower, collards, kale, parsley, and Brussels sprouts can go in after hardening off. Six weeks before your last spring frost date you can plant *indoors* your warm-season flowers and veggies: eggplant, kohlrabi, peppers, strawflowers, tomatoes, and so on.

TREE WARNING • I lost several trees this winter but I am going to take my time replacing them. If you are looking at trees for the first time, avoid box elder (*Acer negundo*), cottonwood, or balsam poplar (*Populus balsamifera*), silver maple (*Acer saccharinum*), and Siberian elm (*Ulmus pumila*, which is different from Chinese elm). These trees can snap in a moment of stress. If you are looking at birches, make sure you get trees that are borer resistant.

WHERE THE TOMATOES ARE • The state that produces the most tomatoes is California.

The March sun raises, but dissolves not.

Much has been written about the Victorian predilection for speaking in flower code, but I *was* disturbed to find out from *The Language of Flowers* (1913) that basil means "hatred." This aromatic herb has always been a favorite, so much so that this year I turned my basement into a basil factory: every kind of scent and color will be represented in tiny seedlings. I hope to have a massive basil garden and also enough plants to give to friends (who I hope don't understand the language of flowers!). Anyway, transplanting will be the first big hurdle for my basilettes; I find the process painful because inevitably I lose a few.

Transplanting is right up there with thinning in my book, a daring and difficult process because it deals with the very young and innocent. Newly transplanted seedlings should be housed in moist but not too soggy soil, and kept evenly moist until they are established. *Always lift your transplant by the leaves—not the stem.* A broken stem is a dead plant. No matter how careful you are, the root hairs are usually damaged in this process so the plant can only absorb a small amount of water at a time. Frequent watering, every day if it's dry weather, will be necessary, along with the usual prayers and crossed fingers.

Always lift your transplant by the leaves, not the stem.

BACKSCRATCH • When your lawn is dry, rake it with a light hand and remove excess debris such as leaves and dead twigs. Raking will also raise the mat up so your lawn can breathe. Aerating machines are a great help in developing a healthy lawn, particularly if used regularly. They puncture holes in the lawn and pull out plugs of soil every 4 to 6 inches. If you aerate properly, root development takes off and you reduce thatch. Oh, yes: give those thatching machines a wide berth. The mechanical rakes seem to damage the grass plants something awful.

USING NEWSPAPER TO KILL WEEDS • Some gardeners like to use newspaper to discourage unwanted grass or weeds. The results vary. A few layers of newspaper, topped with wood chips or sawdust to hold it in place, over time will choke off any vegetation. By the end of the season, the newspaper along with the dead grass and weeds should have decomposed and become humus. *Never use colored newspaper—the funnies and advertising circulars are the worst—because they often contain metals and could be toxic.*

FIRST-TIME GARDENERS • *Seeds will not germinate in dry conditions, so water seed beds or drills before you sow.*

❦ MARCH 4

Caveat emptor: Bat guano has long been a favorite of marijuana growers because of its high phosphorus value (up to 20 percent—read: lots and lots of blooms), and lately more traditional gardeners have been sampling its powers. Most of the bat caves in America were mined in the nineteenth century and are empty now; during the Civil War guano provided nitrate for gunpowder.

The greatest share of modern bat guano comes from unregulated Third World countries. If you unwittingly are exposed to unsterilized bat guano, you can get an infectious reaction ranging from an annoying cough to histoplasmosis—or calcification of the lungs. Though it is doubtless the greatest organic source of phosphorus on earth, it is also not a product to be used without taking precautions.

REMOVE TENTS FROM GERMINATED SEEDS • Covering your pots and seed trays with plastic wrap creates a mini-greenhouse and helps to provide the moisture your seeds need to germinate. Just remember to *remove* the plastic once the seeds have sprouted. The plastic covers can actually promote disease after germination has taken place. Once you've got true leaves, the soil needs to drain to encourage root growth downward and to allow air circulation around the stems. *However, if you're going out of town, you should put the plastic back on your pots and trays. Prop 4 bamboo skewers or some chopsticks in the corners and drape a plastic dry cleaner's bag over your trays and they will stay moist. Just be sure the plants do not come in contact with the plastic.*

PLEASE DON'T CLIP THE CROCUSES • If your crocuses really look a mess, you can deadhead them but don't cut off
the leaves. Those leaves will be needed to make new bulbs for next
spring. Best simply to be patient: the crocus residue will be dried and
gone in a few weeks. Also be grateful. Some of us are still waiting for
our crocuses to come up.

ORNAMENTAL GRASS REMINDER • Once you can work
in the garden, check on all of your grasses. All ornamental grasses
that are not evergreen should be cut back within a couple of inches
of the ground so that new shoots came come up unhindered. Over
the winter their dead stalks provided a measure of protection for the
crowns—now the dead stalks and blades are simply in the way. *Don't
cut back smaller evergreen species at all; just remove any dry dead leaves. Use
your hands to tease the leaves out from the crown.*

A warm March brings a cold April.

❦ M A R C H 5

Garden planning is tricky and I have lots of envelope backs to prove
it. Vegetable gardeners who've been at it for a while know the value
of putting it all down on paper. You can't just go out there with
some seeds in your back pocket and see what happens because what
usually happens is you can't fit everything in. You can't make your
dream come true.

When planning your vegetable garden, first list your early spring
crops and then, using parentheses, identify succession crops in the
same spot, along with approximate planting dates. For instance, your
early spring planting of lettuce might be followed with a May planting of corn, followed by an interplanting in August of lettuce again.
This will not only help you in your initial planning but will keep you
on track through the summer.

Flower gardens are different because you seldom start from square
one. Here sitting in your garden and just s-t-a-r-i-n-g is almost as important as any drawing or list you might make. It is in those moments that you "see" how magnificent a white mugwort might look
here, or how fun an accent of an artichoke plant might look there.

All of which is to say if you haven't taken pencil and paper to your garden, concentrate on your vegetable and herb planning first. You can fudge a little on the flower garden. Flowers are intrinsically beautiful and therefore more forgiving.

WATERED PLANTS RESIST FROST • If you have had an unusually dry spring, give your plants a drink. A sudden frost can seriously damage dehydrated plants.

COUNT YOUR TINES • If you keep getting big clumps stuck in your pitchfork when you turn your compost, try a 5- or 6-tine fork instead of the 4-tine. If the tines are thin and round, instead of flat, the material will shake off easier.

PRESSURE-TREATED WOOD • Railroad ties that have been pressure treated are not recommended for raised beds; some say they leach poison (the pressure-treated-wood people say no, but why take a chance?). The biggest problem, though, comes from sawdust. Some gardeners hand-saw their ties in the yard, leaving minuscule bits of poisonous pressure-treated dust everywhere. *Wood ashes from pressure-treated lumber are suspect for the same reason.*

> *. . . you will find out there are all sorts of ways of learning, not only from people and books, but from sheer trying.*
> —Gertrude Jekyll

❦ M A R C H 6

Are you able to sow seeds outdoors yet? A friend in Colorado has a solution for gardeners who like their rows just so: continuous-feed computer paper. First, rip the perforated edge off the paper. Then lay that edge down so that the edge runs down the planting row. Now simply drop one seed in each of the holes for half-inch sowing, every other hole for one-inch showing, and "sow" forth. *Spice jars with shaker tops also make convenient seed-sowing devices.*

PERENNIAL PURCHASES • When you are selecting perennials, remember that as a general rule, most of them bloom for a 2- to

4-week period. But blooms alone do not a plant make: some perennials have leaves that add color and texture to your border or bed. (Actually, if you have a small garden, you're in trouble if the foliage doesn't carry its own weight.) Look at these plants for foliage interest: lady's-mantle (*Alchemilla vulgaris*) (one of my personal favorites), astilbe heartleaf bergenia (*Bergenia cordifolia*), fringed bleeding-heart (*Dicentra eximia*), barrenwort (*Epimedium spp.*), coral-bells (*Heuchera sanguinea*—actually, there is a whole world of heucheras worth looking into), hosta (another universe of extraordinary plants), peony (*Paeonia spp.*), and lungwort (*Pulmonaria officinalis*).

HASTENING GERMINATION • If some of your woody, hard-shelled seeds refuse to sprout, try lightly scoring them with a file, then soak them overnight in a solution made with 1 teaspoon of of Accent meat tenderizer diluted in a quart of water.

RADISH TIME • Plant radishes as soon as you can. To ensure a mild taste, they should go in in early spring or late fall. Summer-seeded radishes always seem to go to the unpleasant side of *picante*, so do not wait. Keep the soil evenly moist—dry soil will give your radish a tough, woody texture. And remember that the longer the radish stays in the ground, the harsher it will taste. Pluck them out often and before they get too big. They reach maturity in 22 days. *Teatime: Try thin slices of radishes on a slice of homemade bread with sweet butter, a few grains of salt.*

> *Nature does not proceed by leaps.*
> —Philosophia Botanica 1750

❦ MARCH 7
Luther Burbank's Birthday (1849–1926)

I shouldn't complain. For friends farther up north with a *really* short growing season, vegetable gardening is more of a sprint than a hobby. But there are many triumphs. My friends have developed a taste for mustard greens, scallions, loosehead lettuce, spinach, summer squash, and bush snap beans; they all normally mature in less then 50 days (the plants, that is; I'm still waiting on my friends). If your growing season is extremely compact, try Black-Seeded Simpson lettuce, Daybreak pea, Ace pepper, and Tyee spinach from Johnny's Select Seed; these mature in less than 55 days. And, for corn lovers in a hurry, try Seneca Horizon and Spring Dance from Stokes Seeds; both mature in less than 70 days. Burpee has the Early Girl tomato and the Stringless Green Pod bean, which mature in less than 54 days.

Hang your trap just before the fruit blossoms are set to open.

FRUIT TREE WORM TRAP • Here's a recipe for getting rid of fruit tree worms that *really* works. Put 1 cup of vinegar and 1 cup of sugar in a plastic 1-gallon milk jug. Add a banana peel and fill the remaining portion with water. Shake vigorously. Slice a three-inch hole in the upper side of the carton for the worms to "drop in." Hang the jug in the tree just before fruit blossoms are set to open. (Hang as many as you want.) *Spraying insecticidal soap on apple trees when the blossoms first become visible and continuing weekly until the first fruit appears also helps deter canker worms, webworms, and tent caterpillars.*

MOTHER NATURE RESPONDS • By the way, recent studies show that lights illuminating gardens at night can cause spinach and certain other vegetables to bolt.

FERTILIZE DAFFODILS • Fertilize your daffodils when the plants begin to emerge. Spread a general fertilizer such as 5-10-5 on the ground around the plants and wash it into the soil with a good watering. Do not let the fertilizer have direct contact with the unfurling foliage.

> *I remember being asked if I had ever done any work to improve orchids. I stared at the questioner for a moment or two, fumbling for a reply. And then I said, perhaps a little impatiently: "Improve orchids? But who on earth would dream of wanting them improved?"*
> —Luther Burbank

The pansy seems to produce a lot of giddiness in gardeners, or at least in those who name flowers: there is Lady's Delight, Three Faces under a Hood, Tickle My Fancy, Pink of My Joan, None So Pretty, Come and Cuddle Me, Kiss Me, Jump Up and Kiss Me, Meet Her in the Pantry, Kiss Her in the Butt'ry, and so on. I am a Johnny-jump-up loyalist; since childhood its little face has had a place in my garden. If your Johnny-jump-ups have become a bit invasive, give some to a friend. *It's bad luck to toss out a flower that seeds itself.*

PERENNIAL PLANTING SCHEDULE • Japanese anemones and other plants that blossom in late summer and fall should definitely go in during early spring rather than in the summer. Likewise, perennials with silvery or woolly foliage. If you do plant in early spring, make sure you keep the roots watered evenly for the first 2 to 3 weeks so that root production can take place rapidly.

FIRST-TIME GARDENERS • Herbaceous perennials benefit from an annual feeding of commercial balanced organic fertilizer (based on peat or tree bark), composted farmyard manure, or garden compost. The manure and the compost are preferable. If a plant can tolerate lime, it can also be fed with bonemeal, which is rich in phosphorus.

HOW DOES YOUR GARDEN GROW? • If you are in doubt, plant your seed the depth equal to 4 times its diameter.

HAVE PATIENCE, DEAR FRIENDS • If you sow your seeds outdoors earlier than the suggested time, the weather could turn cold again, postponing germination. The worst case is pretty bad, and almost assured: your seeds will just sit in the soil and *rot.*

Another benefit of patience: if you wait to plant a week or two *after* you have prepared your seedbeds, you will give your weeds a chance to come up first. Clear the weeds with a rake or hoe, *then* plant your flower and vegetable seeds.

March winds and April showers
Bring forth May flowers.

Among the cherished images I have of my 98-year-old grandmother is that of her scant form bent over a bed of daffodils, pinching off flowers and tying the leaves into perfect knots. Gardening, for Grandmother, is the imposition of order on beauty. Order comes harder for me. Once they have finished blooming, my daffodils look a little disheveled, as if they just woke up. (Do flower beds look like their owners?) At least I no longer cut them back too soon—the most common mistake first-timers make.

If this is your first year of spring-flowering bulbs, make sure you let them die down as they will. You should allow at least 6 weeks between flowering and clipping or mowing so that the bulb can store energy for the next season. The visual chaos must be endured as long as possible. It is probably best to let all of the foliage die down naturally, though a perfect knot, woven carefully with devoted hands, probably will not harm the daffodils. It never hurt Grandmother's.

RADICCHIO ANOTHER WAY • Lots of Americans have developed a liking for Italian red chicory—otherwise known as radicchio—which for me is a challenge to grow but well worth the effort. Radicchio is tasty in salads but it is fabulous when grilled, even in the oven broiler. If you have some left in your cold frame or decide to grow some this spring, prepare it this way for a change.

GRILLED RADICCHIO

2 heads radicchio, sliced into wedges
2 tablespoons best-quality olive oil
Kosher salt
¼ pound bacon, diced and cooked soft

Line a broiling tray with foil and spray with nonstick vegetable oil. Arrange radicchio wedges on the pan in a single layer. Drizzle olive oil over the wedges and sprinkle with diced bacon. Add kosher salt sparingly, to taste. Broil until the edges are slightly charred, turning once. Serve warm or at room temperature. Serves 4.

FROST LIFT • Some of the perennials, trees, and shrubs you planted in the fall might have fallen victim to frost lift, or frost heave. Check once the soil has thawed to see if the plants have been lifted or loosened. You might need to replant or anchor them with a fresh application of soil.

CRITTER LIFT • Sometimes moles, mice, and other critters nest underground and make little mounds where they've tunneled. Once the ground is dry enough to be worked, pat these mounds gently down.

> To everything there is a season,
> and a time to every purpose under the heaven.
> —Ecclesiastes 3:1

❦ MARCH 1 0

I have entered that gruesome period between catalogue ordering and actually kneeling down in the garden and getting my hands dirty. I keep eyeing the yard, pacing, lamenting in advance that I will not be growing certain plants this year. I mean, what if I go through life and never grow *Campanula glomerata* 'Crown of Snow'?

This is a good time to do some spring garden-shed cleaning and get your work area in order. Lawn mower service centers are eager for business now; take yours in if you need to. Check on your supplies: gloves, cloches, floating row covers (see page 325), insecticidal soaps, tools. It's better than staring at the ground or (worse) dipping back into those catalogues you've *already* ordered from.

TRY, TRY AGAIN

- If your spinach bolted last year, try Malabar or New Zealand.

- If you live in the colder zones and had little luck with turnips, plant them midsummer.

- If cabbage worms are a problem, start your cabbage, broccoli, cauliflower in a cold frame: try to harvest them *before* the infestation.

- If your asparagus was tough, try harvesting earlier this year.

13

RULE OF THUMB • It's pretty easy to play soil doctor if you keep in mind these basics: nitrogen (N) encourages leaf growth, phosphorus (P) helps plants to form good root systems, and potassium (K) benefits flowers. Base fertilizers are high in phosphorus and potassium, and they're added to the soil *before* planting to encourage root formation and sturdy growth. General fertilizers are used as top dressing and lightly forked into the surface as a stimulant during the growing season.

CUT DAFFODILS • Daffodil stems release a saplike substance that harms other flowers. Before you put your cut daffodils in an arrangement, cut the stems at an angle and let them sit in a vase filled halfway with lukewarm water for an hour or two. Discard the preparation water and then add the daffodils to the other flowers. If you recut the stems you will have to repeat this process.

> *What is all this juice and all this joy?*
> —Gerard Manley Hopkins

❦ M A R C H 1 1

If you moved into your house recently and just can't wait to work in the garden, try to restrain yourself. I know that you have all sorts of plans, but you should wait at least a year before you do anything drastic. We moved into our current home a few years ago and I know *exactly* what you are going through. It is frustrating but worth it. Yes, of course, you can cautiously rip out anything you *really* hate. (Be careful, though—there might be bulbs or slow-emerging perennials underfoot.) But by and large you should just watch and take notes.

My first year in our house I was a major container gardener and it provided me with a good outlet for getting my hands dirty and for making beauty. I also spent my first year spying. Check out the neighbors' yards, especially if you are new to the community, and certainly if you are new to the zone. Find out what blooms exactly when. That information will aid immensely in your planning—for next year. Sorry.

MUGWORT CURE • Since the Crusades, a sprig of mugwort (*Artemisia vulgaris*) has been worn in boots and shoes to prevent weariness. Bouquets of mugwort were offered to runners in the New York City Marathon, and none refused.

NOT ALL MANURES ARE CREATED EQUAL • Poultry manure contains 2 percent nitrogen, one of the highest levels of all manures. Horse manure is about .5 percent nitrogen. Cow manure is .25 percent nitrogen. Both horse and cow manure should be aged at least 9 months to prevent burning.

> *Half the interest of a garden is in the constant exercise of the imagination.*
> —Mrs. C. W. Earle

❦ MARCH 12

I am one who believes in leaving the stalks of perennials pretty much intact through the fall and winter, not really for what horticulturalists call winter interest but because of fall laziness: the stalks seem to attract fallen leaves, forming a natural layer of mulch. Now is the time to remove all of that mess, for obvious reasons of aesthetics but also so as not to arrest new growth. Be really careful when you are working in your perennial garden, though. It is easy to harm some of the slow-emerging plants when you are digging around in early spring.

EASTER FORECASTING • The people of the Ozark Mountains believe that if it rains on Easter Sunday, it will rain the following seven Sundays.

IF YOU'RE GOING TO PLANT A TREE • A lot of what happens in nurseries is now done by machine rather than by hand. Oliver's Nursery in Connecticut offers a warning, though: When a tree is planted, cultivated, and dug by machine, it's extremely difficult to keep the proper soil grade against the trunk. Machine-dug trees in wire baskets can be up to twelve inches too deep. Oliver's advises anyone who plants a tree in a wire basket to pull back the soil until a root flare is found. That is where the final grade should hit the trunk. Be sure to remove as much of the wire basket as possible.

I once believed I would never use black plastic mulch, for the simple reason that it's, well, black plastic. (I also had heard that snakes like to huddle underneath black plastic mulch when it heats up in the summer, which reduced its appeal even further.)

My view has changed. I think that 10 or 15 years down the road (when my knees are *totally* shot) I will use it, and gladly, only because I know how extraordinarily effective it is in blocking the growth of weeds. If you plant in wide rows—and put down 3-foot-wide rolls of black plastic between your rows—you'll have room enough for a wheelbarrow and the occasional visitor to move up and down your totally weed-free paths. (You can also use the poke-holes-through-it method—basically making little openings for transplants—and have even fewer weeds.) Black plastic is definitely worth considering. And if you are uneasy about its appearance, you can always crumble soil over it or cover it with wood chips. A covering of mulch will not only anchor the plastic but make that shiny black look go away.

MANURE TEA FOR SEEDS • Manure tea (recipe on page 94) makes an excellent solution for soaking seeds overnight. Ditto: liquid seaweed (pages 361–62).

Thinning is one of the most painful tasks of the gardener, but it is absolutely necessary. If you have a lot of thinning to do, use tiny scissors and clip your excess plants flush with the soil surface. Once the stem is dead, the plant is dead, and the root becomes compost. Clipping is far easier than pulling out plants, hair by hair, but you still need to be careful as you go.

The other point to remember is that if you don't plant too thickly, you won't have to thin. Take your time broadcasting or sowing in rows. That's hard, especially when you are eager in the spring to get out there and garden, garden, garden, but sowing time is not the time to lose your head and dump seed in globs into that soil you've worked so hard on.

If you are compulsively heavy-handed when you sow, especially outdoors, then consider seed tapes. These are much more costly than seed packets and of course the selection is limited, but it might be a cure for the gardener who has a difficult time sowing judiciously and then finds himself thinning like an executioner.

Finally, remember that the little thinnings you pull out—spinach, lettuce, radish, carrots—all can be tossed into the salad bowl.

Use tiny scissors to thin your seedlings.

PEAT POT WARNING • When you transplant your peat pot seedlings to the garden, be certain to either bury the whole pot completely or cut off the lip of the pot, which sucks moisture out if exposed to the open air and wind.

❦ MARCH 15

Ever notice how when you wash black-eyed peas or Great Northern beans before cooking, a dozen or so always rise to the top? Generally, they're broken or mutants and you toss them out. This brings us to the famous soak test. Giving your seeds this wonderfully simple test is a good way to purge the imperfect ones, and it works on exactly the same premise. Before planting, put your larger seeds in a bowl of water. The damaged ones will invariably float to the surface; seeds in good condition will sink.

BEFORE SOAKER HOSES, I GUESS • In Victorian times, gardeners were advised to spit in planting holes before planting parsnips, leeks, carrots, and Brussels sprouts.

PLANTING REMINDER • Subtract 4 weeks from your last spring frost date and plant indoors in flats: cosmos, marigolds, zinnias.

TIRES IN THE GARDEN ARE OKAY NOW • For years gardeners planted seedlings in used tires; the tires collected and released heat, making earlier spring planting possible. Then lots of organic gardeners stopped using them because there was a widely accepted fear that the tires were releasing unwanted chemicals into the ground. Now we know that the tires are not a chemical threat, so you can haul them back out for transplant duty.

BETTER LOOKING THAN TIRES • It serves a slightly different purpose than the tires, but cold-climate gardeners can place large flat rocks between each plant to warm the soil. The rocks release stored heat at night. Later in the season this will help the plants' fruits mature and ripen. The stones are also good for scraping the dirt off your tools.

> *Welcome, O March! Whose kindly days are dry.*
> *Make April ready for throstles' song,*
> *Thou first redresser of the winter's wrong.*
> —William Morris

❦ M A R C H 1 6

I am still looking at mud, but soon enough the weedlets will be poking their little heads into the world. Sometimes I am so happy to see something living and green that I get sentimental and merciful and stupid about the early weeds. When will I learn? Weeding is most crucial in the spring, and the weeding you do through May and June will pay off handsomely in July and August when the thought of weeding in the heat is unbearable.

Weeding is easier when the ground is damp, but wait until the moisture of the foliage has dried so you don't spread disease. Begin cultivation the minute you see weed seedlings appear (but be certain you are not killing newly planted annuals or other friendly specimens). I am a hand-hoe person because I'm so clumsy that I invariably dismember innocent bystanders when operating from a few feet above. When I am down on my knees I have more control, and anyway I like a closeup on what's happening. If you catch your weeds before they flower and go to seed, they can make excellent mulch or compost, so sharpen that hoe and adjust your attitude. The battle will soon begin.

DON'T THROW THAT FISH BACK • In the Northeast, fishing season starts soon, and if you're a fisherman or know one, try to build up an early spring inventory of trash fish. You can freeze the fish and then use them in the garden. When planting time comes, dig a hole 4 inches or so deeper than you would normally and then bury the fish, cover it with soil, and plant as usual. Good for roses, corn, and tomatoes especially.

A garden is a grand teacher.
—Gertrude Jekyll

❦ M A R C H 1 7
St. Patrick's Day

My friend Pip has childhood memories of her mother luring the family out at night on March 17, to plant peas and sweet peas in flannel nightgowns by the light of handheld lanterns. According to legend, peas planted in this manner on St. Patrick's Day will be superior in taste and abundance. The peas, Pip reports, were always excellent. (*Depending on the kind of spring we're having, I generally sow between now and April 1. Pea seeds need soil at about 40 degrees to germinate.*)

ALL ABOUT SHAMROCKS • Shamrocks, among believers and nonbelievers alike, fill schools and pubs and parades throughout the United States on this day. Actually, the shamrock was used by St. Patrick as a teaching tool. To explain the Holy Trinity, Patrick is said to have noted that each point on the leaf of the shamrock is separate and distinct (Father, Son, and Holy Spirit) but that the three points make the whole (God).

In ancient times, the shamrock or trefoil was used in Celtic fertility rites, representing a triad of goddesses. The leaves were burned and dusted over fields to promote growth.

Today, the shamrocks you get in nurseries are usually *Oxalis acetosella* (wood sorrel), *Trifolium repens* (white clover), or *Medicago lupulina* (hop clover, yellow trefoil, black medic).

LET'S HEAR IT FOR OUR TENTH-GRADE LATIN TEACHERS • Were it not for a certain ease with Latin, it would be almost impossible to purchase a China pink. A China pink is a *Dianthus*, specifically *Dianthus chinensis*. Despite the name China pink, it is not a Pink. It is an annual. The variety of *Dianthus* called Pinks is a perennial. *Dianthus* includes sweet Williams and carnations, both of which are Pinks. China pinks are also Indian pinks, another pink which is not a Pink.

❦ M A R C H 1 8

As spring arrives it is wise to gradually remove winter protection from shrubs before the ground gets so warm that it encourages premature growth. The danger, of course, is that premature growth can get killed off by a late frost. Spread the removal process out over 10 days or so, depending on how cold or inconsistent daily temperatures are. Remove the protective layers on a gray overcast afternoon to avoid the sudden shock of bright light, and keep some mats and covers handy in case you get a terrible freeze and need to cloak your plants fast. *Remember, drying out is more dangerous to young trees and shrubs than cold weather.*

CHECK THE ASPARAGUS BED • The first asparagus can be picked just about the time the daffodils unfurl. The spears are ready when they are 6 to 8 inches high, before any tip buds begin to open. They should be about as thick as your fingers, unless you have really thick fingers.

During harvest, sprinkle some kosher salt—about 1 pound per 100 square feet—over your asparagus bed. Make sure it is sodium chloride, rock salt (not the salt used for deicing). It will suppress fusarium crown and root rot. Don't salt first-year plantings (which you shouldn't be harvesting anyway). Water shortly after salting and test the pH (sometimes the salt lowers the pH, and asparagus does best around 7.0, but it is not terribly fussy).

SPROUTING TIP • One method for hastening germination is to soak your seeds in a thermos filled with warm water for 24 to 48 hours before planting. For really hard coated seeds, use hot tea. The tannic acid will soften the outer coating.

❦ MARCH 1 9

When I was a weekend gardener, I fudged here and there in the hardening-off process, and too often my plants suffered from shock. Now that my garden and I have the same full-time address, I can harden off my plants correctly. It's too early for most of my seedlings to go out, but my hardy vegetables will be making their way to the garden: trays of cabbages, spinach, broccoli, and cauliflower. I have a little lattice-protected crawl space underneath my kitchen—an outdoor room, actually, where I can keep my flats for at least 6 days. I begin by setting them in the crawl space for an hour on Day 1, and add an hour every day. The day before I plant them, I skip watering and let them camp out overnight, unprotected. Then I wait for a fair to excellent planting afternoon ("excellent" in most cases means cool, shady, and windless, though some plants do better planted in sunshine), at which point they are ready to be introduced to the garden.

SO LITTLE TIME • Botanists estimate there are more than 330,000 species of flowers.

HOSTA • It is a great testimony to the refinement of gardeners that hostas have become a fad, and that people are collecting them with passion. Hostas are subtle in their beauty; more about leaves than flowers. They are for individuals who can be fascinated with different shades of green—a streak here, a purplish cast there. While some hostas can take full sun, most prefer the shade. Be careful where you plant your shade-loving hostas. The former owners of my house planted a row of them along our peony border. Nice idea, but they can't take the extra hour or so of sun delivered to that spot. If you live in the North, about 2 to 4 hours of morning or late afternoon sun is the *most* you will want for your hostas; in the South an hour of direct sunlight is plenty. Filtered sunlight is best. (*You may be surprised to learn that hosta is edible; the blanched stalks are highly sought after in Japan. Unfortunately, deer love them, too.*)

❦ M A R C H   2 0

Many of us have a flower that called us to gardening as children; mine was the grape hyacinth. I can still taste the dirt from my back-yard in Kansas City, and see that bobbly row of grape hyacinths. It was fun to lie on my stomach and stare at them, purple and from an-other world.

This spring, I forced hundreds of *Muscari*. They'll go into the ground soon, along with secret hopes of snaring one more generation. Although they've been babied somewhat, forced spring-flowering bulbs can be planted after they've been enjoyed indoors. With grape hyacinths, pinch off the heads—not the stems—before they go to seed, and keep them watered in their pots until the foliage dies down. Plant them in full sun or part shade 3 inches deep with a little bulb fertilizer.

THE NIBBLING RABBITS PROBLEM • If you have rabbits nibbling at the bark of your trees, you can take a couple of measures to stop them. The most effective I have found is wrapping the trunk of the tree up to the first branch with hardware cloth. Many garden-ers claim that onions will ward off rabbits, and this practice worked well in my vegetable garden. But our dwarf fruit trees were nibbled to death one year because I trusted chives and onions to protect them. Never again.

Of course, there's always rabbit droppings. Some gardeners told me they make a "paint" of liquefied rabbit droppings and coat the base of their trees with it. The rabbits find this offensive.

SCALLIONS • In many parts of the country now gardeners are enjoying their first harvests of scallions, or spring onions, and I am completely envious. I leave mine in the ground until the day I am going to use them, but if you have a big harvest or want to give some to friends, store them unwashed in the refrigerator; they'll keep for five days.

Scallions have four times the vitamin C and up to 5,000 times the vitamin A as other onions. Many people use just a bit of the green stalk (the source of all that vitamin A), but I generally use the entire onion; why not? They are so mild and delectable when eaten fresh from the garden. Cut them into paper-thin slices and float them in soups, or use them in cottage cheese, or make pancakes with them. They are also excellent braised and served with a leg of lamb.

Spring has come when you can put your foot on three daisies.

❦ MARCH 21

ARIES, March 21 to April 20—*A good time to sow seeds, especially those producing stalks and vines*

Even gardeners in the coldest parts of the country can get a pea in the ground now, but soil, sun, and water are not the only considerations for moon-savvy gardeners. Plant-by-the-moon gardeners scoff at mindless plant-whenever types. I admit to falling into the latter category but I cannot dispute that of all the gardeners I know, the wisest, gentlest, and most methodical ones—who also have the most spectacular gardens—do follow the moon's phases in their gardening.

The basic lunar planting rules are not complex. The 12 signs of the zodiac are divided into 2 main groups—fruitful and barren. During fruitful periods, you plant and do everything you need to do to make your garden produce. During barren signs, you harvest, weed, and thumb your nose at deer and the like.

The fruitful signs are Taurus, Cancer, Scorpio, and Pisces. Capricorn is only somewhat fruitful. Virgo and Libra are fruitful only for the planting of flowers—with Libra being far more productive.

The barren signs are Aries, Gemini, Leo, Virgo, and Libra (except for flower planting), Sagittarius, and Aquarius. Aries, Gemini, Leo, and Aquarius are considered the real lackluster periods. Lunar gardeners would never plant during these dates, though some say Sagittarius is okay for planting fruit crops.

Gardening by the moon.

In addition, lunar gardeners plant according to the phases of the moon. This is easier to get a handle on if you have an *Old Farmer's Almanac*. If you don't have one, race out and get one today because they generally go off sale after the first quarter of the year. The guiding principle is this: Plant annuals and crops that produce their yield *above* the ground (tomatoes, cabbage, etc.) from the New Moon to the Full Moon (the waxing phase), and plant biennials, perennials, and crops producing their yield *below* the ground (bulbs and root crops) during the waning phase, from Full Moon to New Moon. Is this for weekend gardeners? Probably not. But if you have the time and the place, linking your work in the garden to the mysteries of the moon could not hurt, not at all.

> *Sow peas and beans*
> *in the wane of the moon;*
> *Who soweth them sooner, soweth too soon.*

❦ M A R C H 2 2

Apple, willow, peach, maple, and witch hazel make the best dowsing rods for locating water. You can use any branch with a wishbonelike fork in it. Clear the branch of leaves, then walk at a slow pace, branch held straight up. If you've got the touch, you will feel the branch bend when you are near moving water. It will bend straight down, even as you fight it. At least that's what they say. (Let me know if it works.)

WHAT COLOR IS YOUR MULCH? • The color of mulch might make a difference in plant size, yield, harvest dates, and flavor because of the way plants see light, according to a recent USDA study in Florence, South Carolina. The researchers discovered in tests that bell peppers that were grown with red mulch were taller than peppers grown in yellow, black, or white mulch. It was a very particular shade of red so don't try to replicate the experiment until they know why this happened.

INDOOR SEEDLINGS GETTING LEGGY? • If your indoor seedlings are getting leggy, they need more light. Move them up closer to the light source if you are using artificial lighting—the light can be 2 or 3 inches from the plants. If your seedlings are too compact—or not growing fast enough—they might be getting too much light. Light emitted from fluorescent bulbs is at its most intense in the center and least intense at the outside edges. Move your plants around accordingly. *You can also maximize the intensity of the light by placing foil mirrors around the sides of the plants or by painting the shelves beneath a glossy white.*

In the spring, at the end of the day, you should smell like dirt.
—Margaret Atwood

❧ M A R C H 2 3

Clay pots look so much better than plastic pots that a discussion is not necessary. Plastic pots are nondescript and soulless. Clay pots are ancient and beautiful. Clay pots are porous, so you don't have overwatering problems, and bottom watering is much more effective, because clay draws up the moisture so well.

But in the summer, clay pots are a pain; the water evaporates so quickly that you find yourself watering 3 times a day. A clay pot loyalist gave me this suggestion a few years ago and it works wonders: plastic saucers. You can get terracotta saucers that look like clay and function like plastic; scoot them under your authentic clay pots and you have a great-looking, workable container situation. The saucers retain water well so in the summer you can just give them an inch or so of water and the clay pot will draw it up as it needs it.

HIGH TIMES FOR RADISHES • The radish was held in high esteem by the ancient Greeks, and it is said they cast its image in gold for their temple at Delphi.

ANISE SEEDS • It is very difficult to germinate anise seed when it's dried. It is best to use your own fresh seed or some from a friend. Fresh seed is not only potent in cooking but grows better plants.

PROVEN COMPANIONS • The benefits of companion planting (see page 352) are difficult to test, but the following companions have been subjected to scientific inquiry and found to be beneficial. To benefit carrots grow onions, for collards grow tomatoes, for corn grow beans, for cucumbers grow broccoli, for potatoes grow tansy, and for tomatoes grow dandelion.

GREEN MANURE • Researchers have found that green manure (see page 207) cut and left on the soil adds just as much nitrogen as green manure that is tilled under. So if you don't mind the appearance, just let it sit there.

A tree is known by its fruit.

❦ M A R C H   2 4

Raised-bed gardening is an ancient practice, though some of us are just now discovering it. For centuries, farmers in Europe, Asia, and all of the Americas elevated their gardens and for good reason. Raised-bed devotees claim that they get 4 times the yield per acre than commercial farmers do using more traditional methods.

In low-lying areas, raised beds are excellent because they allow water to drain from the soil. Raised-bed plants are not subject to the waterlogging and root rot that can ruin a garden. In the spring, a raised-bed garden has an edge over a regular garden because the soil warms up and dries out so much faster. In colder zones this can mean a few crucial weeks' jump on the season. (The downside is that in the summer raised beds dry out quicker than regular gardens and in a very warm dry zone this could be a problem.)

We used to grow more vegetables than we do now, and what I enjoyed most about my raised-bed gardening was that my weeding time was cut to a fraction of what I experienced in regular gardens. Raised gardens involve close plantings, leaving little room for weeds. Because the plants are so closely packed, they form each others' mulch. It's really a sensational system.

As a final note, raised beds can be truly beneficial for gardeners whose backs and legs aren't as willing as they used to be. For those gardeners, raised beds that are 3 and 4 feet high can offer a chance for more years of gardening than they would have had otherwise. Some retired friends in Washington State have nearly waist-high raised beds and grow all their flowers and vegetables right where they can reach out and touch them—and see them eye to eye.

MARKING YOUR ROWS WITH LIME • You can mark lime-lovers like spinach, beets, and lettuce with a thin line of lime.

LIMESTONE CAUTION • Meanwhile, don't add ground limestone to your compost pile, as it will invariably raise the pH to above neutral and it can also cause ammonia gas to be formed, resulting in the loss of nitrogen. Put limestone in the garden but not in the compost.

FRENCH FRIES • The best potato for French fries is the Idaho or Maine russet because each has relatively low water content.

❦ M A R C H 2 5

Just think, in a matter of weeks—days for some of us—we'll have outdoor plants and flowers . . . and spider mites again! Last season I must admit I had extremely good luck using insecticidal soaps on my bugs. My secret: I used rain water rather than tap water to make my insecticidal soap solution. Okay, so it's not really a secret. Researchers have found that soft water or rain water is essential for effective insecticidal soaps; water with a hardness greater than 20 grains will inactivate much of the soap. And you can see it with your own eyes: with soft water and soap you get a clear solution with lots of bubbles. Hard water gives you a milky white solution with hardly any bubbles.

When you make up a batch, add the soap to the water (not vice versa or you'll get foam city). Spray thoroughly, on both sides of the leaves, until it drips. For soap sprays to work, the wet spray mist must come in contact with the insect. Spray in the evening—never in bright sunlight—to prevent rapid drying. Wash off the residue the next day or before eating, if you are using it on edibles. Don't put insecticidal soaps on plants which are damaged by soap: crown-of-thorns, palms, jade plant, horse chestnut, mountain ash, and Japanese maple to name a few.

NATURAL FERTILIZERS • Fertilizers with high nitrogen content will stimulate the compost's decomposition process, and if you're in a hurry for some compost, you might want to add some good sources of nitrogen to your compost heap now.

••

NITROGEN SOURCES

••

Alfalfa meal	Linseed meal
Blood meal/dried blood	Soybean meal
Cottonseed meal	Fish meal

☙ M A R C H   2 6

I learned a lot of shortcuts while gardening near the mountains, but gardening with plastic milk or water jugs is among my most treasured. I had often seen fields filled with plastic jugs, so it's not as though I didn't know that people *did* that; I just had no idea how effective it was until I tried it myself.

Basically, early spring provides two threats: nibbling animals and frost. By slicing off the bottom of a plastic jug and sinking it down to a depth of 3 or 4 inches over your plant, you can protect your flowers and vegetables and provide a greenhouse-like environment for them for absolutely no money and very little time. You take the cap off for ventilation and if it gets really cold at night, you can drape a towel or sheet scrap over the whole container without crushing the

••

plant. When you want to get an early start or if you live in a cold zone area, this is the ticket.

FIRST-TIME GARDENERS • *Hay and straw are not the same. Hay is cut while green and is a mixture of grasses, legumes, and weeds. Straw is the dried stems and leaves of a grain crop (oats or wheat). Though hay has a higher nitrogen content than straw, it's also much weedier and therefore is less desirable as a mulch. (If you do use hay as a mulch and get weed seed sprouting, just lay more hay on top or roll it over.)*

HARDY ANNUALS • If you harden them off properly, you can put out seedlings of certain hardy annuals when you plant your lettuce and peas. Flowers like sweet alyssum, bachelor's button, calendula, larkspur, California poppy, baby's breath, candytuft, China pink, mignonette, pansy, annual phlox, snapdragon, and wallflower can be put out as transplants and even endure a light frost if they are conditioned. Life in a vented cold frame for about a week to 10 days provides the transitional experience they need before being popped into the garden.

❦ MARCH 27

Best Buy   O.K. Compromise   Waste of Money

Think small. *Sunset* magazine did a comparison of perennials in 6-packs, 4-inch pots, and gallon containers to see how the various containers affected the plants' growth. Three different perennials were tested: delphinium, statice (*Limonium perezii*), and erodium. Within 6 weeks, the 4-inch pots of delphinium, statice, and erodium had caught up with the 1-gallon pots (*and the 4-inch statice and delphinium had more blooms to boot*). *Three weeks after that the little 6-pack delphiniums and statice had completely caught up.* Only the slower-growing erodium 6-pack plant remained smaller during the first season.

From a cost standpoint, there's no question that the 6-packs are absolutely the way to go. If you need faster size and color, you can buy the 4-inch pots, but there is really no compelling reason to buy a gallon-size container ever again—unless your nursery offers little else. If that's the case, investigate mail-order sources for small container plants. To start: Bluestone Perennials, 7411 Middle Ridge Road, Madison, OH 44057, 800/852-5243; Mountain Valley Growers, 38325 Pepperweed Rd., Squaw Valley, CA 93675, 209/338-2775; Milaegers Gardens, 4838 Douglas Ave., Racine, WI 53402, 800/669-9956.

DON'T TILL UNDER TREES • Be careful of tree roots when you plant ground cover under trees. Most tree roots are located in the top 18 inches of soil, and if you till to prepare the soil for planting, you'll damage your trees. (The roots of some, like maples and dogwoods, are very close to the surface.) If you plant ground cover that has been started in beginner 2-inch pots, you can use a trowel or a bulb planter and do the job by hand, which is far more desirable than ripping up ground for a giant 1-gallon-container planting.

PEPPER PARTICULARS • The optimal germination temperature for peppers is about 85 degrees, so it is important to start them in a warm spot in the house. After they germinate, place the flats in front of a sunny window for about 6 weeks or until they're ready to transplant. Pull the flat away from the window if the outside temperature threatens to drop. Peppers like constant, warm temperatures.

❦ MARCH 28

The sooner you can get your compost heap up and running and into your garden, the better. If your compost is ready but you need a really rich compost this spring, cover it with 1 or 2 inches of soil and sow a green manure crop (see page 207) of rye or oats right on top of the compost. As soon as the crop is about 6 inches tall, you can turn it into the compost. A week later, you can put it in the garden.

CHINESE YAM • The Chinese yam, or cinnamon vine (*Dioscorea batatas*), makes a lovely dressing for an ugly wall. If you start its small tubers indoors in pots, the vine will grow up to 25, even 30 feet in the single season. Its white flowers, which appear in July and August, come in clusters and smell like cinnamon.

TOSS EXTRA INOCULANTS • Inoculants are inexpensive, which is a good thing because they don't have a long shelf life. If you have leftovers, give them to your friends and neighbors because they won't be good next year.

TO SLOW DOWN TOMATO GROWTH • A Canadian researcher has discovered that you can slow down the rate of growth for tomato seedlings by directing air to the plants from a gently blowing fan. This slight breeze will arrest the seedlings' growth rate—which is an advantage if it is an especially cold spring and you anticipate having to wait to get the plants into the ground. Give the plants their "breezes" for about an hour a day.

❦ M A R C H 2 9

Big: the largest seed in the world is that of the double coconut, or coco de mer (*Lodoicea maldevica*). It is found wild in the Seychelles in the Indian Ocean. The single-seeded fruit seed can take 10 years to develop and weighs up to 44 pounds.

AH, TO HAVE THE SPACE • The dimensions of Thomas Jefferson's nasturtium bed: 10 yards by 19.

DOG FUR USES • Dogs are now shedding their winter coats. Save that fur! The fur can be strewn around the garden and it will not only deter certain other furry creatures but also release nitrogen into the soil.

FIRST-TIME TRANSPLANTERS • If you put your transplants in poor soil, they are that much more vulnerable to insect attack and disease. To help them through the stressful transplanting period, prepare the hole with a scoopful of compost. Plants in weak soil develop more carbohydrates and less protein—and insects love carbos.

DAFFODIL REMINDER • When the daffodils start to emerge, combine ½ cup Epsom salts with ½ bushel of wood ashes and sprinkle around the green shoots. You will be contributing potash, lime, and magnesium to the soil.

❦ M A R C H   3 0

Nabel's, my favorite local nursery, is brimming with semihardy primrose (*Primula*), and on this rainy day it is the primrose plants that signal the end of this endless gray.

Primrose, from *primus*, Latin for "first," are among the first flowers of spring, be it by nature or by force. The primrose is a symbol of early youth, and "a walk down the primrose path" connotes a life of pleasure and self-indulgence. I take my deep violet and crimson and yellow and fuchsia primrose home now, and put them in baskets with other forced and coddled wonders like the Transvaal daisy (*Gerberium*) and grape hyacinth. What cheer! Last year, when the temperatures evened out to the 50s and 60s, I moved the primrose outside to a sunny, cool protected corner and gave them a bit of organic fertilizer, and they bloomed amicably for weeks. I have yet to see signs of their return, but it's still a little early. And I can always try again.

FIRST-TIME GARDENERS • As a rule, your seedling is ready to transplant when its first true leaves appear (these come after the initial leaves, or cotyledons). I use a spoon handle to pry up the plant, and then pick up the plant by the leaves. Of course for Northerners, it's too early to put most plants into the garden. But when the time comes, I will be sure to set the leaves barely above the soil line in the prepared hole. By planting the seedling deeper, you encourage outward growth and end the spindly growth caused by a long stay in the flats. Tomatoes should be transplanted very deeply (not now, cold zoners!); peppers and cabbage should be transplanted only an inch lower than their previous level. Slight wilting is normal. If you are in a warmer climate and your plants are going into the ground, protect them from sudden exposure to light and wind.

Friends from China share this method for deterring birds from the garden: hang sliced onions from nearby trees or on stakes around your plantings. The birds do not like the scent. Another suggestion is to hang bright streamers from the tree to unsettle the bird population. If you are planting and the birds won't leave you alone, interplant garlic and they will be put off. Interestingly, many birds are also repelled by lavender.

If you hang onions from the tree, the birds will not come.

SIGNALING • Early spring begins when the wood anemone (*Anenome quinquefolia*) flowers and ends when the leaf buds of the horse chestnut (*Aesculus hippocastanum*) and European white-bark birch (*Betula pendula*) open.

MOISTURE-OMETER • Plan on putting a few chrysanthemums here and there in the garden, if not for aesthetic reasons then for the information they provide about the water content in your soil. Chrysanthemums are the first to wilt when water is scarce. If you see your mums drooping it's time to start watering.

OKAY TO COMPOST • Even though rhubarb leaves, potatoes with green skin, and tomato leaves are said to be toxic, it is safe to add them to the compost heap. The items may be toxic to humans but are not to plants.

WORLD'S LARGEST RADISH • The largest radish on record was grown by the Litterini family of Tanunda, South Australia, in 1992. It weighed 37 pounds, 15 ounces.

❦ *April* ❦

Flower of the Month: Daisy

❦ A P R I L 1
April Fool's Day

If you are a beginner and running in circles now that spring has arrived, don't worry that Farmer Jones has already planted his early spring crops, and forget what Pip said about planting peas on St. Patrick's Day.

Early plantings can vary enormously among neighbors, seasons, years, and families. Within a 5-mile radius, microclimates can vary so dramatically that planting and sowing dates could be as much as 2 weeks apart.

The most reliable timepiece for the spring gardener is the garden itself. Instead of clinging to a number on the calendar, look to nature. When the daffodils and forsythia have bloomed, your garden is ready for all its hardy seeds like peas, carrots, lettuces, onions, and so on. When the dogwood and common lilac blooms begin to unfold, you can gingerly put out hardy seedlings that you've started indoors.

April, for me, is about hardy annuals. I have to wait until May to put out the tender seeds and plants, but my calendar is not as telling as my next-door neighbor's wisteria and spirea. Once they bloom I sow seeds that need warmer soil to germinate—nasturtium, morning glory, zinnia, and sunflower. The most vulnerable tender seedlings— my tomatoes, peppers, tender herbs, and other such annuals—will not come up from my brightly lit seedling factory in the basement until all danger of frost is past. And of course I will take great care to harden them off properly (see page 21).

Meanwhile, perennials won't show themselves until the weeds do and, in any case, it is unwise to toy with your perennials too early be-

34

cause you could unwittingly damage their root systems. On the other hand (actually, there are a lot of "on the other hands"), you *will* want to divide some perennials early in the spring, especially invaders. A final word to beginners: Don't ever let a string of warm days lull you into thinking you can plant before your frost-free date (and if you are unclear about the date, ask your cooperative extension service or your local nursery). Out of nowhere will come a chilling night, and your little plants will pay the price.

Besides, what's the rush?

I THINK THAT I SHALL NEVER BUY • A tree is not an impulse buy. And people who sell trees are not always expert. Before you head for the nursery, make sure you know as much as you can about your grounds. Do a bit of research into the kind of tree you are interested in; check out trees at the nearest botanical garden; read up. Unless you are dealing with a foundation planting, never plant a new tree closer than 30 feet to your house. Roots can eventually cause serious damage to your foundation, which is sometimes no more than 10 inches thick.

> *If it thunders*
> *On All Fool's Day,*
> *It will bring*
> *Good crops and hay.*

❦ A P R I L 2

Dancing with nature requires perfect timing and I'm no Gene Kelly. I have created the healthiest, most gorgeous seedlings of my life, all ready for planting in March, when even looking out the window could have killed them. Then there's the season I had about 400 little seedlings, begging to be transplanted, and me walking out the door with the kids for an impromptu trip to Florida.

Basic bad calls and life's little exigencies are always going to play havoc with the plants of the seedling farmer, but there is a trick you can use when your seedlings are ready but you—or the garden—are not. Without going to an extreme, you can ease your seedlings into a period of semidormancy by withholding water and putting them in a cooler place. Don't let them die of dehydration, of course; just slow the watering down a bit. This is a great method to employ if you are hit with an April 15 blizzard or some other fluke that throws your planting calendar off.

TRICKS FOR YOUR HOLLY PLANTS • Holly (*Ilex*) grows best in full sun but it can tolerate shade, which makes it a versatile plant for hedges, screenings, and foundations. But it is dioecious—male and female flowers are on separate plants—so to produce showy fruit, you have to plant male specimens in the same vicinity as female specimens. If you don't have a male holly near your female, use some artifice: place a few branches of male holly in a soda bottle. Tie a string around the neck of the bottle and simply hang it down from a female branch. With a little luck, bees will come and do the job for you.

STORING GREENS • Put garden lettuce—roots and all—unwashed, in a plastic bag and store in the refrigerator. Looseleaf lettuce should be spritzed with water, then set on paper towels, wrapped in plastic wrap or put in plastic bags, and then refrigerated. To recrisp wilted lettuce, put it in the freezer for about a minute or soak it in really cold water for a couple of minutes.

❦ A P R I L 3

One of the first greens to come up in the spring is poke (*Phytolacca americana*), also known as pokeweed or inkberry. Although the mature plant is unpalatable and maybe even poisonous, the very young shoots are edible and delicious when eaten like asparagus. During the 1844 presidential campaign of James K. Polk, his supporters wore sprigs of pokeweed to show their allegiance, causing many people to assume Polk was its namesake. He wasn't.

SHRUB AND TREE ROOTS • One of the biggest mistakes beginning gardeners make in planting container-grown shrubs and trees is thinking the roots should be treated with great care, as if they were tiny plant seedlings. The opposite is true. The roots need to be released and opened up, moved around, liberated, or your tree or shrub will die during the dryness of summer. It is imperative that you give your roots a workout before you plant. (This does not apply, of course, to the roots of wildflowers or rock plants, which do need Tender Loving Care.)

Loosen up your shrub and tree roots before planting.

STAKE YOUR PLANTS EARLY • Be sure to stake all your peonies and other early growers before they get too big, as they tend to flop. Good doses of liquid seaweed will also strengthen stems.

RULE OF THUMB • Roses that need to be pruned during dormancy—hybrid teas, grandifloras, and florabundas—should be pruned once the forsythia bloom, in the spring. *Do not prune until the leaf buds have swelled.* When the rosebush goes into action, you do too. (In mild climates timing is not so important, but for cold zones it is crucial.) Meanwhile, climbers and ramblers should be pruned after flowering.

> *Here tulips bloom as they are told.*
> —Rupert Brooke

❦ A P R I L 4

Buying a perennial is like buying anything; whatever it is, you need to give it a good once-over, and check under the hood. Checking under the hood in perennial purchasing is sneaking a look at the roots. Many times the larger perennials are not a good choice because their roots are not as vigorous; the roots closest to the sides of the pot are discolored or dead. What you want is a thriving, vital plant, not one that has spent its energy adjusting to a dreary plastic pot. Check out the roots: if they are healthy they will be a white color with tiny, wispy root hairs (some roots have different colors but your eye will tell you immediately if the plant is healthy).

GIVE YOUR FORCED BULBS ANOTHER LIFE • All of those wonderful forced bulbs (except paper-white narcissus) can have a double life if you treat them right. After they've bloomed, keep them well watered and give them lots of light, along with some organic fertilizer. When the foliage starts to yellow, gradually slow down your watering. Once it has browned and withered completely put the bulbs in a dry place, labeled, where they can stay all summer. In the fall, you can plant them outdoors with your other bulbs as usual.

TROWEL HANDLE COMFORT • To soften the feel of your trowel or tiller, cut up some foam from one of those insulated can holders—the kind that keep your sodas cold—and tape it to the handle with a strong adhesive like electrical tape. You'll be able to do a lot more work before you get your first set of blisters.

WATCH WHAT YOU MULCH • Mulch is usually a great boon to gardeners, but some people put it on indiscriminately. If the soil isn't warm enough, wait to mulch. Mulching too early will actually keep in the cold. This would be especially dangerous for plants that need soil to be well on the warm side (e.g., eggplants, tomatoes, and peppers).

April borrows three days from March and they are all ill.

❦ A P R I L 5

Ralph Waldo Emerson said, "A weed is a plant whose virtues have not yet been discovered." In some cases, I'd suggest, their virtues have been discovered, and found wanting. But most certainly weeds are better understood than loathed.

Weeds, like flowers, come in two varieties: annuals and perennials. Chickweed, lamb's quarters, purslane, and spurge are common annuals. Bermuda grass, bindweed, crabgrass, and quackgrass are typical perennials. If they are invading your garden, the most reliable tactic—besides serious mulching—is to level the soil with a hoe between rows every time the seeds reach ¼ inch high. This decapitates the weed and weakens its root systems. It also exposes the weed seed to sun and air, and dries it out.

If perennial weeds are your main problem, laying down black plastic after tilling works wonders. Most perennials need at least ½ inch of foliage to properly revive their root system. Weeds between individual plants are most effectively eliminated by the old gloved hand. It's least disruptive to pull weeds out when the ground has just been watered. Make sure when you water that you don't get the leaves wet, to avoid the spread of disease.

GROWING FRENCH TARRAGON • French tarragon (*Artemisia dracunculus*) was known as "Little Dragon" (from the Latin *dracunculus*) because it strangles itself on its own roots if it is not divided and separated every few years. It does not set seed. To grow it, you'll need to get a cutting from a friend or find a pot at your nursery.

RULE OF THUMB • Seedlings should be about as wide as they are tall at planting time.

• •

FLOWERS THAT LOOK GREAT IN BASKETS

• •

Sweet William (*Dianthus barbatus*)   Nasturtium (*Tropaeolum majus*)
Impatiens (*Impatiens wallerana*)   Annual phlox (*Phlox drummondii*)
Ivy geranium (*Pelargonium peltatum*)   Verbena
Petunia   Lobelia
Moss rose (*Portulaca*)   Lantana
Creeping zinnia

• •

SOME VINES FOR BASKETS

• •

English ivy (*Hedera helix*)
Variegated vinca (*Vinca variegata*)
Peppermint geranium (*Pelargonium*)

TINSEL DETERS BIRDS • If you tie Mylar Christmas-tree tinsel to stakes here and there in the garden, birds will not peck at your seeds. Once the seedlings are established, remove the tinsel and save it for your next sowing.

Hoe while it is spring, and enjoy the best anticipations. It is not much matter if things do not turn out well.
           —Charles Dudley Warner

• •

One of the shortest relationships of my life was with a landscape designer. I told him I envisioned, among other things, a planting of lilacs (*Syringa*) at one corner of my yard, and he looked at me as if I had requested a flock of pink flamingos. How sad for him. Lilacs have good karma. I have only a couple of varieties in my yard, but they give me enormous pleasure.

The best lilacs are grown on their own roots; if you purchase one that has been grafted, plant it deeply. Your lilac will need a dormant period in order to bloom, which is no problem if you live in a colder zone. In places like California, a dry period can sometimes serve the same purpose.

Lilacs are easy to grow if you have the right conditions. They need several hours of full sun a day or they will not bloom. A very old lilac can be stimulated to bloom by pruning it severely after blooming time. If your lilacs are growing nicely, just prune them moderately after they blossom. Deadheading is excellent for the plant.

Sprinkle wood ashes around your lilacs when you give your lawn the first cutting in the spring.

NINETY-NINE BOTTLES OF KUDZU ON THE WALL • Extract of kudzu (*Radix puerariae*) may decrease alchoholic intake in hamsters. Researchers Bert Vallee and Wing-Ming Keung of Harvard Medical School tested the extract on hamsters and found it lowered the amount of alcohol the hamsters consumed by free choice. Modern science, as usual, is a little behind the times. In China, the extract has been used to cure alcoholism since the seventh century.

REMINDER: EARLY SPRING LAWN CARE • For rapid greening, add a light application of balanced lawn fertilizer. In early summer apply another slow-release fertilizer to carry you through the summer months.

RULE OF THUMB • If you are sowing successive crops of greens like lettuce, spinach, and so on, keep rows grouped in their own areas, based on *when* you plant them. In other words, don't have mature lettuce heads at one end of the row and new seedlings on the other end—or even running parallel—because the watering needs of the plants vary so dramatically.

STONE WALLS AND VINES • If you are fortunate enough to have a stone wall, vining nasturtium or morning glories cascading down the sides look sensational.

No April is so good it won't snow on a farmer's hat.

❦ A P R I L 7
National Garden Week, April 7–April 13

My first garden was a 10-by-20-foot plot in Dallas that ran next to a detached garage painted white. I can still see the dead plants, all lined up in neat rows, the victims of a highly reflective white surface and a big merciless Texas sun.

I often think about that little garden and the grounds around the cottagelike house. In Texas, I learned one thing quickly: if you live in a hot weather zone you should plan to plant your summer crops in the corner of the garden that gets some afternoon shade or make your own shade with an old sheet stapled to stakes or posts. Also I learned the value of compost. Once I got the hang of things I added 2 to 3 inches of compost and other organic mulches to help my soil retain moisture and to insulate my plants from the sun. After a while things grew, especially my love for gardening.

FAVORITE WAY TO EAT ASPARAGUS • My asparagus recipe collection has its own shelf. When asparagus is in season, I like to eat it every day. Asparagus can go a thousand ways but I still like it best with a thin cheese sauce on buttered wheat toast. I also eat it steamed and then quickly stir-fried with a drop of sesame oil and hot red pepper flakes. Although it stores pretty well, there is nothing like fresh-picked asparagus cooked within an hour of harvesting. Pick it fresh and eat it right away.

MULTIPLY YOUR MUMS • If you have mums in the garden and want more, there is no need to go to the nursery and pay good money for them. Chrysanthemums are quite simple to propagate. In the spring, carefully dig up the shoots and replant them directly in the garden (or in a nursery bed until you are ready for them). You'll not only get more mums but will be doing a favor to the existing plants, which need to be divided anyway.

If you have potted *hardy* chrysanthemums you can also take cuttings from them. After the plant flowers, wait for the new growth to come in and then clip away—at the third set of leaves. You can start the cuttings out in a nursery bed or a cold frame.

PLANTS FOR CONTAINER GARDENING IN HOT WEATHER • Container gardening opens up a new universe of planting possibilities, but the containers need constant monitoring for moisture. If you live in a hot weather zone this can mean watering twice, even three times a day, at the peak of summer. Consider these drought-resistant perennials for your containers: *Amsonia tabernaemontana* var. *montana* 'Willow Blue Star'; *Asclepias tuberosa* (butterfly weed); *Gaillardia spp.*, *G. x grandiflora* 'Baby Cole' (blanket flower); and *Yucca filamentosa* 'Golden Sword' (yucca).

I stick to asparagus which still seems to inspire gentle thought.
—Charles Lamb

❦ APRIL 8

I first became aware of Arbor Day as a student living in Ann Arbor, where I suppose it is a bigger deal than in most places. Arbor Day is usually observed quietly, with goodhearted garden club members planting a tree here or there to acknowledge the occasion.

But a hundred years ago, Arbor Day had a passionate, moralistic edge to it. The earliest observance of Arbor Day was April 10, 1872, in Nebraska. J. Sterling Morton migrated from Detroit to Nebraska in 1854, and when he got there he was shocked, shocked at the treeless territory. As editor of Nebraska's first newspaper, he became an outspoken proponent of conservation, and suddenly planting trees was about good and evil. As it turned out, Nebraskans are such *good* people that on the first Arbor Day they planted 1 million trees. If you are interested in observing Arbor Day, find out when your state officially proclaimed it a holiday; the date varies from state to state.

ASPARAGUS NIGHTMARE • If your asparagus stalks turn a rusty color, they might have asparagus rust. Use pruning shears that has been disinfected in a 1-to-1 solution of bleach and water, and cut off and burn any affected stalks. Do this early, or the fungus will eventually reach the roots.

SWEET POTATO SHOOTS • If you haven't tried growing sweet potatoes before, you can easily create your own seedlings. Just buy 1 full-sized sweet potato at the grocery store—1 potato can yield up to 50 shoots! Poke toothpicks into the potato so that it can be suspended in a glass of water that covers the potato halfway up (the "Spudnik" look). After 2 weeks, you should have many shoots growing out of the potato. Clip them off and transplant them in flats. Feed them with fish emulsion and keep them under bright lights. When they are sturdy seedlings, plant them in the garden. Even if you don't like sweet potatoes, the plant makes a delightful ground cover.

Early insects, early spring, good crops.

❦ A P R I L 9

All is fair in love and gardening, and I use pots of flowering annuals and tender herbs as a cheating device, quite successfully. You can fill in almost any bare or boring spot in the garden with pots used in odd numbers. I use odd numbers, usually 1 or 3, because two pots, lined up side by side, tend to look goofy. The pots not only cover up mistakes but allow me to experiment with color. If I am thinking of adding a sweep of perennials in a certain color, I can get a preview by growing from seed a similarly colored annual.

Pots are also great labor savers. One woman I know puts pots of small dahlias around, with great effect. Once the foliage dies down in autumn, she puts all of the pots in the garage and covers them until early spring, when growth reappears. After her last frost date passes, she sets the pots out in her garden again for another glorious season.

KEEPING SEED BEDS MOIST • One idea for keeping seed beds moist: put wet burlap or watered wooden boards over the seeds until they come up. The day they sprout you obviously have to remove the covers, so keep a close watch. The board method also works well for fall plantings of crops like broccoli that are tricky to germinate when it is so hot and dry. Sow seeds thickly and then thin once you take the boards off.

FIRST-TIME GARDENERS • *Roses should be planted when dormant. Spring planting is safest in the cold zones, and winter planting best in the South. Late fall plantings work for some states like Maryland and New Jersey. Check with your local nursery.*

HARVESTING LOOSELEAF LETTUCE • There are two ways to harvest looseleaf lettuce. You can pull off individual leaves as needed or, if you need a lot of lettuce at once, you can employ the "cut and come again" technique where you cut the lettuce off at the crown of the plant when it is about 5 inches high. You'll get a second harvest in several weeks.

PINE NEEDLES AS MULCH • Pine needles, about 2 inches in depth, make a handsome mulch and are excellent for acid-loving azaleas and rhododendrons. But the terpene in pine needles can arrest seed germination, so be careful how you use them.

STORING RHUBARB • Rhubarb not only makes delicious pies and sauces but it is a handsome presence in the ornamental garden. You can harvest rhubarb over a 2-month period in the spring once your plants are established; stop when the stalks thin out because that indicates their energy is waning.

Pull the stalks from the plant (don't cut), and don't harvest more than half of the plant's leaves. Store rhubarb stalks in the refrigerator with the leaves attached, wrapped in plastic, up to a week. (Don't eat the leaves; they contain toxins.)

RHUBARB CRISP

1½ pounds rhubarb, cut up (4 cups)
½ teaspoon salt
1⅓ to 2 cups of sugar (varies according to tartness of rhubarb)
¾ cup all-purpose flour
1 teaspoon ground cinnamon
⅓ cup (5⅓ tablespoons) butter

Preheat oven to 350 degrees. Arrange rhubarb in an ungreased 8 × 8 × 2-inch baking dish. Sprinkle with salt. In a medium bowl, mix sugar, flour, and cinnamon. Cut in butter until the mixture is crumbly. Sprinkle over rhubarb.

Bake uncovered until the topping is golden brown and rhubarb is tender, about 40 to 50 minutes. Serve warm with vanilla ice cream. Serves 6.

Compared to gardeners, I think it is generally agreed that others understand very little about anything of consequence.
—Henry Mitchell

APRIL 10

Authors Bridget and Maureen Boland insist that amazing benefits follow from planting animal fat underneath rose bushes. This is not a practice that works where there are inquisitive rodents, but the Bolands say any city gardener would be foolish not to try it. Apparently in London after the war, a thick cake of fat formed on the manhole cover outside the Bolands' kitchen window, and as food rationing was still in place and the clump of goo looked somewhat edible, they decided to bury it in the yard so that a hungry passer-by would not think it worth trying to eat. At least that's what they said. They buried it near a climbing rosebush, which performed "stunningly" that year and every year thereafter. They continued the practice with excellent results, using scraps from the butcher, until they moved to the country and little foxes dug up the pieces of fat.

BITTER HERBS • Though there is a bit of a dispute on the subject, the original bitter herbs of Passover are often said to be: horseradish, coriander, lettuce, horehound, and nettle. Another list includes lettuce, chicory, dandelion, sorrel, and possibly mint or watercress.

GARDENING IN STONE PATHS • Here's an aromatic idea for flagstone walkways. If yours is in a sunny area, plant creeping thyme (*Thymus serpillum*) between the stones. The thyme does not mind being trampled upon and it releases a pleasing scent as you crush it with your heel. Another plant that does not mind heavy traffic is chamomile (*Anthemis nobilis*), which makes a lovely walkway plant.

SWEET GREENS • Most garden plants need a deep watering once a week. Lettuce is the exception—it needs more frequent watering. Keep your lettuce seedlings constantly moist. They are very shallow rooted and can dry out easily. Mulch is important, but you'll still have to water. If you don't provide even watering, the greens will turn bitter.

HI HOE, HI HOE • Although regular hoeing may not always destroy underlying weeds, it is still an effective way to discourage weeds from growing without destroying the root systems of desirable plants. Don't hoe deeper than an inch, though, or you'll endanger your good roots.

❧ A P R I L 1 1

Nothing is more valuable than a backyard pile of compost but, invariably, when my garden is ready, the compost is not. You can speed up the action in your compost heap by turning it more frequently with a spading fork. Turn it a few times a day over the course of a couple of weeks and you'll see excellent results. After you turn it, make sure to create a saucer-like shape to allow the rain to soak in better. Water it on your own if you need to. You can also find some specially formulated accelerators at the nursery and from gardening catalogues, which will heat up your compost pile more quickly. Leaf shredding machines are invaluable for hastening the degrading process. If you don't want to invest in one (they can be expensive), rent one from a local dealer.

HERBS FOR SHADE

Allium schoenoprasum (Chives)
Angelica archangelica (Angelica)
Anthriscus cerefolium (Chervil)
Galium odoratum (Sweet woodruff)
Levisticum officinale (Lovage)

Melissa officinalis (Lemon balm)
Mentha sp. (Mint)
Myrrhis odorata (Sweet cicely)
Petroselinum crispum (Parsley)
Symphytum officinale (Comfrey)

RADISHES AS MARKERS • Radishes make great markers for slower germinating root vegetables like parsnips. Plant the radishes and other root vegetables together. The radishes will come up first, allowing you to cultivate to your heart's content, knowing you won't damage the slower-growing vegetable.

PLANT SOME CHAMOMILE • Chamomile (*Anthemis nobilis*), translated from the Greek, means apple of the ground. Throughout history it has attained "best-all-around" status as an herb that can be used for everything from clothes freshener to eye lotion to stomach cramp reliever to face wrinkle remover to hair rinse to sedatives. April is a good time to plant chamomile in many zones. It's an annual, and if the conditions are right, plant it in a sunny spot with light, moist soil. Chamomile is said to revive ailing plants when planted in close proximity. It is a friendly little flower with light, lacy leaves, but I grow it mainly for the virtues of its tea. *To make the tea, add 1 ounce of fresh leaves to a pint of boiling water. Add 2 tablespoons of honey if you like it sweetened.*

> *Here are sweet peas,*
> *on tiptoe for a flight*
> *With wings of gentle flush*
> *O'er delicate white.*
> —John Keats

If you purchased one of those Easter lilies from the grocer and are trying to figure out whether to toss it or not, give it the summer to prove itself. More and more Asian lilies are being sold at Easter, and they tend to be a better bet long-term than what we ordinarily get at the grocer's. Here's what you do: Once you've finished enjoying the plant indoors, plant it outside and let it form a new bulb for next year under natural conditions. If it forms another bulb, you'll get another bloom next year; if not, it's history.

SPRINKLE COFFEE GROUNDS ON YOUR CARROT PLANTS • Root maggots are repelled by coffee grounds spread around your carrot plants. Sprinkle a little lime to ameliorate the acidity of the grounds.

REMINDER: BULB MAINTENANCE • Bulbs exhaust their nutrient reserves when they bloom. To grow—and to bloom again—they need to replenish their systems, which is why it is inadvisable to trim the foliage, no matter how unattractive. The plant needs the foliage to carry on the photosynthesis process. Once half the leaves turn yellow, you can transplant the bulbs if you want. It's a good time to do it because they are still easy to locate and the leaves serve as a handle. Separate them and replant them in well-drained soil enriched with compost and a sprinkling of organic fertilizer.

Once the leaves are totally yellow, cut out the watering and let the plant die down. When the leaves are brown and crinkled, you can cut them off or mow them down. You'll know it's time if when you tug at the leaves by hand they come away from the bulb easily and cleanly.

TOBACCO SWEEPINGS • If you live in the tobacco belt, try tobacco sweepings as a natural insecticide for your rose plants. In the spring, gently work the sweepings into the topsoil of established plants, being careful not to damage the root system. Don't apply it to new plants until they are at least a month old. The plants will slowly absorb the nicotine, which is fatal to leaf-chewing insects. Don't use tobacco on anything but roses, as it tends to spread viruses.

PRUNING FLOWERING SHRUBS • Your lilacs, rhododendron, laurel, and other spring-flowering shrubs should be pruned after blooming but before new growth begins.

❦ APRIL 1 3
Thomas Jefferson's Birthday (April 13, 1743–July 4, 1826)

If you are wondering whether your compost is ready, give it the sniff test. It may not be terribly sophisticated, but if your compost smells at all foul or like garbage, it's not ready. Get close. It should smell like fresh earth. Putting in compost prematurely can be counterproductive; your seeds will not germinate as well and you will not deliver the needed nutrients to your soil. If it needs more time, give it more time.

PINCH YOUR GARLIC SEED HEADS • To help along your garlic bulbs, pinch off seed heads to keep the plant's energy focused on healthy bulb production. Garlic thrives in a well-drained, compost-rich soil, in full sun.

FIRST-TIME PRUNERS • Never strain your pruning shears. If you try to cut a woody perennial that is too thick for your shears you'll ruin the shears and won't do your plants any favor, either.

❦ APRIL 1 4

Don't let a tiny plot stop you from having a pumpkin patch. Plant pumpkins, squash, melons, or cucumbers in your lawn. My neighbor, Spencer, planted her pumpkins in a sunny corner of the lawn and it looked as natural and plausible as it could be. A week or so before you plant your seeds or put in your transplants, prepare the soil by digging a really deep hole that is about 1 foot square. Work the soil, adding compost and some bonemeal. Give the dirt some liquid seaweed and let it sit for a few days. Then plant. Once your plants are

*Plant your pumpkins
in the lawn.*

really up and going, mulch them well so the lawn doesn't encroach on the area and absorb the water and nutrients. I would also recommend marking *exactly* where you planted the seeds, using a short stake or plant identifier; otherwise, once the vines start to fill in, you'll have no idea where to water.

RULE OF THUMB • Sometimes plant names can give you a clue as to shade or sun requirements. If the name has "hel," derived from the Greek *"helios,"* it won't work in your shade garden (e.g. *Helianthis*, or sunflower).

OTHER USES FOR TOMATO CAGES • You can also use your tomato cages to stake plants like dahlias, peonies, and sweet peas.

MAJOR SNOWFALL • On April 14, 1921, it snowed for 24 hours in Silver Lake, Boulder, Colorado, netting an accumulation of 75.8 inches for a U.S. record.

Oh, the lovely fickleness of an April day.

❦ A P R I L 1 5

A rose is a rose *is* a rose. Unlike most flowers, "rose" has no known meaning. In Greek it is *rhodon* and in Latin *rosa*, and both of these words have come to mean red, rose, or pink. Other flower names have more complex origins. The iris acquired its name from the Greek goddess of the rainbow, who was a member of Juno's court and charged with receiving the souls of dying women. Gladiolus derived its name from the Latin *gladius*, meaning sword, an allusion to its spikelike stem. Tulips were so-named for their imagined likeness to the *tulbend* (turban), headgear worn by the Turks.

The orchid's name is from the Greek *orchis*, or testicle, because of its tendency to be anchored by two swollen roots. Nasturtium is from the Latin *nasus torqueo*—or nose twister—apparently a reference to its scent, which is found by some to be disagreeable. And mistletoe, customarily a signifier of love, or at least kissing, actually translates in Old English to *mistil tan*, or "twig with the bird dung on it."

Aconitum spp. (Monkshood)
Alchemilla mollis (Lady's mantle)
Aquilegia spp. (Columbine)
Aruncus dioicus (Goatsbeard)
Astilbe (Astilbe)
Bergenia cordifolia (Bergenia)
Cimicifuga racemosa (Bugbane)
Convallaria majalis (Lily-of-the-valley)

Corydalis lutea (Corydalis)
Dicentra spp. (Bleeding heart)
Epimedium (Barrenwort)
Helleborus niger (Christmas rose)
H. orientalis (Christmas-Lenten rose)
Hosta spp. (Hosta)
Macleaya cordata (Plume-poppy)
Mertensia spp. (Bluebells)
Primula spp. (Primrose)

COMPOST SPEEDER-UPPER • Some gardeners insert lengths of PVC pipe—the ones with all the holes in them—into their compost piles to speed up the decomposition process. The pipes allow more air circulation in the pile, therefore delivering the benefits of constant turning. Insert them into the pile at an angle to affect the largest possible area.

Tulips open their petals when the temperature rises and close when the temperature falls.

🐛 APRIL 16

Every large bed needs some clear pathways; if you haven't put down brick or flagstones or mulch or straw hay—or *something* to take the tippy-toeing out of your gardening life—get that done this week. You've got to be able to get in there and work without worrying about crushing a seedling or picking up gigantic cakes of mud on your boots. Most professionals recommend a 3- to 4-foot walkway.

BUY YOUR ANNUALS AT THE RIGHT TIME • Don't buy your annuals from the nursery when they are in full bloom—buy them when the buds are just forming or they will be spent by July. If you buy the plants already in bloom, cut off the blooms so they can thicken up and form new buds. Deadheading (see page 123) will also keep your annuals in bloom.

Aster spp. (Aster)
Calendula (Pot-marigold)
Callistephus chinensis (China aster)
Campanula spp. (Bellflower)
Centaurea cyanus (Cornflower,
  bachelor's button, basket flower)
Chrysanthemum (Chrysanthemum)
Commelina spp. (Dayflower)
Coreopsis spp. (Coreopsis)
Cosmos spp. (Cosmos)

Helianthus annuus (Sunflower)
Phlox drummondii (Phlox)
Portulaca grandiflora (Moss rose)
Rudbeckia spp. (Black-eyed Susan)
Scabiosa atropurpurea (Scabiosa)
Silene spp. (Campion)
Tagetes spp. (Marigold)
Verbena hybrida (Garden verbena)
Zinnia elegans (Zinnia)

ONION CLINIC • To prevent seed heads from forming on your onions too early, water them consistently. Cut off flower heads as soon as you spot them; once onions go to seed, they never quite dry correctly. Also, planting onions too early can create trouble, but for most zones (depending on the weather, of course) your onions can be in the ground now.

RULE OF THUMB • If you live in the Northeast or the Midwest, you should plant most bare-root trees and shrubs in the spring. Balled and burlapped trees and shrubs, or those grown in containers, can be planted early in the fall—when the ground isn't frozen—but I still find spring planting optimal.

> April wet or April dry
> Always brings head of rye.

🌿 APRIL 17

Most herbs do *not* benefit from inorganic fertilizers. If you are a first-timer, hold back on the Miracle-Gro. Once an herb receives a strong dose of nitrogen-rich fertilizer, the plant undergoes a period of rapid growth, which has the effect of making its leaves less flavorful and reduces its aromatic and medicinal properties. Instead, think compost.

Compost's ability to absorb heat, aerate, and retain water and nutrients provides herbs with precisely what they need.

DIATOMACEOUS EARTH FOR WHAT AILS YOU • Diatomaceous earth (DE) is essentially finely ground shells from the sea that feel somewhat like baby powder to the touch. To a tiny predator, however, DE is like taking a razor to the digestive tract, which is why DE is extremely useful in discouraging slugs, flea beetles, and root maggots, among others. You can get it at the nursery. Read the directions before using and handle carefully.

EASY ON THE WATER • Plants need even, consistent moisture. Too much water not only deprives the plant of oxygen but promotes root rot. Plant a tin can halfway in the ground to measure how much water your plants are getting. It should fill to about an inch a week.

FLOATING ROW COVERS • I use floating row covers (described on page 325) on almost everything. Right now the sheeting protects my new lettuce seedlings from wind and harsh rays while boosting temperatures just a bit. Some gardeners use row covers for insect control but you have to make sure no insects are present before you put them down, and you have to seal the sides and ends completely, or you will have just made a cool tent for bugs.

❧ A P R I L 1 8

If you've been *meaning* to get the hose situation worked out, this is an excellent week to get it over and done with. Home gardeners are at the mercy of their watering systems, and if you take measures to refine your system now, you will find yourself grumbling less about that stupid hose come July.

Inexpensive hoses are wasted money. They bend and crack easily and they are a daily reminder that you were cheap and foolish when you bought them. If you are buying a new hose, spring for the best you can possibly afford. Then put in hose guides at the corners of your beds and borders so you don't smash the fragile transplants you've been nursing for weeks. I have a wonderful wooden post with a carved rabbit on it that always topples over the moment the hose comes around the bend. It will have to go somewhere else this year. Instead, I will install a solid 2-foot piece of galvanized pipe or even something taller that I can send a vine up. (Metal guides can also be beautified by putting a length of bamboo over them; sand the top edge so you don't scrape your leg on it.)

Another investment to make is in soaker hoses, if you don't have them already. They are totally efficient and will help you save on water bills (evaporation typically occurs when you use an overhead sprinkler). Another problem with overhead sprinklers: they wet the foliage, which in turn spreads disease. Soaker hoses are slow and gentle. They don't compact your soil like a giant glop of water from a watering can.

WHEN YOUR STRAWBERRY CROP GETS A SPRING FROST • One way to save your strawberry crop from complete devastation when hit by an untimely frost is to hose the ice off before the sun rises. Some plants will be damaged but you'll save more than you might have otherwise.

APHID TIP • One of the simplest methods of ridding your garden of aphids is to squish a few in your hand next to the affected plant. The dead aphids release a chemical signal that causes the other aphids to drop to the ground and abandon the plant.

LET'S HEAR IT FOR THE INVENTOR OF THE THERMOMETER • In ancient times, it was a standard practice to remove one's trousers and sit on the ground before seeding, to determine whether the soil was ready to be planted. If the flesh found it discomforting, it was too early to sow.

> *Good gardening is very simple, really. You just have to learn to think like a plant.*
> —Barbara Damrosch

Waging war with beneficial bugs has its toy soldier aspects, and it is not only fun (I always wanted a private army) but extremely effective. Timing, however, is critical. If you release your green lacewings, lady-bugs, praying mantises, or fly parasites too early they won't have anything to feast on; if you wait too long they may be overwhelmed by the infestation and unable to wage a serious battle. You have to read up and ask up before you play soldier; I found our local county extension agent most helpful and of course your bug broker should be a great help. Oh—and be careful about spraying your plants with toxins once you've released the bugs; the toxins may affect the good guys, too.

Timing is important when waging war with beneficial insects.

WHEN REMOVING TREE STAKES • Once your young tree can support itself without a stake, the stake can go. But don't pull it out of the ground willy-nilly. Saw it off at ground level or you could injure the tree's roots.

NUMBER ONE ANNUAL • Impatiens, lovers of shade, account for almost half of all annuals purchased in the United States, with the annual vinca coming in number 2.

PEPPER PLANTING TIP • Pennsylvania master gardeners Ann and John Swan recommend using 6-inch plastic pots to protect pepper seedlings from wind and cutworms. First plant the seedling, then take a plastic pot, with the bottom cut off, and twist it down into the ground over the plant. The bottom rim goes about 2 inches deep into the soil. Water slowly so the pot doesn't get dislodged. At night, if the temperature dips below 50 degrees, the Wards recommend putting empty 3-gallon plastic pots over the plants for protection. Once the pepper plants take off, the Wards cage them—using the cages as windbreakers and to support the limbs, which in their case are laden with fruit. The Wards use salt hay as a mulch, which is excellent for their climate; clear plastic is better for colder zones.

❦ A P R I L 2 0

One of my favorite ways of encouraging ants, aphids, and fleas *out* of my garden is to serve them mint tea. I drink it all the time and save the leftovers. Bugs do not like the odor of mint. You can either scatter mint leaves and stems around the garden or water your plants with mint tea and you will get excellent results. Be careful if you scatter the mint leaves and stems, though—your garden might turn into a mint bed, as the cuttings propagate easily.

MOST FRAGRANT PERENNIALS • The New York Botanical Garden created a Fragrance Garden in 1955. Its original hardy perennial plantings included the following:

Achillea ageratum (Sweet yarrow)
Cheiranthus allionii (Wallflower)
Chrysanthemum balsamita (Costmary)
Convallaria majalis (Lily-of-the-valley)
Dryopteris nevadensis (Fragrant fern)
Dianthus deltoides (Maiden pink)
Nepeta hederacea (Gill-over-the-ground, runaway robin, ground ivy)
Hemerocallis citrina (Long yellow daylily); *H. flava* (Tall yellow daylily); and *H. minor* (Dwarf yellow daylily)
Hosta plantaginea (Fragrant plantain-lily)
Lavandula officinalis (Lavender)
Melissa officinalis (Lemon balm)
Mentha piperita (Peppermint); *M. spicata* (Spearmint)
Nepeta mussinii (Persian catmint)
Paeonia (Peony)
Papaver alpinum (Alpine poppy)
Petasites fragrans (Winter heliotrope); *P. hybridus* (Purple butterbur)

Salvia officinalis (Sage)
Santolina chamaecyparissus (Lavender cotton)
Saponaria officinalis (Bouncing Bet)
Sedum spectabile (Showy stonecrop)
Tanacetum vulgare (Tansy)
Thymus citriodorus (Lemon-scented thyme)
Trifolium repens (White clover)
Viola odorata (Sweet violet)

CUTTING TULIPS • Tulips are a splendid cut flower, and should last at least a week in the house. The Netherlands Flower Bulb Information Center suggests you trim the stem ends with a sharp knife or shears to open up the channels for water intake (they close down when the stem is dry). Wrap the bunch snugly in newspaper with the lower stems exposed a couple of inches below the paper's edge. Put the bunch in a bucket of cool to lukewarm water deep enough the cover the stems but not the paper. Keep it in a cool location for an hour or two. The stems will draw water up and also they will stiffen. (If the flowers droop, repeat this procedure.)

When arranging spring flowers use only cool water filled about one third up the vase, and refill daily to that level. Cut tulips will continue to grow in water, sometimes adding nearly an inch to their height in the vase. Darwin hybrids grow the most.

> *To dig and delve in nice clean dirt*
> *Can do a mortal little hurt.*
> —John Kendrick Bangs

APRIL 21

TAURUS, April 21 to May 21—*A time for sowing root crops*

In the vegetable garden, mixing plants that have different light requirements is an excellent way to create mini-environments perfectly suited to your plants' needs. You might have some spinach in the ground now; if there is space, how about planting your peppers in the same row? The peppers will shade the spinach and soon enough, when the spinach is through its life cycle, there will be room for the growing peppers. Celery and leeks, both potash lovers, are well paired for similar reasons. Corn and pumpkins (or squash) planted together will also maximize space, light, and nutritional amendments.

GET YOUR FREE COMPOST HERE • I never produce as much compost as my garden needs at any given moment, which is why I rely heavily on the village sanitation department for the free compost they offer throughout the growing season. We load up the van with bags and bags of the stuff, and it's like Christmas. Your municipality probably offers free compost; if not, you should be able to find a town within driving distance that does offer it.

EAU D'LOCKER ROOM • The herb valerian and the oxeye daisy contain valeric acid, a compound found in human perspiration.

ROLY POLY BUGS • Compared to other insects, roly poly bugs, aka wood lice, aka sow bugs, aka pill bugs, aka doodlebugs, are low on the enemies list. They usually dine on decaying organic matter so when they are present it means that something else has gotten to your plant first. But it is also true that they enjoy tender stems and the growth of very young seedlings. If you have an infestation with your early spring or summer crops, you can try sprinkling corn meal, diatomaceous earth, or washed and crushed eggshells on the problem site.

SPRING MULCHING • If you are spring mulching new plantings of flowers and vegetables, wait until the soil temperature warms up to 55–60 degrees. This may occur as late as June in some Northern zones. When you mulch, be serious. Fine-textured materials like sawdust are so dense you need only a couple of inches of mulch. Shredded leaves or chips should be laid down in 3- or 4-inch layers. Unshredded leaves or salt hay can be laid down as deep as 8 inches. Newspaper mulch should be 8 or so inches deep, anchored with dirt and rocks. Don't mulch too close to the plants' bases or the stems will rot. Give stems about 3 to 5 inches of breathing space.

I gardened for years in a pretty cold zone (put it this way: the leaves start turning in late August) and I had to employ a lot of tricks to extend my gardening season. Though my gardening circumstances have changed I still find myself using these tricks when we have an abnormally cool spring or when my seedlings sown indoors are ready for the garden but the garden is not ready for them. If you want to get your warm-season crops in now—and if it's not really warm enough yet—try these measures:

First, warm the soil. To do this, spread clear (not black) plastic over the planting bed for 10 days. Once the soil temperature is up to 60 degrees for tomatoes and cucumber or squash seeds, 70 degrees for peppers, 75 degrees for cantaloupe or okra, you can plant accordingly. Cover the seed beds with floating row cover (page 325). When your tender plants (tomatoes and peppers) come up, you can put "Wall O'Water" cloches around them. These clear plastic water-filled tubes need to be staked if winds are violent. Another mini-greenhouse can be created by covering cages with clear plastic and staking this into the ground to protect your plants. With determination you can gain a week or two, but most important is the ability not to *lose* a week or two to unseasonable weather.

CROW DETERRENT • To keep crows out of your garden one Virginian suggests tying monofilament fishing line 7 or 8 feet off the ground around the garden, attached to stakes and crisscrossed several times.

TO KILL COMPOST ODORS • It's rare to have bad odors in the compost heap, but if the problem arises, add a layer of torn-up newspapers, 1/2 cup of household ammonia (adds nitrogen, too), a sprinkling of soil mixed with a little ground agricultural lime, and some coffee grounds or tea leaves. The problem will disappear almost at once.

I used to shoot a lot of black-and-white photographs, but now my photography is confined to color images of my family and garden. Shooting vignettes, lovely color combinations, a specimen that has come of age, a vegetable that is gigantic or just plain beautiful is a favorite pastime. I also think that the process of studying the garden through a lens gives me visual insights I would not have had otherwise.

When you take pictures of your garden, don't make the mistake of standing miles away to cram in every last flower. Shoot scenes from your garden instead. Compose the picture: Should it be vertical or horizontal? Will the subject look best close up or from a slight distance—and where should it sit in the frame, on the left or right or even in the center? (Unless it is a close-up, don't put your focal point smack dab in the center; it looks dumb.) Should you look down on your flowers for an overview? Or kneel and shoot it straight on from a 4-year-old's point of view?

A bright sunny day is not the best time to photograph your garden: everything will look washed out by the intensity of the sun. So don't shoot at noon. Try to pick a day with a little cloud cover and shoot in midmorning or midafternoon. Another fun photographic adventure is to pick a location and shoot pictures from the same spot in weekly increments. You will be amazed at how many transformations take place in your garden in just a single season.

BEFORE YOU GET OUT YOUR SHOTGUN • Rabbits probably have discovered your tender lettuces by now, and if *hasenpfeffer* is not your favorite spring dish, put in a fence. Use ¾-inch chicken-wire that is buried at least a foot to discourage the creatures from burrowing under. The fence doesn't have to be high—30 inches will do—but you should bend the top of the wire outward about a foot over the ground to discourage hopovers.

PEA HARVEST • Peas are ready to harvest 3 weeks after the first blossoms appear. Use little scissors or pinch them off by hand. The tips of the pea vines are edible and work beautifully in stir fries. Harvest often. They'll produce more.

UNCOVER PLANTS IF TEMPERATURES GO UP • Playing with cloches and row cover requires vigilance. If you get a string of warm days, be sure to remove the protection or your plants may overheat and burn.

It's a way off, but if you want to grow gigantic slicing tomatoes, there are a few tricks you might want to play—at least on one plant. First, when your tomato plant begins to form its initial sets of flowers, pick off all the flowers. I'm not kidding. What happens when you do this is that the plant goes back to its work of setting roots and establishes itself better than if it went right into the fruit-making process. In the peak of summer it will handle stress much better than your other tomato plants (and believe me, it is going to have stress when you start encouraging atomic tomato growth). When the plant begins setting fruit again and the little tomatoes are about ½ inch in diameter, pluck off all but 2 per cluster. You should do this to all the clusters on the plant, all season long. By harvest time, you should be lugging major tomatoes into the kitchen.

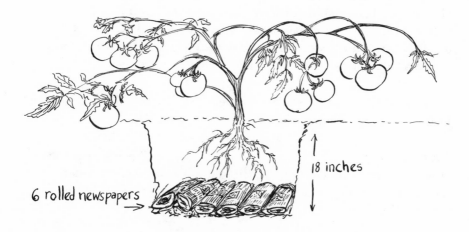

Create a time-release watering system.

P O O R M A N' S P O L Y M E R S • Squash, melons, cucumbers, and tomatoes all require a lot of water. One way to keep a steady supply directed to the roots is to create an underbed of newspaper. Take the daily newspaper and roll 3 or 4 sections together very tightly; tie with string every 6 inches or so. Dig a hole approximately 18 inches deep where you are going to create a hill or plant your tomatoes. Place the rolled newspapers—about 6 of them per plant—horizontally in the bottom of the hole, side by side. Each newspaper roll will absorb nearly a gallon of water. Layer on about 6 or 7 inches of good soil and a handful of compost, and then put in your seedlings. With deep, periodic watering, the roots will have access to water all season long.

> *What a man needs in gardening is a cast-iron back, with a hinge in it.*
> —Charles Dudley Warner

❦ A P R I L 2 5

Be careful when selecting seeds and specimens for fragrance. Many of the "new and improved" varieties have had their fragrance bred out of them. When selecting sweet alyssum for fragrance choose *Lobularia maritima*, the original white variety. Stick to the old-fashioned tobacco plants, too. The jasmine tobacco plant (*Nicotiana alata*) is lovely, grows to be 3 or 4 feet tall, and is strongly scented; so also is the 6-foot woodland tobacco plant (*N. sylvestris*), which thrives in sun or partial shade and is powerfully fragrant at night.

ST. MARK'S DAY • The evangelist St. Mark is the patron saint of mildew. I don't know why. Today is his feast day.

CROWDED SEEDLINGS • Don't buy seedlings that are overcrowded. Not only will they be stressed out from their crowded conditions, but when you try to separate them you will probably damage the tangled roots.

SMALL SEED TRICK • One way to sow those tiny, tiny seeds is to wet a cotton string and roll the wet string in a dish of the tiny seeds. The seeds will stick to the string—all you have to do is lay the string in the planting furrow and cover with the appropriate amount of soil, if any. Eventually, the string will decompose.

TAKING THE TEMP OF YOUR SOIL • All seeds have a minimum temperature requirement for sprouting, and in order to determine the temperature of your soil you really do need a thermometer. Some people use a meat thermometer in the garden. You can also order a soil thermometer from catalogues or get one at a good nursery; they're very helpful if you want to get your seeds in at the earliest possible moment (and not rely strictly on the calendar for sowing), and they also are good for taking the temperature of your compost pile. Take a reading on your soil *at the depth you will be planting your seed*, and do it once early in the morning when it will be coldest and once as the sun begins to set, when the soil will be warmest. The average of the two will be the measurement you go by. Test three days in succession for good measure.

❦ A P R I L 2 6

When you stake your flowers, make sure you use stakes that are tall enough. I remember A Real Bad Day when I came home and all my sunflowers were snapped off at the knees because of strong winds and stubby stakes. The tall stakes are an eyesore at first but they soon disappear in foliage and blooms. (Anyway, there is no sorer sight than a pile of broken sunflowers.) Insert the stakes about 6 inches from the plant's crown. Each stem should have its own stake (important especially for plants like delphiniums). The stake should go down about a foot to anchor it properly, and when there is growth, tie it in place every 12 inches or so. If you are using white string, which looks kind of dopey, you can stain it by letting it sit in a pot of old coffee overnight.

SAVE OLD SHEETS • You can use old sheets as your floating row cover to prevent damage from early or late frosts. You shouldn't use row covers in the heat of summer because they raise the temperature around your plants even higher. You, can, however provide *shade* for your plants in the heat of summer using old sheets as a canopy, several feet above the ground to allow air to circulate freely.

COLORED PEPPERS • If you have a short growing season and want to grow some colored peppers, choose Northstar (green to red) or Gypsy (yellow to red). Give your peppers some nutrients at planting (a 2-5-2 or rough equivalent) and when the blossoms appear, feed the plants with some 5-2-5. Get peppers into the ground as soon as conditions allow—but not before!

RULE OF THUMB • If your perennials deliver only one flush of blooms over the course of the season, don't deadhead them after flowering. Cut the plant back about a third down from the top after flowering and then leave it alone.

❦ A P R I L   2 7

With the great spring harvests come many hours of puttering in the kitchen—and greens have my full attention now. Greens are nutritional godsends, but I am mostly interested in them because they take beautifully to mere culinary suggestions: a slice of garlic, a splash of flavored oil, a dusting of grated cheese. For the best flavor, eat your fresh-picked greens as soon as possible. When you are ready to cook, wash them in tepid water to get rid of the soil and aphids, if present. Wash them several times, as quickly as you can. Be sure to get all of the grit out. Nobody likes grit. Use a nonreactive pot or pan when you cook greens. And remember that an armful of greens cooks down to absolutely nothing in the pot, so cook much more than you think you'll need. You'll definitely want seconds.

FOIL REFLECTORS FOR TOMATOES • If you plan on growing tomatoes in less than 6 hours of sun, try putting down some foil reflectors once the soil has heated up. By placing aluminum foil on the soil, shiny side up, under the tomato plants, you increase light exposure dramatically. You can anchor the foil with rocks or dirt— just be very sure the soil is warm enough before you lay down the foil "floor." Planting tomatoes next to a white wall will also boost light exposure.

IF YOU ARE ALLERGIC TO BEES • I know some gardeners who are allergic to bee stings, and for obvious reasons gardening is a dicey pastime for them. The best way not to attract bees to the vegetable garden is to stick to plants that you harvest before flowering, like lettuces, cabbages, and all of the root vegetables. Unfortunately, with a few exceptions, most herbs and flowers are bee attractors. The exceptions are chrysanthemums, lilacs, and forsythia; bees also don't much like tulips or daffodils.

I still get the creeps about using pathogenic insecticides, though they are logical, effective, and well within the rules of nature. Pathogenic insecticides are essentially a means of conducting organic germ warfare against the insects that plague your garden. It is selective, because these microbial insecticides do not harm other insects, birds, and animals. It is organic because these substances occur naturally and readily break down in water. The two most common are *bacillus thuringiensis* (BT) and *bacillus popilliae*, also known as milky spore disease. BT can infect more than sixty species of insects, including potato beetles, corn earworms, cabbage worms, and loopers. Milky spore disease is best known as a slow-acting but long-term insecticide for Japanese beetles.

Do some research on these two methods before you use them. It's not just a simple matter of one application and boom! your troubles are over. But they are enormously effective and well worth your investigation.

DAFFODIL CLINIC • If you need to separate your daffodils this year, wait until all foliage has turned brown and the bulbs are in dormancy. After separating the bulbs, either replant immediately or store in a cool dry area sprinkled with ground sulfur.

EAT YOUR BROCCOLI • Broccoli contains sulforaphane, a substance that has been identified as an anti-cancer agent.

TOMATO MANIPULATION • To encourage tomato seedlings to be shorter and stockier (which is desirable for a smoother transplanting experience), brush the seedlings that you have indoors in flats. You can use a child's thick paint brush. For some reason, brushing them every few days causes their growth to be somewhat arrested and you get healthier transplants.

There is an art to watering plants: when, where, and how are lessons learned over time. First-time gardeners tend to water frequently and lightly. This is good for seedlings, which can only take in so much water at a time, but it is unproductive for more mature plants. Mature plants need thorough watering, which means to a depth of 6 to 8 inches.

If you have soaker hoses, you are already ahead of the game. If you don't, the best way to get a thorough, deep watering is to water once with your hose and then repeat the process.

If you come home in the evening and find your plants doubled over, resist the temptation to flood them that night. A few more hours of thirst won't kill them, while watering them at night when they are stressed out and more vulnerable to fungus is more apt to damage the plant.

When you water, aim your hose at the base of the plant. Avoid getting the leaves of your plants wet, again to inhibit the spread of disease.

BROCCOLI PLANTING • When you transplant broccoli outside, position the seedlings 18 inches apart and plant 2 seeds between them. This way you'll get both an early and late crop. (If you've already planted yours, just tuck the seeds in now. Broccoli grown from seeds planted directly in the garden is tastier than broccoli grown from transplants.)

CUTWORM COLLARS • When your cabbages and broccoli are young, place little collars around the stems. Paper cups or tuna tins with tops and bottoms removed will work well. Bury the collar at least an inch deep.

FIRST-TIME GARDENERS • In general, cut flowers last longest when cut in the full-bud or half-bud stage. Most flowers should not be cut when they are fully open. Delphinium, gladioli, and other spiked flowers are normally cut when the first floret opens.

When it says on the back of the seed packet to plant cucumbers or squash or pumpkins in hills, the hills refer to mounds raised 8 to 10 inches from the ground level, where drainage is a problem. If drainage isn't a problem the "hills" are not hills at all, but merely a reference to seeds planted together.

COMPOST NO-NO'S • Meat is a primary no-no in composting. The meat and fat take forever to decay and they also attract unwanted animals. Cheese and other fatty dairy products are also best left out, for the same reason. Animal manures, except those from pets (they harbor disease), are all excellent. Also: leave out all difficult weeds, and diseased and chemically treated plants.

FIRST-TIME GARDENERS • *Don't pinch peppers back to produce more foliage. You will get more foliage but you won't get peppers.*

ALFALFA FOR ROSES • You might give your roses a hormonal boost by sprinkling alfalfa rabbit food—the pellet kind—on your rose beds. Just toss a handful around each rosebush at the base and let the rain dissolve it. This might not be a good method for gardeners plagued with rabbits.

STORING ASPARAGUS • Dutch researchers have learned that asparagus spears stay fresh and firm for sixteen days if the cut ends are placed in wet tissue paper. Spears stored dry lose their moisture rapidly, and soften in less than a week.

Give me flowers while I live.

❦ *M a y* ❦

Flower of the Month: Lily-of-the-valley

❦ M A Y 1
May Day

One of the first tricks most of us learned about container gardening was to put in a layer of gravel, broken clay pots, or marbles in the bottoms of our containers. The idea was to assure good drainage and avoid root rot. Only it isn't necessary. All the gravel does is use up valuable space that is better devoted to nutritious soil.

As long as there is a hole at the bottom of the pot, you don't need to worry about drainage. The only good reason for putting rocks in the bottoms of containers is to anchor them from strong winds, although if the winds are so strong they are going to blow your pots over, you might want to rethink where you have your plants in the first place.

ALL HAIL FLORA • In ancient Rome, April 28 to May 2 was a feast period devoted to the worship of Flora, the goddess of flowers, in whose honor the celebration of Florialia was held. Happy May Day.

FLOWERS THAT ATTRACT HUMMINGBIRDS • Hummingbirds like bright red and orange colors. They also like tubular shapes. You can make a hummingbird solution easily: Add 1 cup of sugar to 4 cups of water and bring to boil. Boil for several minutes, and then cool. Put the solution in a feeder that is tinted red (*don't* use red food coloring). Some people add a drop of baby vitamins for extra nourishment but I have never tried it. In intensely planted hummingbird gardens, gardeners can go out in a red cap or T-shirt and the hummingbirds will seek them out! To attract some to your yard, plant the following near a window—so you can peek:

Bee balm (*Monarda didyma*)
Butterfly weed (*Asclepias tuberosa*)
Cardinal flower (*Lobelia cardinalis*)
Columbine (*Aquilegia*)
Fuchsia (*Fuchsia*)
Hollyhock (*Alcea rosea*)
Impatiens (*Impatiens*)
Indian paintbrush (*Castilleja coccinea*)
Jewelweed (*Balsaminaceae*)
Phlox (tall) (*Phlox maculata*)
Lantana (*Lantana camara*)
Salvia (*Salvia officinalis rubriflora*)
Tiger lily (*Lilium tigrinum*)
Trumpet vine (*Campsis radicans*)

Flowers are the sweetest things God ever made and forgot to put a soul into.
—Henry Ward Beecher

❦ M A Y 2

My sister Ginny puts copper pennies in her vases of cut tulips and she insists that she gets an extra couple of days' pleasure for her efforts. I know people who add a little bit of Seven-Up to their vases (a teaspoon of sugar is a corresponding tactic); others put in a thimbleful of gin. Still others add a crushed aspirin.

Everyone seems to have it half right. The package of chemicals you commonly receive from the florist along with your bouquet is a sugar-based substance that functions as an energy source and as an antibacterial agent. When bacteria multiply rapidly, they can clog the water-conducting vessels in the stem, shortening the life of the flower.

In the heat of summer, I sometimes add to a quart of hot water 1 teaspoon of household bleach and 2 teaspoons of sugar because it seems to arrest the bacterial build-up and goo. If they are really special blooms, I put the vase of flower somewhere cool and dark for several hours before displaying them. If I don't use the sugar-bleach mixture, I use this formula: *Change the water every day, and cut the stems about an inch daily. Remove the dead and dying stems as you go along.* It's boring, I realize. But it works.

HARVESTING CHIVE FLOWERS • Chive flowers are too often viewed as mere spiky purple things at the tops of chives. This is a terrible oversight! Let your chive flowers bloom—but don't let them go to seed. Pick them before the papery coat begins to open. If they have opened, you can use them in bouquets. But they also are an interesting edible. They add excellent flavor to roasted chicken. You also can use them in a stir-fry with sesame oil.

I like them in seasoned vinegar. Pack the flowers and stems into a jar and fill it with rice wine vinegar. Let the vinegar stand for a couple of weeks, and then strain it. It will turn a violet color, and is lovely with a little olive oil used to dress fresh greens.

All gardens are a form of autobiography.
—Robert Dash

❦ M A Y 3

A lawn, to me, is somewhere I don't get to plant flowers. Unfortunately, as long as my husband plays croquet and the children play soccer, I am going to have a lawn. One of the transformations in lawn upkeep, however, makes me more tolerant: as long as you don't have a thatch problem (a very thick buildup of dead grass parts at the soil surface), you no longer have to pick up your lawn clippings. (If you have a thatch problem, skip the next paragraph. Lawn clippings will exacerbate it.)

Lawn clippings are mostly water and they decompose rapidly. When you leave the clippings on the lawn, it adds the equivalent of 15 to 18 percent of the nitrogen fertilizer you apply. Free nitrogen! Less work! So if you are still raking and bagging, you can stop now—unless, of course, it is for a good purpose like mulch or compost.

The other good thing about lawns is how good they smell when they are freshly mown. Happy lawns are shorn lightly—no more than one third the height of the leaf blade—which means often. Don't try to save work by doing a buzz job on your back forty or it will send the root system into shock. Your lawn will thin out and be an open house for weeds. If you can't mow every week, let it grow out a bit, especially in the heat and dryness of high summer. Taller grass shades itself and the ground. It also grows deeper roots, which need less water.

DEADHEAD YOUR RHODIES AND AZALEAS • Once they've finished blooming, deadhead (page 123) your rhododendrons and azaleas. An estimated 70 percent of a rhododendron's energy goes into the formation of seed. I use a whisk broom to lightly dislodge the dead blooms of my azaleas. The rhododendrons get the gloved hand treatment.

SAVE YOUR ONION SKINS • Instead of tossing onion skins in the compost heap, spread them over your cucumber patch. The scent will disorient squash bugs and striped cucumber beetles.

Add Epsom salts to help your roses grow.

ROSE BOOST • To stimulate new growth, give each rosebush 1 tablespoon of Epsom salts in May and June along with regular monthly feedings. The magnesium in the Epsom salts assists in the metabolic process.

PREPARE YOUR SOIL TO RETAIN MOISTURE • To avoid the consequences of a drought this summer, prepare your soil properly. The effort you put in now will pay big dividends in July and August. Work peat moss into your soil well; its water-holding capacity is superb. Also, mulch. Decide on a mulch that looks right and get it on your garden once the soil is warm. I use salt hay on my vegetable and herb garden and I generally have to water only a few times during the entire month of August.

If you use a year-round mulch, don't just pile new mulch on top of it. Freshen it by raking it around and fluffing it up before adding new mulch.

Plant four seeds when you make your row:
One for the pheasant, one for the crow,
One to rot and one to grow.

❦ M A Y 4

Cool nights can be a problem for warm-weather crops like eggplants, peppers, and tomatoes. Though a 40-degree night won't kill your plants, it will retard growth. In general it's much better to wait until the lowest temperatures don't go below 50 degrees before putting in your warm-weather vegetables. Vegetables planted later will yield earlier—and more abundantly.

WINDOW BOX MAGIC • If you're still doing Boring Containers, this is a great month to experiment with a set of pots. You can create a whole cosmos out of pots on a porch or terrace, and you are limited only by your imagination. Go beyond the usual herbs, verbenas, pansies, and nasturtiums—and experiment with leaves, textures, and oddball flowers. Let some ornamental edibles into your pots and let them go to seed. This is the place to check out intriguing annuals and daring color combinations. You can try almost anything you want in a pot!

PEA CLINIC • If your blossoms aren't producing pods, give them some encouragement. Often brushing the vines with a soft cotton cloth can spread the pollen on this self-pollinating plant.

COLORS FOR ATTRACTING BUTTERFLIES • Next to purple flowers, butterflies like concentrations of yellow flowers (like coreopsis) best.

WORMS DO NOT LIKE ONIONS • Worms are great for compost. But if you have worms in your compost heap, don't add onions. The worms will actually crawl out of the heap if it has onions or other intensely acidic food particles in it.

A wet May makes a load of hay.

MAY 5

Many gardeners are enamored of Citrousa (*Pelargonium citrosum* 'Van Leeni'), the so-called mosquito plant, not particularly for its physical attributes but for its purported ability to repel mosquitoes. A cross of lemon grass and a scented leaf *Pelargonium* (geranium), the plant grows up to about 5 feet high and sends wafts of lemon about in gentle breezes. But researchers have concluded it doesn't repel mosquitoes. Castor beans are also said to repel mosquitoes, though they can do worse to humans; 6 seeds can kill an adult. *Fisherman's secret: Avon Skin-So-Soft bath oil. Rub a few drops on your arms, face, and neck, and flying insects will have nothing to do with you.*

TOMATO COMPANIONS • The following plants in your tomato patch may ward off disease, encourage growth, and improve flavor: carrots, leaf lettuce, nasturtiums, parsley, onions, chives, and marigolds. Do not plant tomatoes with cabbages, fennel, potatoes, or kohlrabi.

INSTANT SHADE • When you are transplanting, use light lawn furniture propped here and there to create shade for your plants as they get accustomed to their new location.

WEED-FREE ZONE • If you would like to develop a new bed or correct a bad weed situation you see developing, you can solarize the weeds away. Just pull a sheet of clear plastic over the area that you want completely weed-free and weight down the edges. Let it sit for a few months in the hot sun. This process should not only kill the weeds at the surface, but knock out the weed seeds on the top couple of inches as well. You'll get a nice fall garden out of it this year.

No poet I've heard of has written an ode to a load of manure. Somebody should, and I'm not trying to be funny.

—Ruth Stout

❧ M A Y 6

One *can* have too many eggplants. Last year, we had eggplant for breakfast, lunch, and dinner, but it will be difficult *not* to put in my usual 10 too many; no fruit is quite as beautiful. If you have an extravagance of eggplants later in the season—and wish to discriminate—one grower recommends you check the scar at the blossom end. The blossom scar on a Black Beauty eggplant will be either round or elongated. The round blossom-end scar will be mild. The elongated blossom-end scar will be somewhat bitter. Both kinds have their defenders, though I prefer the milder eggplants. Keep what you like and harvest the rest—for neighbors. *Eggplants like to be kept evenly moist; they do not respond well to drought.*

WHAT TO DO WITH A SPENT TULIP BED • Maybe it's old age, but I am getting more and more relaxed about the appearance of spent flowers. However, if you are still young and not as lax, or if you have a major tulip bed and find those final days of tulips an unbearable sight, then dig them up. Without harming the bulbs, you can dig up your tulips and trench them in a holding bed until the leaves all die back. Then simply sort out the bulbs and store them in mesh bags in a cool dark place with good air circulation. Replant in the fall.

MIXING APPLES AND ORANGES • If you are not collecting and saving seed for next year, you can plant different varieties of squash and melons in close proximity. While cross-pollination prevents the seeds from reproducing true, fruits usually aren't affected. This holds for most vegetables and fruits, except corn and other plants where what you eat is the seed.

REMINDER: EARLY SUMMER LAWN CARE • Toward the end of early summer, apply a liquid or granular general-purpose fertilizer to your lawn.

NEW PEPPER ON THE BLOCK • A yellow jalapeño, called Jaloro, is here—from the experimental laboratory of Benigno Villalon, Ph.D., of the Texas Agricultural Experiment Station. This one is super-hot, disease resistant, and fabulous looking. "It's as hot as any jalapeño we've tested," Villalon says. Seed information is available by writing Texas Foundation Seed, Texas Agricultural Experiment Station, College Station, TX 77843.

FIRST-TIME GARDENERS • *Whenever you are scratching fertilizer into your established beds, be sure to avoid fertilizer contact with the plant foliage.*

Old gardeners never die, they just spade away.
—Muriel Cox

❧ MAY 7

Growing vines up tree trunks can be a wondrous thing, and there are combinations that are pure poetry. But certain vines growing up tree trunks can cause terrible damage, and are best left to inanimate surfaces. Poison ivy, for instance, can overwhelm a tree completely and choke off its supply of food. Other vines to keep from your trees are wild grape, wisteria, honeysuckle, and bittersweet.

Many vining annuals, meanwhile, take beautifully to shrubs. Last summer, I grew moonflowers (*Calonyction aculeatum*) on my yews and the effect was glorious. Morning glories and trumpet vines also wander happily on the shrubs.

FOR SUPER TOMATOES • To boost your tomato yield and increase fruit size, sprinkle a teaspoon of Epsom salts into your planting hole. Tomato plants love the magnesium in the salts. Also, researchers at the University of California suggest planting tomato seedlings in midafternoon. Seedlings set out on cold mornings are more susceptible to chilling injury because their metabolic reserves have been depleted during the night.

SOME TIPS ON LAVENDER • You will get good flowering lavender all season long if you hold back on fertilizer (I fertilized heavily one year and got virtually no blooms at all). Cut the flowering stalks periodically and deadhead continuously. The stalks look great in summer flower arrangements, and when they begin to lose their looks you can throw the whole thing, stem *and* flowerhead, into a basket to dry. The stalks have a fragrance, so you can use both stalk and flowerhead in your potpourri bowls, if you are a potpourri person. (Did you know potpourri means "rotted pot"?)

Plow deep while sluggards sleep.

❦ M A Y   8

When your tomato seedlings have about 5 to 7 true leaves, it's time to plant them in the garden—that is, if your soil is at least 50 degrees. If you let your seedlings overharden or get too large before planting, you'll tend to get poor plant growth and smaller tomatoes. (If you did plant your seeds a little early and your plants are ready but your soil is not, transplant the seedlings to larger pots so they do not become stunted and rootbound. This is very important.)

Plant your tomatoes deeply unless the soil is still a bit too cold, then trench them so that the roots are closer to the warmer soil at the surface. To do this, just lay the plant down on its side, burying most of the stem including the lower leaves. This will give you a strong root system. Once the ground has warmed up, mulch heavily around the stems. Foliar-feed (spray the leaves of your plants) every 2 weeks. Don't give the plant too much nitrogen or you'll get beautiful leaves and nothing else. Once the plant begins to flower, hold off on all fertilizer. When the fruits begin to ripen, cut back on the water.

HOT ONIONS • If you like your onions on the hot side, add sulphur to your soil.

AN EASY EVERLASTING • Chinese lanterns (*Physalis alke-kengi*) are one of the easiest and best-loved flowers among everlasting devotees. Their orange "lanterns," which are often used in fall arrangements, are actually the fruits of the plant. Inside the little papery husk is a fruit very much like its relation, the tomatillo, a staple of Southwestern cookery. Chinese lantern tends to be invasive. Plant it where it can grow without disturbing others.

ON THE SUNNY SIDE • Wind pollination can complicate the life of the home gardener, especially if space is limited and you want to grow different varieties of corn. An Amish farmer had an good idea: he planted his popcorn and sweet corn on the same plot but interplanted sunflowers to prevent cross-pollination. The sunflowers served as a barrier so that wind-pollinated corn stayed pure.

An apple-tree puts to shame all the men and women that have attempted to dress since the world began.

—Henry Ward Beecher

🐛 M A Y 9

This great idea for getting a second crop of scallions comes from a friend who uses scallions on everything. When you harvest your first crop, be very gentle—*do not disturb the roots*. Take a sharp knife and cut off a short section of the root end—about ½ inch—and plant the scallion tip immediately, about 1 inch deep. Water lightly. In a couple of months, you'll have a second scallion crop!

PREVENT YOUR GREENS FROM BOLTING • To delay the inevitable—spent mustard greens, lettuce, and cress—keep your greens evenly watered and put some floating row cover (page 325) over your plants. Anything you can do to keep the heat off the backs of your tender greens will put a damper on the bolting process.

BEANS ARE YOUR FRIENDS • Even if you are only mildly fond of beans, they are an excellent guest in the garden. Not only are they delicious, but they deliver bonus nutrients to your soil as a member of the legume family. I prefer pole beans to bush. Pole beans take longer to bear—a total of 10 to 11 weeks—but once they produce you'll have a steady supply of delectable beans out of a relatively compact area until frost. Cut one 8-foot pole for every 5 seeds you plant. Place the poles 3 feet apart and drive them deeply into the ground. Plant 5 seeds around the base of each pole, about 1 inch deep. If you have a windy garden, create a tripod instead. Three poles, buried at the bottom and crossed in the middle—not at the top—provide good disease resistance and also will make for easier pickin's than three poles simply tied at the top. Whatever you build, don't try to grow the beans horizontally or they will choke themselves. *Since bean roots actually leave nitrogen, I like to follow them with broccoli or corn or other heavy users to take advantage of the free nitrogen.*

RULE OF THUMB • Organic fertilizers feed the soil. Inorganic compounds—which occur naturally in mineral deposits or are produced synthetically—are not derived from living organisms, and feed plants directly.

SOIL LEAKS OUT OF CONTAINERS • If you get a little stream of soil running out of the drainage holes of your containers, you can stem the tide by laying a remnant of screening material inside the pot. (*Now* I tell you.) The soil is more likely to stay in place and pests will also be discouraged from coming in through the bottom.

> *A cold May is kindly*
> *And fills the barn finely.*

The first Mother's Day was observed in a church service in Grafton, West Virginia, on May 10, 1908, in honor of Anna Jarvis's mother. Carnations were Mrs. Jarvis's favorite flower, and soon afterward the custom of wearing red carnations for a living mother and white ones for a deceased mother became widespread, lasting in some parts of the country to this day. By 1911, every state in the country had issued formal Mother's Day proclamations.

LET THEM EAT RINDS • Try cutting down on sow bug populations with orange rind halves. Leave the rinds out overnight; the next morning you should have a small sow bug convention which you can dispose of easily in plastic bags. You can also use washed, crushed eggshells and cornmeal to get rid of sow bugs (separately, on separate occasions). The eggshells cut their bodies and cause them to dehydrate and die. The cornmeal is difficult to digest and causes their demise as well.

FAVORITE TOMATO • Romaine J. Breault of Minneapolis, Minnesota, the 1993 winner of the Tomato Club's Super-Grower competition, stated after much deliberation that if he had to choose just *one tomato* as his favorite it would be "Radiator Charlie's Mortgage Lifter."

According to the club's newsletter, M. Charles Byles of West Virginia created the plant in the 1930s after breeding four of the largest varieties he could find. Byles, also known as "Radiator Charlie"—he repaired trucks—was able to sell his new variety for $1 a plant in the early 1940s ($11.35 in 1990 dollars). The plants sold so well he was able to pay off his mortgage in a few short years. Breault points out that the Mortgage Lifter produces large tomatoes, from 1 to 4 pounds, and can average 2 to 4 pounds in prime conditions. (For seeds, try Southern Exposure Seed Exchange, P.O. Box 158, North Garden, VA 22959 or Totally Tomatoes, P.O. Box 1626, Augusta, GA 30903.)

Are your dandelions trying to tell you something? Dandelions are calcium accumulators; they bring it up to the surface of the soil. If the lawn is blanketed with them, one theory suggests that the deep-rooted weeds are simply compensating for your soil's state of calcium deprivation. To still the dandelion's activity, one might spread bonemeal for temporary help and ground limestone for long-term correction. Actually, I have never found the dandelion to be offensive (I am more likely to find the too perfect lawn offensive). Unlike many weeds, dandelions don't compete with the lawn for nutrients because of their long taproots. And they are cheerful.

MORE ABOUT DANDELIONS

- Dreaming about dandelions brings bad luck.

- Blow on the seed heads twice and however many seeds are left gives you the hour of the day.

- Dandelion blossoms close before a rain.

- Dandelion comes from *dent de lion*, or lion's tooth, referring to the jagged shape of the leaf.

- Dandelion greens are delicious and packed with vitamins and nutrients, but be cautious about eating young leaves straight from your yard, especially if it has been chemically treated in recent seasons.

••

WARM DANDELION COUNTRY SALAD

8-ounce slab of bacon, rind removed and cut into ½-inch dice
¼ cup balsamic vinegar
1½ tablespoons Dijon mustard
2 tablespoons honey
3 tablespoons olive oil
Salt and pepper to taste
8 cups of tender young dandelion leaves, rinsed and dried
3 ounces goat cheese, such as Montrachet, crumbled

••

Fry the bacon pieces in a medium skillet until crisp. Remove with a slotted spoon and drain on paper towels. Pour all but ⅓ cup of bacon fat from the skillet. Whisk in vinegar, mustard, and honey, then add olive oil. Season with salt and pepper. Keep warm.

Toss dandelion greens with cheese and bacon in a salad bowl. Pour warm dressing over the salad and toss to coat. Serve at once. Makes 4 to 6 servings.

⸱⸱⸱

MEASURE OFF STEPPING STONES • Before you order and lay down stepping stones in or around your garden, pace them off with a natural gait. Stones that are too close or too far away will drive you nuts.

A fallow field is a sin.
—John Steinbeck

❦ M A Y 1 2

Give a little thought to where you put your compost pile. If you live in a very dry area, it is best placed under a tree that provides shade but also lets some sunshine through. (Exceptions: pine, eucalyptus, bay laurel, juniper, black walnut, and cypress, all of which produce growth-inhibiting acids.) In colder zones, you should put your pile in direct sunlight.

Don't put a compost heap next to a wooden fence or you'll lose the fence to rot. If you have space, put the heap in a spot where you want to plant next season and let that black gold ooze in; you'll get a running start on soil fertility.

JAPANESE BEETLES HATE RUE • Rue is a natural deterrent to Japanese beetles. You can either start rue from seed in early spring or buy the plants at your nursery. The bluish-green foliage makes a good-looking border, though the plant's scent is quite strong and could end up deterring you.

PINCH OFF YOUR NEW STRAWBERRY PLANTS • It's no fun, but if you pinch off all the flowers from your newly planted strawberries—and lose your first year's crop—you'll be rewarded with healthier and more abundant plants in future years.

⸱⸱⸱

HMMMM . . . • A gardener from upstate New York recommends a homemade spear for getting rid of slugs. He inserts a sewing needle into a 15-inch-long ⅜-inch-thick dowel rod with a pair of pliers. Spear in hand, he goes out at night and stabs the slugs, scraping them off the needle into a coffee can into which he has poured a couple of cups of water and a thin layer of gasoline or kerosene.

TEA BAGS FOR ROSE BUSHES • Veteran rose growers toss tea bags and tea leaves into the soil in their rose beds. The roses like slightly acid soil and the tea contains tannic acid.

Plant corn when the apple blossoms fall.

☙ M A Y 1 3

Japanese beetles usually come out from early May to early July—and do their worst damage between July and August. You can take a variety of measures to combat them.

The most debatable method is the Japanese beetle trap, which you can purchase at any garden center. Some say that by putting out the traps you simply attract more beetles to your own garden—beetles that would have been happily munching on your neighbor's plants if you hadn't issued an all-points bulletin. Manufacturers say that if you put the trap several feet upwind from the plants you're protecting, your garden will be safe.

A different approach is to have your plants kill the beetles. White geraniums, castor beans, four-o'clocks, and red buckeyes all will poison the beetles. These plants are also poisonous to humans.

I go after them with angry fingers (my own). In the morning, when the dew restricts their ability to fly away, I hand-pick or shake clusters of the beetles into jars of kerosene (you can also use soap solution). I also try to keep the soil well cultivated in both the fall and the spring to expose the larvae to grub-loving birds. That seems to do it for me.

If you've got a really bad infestation, try milky spore disease (*bacillus popilliae*). The germ warfare route works best if the whole community uses it and it does take almost 5 years to really take effect. Don't use chemical soil insecticides after applying milky spore.

LET THEM SMELL FOX URINE • If you have a squirrel problem, fox urine may be your cure-all. Fox urine is now available through catalogues and at garden centers. If the squirrels are getting into your garbage or raiding your bird feeders, apply fox urine every few days. The smell is awful, and one wonders how it is collected. But it works.

SHOWY PEONIES • To create a larger peony flower, remove the side buds. You can experiment with your peonies—and also dahlias, chrysanthemums, and carnations—to see how grand a bloom is possible.

TUCKING IN COLOR • One of my favorite plants is garden verbena (*Verbena hybrida*), an annual, which comes in many wonderful colors. If you have blank spots in the garden or places that need a touch of color, tuck in a few verbena plants here and there for a lovely effect. Verbena requires very little care and blooms all summer long in sun or light shade.

One of the most endearing qualities of gardeners, though it makes their gardens worse, is this faculty of being too easily delighted.
                                                                    —Henry Mitchell

❦ M A Y 1 4

Bees are attracted to colorful floral patterns—no surprise, but good to remember when you're out in the garden. You won't gain the bees' attention when you dress in neutral colors. Also avoid wearing perfume and hair sprays; they like the scent. When the bees start to swarm, I do my best imitation of a Buddhist monk and keep perfectly still. It runs totally contrary to impulse, but has gotten me through twoscore years unstung.

CUCUMBER COMPANIONS • Cucumbers enjoy the company of beans, peas, and corn. Like potatoes, cucumbers are subject to phytophthora blight, so keep them far from your taters.

DOLPHIN-IUMS • Delphinium comes from the Greek *delphi-*

nion, or little dolphin, as the long nectary resembles the nose of the *delphis* or dolphin.

REMINDER: LILAC BLOOMS • Once your lilacs bloom, pick off all the spent flowers so your plants don't put effort into the seed manufacturing process. It will help your bloom production next year.

RULE OF THUMB • Don't fertilize your pepper plants until the fruits actually form. With tomatoes, you should fertilize lightly before the fruit forms. On peppers and tomatoes, use fertilizers low in nitrogen and heavier on phosphorus.

....

HERBS THAT SELF-SOW

....

Borage (*Borago officinalis*)
Caraway (*Carum carvi*)
Chervil (*Anthriscus cerefolium*)
Cilantro (*Coriandrum sativum*)

Dill (*Anethum graveolens*)
Fennel (*Foeniculum vulgare*)
Lemon basil (*Ocimum basilicum* '*Citriodorum*')

Weed your own garden first.

❦ MAY 15

The grass is always greener after a thunderstorm because it receives electrically charged air which converts its nitrogen content (78 percent!) to water-soluble form.

Liberated nitrogen is a good thing, of course, and as a practical matter you can tap into it by tying your tomato plants with metal poles or trellises (you can use concrete reinforcing wire bent in an inverted V shape, with a row of tomato plants on each side). Tie the tomato plants to the poles with nylon strips cut from discarded panty hose. The metal supports will attract static electricity. One study has shown that 250,000 tons of natural nitrogen are produced in the 1,800 thunderstorms that take place worldwide, daily.

....

TO BLANCH OR NOT TO BLANCH • Recent research has shown that horticultural blanching—the process of covering growing plants to "whiten" them—robs vegetables of certain nutrients, and lately people have been moving away from the process, though certain vegetables look terrific in this pristine state. If you ever wanted an excuse not to mess with the process, this is it.

WET THAT FINGERTIP • Pick a still day to spray your plants with insecticidal soaps, and check the weather forecast to be sure your efforts will not be followed soon after by rain.

EARWIG ERADICATION • Earwigs get into cracks in your house, hide under your buckets, hang out in metal arms of lawn chairs and coiled garden hoses. They prefer stressed-out plants to healthy ones, so the first move you can make to protect your plants is to keep them in tiptop form. Then you can try this: Roll up several thicknesses of newspaper and leave it outside overnight. The next morning, plunge the newspaper into a bucket of hot water. It will be disgusting, but you'll have drowned a ton of earwigs. The problem is, you have to do this almost every night, which is a pain.

Another method you might try is putting Twenty Mule Team Borax in areas they seem to like.

If you are losing the earwig war, you can take some comfort in that earwigs do have their beneficial side. They eat aphids, fruit worms, spider mites, caterpillars, and thrigs, among others.

❦ M A Y 1 6

Hot peppers, it's been proven, are habit-forming. They certainly are one of my addictions. I'm not a nut (like that man in San Antonio, Texas, who went for the world record by devouring 29 jalapeños in 2 minutes flat) but I do like my peppers. Whenever I'm feeling a little blue, day or night, I get out a jar of jalapeños and some saltines and a glass of iced tea. Two peppers later, without fail, I'm back in the game. If you want really, really hot peppers, plant them in the sunniest spot in your garden. To get maximum flavor, they must reach full color while on the plants. Peppers harvested in cooler, fall weather aren't as hot, so time your planting for a warm-weather harvest. Don't be too ambitious: pepper plants have high yields, and unless you devour peppers routinely, you can end up with too many peppers and not enough neighbors to give them to. Final tip: If you've followed these directions and end up in August with peppers that are too hot, don't put out the fire with a glass of water or iced tea. The heat in peppers comes from an oil-based substance that won't be affected unless you eat a piece of bread or cheese or a saltine.

OAK LEAF ALERT • When the oak leaves are the size of a mouse's ear it's time to sow corn and cold-tender annuals.

WHAT SLUGS HATE • A book called *Bugs, Slugs and Other Thugs*, by Rhonda Massingham Hart, states that slugs react negatively to azalea, apricot, basil, bean, corn, chard, Jeruselum cherry, daffodils, fuchsia, freesia, grape, ginger, holly, hibiscus, rose of Sharon, Swedish ivy, Peruvian lily, parsley, pumpkin, plum, sage, sunflower, and rhododendron. She suggests including these plants in your garden if you have a slug problem.

••

Mid-Spring Vegetable Planting Checklist

••

Beet   Chard
Broccoli   Early potato
Carrot   New Zealand spinach
Cauliflower

Of the seven deadly sins, surely it is pride that most commonly afflicts gardeners.
                                                    —Michael Pollan

❦ M A Y   1 7

I have come to an understanding with my invasive herbs: I give them all of the rights and privileges of my garden if they will agree not to venture from the plastic pots I have prepared for them.

Plants like bee balm, mint, and costmary agree cheerfully to this program. I use big plastic pots and cut out the bottoms before planting my seedlings. (You can also use chimney flues for this, which would be easier because you don't have to cut anything. But since I

••

have about two hundred plastic pots in my garage, I use the pots.) Then you simply bury the pots—or flues—in the garden. When you bury them, leave about an inch of lip showing above the ground and that's it. The herbs stay mostly in their place.

Use bulb planters for annuals.

USE BULB PLANTER FOR ANNUALS • Use your bulb planter to dig a hole for those little annuals that come in the plastic six-packs. It makes a perfect hole with just a couple of quick twists.

CROPS THAT REQUIRE THE MOST WEEDING

Carrots
Lettuce
All members of the onion family

TOMATOES IN THE COMPOST • Growing tomatoes in your compost heap is almost cliché—but in case you haven't tried it yet, make it a point to drop a few seeds right at the edge of your pile. Tomato seeds are so durable they pop up as volunteers as a matter of course in most compost heaps—and the tomato plants that result are extraordinary producers. Cherry tomatoes are a good choice if you are actually planting seeds; they can be staked right to the sides of wire bins. Some people encircle their compost piles with three or four plants and let the run-off compost fertilize their tomatoes all summer long.

A day lost is never found.

Asian immigrants have reintroduced a spectacular growing method to the United States in recent years: trellis gardening. Trellis gardening is ideal for people with limited space—and some of the trellis gardens I have seen are visual feasts as well as highly prolific producers of vegetables.

A variety of trellis forms can be made out of bamboo, but any untreated wood will do. You can create a simple A-frame shape and have a sun and shade garden both at once. On the A-frame trellis you can grow cucumbers, tomatoes (cherry tomatoes are most successful), Malabar spinach, pole beans, small pumpkins, small watermelons, and gourds. Under the trellis you can grow lettuce, selected herbs, and onions.

No matter what you grow, trellis gardens are intriguing, secretive, and wonderful to look at. Don Lambert of the Dallas Civic Garden Center recommends intermingling flowers and flowering herbs with vegetables: gourds with a wisteria, trailing red honeysuckle or passion fruit vine with pole beans or pumpkins, or brightly colored chili peppers, dill, and cilantro under a trellis covered by trumpet vine and scrolling cucumbers.

Beyond beauty and space considerations, trellis gardens produce crops that are both accessible and generally less prone to disease.

TO DISCOURAGE ONION MAGGOTS • Onion maggots are a nightmare, but an avoidable one. A top dressing of wood ash will put them off, and sowing radishes nearby also helps. You can intersperse onions throughout your garden and put them in a state of confusion. You can also plant their least favorite onion—the red onion—and discourage their presence.

COMPOST PH • Most composts have a neutral pH, but some are up near 8.5 and can damage acid-loving plants. Be sure to test your compost's pH before adding it to soil (test just as you would your soil); if you need to, adjust pH by mixing in other high- or low-pH waste materials.

There can be no other occupation like gardening in which, were you to creep up behind someone at their work, you would find them smiling.
                                                    —Mirabel Osler

I use my children's plastic sled for everything. If you have children, borrow theirs; if you don't have kids, look out for plastic sleds at garage sales. Plastic sleds—shaped like a shallow, oblong saucer—are great for hauling compost or mulch, and for carting away debris, weeds, anything—and you can't beat them for hauling around firewood in the winter. They are much easier to load and unload than a wheelbarrow—perfect for the small, daily gardening jobs that come up.

For dragging leaf piles, you can use old blankets or dropcloths. This way you don't have to lift "up" to a wheelbarrow.

PLANTING BEANS • When you plant beans, plant the seeds with the eyes looking down.

DON'T THROW THOSE SHOES AWAY • If you have rabbits, you can often get them off your grounds by placing old shoes around your plants. The smell puts off the little munchers. Rabbits also find onions and garlic distasteful.

GARDENIA BLOSSOMS • When you are cutting gardenias for display be sure to handle them carefully because their petals bruise quite easily. Since their stems don't draw water once they're cut, you may want to wrap wet tissues around the flowers and put them in a cool place during the evening. For a pretty effect, float them in bowls of water.

RAISING CANE • The average American consumes 75 pounds of sugar, 45 pounds of corn, 30 pounds of citrus, and 7 pounds of shelled peanuts each year.

HERBS THAT WORK WELL IN BOUQUETS • Cut flower arrangements are limited only by your imagination. I use many unexpected plants in my bouquets.

Basil (especially cinnamon)	Lavender
Borage	Mint
Bee balm	Sage
Chamomile	Scented geranium
Dill	Thyme
Hyssop	

PLANTS THAT LOVE EPSOM SALTS • African violets, peppers, and tomatoes all benefit from a helping of Epsom salts. Mix 2 tablespoons of Epsom salts to 1 gallon of water. Give plants a single application right after they form their buds. Epsom salts will accelerate tomato growth and deliver an earlier harvest.

Adam was a gardener, and God, who made him, sees that half of all good gardening is done upon the knees.

—Rudyard Kipling

❦ M A Y 2 0

Now is a good time to concoct a reliable home brew for insects. Since insects are dependent on their sense of smell, garlic is an excellent repellent because it totally disorients them. Here's an all-purpose recipe for a garlic–red pepper spray that will not poison your children or your dogs or your spouse, but *will* knock out your tiny enemies.

Take 1 cup of chopped dried hot pepper and 2 cloves of crushed garlic and mix with 1 cup of water. Cover and let steep for 24 hours. Strain. Dilute with 2 cups of water. Pour the concoction in a spray bottle and aim. You can also take the equivalent of a bulb of minced garlic and let it soak in some mineral oil for about 24 hours. Add 1 tablespoon of garlic oil to a pint of water, to which 1½ teaspoons of unscented liquid soap has been added.

You have to be careful with these brews. They could cause severe irritation of your skin and eyes. Avoid spraying the solutions on seedlings, as well. *This spray is for established plants only and should be tested on a leaf of the plant in question and then sprayed 24 hours later only if the plant finds the spray agreeable.*

DON'T LET YOUR LETTUCE BOLT • Lettuce naturally bolts in warm weather. If you planted yours in a shady area or under the leaves of a larger plant or a tent made out of old sheets, you are ahead of the game. If your lettuce is bolting in the shade, I suggest you try new varieties to plant. *Mantilia*, from Shepherd's Garden Seeds catalogue, is a slow-bolting butterhead you will enjoy. From the same catalogue, I recommend a looseleaf called *Red Oakleaf*, which is also good in hot weather.

STAKE YOUR FLOWERS NOW IF YOU HAVEN'T
ALREADY • Once your balloon flowers, delphiniums, monks-
hoods, shasta daisies, and veronicas (and so on) get going, you
should use thin bamboo or metal stakes to support a vertical cluster.
For a group planting, closely surround your plant with four wooden
stakes and then tie a string—I use fishing line—around the entire
mass.

> *When the sun goes to bed red.*
> *'twill rain tomorrow, it's said.*

❦ MAY 21

You planted some nasturtium seeds, didn't you? I don't think a garden
is complete without nasturtiums ambling down the edge of a border,
or growing in containers where they do so well. Nasturtiums in low
containers are not only wonderful to look at but handy. The plant repels cucumber beetles, squash bugs, and white flies so it is very effective when dispatched to infested areas and used in connection with
insecticidal soaps or other solutions.

Nasturtiums also attract aphids, which makes them a good trap
crop. If, for instance, aphids attacked your young fruit trees last year,
plant some of the trailing kinds of nasturtiums at the base of the
trees this year. I always have a fleet of nasturtiums in pots to dispatch
to troubled sites. Once nasturtiums "trap" the aphids, move the containers to a porch or driveway, hose off the aphids, and place the
plants back in your garden where they are most needed.

BIRDS THAT WILL EAT YOUR BUGS • Birds consume in-
sects at an astonishing rate but they are discriminating about what
they eat. Bluejays and blackbirds love cutworms; chickadees eat
aphids, Colorado potato beetles, leaf miners, loopers, and slugs; war-
blers eat aphids; wrens dine on cutworms and leafhoppers. Wrens can
feed their babies up to 500 bugs in a single afternoon. A brown
thrasher consumes about 1,000 bugs a day.

MULCH YOUR CONTAINERS • Containers—especially
clay pots—tend to dry out quickly and can be rather onerous in their

demands for water. So mulch them! You can mulch by adding a layer of finely shredded wood chips or a fine gravel to the soil surface with excellent results.

LAZY GARDENER TIP • If your garage or garden shed is a far piece from your garden, store your garden tools in an old trunk or a plastic children's toy box. The bright colored toyboxes don't look like something you'd see at Walden Pond, but if you tuck yours in an unobtrusive spot in the garden and surround it with plants it will provide not only a good storage spot but a place to occasionally rest your bones.

As a matter of fact, you know I am rather sorry you should see the garden now, because, alas! it is not looking at its best. Oh, it doesn't compare to what it was last year.   —Ruth Draper

❧ M A Y 2 2

GEMINI, May 22 to June 21—*A barren sign, but good for sowing melon seed*

Author Allen Lacy, who writes so eloquently about the garden (please treat yourself to his book on vines and groundcovers, called *Gardening with Groundcovers and Vines*), also has a handle on the mundane. He recommends baking powder for reducing ant populations. His method, which he inherited from his mother-in-law, is no more complicated than this: sprinkle baking powder here and there, and within 24 hours, the ants will be gone. I tried it and sure enough, *no ants.*

Over time, I have learned that ants are easily disoriented—or repelled—by many common household products. Bay leaves work (expensive, unless you are plucking them from your own plant); so do a host of other easily obtained products: coffee grounds, vinegar, ginger, charcoal, mineral spirits, lemon juice, and mint.

A gardener from the Blue Ridge Mountains recommends 1 tablespoon boric acid powder, 1 tablespoon sugar, and ½ cup water. Wet cotton balls, and wipe infested areas. Wipe again from time to time.

Use baking powder to get rid of ants.

USE LIQUID FERTILIZERS IF YOU'RE HAVING A
DRY SPELL • If you are having a dry (but not too stressful) spell
and need to fertilize, use a liquid fertilizer which can be applied to
the soil or sprayed on the leaves of the plants. Liquid fertilizers contain varying amounts of nitrogen, phosphorus, and potassium, and will
encourage balanced growth. In addition, they will be absorbed more
quickly because they don't need extra moisture to dissolve. If it is hot
and dry—i.e., drought conditions—don't fertilize at all. During
droughts, your plants need to go into a rest mode.

*Our vegetable garden is coming along well, with radishes and beans up, and we
are less worried about revolution than we used to be.*
                                                        —E. B. White

☙ M A Y 2 3

Have you tried those insect sticky traps? I've had uneven success with
them but I always use them because (1) they are inexpensive; (2) a little goes a long way; and (3) anything is better than having to spray.
The yellow ones are great for winged aphids, leafhoppers, fruit flies,
white flies, fungus gnats, male winged mealybugs, leaf miners, and oth-

ers. Leaf miners, my enemies, get the sticky tape treatment and I always have a trap near my beautiful columbines. One 3 × 5-inch trap will work for 25 to 50 square feet of garden—which is a big range; err on the low side. You can use 1 trap per about 6 or 7 tomato plants as a general rule.

RECIPE FOR MANURE TEA • One of the finest brews available to gardeners is manure tea. You can make it easily with a 30-gallon plastic garbage can and a homemade "tea bag." Put four shovelfuls of manure in a porous bag, knot it, deposit it in the garbage can, and fill it with water. Swirl your tea bag daily for three weeks to promote aerobic decomposition. Then remove the bag (toss it on the compost pile) and siphon the nitrogen-rich liquid onto the plants that need it most.

KEEPING CUT ROSES FRESH • The trick to prolonging the life of a cut rose is to keep air from being drawn up into the stem. Cut the rose in the morning—preferably before 10 A.M.—just above a 5-leaf cluster, then place the stem in tepid water. (Be sure to leave at least 2 leaves between the cut stem and the cane to allow for rejuvenation.) Once you've returned to the house, recut the rose under warm running water, forming a 1- to 1½-inch angular cut along the stem. Then plunge the stem into a vase filled with warm water.

What I enjoy is not the fruits alone, but the soil itself, its nature and its power.
—Cicero

❦ M A Y 2 4

If you are looking at your garden and it seems to be too much of a hodgepodge, it probably needs a focal point. Some gardeners successfully add a large rock or some tall ornamental grass, shrubs, or a tree to create some visual coherence. Once the focal point is in place you can make myriad little "moments" in your garden.

HOMEMADE FACIALS • If you have a little space, tuck in some herbs that will make a soothing facial later in the summer. A half cup of the leaves of chamomile, mint, lady's-mantle, calendula, and comfrey, mixed well and soaked in a bowl of boiling water, will exude a wonderful fragrance and restorative steam for your face. Simply lean into the steam and drape a fresh towel over your head to create a little sauna. Breathe in the steam carefully at first; it can burn your nostrils. Stay there 8 to 10 minutes, and relax. (The recipe above is for people with dry skin. If you have oily skin, grow lavender, lemon balm, and yarrow and use those herbs in the same way.)

VEGETABLE SEEDLINGS • If you buy vegetable seedlings from a garden center, be sure not to purchase any that are bearing fruit or flowers. Young tomato, eggplant, and pepper plants should not be flowering or fruiting; any such behavior indicates the plant has been stressed in some way.

❧ M A Y 2 5

Keep your crops moving. Most early spring crops have died down and new plantings for warm-weather crops should be in by now. With succession planting, the sequence is cool-weather crop, warm-weather crop, cool-weather crop. In most zones, you should get three good harvests per year (and even more, of course, in the very mild climates). Supplement the soil with a light fertilizer and rotate your crops carefully.

RACCOON TIP • Ralph Snodsmith, gardener of *Good Morning, America* fame, offers this tip for gardeners whose corn crops are plagued by raccoons: talk radio. Raccoons apparently are confused and put off by the cacaphony of human voices, and if you place in your garden two portable radios, set on different talk-radio shows and encased in plastic bags, the critters will stay away from your corn and other delectables. Snodsmith says that music is not a deterrent; this technique is only effective with talk radio. You should set the radios out about a week before the corn is edible.

ANOTHER OLD WIVES' TALE • Don't bother removing the suckers growing from the base of corn stalks. It's just an old wives' tale. Suckers actually provide the plant with strength.

SPINACH CROP • I am looking at some very handsome spinach here, and nothing could make me happier except, perhaps, if someone in my household would eat it. I have been semisuccessful sneaking steamed chopped spinach onto pizzas, using feta cheese and oil-cured black olives to obscure the taste. (It's hard to pick out the spinach from the cheese, so at least some of it goes down.) Mostly I just eat it myself. This is how I like it, especially next door to a piece of grilled fish.

COLD SPINACH WITH SESAME AND GINGER

1½ tablespoons Asian sesame oil
1½ tablespoons rice wine vinegar
1½ tablespoons minced fresh ginger
1 teaspoon sugar
1 teaspoon hot red pepper flakes
White pepper to taste
1 pound of spinach, rinsed, steamed lightly, and cooled
2 tablespoons white sesame seeds, toasted

Make the dressing by combining the sesame oil, vinegar, ginger, sugar, hot pepper flakes, and white pepper, and mixing well with a wire whisk. Taste and adjust if necessary. Pour the dressing over the spinach and toss several times to mix well. Sprinkle the toasted sesame seeds over the top. Serves 2 spinach lovers, or 4 as a side dish.

❦ MAY 26

One of the first disputes my husband and I had was about color in the garden. I leaned to a mix of softer colors and secondary hues, while he favored bold, primary colors, those you might see in the planters at toll booths or in berms at filling stations. (That was unnecessary, but you get the picture.) We then decided that I would be the gardener and he would be the fisherman, and sort of left it at that.

I recently read a report by the National Garden Bureau that gave a reason for this dispute. The Bureau stated that men tend to favor yellow-based reds, like scarlet, while women tend to favor blue-based reds, like burgundy. This explained the conflict in my marriage but not the fact that some of the most riveting gardens I have seen were created by men, and included pastels and burgundies and not one *Salvia splendens*.

The bureau also advised that plantings of bright red and yellow flowers will create a powerful visual distraction, and can be used to pull the eye away from an architectural or landscaping flaw. Also worth noting: homes with bright yellow borders sell faster.

COLORADO POTATO BEETLE • One of the classic controls for the Colorado potato beetle is derived from trees you might have on your own property. Take a few cedar branches, break them into 12-inch lengths, and boil them in a stockpot until the water changes to an amber color. Drain the liquid, allow it to cool, and then simply spray on the affected plants. Also: lady bugs, ground beetles, and toads are natural predators.

BEAN CLINIC

- If your beans don't germinate, you might have planted them too early—or not deep enough.

- Bean rot is a frequent problem when the soil is wet.

- If bean blossoms drop, it might be due to a sudden shift in weather patterns.

- Beans that don't mature might have been planted too late.

- Poor-tasting beans probably sat around in wet weather.

- Low production is most often caused by lazy harvesting. Pick them often!

HERBS THAT LIKE A LITTLE LIME

Aloe vera	Lavender
Artemesia	Tarragon
Coriander	Rosemary
Fennel	

I take chemical pesticides very seriously and neurotically. Research, common sense, and having children about make chemicals an unwanted presence in my garden; and my plants are all the better for it. If you are still using chemicals—or just starting out and seeing chemical pesticides as a quick fix—do a little reading about the true effects. Chemicals are not your friend.

And whether you are using a really lethal pesticide or your own red pepper–garlic spray, take precautions when using sprays. Always wear disposable gloves; you can get plastic gloves for about a dime a pair at hardware stores and outlets. Keep a big box of them and use them whenever you are working with pesticides—organic or otherwise. Have special measuring spoons designated for pesticide use. Wear a hat, long pants, a long-sleeved shirt (even in July), goggles or sunglasses, at the least, and a breathing mask, if you have one. Wash your clothes as a separate load when you are finished. And clean out your sprayer thoroughly when it is empty, dumping the rinse water outdoors (if you have a well, ask your local sanitation department for disposal advice). Don't pour rinse water down drains—it is a contaminant.

BLACK PLASTIC MULCH WARNING • Remember not to let your fruits and vegetables "sit" on black plastic mulch; they might rot. Make a little nest of newspaper or straw for melons, low growing tomatoes, cucumbers etc.

FOXGLOVE REDUX • You can get a second flowering from your foxglove (*Digitalis*) this year by cutting off the main flower stem after its initial bloom. After the second bloom has faded, deadhead all but a few flowers for self-sowing. Remember, foxglove is poisonous.

GETTING RHODODENDRONS TO BLOOM • The best fertilizer to use to encourage your rhododendrons to bloom is one that is high in phosphorus content. Use something like a granulated 0-18-0 mix, and to maintain the soil's acidity, spread spent coffee grounds or tea leaves around your plants. After the plant blooms (in a year, one would hope), you can switch to a water-soluble 15-30-15 mix.

CONTAINER FERTILIZING • Your container plants need more frequent fertilizer treatments than your garden plants; make sure you have them on a regular schedule. Container herbs, which do not need huge amounts of fertilizer, benefit from an organic treatment like Electra, which you simply scratch into the soil once a month.

❦ M A Y   2 8

I am a proponent of common sense when it comes to the question of using organics. It makes sense to me to use organics whenever possible, but I also don't think using Miracle-Gro is a sin. Inorganics give your plants a blast of vigor and energy, not unlike a candy bar, but you can't live on candy bars. If you use inorganics you certainly don't have to wear a paper bag over your head. Just don't use them in excess.

Inorganic fertilizers contain salts that can draw out much of the moisture from a plant when used in excess, causing dehydration in the worst cases. Overdoses of fertilizer can also cause forked carrots or eggplants that never bloom. That's why common sense dictates nourishing the soil organically, over time, rather than dumping a lot of inorganics into your garden to fertilize the plants directly.

With inorganics, after the initial dose is applied in the spring, you should apply a second top-dressing only after the vegetables are half grown. Foliar feeding is even better. Balance out the use of chemical fertilizers with the addition of manure or compost and peat moss and you will be just fine.

PREGNANT WOMAN CRAVES BELLFLOWERS •
When she was pregnant, Rapunzul's mother craved *Campanula rapunculoides* (bellflower). The craving was so overwhelming that she had her husband steal bellflowers from the nearby witch's garden, and we all know what happened after that. Rapunzul was named for *C. rapunculoides* (also called rampion), an excellent, radishlike root vegetable.

WEED TEA • Fresh-cut weeds—gathered *before they go to seed*—make an excellent nutritious tea for plants. Gather a big armful and put them in a 5-gallon container, cover with water, and let the tea sit for a week or two. You will have a concentrate that can be diluted with 3 or 4 parts water. Sprinkle the tea as a fertilizer over your garden as needed.

ROW COVER USE AND REUSE • After a season of pro-
tecting early spring transplants, used floating row covers (page 325)
look pretty shabby. If they are basically in good shape, you can clean
them by hanging them on a clothesline and watering gently with a
hose. You can't really wash the material but you can give it a good
soaking. Once the covers are totally trashed, some gardeners cut
them in squares and use them as wraps for vulnerable fruits like cantaloupes (tie with pantyhose scraps). The leftover cloth is also excellent
as the material for pond filters.

❦ M A Y   2 9

A few seasons back I spread salt hay as a mulch. First reaction: big
mistake. My mulches had always been dark. Suddenly, my garden was
a blonde. The whole effect was blinding.

Having lived with it for that first season, I now wouldn't garden
without it. Salt hay is actually a coastal grass that grows in saline conditions but contains very little salt—and very few weeds (The light-
mulch look does take a bit of getting used to but it is not unattractive; in fact, now I think it makes my vegetables and herbs look
sensational.)

If you want to try it in doses, start with your tomato plants. While
neighbors are pumping their hoses all summer long, I am able to
keep watering to a minimum, even with water hogs like tomatoes and
squash. Some gardeners actually support their tomato plants with
hay—mounding up the hay almost to the top of 12-inch seedlings.
This not only acts as a support but cushions the fruits and vines that
grow all over the place. (Give your plants plenty of space if you try
this method.) Anyway, I am a convert to salt hay, and I think I'm
having more fun.

RESTRAINT, EVERYONE • Especially for first-timers: Don't
pack your plantings in too tightly. The seedlings you just bought at
the nursery look puny now, but in a few weeks they will be bushy
and grand. There is a temptation to "fill it all up" and make your
May garden look like a July garden; don't try it. Your plants need
space. In general, perennials need more space than annuals; over time
perennials will grow larger and spread farther. Plants need good air

circulation, and overcrowding fosters disease. Remember, it is not for nothing that the single most important device in a greenhouse is a fan. Plants need air. Give them space!

MAKING POTTING SOIL OUT OF MOLEHILLS • If you are overrun with moles—and molehills—you can at least grab up the finely crumbled soil, mix it with a little sand or whatever it might need, and use it as nonsterilized, free potting soil.

So that's what hay looks like.
—Queen Mary

🍂 M A Y   3 0

Hollyhocks are celebrities in the cottage garden, and they never fail to charm. I like the single-petal varieties best. One British gardener said he had a row of hollyhocks that grew to 18½ feet after he watered his plants with the residue of his home brewery (though possible effects of the brew on the storyteller must also be taken into account). Plant hollyhocks next to beehives—the nectar is said to make an exceptional honey. And if you have a true extravagance of blossoms, strew them around the edge of a flea-infested room. They have been thought to repel the wee beasts.

WHEN PLANTING MINT • Don't mix wood ash with the soil when you are planting mint. It might be advantageous for many herbs but for mint it is a disaster.

One of the healthiest ways to gamble is with a spade and a packet of seeds.
—Dan Bennett

The oldest story about the origin of Memorial Day goes back to April 25, 1866, and, not surprisingly, it is a story about flowers. On that day, a former chaplain in the Confederate army escorted a group of women to a cemetery just outside of Columbus, Mississippi, where 1500 Confederate soldiers and 100 Union soldiers were buried. The town was occupied by Union soldiers, and there was some apprehension that the women, carrying armfuls of flowers for the dead, would be misunderstood. But the women were not going to honor just their own but all of the dead. Instead of creating more friction, they created a fragile harmony with their gesture, strewing flowers on the graves of Confederates and Union soldiers alike.

GREEN PEPPER CLINIC • Green peppers are finicky about temperature. In rare cases, extremely hot conditions will stunt fruit production; more commonly, the same problem will occur when the temperatures are too low. There is little one can do about the hot temperatures except wait for the cooler season. If you have a cold spell, make sure you mulch well to help the soil retain its heat.

Fruit production is also stunted by too much nitrogen. You'll get all foliage and no fruit if you overfertilize your peppers with nitrogen.

FIRST-TIME GARDENERS • *Don't despair if your newly planted fruit trees don't bear in the first few seasons. Peach trees normally don't bear before the third year. The average cherry and plum start after about 6 years. Poor health can significantly delay fruit production beyond the usual period.*

MOSS GARDEN TRICK • To make a moss garden, purée some moss in a blender with 3 parts beer to 1 part sugar. Spread the mixture on rocks, old logs, aging wooden fences, or bare soil to get it started.

Summer

🌱 *June* 🌱

Flower of the Month: Rose

🌱 JUNE 1

Nature has its many wonders, but the symbiotic relationship between ants and peonies is not one of them. For years, like many Northeasterners, I marveled at the notion that the little ants who lick the gummy nectar on peonies were in fact ungluing the petals so the plants might bloom. I found the idea charming, and welcomed the ants each spring, brought them into my house on the blooms, did everything short of thanking them in my prayers.

Turns out ants don't have anything to do with the opening of the peony buds. The more ants a plant has, the more profusely it will bloom because healthy plants with big buds produce more nectar, and therefore attract more ants. This is indoubtedly why this lore has endured; and why there is *so* much to learn about gardening.

WHILE WE'RE ON ANTS • Meanwhile, the presence of ants often indicates the presence of aphids. Ants protect and feed off aphids, and in the process transport them to different plants.

DON'T REMOVE THORNS ON CUT ROSES • Modern florists remove the thorns from the stems of cut roses; there is evidence that this practice reduces the indoor life of the rose by 1 to 3 days.

SCARECROW WARDROBE • Dress your scarecrow in red. More birds are put off by red than any other color.

104

Recalling Thomas Jefferson's great line "Though an old man, I am but a young gardener," I wonder, in gardening years, how old that makes me. I just returned from my traditional Unseemly June Binge where I buy lots of plants—plants that have nothing to do with my garden! A plume poppy? *What was I thinking?*

Try *not* to do what I just did. You go to your favorite nursery—or even more dangerous, a famous nursery—and you start looking at specimens. It is early June and not all of your plants have filled out and you still can see a little more mulch than plants, and after all it's a lovely morning, so you think, "Ah! I'll go see what's happening at Sunnybrook Farms." Three hours later, dazed, you pull into your driveway with the backseat and trunk positively brimming. Thomas Jefferson never would have done that.

Well, someone has got to show some self-restraint around here, and I just hope it's never me. Scootch over everybody. I'd like you to meet *Scabiosa* 'Butterfly Blue'. . . .

> *What was Paradise?*
> *but a garden,*
> *an orchard of trees*
> *and herbs, full of*
> *pleasure, and nothing*
> *there but delights.*
> —William Lawson

We had a tough winter last year, which left our village with many fallen trees and awkward-looking stumps. One particularly inventive neighbor used her stump to do a little container gardening—she hollowed it out, filled it with dirt, and planted it with flowering annuals and vines. It looks delightful.

VINE TRAINING TIP • If you are training a vine on a trellis or an espalier, use snap clothespins to keep the vine in place. Remove the pins at pruning time.

Welcome a toad into your garden.

CHEZ TOAD • Toads are easy to attract to your garden and they are big allies in the pest wars. You can purchase toad huts from gardening catalogues or fashion your own. Simply set out some old clay pots, inverted, and crack a small 2- to 3-inch door in the side to give the toad entrance.

REMINDER: EARLY SUMMER LAWN CARE • In early summer apply a liquid or granular general-purpose fertilizer to the lawn.

To dream of strawberries is a good omen.

❦ J U N E 4

Cucumbers need consistent moisture over the growing season to grow big and sweet. One way to make certain your cucumbers get the moisture they need is to get a large empty 64-ounce juice can. Remove the lid with a can opener and poke about 8 tiny holes with an ice pick in the sides. Now bury 1 can in each cucumber hill, leaving a 1- or 2-inch lip extending up. When you water, fill the can up to the brim with water and the liquid will seep into the cucumber hills as needed all day. To prevent loss of water due to evaporation, you can put flat rocks on top of each can.

- Squash bugs can be hand-picked and doused in kerosene. You can also deter them by rotating your crops, growing resistant varieties, and timing your plantings to miss infestation periods. Also, plastic mulch will help.

- To discourage the squash vine moth from laying eggs on your cucumber, melon, pumpkin, and squash stems, wrap small strips of pantyhose or aluminum foil around the base of the plant.

- Striped cucumber beetles don't like radishes. Before you plant or transplant your cucumbers, squash, melons, and beans, sow radishes in the same area.

BE CAREFUL MULCHING AROUND TREES • When you mulch your trees or plants that are growing around trees, be careful not to get the mulch up against the bark or it will promote rot and disease in the tree itself. Trees that are mulched too deeply also invite mice to come and nest. To avoid all of this, leave a few inches between the bark of the trunk and the mulch, and keep the mulch nearest the tree no more than ½ inch or so deep. From there you can mound the mulch up to 2 or 3 inches—no deeper, to discourage rodents.

RECYCLE THOSE WORMS • Once you empty your compost pile, all those lovely and helpful worms go with it. If you use a bin, and want to save some worms for future compost, you can do so by leaving the lid off for a day or two *before* emptying it. Worms don't like light, and will burrow down to the bottom of the pile if they are exposed. (Shining a light on the top of the pile for several hours will accomplish the same thing.) Unload the compost and as you approach the bottom of the pile you'll start seeing your worms. If the worms are still near the surface, expose them to additional light before unloading the pile.

> *Gardening is not a rational act.*
> —Margaret Atwood

I had always been told that one should harvest herbs in late morning—before the day gets hot and when the oils reach their peak intensity—but I used to pick my herbs, well, *whenever*. Then I did an experiment—nothing fancy, just a straight side-by-side tasting of herbs picked *whenever* compared to herbs picked on a cool sunny morning at about 10 A.M. Try it—or take my word: you can truly tell the difference, so much that only an emergency pesto would cause me to pluck my herbs at any other time of day.

They're all picked and flavorful—so now what do you do with them? Well, if I am not going to use them that day, I usually hang some in the kitchen against my brick wall because I like how it looks. But for the *real* harvest, I have become an enthusiast of the microwave process. It takes no time and delivers a good clean batch of herbs. Detach the leaves from the stems, put them on four thicknesses of paper towels, place in the microwave for 2 minutes on High, flip the leaves and give them another 2-minute blast. They should be dry—if not, give them another 1-minute blast and do so until you are satisfied. You don't want powder, obviously, but you do want to be able to crumble them when the time comes.

By the way, you can put your fresh-cut herbs in a mug or glass with fresh water, just as you would put flowers in a vase, and they will keep quite well for 2 or 3 days—and also give you the pleasure of their presence.

FERTILIZING PEONIES • It is almost impossible to ruin a peony border, but you can err in the fertilizing process. Peonies should not be overfed with nitrogen or manure. When the flowering is done, use a handful or so of granular 5-10-5 around the outside of the clump. Check soil pH, too. It should be between 6.5 and 7.0.

Love of flowers and vegetables is not enough to make a good gardener. He must also hate weeds.

—Eugene P. Bertin

Moles are blind rodents that make tunnels in your yard, and eat your grubs, slugs, earthworms, and insects along the way. No one would miss a grub or two, but unfortunately, the tunnels the moles make separate plant roots from the soil; the roots dry out and the plants die. As a result, I would say that moles are definitely in the category of top five most hated rodents of all time. Unless you are into traps, moles are quite difficult to eliminate. Luckily, a few simple off-the-wall methods seem to be getting satisfactory results.

For instance, some gardeners report excellent success placing soda bottles in the moles' holes. The bottles whistle when the wind blows and the moles do not like the sound. You also can stuff your thorny rose prunings into mole holes, and they will find it annoying enough to leave.

Another solution is the famous Juicy Fruit trick. Wearing gloves so that the moles cannot detect human scent, unwrap the gum, roll it up, and stick it in their holes. They'll eat it but are not able to digest it, and the gum eventually kills them.

A third solution is a bit more obtrusive. At various garden centers and from catalogues, you can purchase little windmills for about $20. When the wind is up, the windmills generate vibrations and the moles scatter. Moles hate vibrations. Or maybe they don't like little windmills.

SOFT-WATER TROUBLES • If you're using water treated by a water softener (or have naturally soft water) you'll need to replenish certain essential elements that have been filtered out in the process. The first step is to test your soil and make sure your pH is within the range of normal. If it's normal, you can begin to uncover and remedy the effects of the soft water. For instance, chlorosis, characterized by yellow or blanched leaves, can often be traced back to this source of nutrient deficiency. To remedy this condition, periodically add magnesium and calcium to the soil. Magnesium can be obtained through Epsom salts and calcium from gypsum. (If when you test your soil you discover it has a low pH, indicating high acid content, add dolomite. It contains both nutrients and will increase the soil's alkalinity.)

ABOUT CANDYTUFT • Candytuft (*Iberis*), according to the Oriental language of flowers, means "indifference" because it can adapt to many differing climates and conditions.

Here are some Latin descriptions of habitat to help you in your decoding process:

alpinus	alpine
arenarius	sandy
halophilus	salt loving
maritimus	of the sea
montanus	of the mountain
muralis	of walls
nivalis, niveus	relating to snow
palustris	of swamps
pratensis	of meadows
saxatilis	of rocks
sylvatica	of woods
uliginosus	of wet places

❧ J U N E   7

I am capable of getting overwrought about little things gone wrong
in the garden, like the time the stem of my *Gerbera* daisy broke in
half, after I had cajoled it into wintering over and blooming again.
Luckily I am trained in flower first aid and was able to make a splint
right away. All you do is slice a drinking straw down the side, place
it over the injured stem and seal it with some tape. Nine chances out
of ten the stem will heal and be good as new. Use clear straws so
the splint isn't noticeable.

METAL SHEETING MAKES GOOD NEIGHBORS • In
past lives, I had a couple of instances where a neighbor's roots in-
vaded my borders and created a bad situation. As long as it's not an
aggravated attack of bamboo, the neighbor's plant problem is usually
easily dealt with by having a nice, well, "neighborly" conversation—
and then digging a deep trench along your boundary line. After you
dig the trench, insert metal sheeting or any other barrier that won't
decompose.

FERTILIZE THOSE CONTAINER PLANTS • Just a reminder: your container plants need to be fertilized more often than plants grown in the ground. Water has a tendency to leach out the fertilizer rather quickly so it's best to use diluted fertilizers, and use them more often. Fish emulsion is a good choice.

DISAPPOINTING PEA CROP • If your peas tasted somewhat lackluster and the texture seemed off, you probably harvested them too late. The best way to tell when peas have reached their prime is to continuously harvest them until they taste just right. There's no magic test. You just want peas that are young, sweet, and tender.

Arranging a bowl of flowers in the morning can give a sense of quiet in a crowded day—like writing a poem or saying a prayer.
—Anne Morrow Lindbergh

❦ J U N E 8

My current garden is a study in small spaces, which instead of constricting me has actually expanded my ideas about gardening. What mostly have evolved are whimsical and lovely combinations of plants I never before would have thought to mix. When I was gardening in the country, a parsnip was just a parsnip. Now I see in the parsnip a wonderful cut flower as well as a tasty root vegetable. Sweet potato vines now serve as a ground cover. I have a wispy lane of dill and fennel and cosmos where fairies certainly live. My herbs and vegetables no longer dwell solely in row-after-row-after-row, and while the result is sometimes chaotic, it is also, mostly, beautiful. Do not be afraid to put red lettuce in the flower garden or purple basil anywhere you need a deep, rich foil. When your greens bolt, enjoy their blossoms for a while. Your garden is your invention, and while there are many techniques, there are no rules.

A TEA FOR CUT FLOWERS • A tea made with foxglove (*Digitalis*), a charming garden flower, is said to keep your cut flowers fresher, longer. But don't drink it. For humans, it's toxic.

DROWN YOUR SLUGS • If you've got some expired yogurt in the fridge and some slugs in the garden, bury the container so that the rim of the cup is flush with the surface soil and the slugs will eventually find it, slip in—and drown.

BLAND STRAWBERRIES • Some strawberry varieties look great but don't measure up in the flavor department. If yours are large and healthy looking but bland tasting, look for another variety. Breeders have created larger, more sumptuous berries at the expense of taste.

If on the eighth of June it rain,
It foretells a wet harvest, men sayen.

❦ J U N E 9

I always took my children for regular haircuts because I had been told that hair grows in thicker if you do that. To tell the truth, I don't think it made much difference except to the barber, whose wallet grew thicker. However, with plants it is a completely different story. Plants respond magnificently to being cut back, and now is the time to stay vigilant.

Annuals, in particular, require pinching back. If you don't do it, they will grow tall and spindly. At least twice during the summer, you should pinch your blooms back halfway—though not all at once, of course, or the plants will look barren. In about 3 weeks' time your plant will have a whole new set of blooms and will get bushy and lush, just the way they look in the catalogues.

Pinch! Cut! Pick! Clip!

112

Perennials like delphiniums should be cut back after blooming; if they set seed they'll think the summer is over and that they don't have to flower again. Herbs, well, we've talked about herbs. You have to keep the flowering ones in check because they are eager to fulfill their destinies and set seeds. If you want the seeds, that's one thing. But if you want the fragrant leaves, you have to keep the plant in its present stage of lush growth. So get ready to pinch! Cut! Pick! Clip! You will be repaid well for your efforts.

OKRA PLANTS • Okra plants have tiny hairs which some people find irritating to the skin. If you get an allergic reaction to okra, keep your hands dry and cool. Hot, perspiring hands will only aggravate the problem. Wear gloves and pick okra in the morning.

TO STORE FRESH HERBS • Wrap clean herbs in a paper towel. Spritz with water and put in a plastic bag. Refrigerate.

FIRE ANTS • A veteran fire ant fighter from Arkansas advises that successive glops of boiling water on fire ant mounds will rid you of serious infestations. The water has to be boiling—or thereabouts. Pour about 3 gallons of boiling water onto a small-sized mound; then repeat a week later. If you have large mounds, repeat the applications on a weekly basis until the problem is solved. *Another fire ant remedy: feed them instant grits. The grits swell up and the ants explode. Still another: Epsom salts sprinkled on hills.*

❦ J U N E 1 0

If you are laying down sod on your own, make sure you prepare the to-be-sodded area properly. Remove the weeds or existing lawn and then broadcast lime or sulfur (only if you need it—test first). Add some compost and then till it. Make sure you have some texture at the soil surface; don't till it until it's a fine powder. After you lay down the sod, roll or tamp out the air pockets. Water it to a depth of about 6 inches. If the newly sodded area is near pavement (like a driveway or concrete walkway) you will have to monitor the watering situation carefully, because it will dry out much faster in those spots than in the center lawn. Try to keep kids, neighbors, letter carriers, and dogs off the newly sodded areas for at least a month or two.

Chickadee	Bluebird
Wren	Vireo
Swallow	Woodpecker
Native sparrow	Nuthatch
Phoebe	Nighthawk

KITCHEN COMPOST ODORS • Sometimes odors develop when you are collecting kitchen scraps and storing them in a bucket or milk carton on the counter in the summer heat. Sprinkle alfalfa meal on the scraps, in layers, to rid the kitchen of the odors and also to add nutrients.

Still—in a way—nobody sees a flower—really—it is so small—we haven't time—and to see takes time, like to have a friend takes time.
                                                        —Georgia O'Keeffe

❦ J U N E 1 1

I have mixed feelings about edible flowers. Of course a salad with nasturtiums looks and tastes divine, but I have a hard time stabbing delicate petals with a fork. Flowers in syrups and vinegars and honeys are another story, and I count them chief among my summer pleasures. Especially the honey-making. It's so easy and fun to do.

Flowers you can eat or brew include: chrysanthemum, daylily, geranium, hollyhock, Johnny-jump-up, nasturtium, pansy, peony, rose, sunflower, tulip, and violet.

You can make a delicious spread by adding chopped petals or leaves to some mild honey. Proportions are completely up to the individual. I use about ⅓ cup of flowers to 1 cup of honey. Put the mixture in a jar, and set it in about 3 inches of boiling water; keep the water at a gentle boil for about ½ hour. Cool and store for 2 weeks before serving. On toasted, lightly buttered bread it is ambrosial! This makes a good hostess gift, too. Just doll up the jars.

Another summertime delight is flower-brewed tea. Take 2 or 3 teaspoons of fresh or dried petals per cup of boiling water. Steep the petals in the water for 3 to 8 minutes, depending on your preference. Strain it and serve hot. I've never tried it cold, but that might taste good, too.

For obvious reasons, make sure the flowers you are eating are not poisonous. (For instance, some jasmine is edible; Carolina jasmine is not.)

POWDERY MILDEW SOLUTION • I am sorry but I cannot even tap out the words P-O-W-D-E-R-Y M-I-L-D-E-W without having a physical reaction. PM is my declared enemy. But I *have* found a splendid ally in sodium bicarbonate. I will not say it has worked 100 percent, but in the majority of cases, a tablespoon of sodium bicarbonate (baking soda) mixed with a gallon of water, sprayed on plants the moment you see the dreaded gray traces, works. While the baking-soda-only formula works well, researchers have now added horticultural oil to the mix, with stunning test results. Here is the improved formula (*be sure to test this solution on a few leaves to be certain your plant can tolerate it*):

Cornell Fungicide Formula: Combine 1 tablespoon of baking soda with 1 tablespoon of light horticultural oil (like Sun Spray Ultra Fine Oil) or vegetable oil. Add to 1 gallon of water. If you use vegetable oil, add some insecticidal soap (amount appropriate for 1 gallon of water). Shake well before using and also occasionally while applying.

This baking soda–oil spray has been tested and proved better than a variety of commercially available polymer coatings and fungicides. It is important to spray both sides of the leaves, and to reapply after a rain. If the weather is humid, spray both sides of the leaves every 5 to 7 days. The moment you see signs of the disease start your spray program. Good luck to all of us.

PEPPER NUTRITION • Colored peppers have 10 times the vitamin C content than the traditional green pepper.

Flowers smell best just before a rain.

If you love blue flowers, and haven't planted borage before, cancel your afternoon plans, go to the nursery, and buy a packet of seeds. Borage is not only a marvelous old-fashioned garden plant, but it is reputed to bring happiness and courage to those who eat it. What more could you ask from a flower?

Borage can grow up to about 3 feet, reseeds itself, and both its leaves and flowers are edible. The leaves have a cucumber scent and should be eaten when very young. The flowers float in iced tea or can be used in salads, if you are a flower eater. I use the flowers in arrangements and they add a sense of nostalgia, though for what I am not sure. They just look great, that's all. Borage is not to be passed by; there is a reason the Welsh call it *Llawenlys*—the herb of gladness.

COUNT YOUR PEAS • Pea harvesters can determine their fortune by counting the peas in the pods. It is good luck to find a pod with a single pea in it (unless you are very hungry). But it is even better luck to grow a pod bearing nine lovely peas.

Count your peas.

DAMASK ROSE • The damask rose (*Rosa damascena*), grown for its essential oil (attar of roses), is one of the most ancient roses of all. Archaeologists have uncovered walls in the Palace of Knossos, Crete (circa 2000 B.C.), depicting the damask rose.

Many things grow in the garden that were never sown there.
—Thomas Fuller

The strawberry is such a perfect creation that only a scientist with a government grant would try to figure out utilitarian purposes for it. But if you have strawberries in great abundance this year, even without a grant you might want to experiment with some novel uses.

Strawberry tea, for instance, made from boiled leaves, is said to relieve rheumatic discomfort. Or if you have stains on your teeth you might find profit in rubbing strawberry juice on them, allowing the juice to penetrate the stain for 5 minutes. Then rinse with a solution of baking soda, about a teaspoon, stirred well in a cup of water. The discoloration will fade. A cut strawberry will also lighten sunburned skin. Apply the strawberry to a freshly cleaned face to reduce the intensity of the red marks.

GUIDELINE FOR IDENTIFYING AND KILLING SMALL CREATURES • A panelist on the BBC's "Gardener's Question Time," when asked how to identify and respond to small creatures in the garden, said he was told as a young gardener, "If it moves slowly enough, step on it; if it doesn't, leave it. It will probably kill something else."

IRIS BLOOMS • When your irises finish blooming, be sure to cut the flowering stalk down as close to the rhizome as you can get. Don't trim the blades of your irises in a fan shape at this time—the plant needs the green leaves to nourish the rhizome for next year. You can cut the brown tips just a bit if they bother you.

Divide your irises sometime between 2 and 4 weeks after flowering. Don't wait. The plant needs the time to regroup after you thin the extra rhizomes. Remember to leave the rhizome almost sitting on top of the soil.

BIRD WEB • If birds are attacking your fruit trees or bushes, create a web out of heavy black thread, woven in and out of limbs and branches. The birds are frightened by the possibility of entanglement and they will leave your buds, blossoms, and fruit alone.

The daisy shuts its eye before the rain.

Flag Day

Our catmint patch is a highly smashed affair. Our calico, Franny, spends most of the day idling in the patch and when she leaves, despite whatever territorial markers she has imposed, the neighborhood cats come over for catnaps, as it were, or simply to frolic.

If you want to grow *Nepeta cataria* but local cats ruin the plants before they get established, sow directly into the garden instead of setting out seedlings. When you handle the plants the scent is released and seedlings grown in place are more likely to be ignored. Catmint (catnip) is also bee-nip; it attracts bees, and old-fashioned beekeepers used to rub the leaves inside the hives to encourage new swarms. In addition, the plant contains nepeta-lactone, which is a natural insect repellent, though I don't know how that figures with what I just told you about the bees.

If you do want to grow *Nepeta* and don't want it to serve as a cat hangout, one gardener suggests putting the inner tube of an old bicycle tire near your garden. She says the cats, thinking it's a snake, keep their distance. Another option is to use a lemon-scented form of catmint, which has less appeal to cats.

MULCH YOUR TOMATO PLANTS • There are 1,001 excellent reasons to mulch. Okay, maybe a dozen. But for tomatoes it is *critical* to mulch, and if yours aren't mulched now—go out today and just do it. For one thing, you won't have to water nearly as much, and tomatoes need a *lot* of moisture. They also need *even* moisture, or they will split and crack—and by mulching you will assure some consistency, especially during the heat and dryness of late summer. In addition, your weeding will be reduced to practically nil when you layer on a good mulch.

Postscript: if you stake rather than cage your tomatoes, a salt hay mulch in particular creates a good-looking, clean, and comfortable nesting ground for all of your inevitably sprawling vines and fruits.

> *There was a dormouse who lived in a bed*
> *Of delphiniums (blue) and geraniums (red)*
> *And all the day he'd a wonderful view.*
> *Of geraniums (red) and delphiniums (blue).*
> —A. A. Milne

Succession planting isn't just a matter of sowing in intervals of 2 to 3 weeks throughout the summer. The heat and customary summer dryness add a kink or two to the germination process, so there are some adjustments to make when you sow. First, make sure that you water the soil down several inches before planting. If your dirt is really dry, water a few days before planting, and when you sow, do it a little deeper than you normally would, an extra ¼ inch for fine seeds and as much as ½ inch more for big seeds. After you sow, throw some dried grass clippings over the bed to keep the soil temperature down. If it is really hot, sprinkle the bed gently with water every 24 hours. I've had too many seeds sprout in June and July and then dry out and die because I didn't monitor the moisture carefully.

On the other hand, don't go crazy and make a rice paddy. Overwatered soil doesn't contain enough oxygen for seeds to germinate. Once you've got your sprouts, cut back on the daily watering, and water deeply when you do. Shallow watering is the worst for developing seedlings because the roots go up to the surface for the water instead of seeking it underground.

LAVENDER BLUE • Lavender (*Lavandula officinalis*) is a gem in the garden. If you want to produce a plant rich in oils, plant it in poor soil. In good soil, the plants are lush but their fragrant oils are diminished.

Plant a banana peel beneath each rosebush.

BECAUSE THEY HAVE APPEAL • Bananas make a great vitamin for your roses. Dice or slice the peels and bury about 3 around each rosebush. They are high in phosphorus and potash.

My house is spare on furnishings, and cut flowers take center stage in the spring and summer when they come inside. It always amazes me to see a vase on the dining room table exploding with magnificent flowers from my garden—they are really here, with me, this is it: June!

Morning is the best time to cut flowers, and for roses especially no later than 10 o'clock. If you wait until late in the day the heat may have drained them, so don't tarry.

I like to go out with a plastic bucket and, using a sharp knife, slice the flowers at the stem on an angle and plunge them immediately into the bucket of water. Rain water is ideal; soft water is not great for cut flowers. In general the water should be room temperature, though some plants, like violas and violets, are said to like really cold water. (It's never easy, is it?)

Once the flowers are cut, I bring the bucket inside and let the flowers sit for about half an hour, enough time for some coffee and the newspaper. Then I make an arrangement, although "arrange" sounds more artistic and deliberate than what I do. If you are cutting woody stems, you can make 2-inch gashes in the stems so that they split open and absorb water more readily. The flowers of poppies, hollyhocks, and milkweed all benefit from having their stem ends burned before placing in water. Strip off all the leaves that will fall below the water line to prevent bacteria buildup.

Oh, yes: don't put your cut flowers near a sunny window. Some light is okay but heat and sun are not.

IVY TRICK • To grow lush ivy foliage, add ¼ teaspoon of ammonia to 1 gallon of water, and water with this solution every few weeks.

RULE OF THUMB • Sometimes it's necessary to play Doctor Dirt. Here are a few tips for diagnosing deficiencies in your soil. They are very general guidelines, so check with your extension agent or nursery advisory to confirm your diagnosis.

In all cases of nitrogen, phosphorus, and potassium deficiencies the plant will be dwarfed. Without enough nitrogen, the older leaves will turn from green to yellow and finally to brown. Cases of phosphorus deficiency can be seen with leaves turning a dull dark green. In some cases, the stem and/or the area around the veins of the leaf will turn purple. Potassium deficiency is indicated by a yellow color at the leaf's margin in the lower foliage area. While the plants may look pretty bad, all deficiencies, if caught early enough, can be remedied.

COLOR COMBINATIONS THAT WORK • When you combine colors, be careful about the hue of each plant: there are a hundred purples, and not all of them will look good with any yellow. As a primer though, here are some color groupings to work with.

Red, Pink, and Rose
Pink, Purple, and Blue
Purple and Yellow
Blue and Pale Yellow
Blue and Orange
Blue, Purple, and Yellow
Red and Purple

❦ J U N E 1 7

Many gardeners in our village alter their soil to create the bold, blue color in their hydrangeas, but to me it recalls bad corsages. I just don't care for it. This is our third season in this house, and I have tried to soften the blue color in our hydrangeas by omission—and haven't added a bit of elemental sulfur (aka flowers of sulfur), which is usually used to generate the big blue blooms. The color of hydrangeas is determined by the amount of aluminum in the soil, which is determined by pH. For blue blooms you need a pH that is acid, from about 4.5 to 5.5. For pink blooms you want a more alkaline soil, within a range of 7 to 7.5.

This year I added some lime to move the plants back to their pink coloration, and soon enough we will see the result. In Victorian times, gardeners called their hydrangeas "changeable," and to create the blue color they ground up old blue slates, digging the slate dust in around each bush.

DON'T FORGET THE PAPER TOWELS • I have a major guilt complex about the quantity of paper towels our family goes through, some of which is alleviated by the practice of putting the wet paper towels into the compost heap. Obviously, if there are gigantic globs of grease or harsh chemicals on the towels, I don't put them in—but with garden-variety grunge, they make a fine addition.

I think this is what hooks one on gardening: it is the closest one can come to being present at creation.
                                                    —Phyllis Theroux

❧ J U N E 1 8

My most treasured plants are from my gardening friends, even if I still don't have the ideal spot for the Siberian iris and evening primrose I received a few seasons ago. Sharing plants is one of the most congenial acts in a gardener's repertoire, but it can be tricky sending plants to friends across the country. Packing is crucial to their safe arrival.

I learned how to pack by observing the way the best nurseries sent me plants, and have tried to duplicate it when I ship transplants to friends.

Here is an easy, reliable method for most journeys. First, use lightweight plastic pots, which will hold moisture well. Water the plants a day or so before packing, or they will be too soggy. Wrap them carefully in newspaper. Tape newspaper over the soil surface to keep the dirt in place, then wrap newspaper around the entire plant and tape it well.

Now wrap the entire newspaper-packaged plant in plastic (I use saved-up dry-cleaner bags) so the plant will retain its moisture. Pad a box with newspaper on the bottom, and place the plant in the box. Use packing materials to keep the plant in position for its journey, assuming the handlers will pay no attention to your touching notes of "This side up" or "Handle with care." Cross fingers. Mail.

ANIMAL ZAPPING • Zappers are not just for bugs, according to one formerly frustrated gardener. Here's a man who had been through every technique for ridding himself of deer, raccoons, and woodchucks, from aluminum pie plates to plastic grocery bags flapping in the wind to mothballs to radio. Determined, he made one last attempt. He got miles of extension cords and put his bug zapper out in the middle of his corn patch. Zit. Zit. Zap. Zap. Guess what? No raccoons. No deer. No woodchucks.

TOMATOES IN THE SHADE • Reports are in that Burpee's Big Girl will deliver beautiful *major* tomatoes with no more than five hours in full sun.

WHAT COLOR IS MY COMPOST? • With compost you want a balance of wet, green materials like food scraps and grass clippings, and dry, brown materials like dry leaves and woody materials. If you have only brown materials, the decomposition will slow to a halt because it won't create enough heat. Adding only green materials without dry agents can cause odors to develop. Try to keep a balance through the summer months (See July 1 if you are low on brown materials.)

> *What if you do have a few bugs?*
> —Catherine Osgood Foster

❦ J U N E 1 9

The first Father's Day was actually planned for June 5 by Mrs. John Bruce Dodd of Spokane, Washington, whose father was born on that day. Apparently, the minister of Mrs. Dodd's church needed more time to prepare his sermon, so they changed the celebration to the third Sunday of the month, which was June 19 that year, where it stuck. Mrs. Dodd's suggestion for observing the day was to wear a red rose for a living father, and a white rose for a dead one.

FIRST-TIME BLOSSOM REMOVERS • Deadheading is removing faded and spent flowers, and it is crucial to summer garden maintenance. But there is more than one way to remove blossoms. Plants with foliage on the flower stems like the shasta daisy (*Chrysanthemum maximum*) and yarrow (*Achillea*) should be cut off just above the new flower buds. With spring-flowering bulbs, hostas, and day lilies, which have leafless flower stalks, the stems should be cut close to the ground.

Plants with attractive seedheads like *Sedum spectabile* 'Autumn Joy,' globe thistle, and rudbeckia don't need to be deadheaded and can be left for winter interest.

LADDER FOR A PLANT STAND • An old stepladder makes a whimsical plant stand for your container garden. You can sand it and paint it a deep, dark green or a bolder color, or even leave it with a weathered appearance, all with great effect. Clay pots with vining plants arranged on the steps will look terrific. Put it on the lee side of a building if winds are a problem and you don't want pots sailing off the steps. If there is a chance the ladder could topple, simply stake it as you would a swing set.

I have also seen aging ladders with hinges removed and laid down flush with the soil to create mini-raised and enclosed beds, an especially appealing arrangement for herbs.

BEE STING REMEDY • A member of the Garlic Seed Foundation claims that you will get instant relief from a bee sting if you apply the cut side of a peeled garlic clove to the affected area. Baking soda mixed into a paste with a little water is also a good poultice.

Wet June,
Dry September.

❦ J U N E 2 0

Black-eyed peas are a staple at our house. Southerners eat them for good luck on New Year's Day, and we have them every couple of weeks. I guess it works; we're a pretty lucky family.

I don't grow black-eyeds up here; the season's too short. But in the South, the peas are commonly pollinated by wasps. If you are lucky enough to grow them, the best time to gather your pods is in the early morning while the wasps are still drowsy from the night's cool temperatures. The black-eyed pea is one of the most versatile foods put on this planet, and I would suggest that anyone who can grow them ought to give it a try. You can prepare them in a number of ways, but my family seems to like them in a salad best of all.

SUMMER SALAD OF BLACK-EYED PEAS

If using dried or store-bought peas, soak them overnight. Drain, cover with fresh water, and boil slowly for 30 to 45 minutes or until tender. (Don't let the water boil too rapidly or the skins will come off and the beans will get mushy.) Drain the peas and let them cool. Here's where you improvise: Add chopped parsley, chives, diced cucumbers, tomatoes, carrots, radishes, celery, scallions, or anything else that you have handy and that sounds good. Salt and pepper to taste. Pour a garlicky vinaigrette over the peas and vegetables and then refrigerate for at least an hour. Toss once more and check your seasonings. Crumble feta cheese over the salad before serving, and eat healthy.

HERB HARVESTING • Keep on top of your herb harvest. When you harvest most of your perennial herbs, cut about a third off the top. The exceptions to this would be chive, oregano, sweet marjoram, thyme, and mint, which should be clipped almost to the ground. Stalks of annuals like caraway, parsley, chervil, and lovage should be cut to the ground at the outside edges of the plant (in other words, don't disturb the crown). Dillweed and fennel stalks can be cut back to the main stem.

Spray your clean shovel with a vegetable oil cooking spray.

SHOVEL CLEANER • Lots of gardeners recommend using dried corn cobs to clean dirt off shovels. After you get a clean surface, spray the shovel with Pam or another vegetable cooking spray so the dirt won't adhere so easily.

Summer Solstice

Watch how you use water. Keep a plastic gallon jug by the kitchen faucet. While you're waiting for the lead to clear out of your pipes in the morning or for the water to heat up, you'll be amazed at how much water you can save in your jug. Use your jug for watering outdoor container plants and house plants.

....

WEEDS THAT GROW IN ACID SOIL
....

Dock (*Rumex acetosella*)
Knotweed (*Polygonum*)
Wild strawberry (*Fragaria virginiana*)
Cinquefoil (*Potentilla canadensis*)
Sorrel (*Rumex acetosella*)

....

WEEDS THAT GROW IN ALKALINE SOIL
....

Broom sedge
Yellow toadflax (*Linaria vulgaris*)
Quackgrass (*Agropyron repens*)
Wild mustard (*Brassica kaber pinnatifida*)
Pineapple weed

START PRESSING FLOWERS • One year I got a little carried away with my flower pressing and ended up with hundreds of beautiful flowers, but then what do you do with them? Many people glue them to fine-quality cards to make stationery and even frame them. I ended up gluing the dried flat blooms to pastel Easter eggs and they were exquisite. The earlier blooms of summer tend to be more pastel and are gorgeous on the eggs.

> In counterpoint
> Of clover and Queen Anne's lace
> Summer sings to me.
> —Lois O'Connor

....

CANCER, June 22 to July 22—*The most productive time for sowing and transplanting*

Roses look even more lush if you underplant with carpetlike flowers that are no more than about 18 inches tall. Many people use white alyssum to this end, but you can also use certain verbenas (they come in all colors so you can plant in different-colored drifts to complement the different-colored roses). Lobelia and forget-me-nots are also excellent, though forget-me-nots have a shorter bloom period.

ABOUT DAISIES • Daisy means "day's-eye" from the Anglo-Saxon *daegeseye*, so named because the pink and white English daisy closes at nightfall and opens at sunrise. When you pick a single daisy, you are actually picking a bouquet. Pull a blossom apart. Each flower is actually many little flowers. Daisies belong to the Compositae family, which includes asters, marigolds, goldenrod, hawkweed, thistles, sunflowers, and dandelions.

FOR DEEP ROOT DEVELOPMENT • If you are planting a new tree, or for that matter any plant, and you want to encourage its roots to grow downward, locate a 3- to 4-foot pipe that is wider than a hose nozzle. Stick the pipe into the soil, right alongside the stem or trunk, with the top of the pipe flush with the ground. About once a week, pour water into the pipe with a very slow hose for about a quarter of an hour (cut off the water before it gets too flooded) and you will create a steady, deep watering system that boosts root development tremendously.

RULE OF THUMB • For the most part, plants that have glossy, tough leaves have fewer leaf diseases because the waxy coating is tough to penetrate. Plants with little hairs on the leaves are safe havens for diseases spores, and therefore are more disease prone.

Gardening can become a kind of disease.
—Lewis Gannit

❦ J U N E 2 3
Midsummer's Eve

WHERE IS THAT ST.-JOHN'S-WORT WHEN YOU NEED IT? • This is the night when witches and fairies stir in the garden. The traditional midsummer bonfire is lit to burn yarrow, ivy, corn marigold, plantain, and St.-John's-wort (the herbs of John) and to protect herb burners from evil.

HORTICULTURALLY INCORRECT • The classic suburban lawn is the new leper in horticultural circles, *very incorrect*. For the environmentally conscious, a smaller lawn, or use of alternative plantings like ground cover, is the preferred option. According to the EPA the amount of pollutants generated by running a gasoline-fueled lawn mower for 1 hour is comparable to the amount of pollutants produced by a typical automobile driven 50 miles. (Gas-fueled chainsaws are even worse. They produce pollutants four times faster than lawnmowers.)

CAVEAT ON MARIGOLDS • Marigolds attract slugs. If you have a serious slug problem you might want to go light on marigolds in your garden—at least until you are able to reduce the slug population significantly.

CHINESE CABBAGE LORE • According to lore, two days following the summer solstice is the best time to plant Chinese cabbage. Science bears out the practice. The plant prefers days as they become shorter and tends to bolt when the days get longer.

MOTHBALLS WILL DETER DOGS, CATS, AND SQUIRRELS • If neighborhood animals are claiming your yard for their territory, put some mothballs around your shrubs and plants. Push them into the ground and you will offend a good number of local pets. Also, try "planting" mothballs in your garden if you have a slug problem.

A swarm of bees in June
is worth a silver spoon.

❦ J U N E 2 4

All too often brand-new concrete ornaments in the garden look forced, and call too much attention to themselves. (Hi. I'm a pillar.) One way to help the ornament blend in quickly is to paint the concrete with a "fertilizer" made up of 1 part buttermilk or yogurt and 2 parts water. If you give it the buttermilk coat and then two weeks later paint it with plain water it will start to develop a moss or lichen coat. You can add more fertilizer and an application of water every few weeks if you need it.

This also works on new stone walls that need some instant weathering.

ROSE PROBLEMS • Rose gardening can be tricky. If nothing you read in the books is helping you to solve a pest problem, or if you want to grow roses but don't know how to get started, contact the American Rose Society, P.O. Box 30,000, Shreveport, LA 71130. In most communities there are local rosarians who will gladly assist gardeners with questions and problems *free of charge*.

CUT BACK WORN PERENNIALS • If your perennials start to get that Johnny Cash look—the leaves are looking brown or wilted and a little the worse for wear—cut them back. They will start over again and come in much healthier (unless there is an insect or disease problem we didn't know about). In colder zones you can cut your perennials back until about the middle of July. Southern gardeners have a lot more leeway and can cut back until the end of the season.

❦ J U N E 2 5

Making potpourri from your own garden is a sensual and civilized thing to do. Most gardens already have many of the classic ingredients: rose, lavender, jasmine, violet, lemon balm, lemon verbena, heliotrope, rosemary, marigold, delphinium, pansy, thyme, and geranium. Pick the flowers in the morning, just after the dew has dried, and when the flowers are either in bud or just beginning to open. Spread the leaves and petals on large sheets of cheesecloth and place in a dry airy room out of direct sun. Carefully turn the petals every day for a week or until they are dry. Aren't they beautiful? Put the petals in an airtight container. If you wish, you may also add ½ teaspoon each of crushed cinnamon sticks, whole cloves, whole coriander, or ground mace per quart of leaves. To preserve both the scent and color of the leaves and petals, add 1 ounce of orrisroot, ambergris, or violet powder per quart of potpourri. Store the leaves and petals for a month in a cool, dry place. When the fragrance fades, you can rejuvenate it with a teaspoon of brandy.

KEEPING CONTAINERS MOIST • When the heat begins to pour on, we'll be watering our container plants—especially those in clay pots—daily. If the plants in your smaller pots need more than a daily watering, give them ice. Water as usual in the morning, and then put ice cubes on the soil surface. The time-release moisture will tide the plants over until the next day.

When you give your plants a gentle hosing, spray the sides of the clay pots as well.

❦ JUNE 26

I have always gotten confused about coriander and cilantro, especially since they are the herbs of choice in so many Chinese, Indian, Caribbean, and Mexican food preparations.

What we commonly call cilantro is the fresh green leaves of *Coriandrum sativum*, and that's what most of us grow. (It's known to Dominicans and Puerto Ricans as cilantrillo.) The dried seeds are called coriander and have an entirely different taste. The home-grown variety of cilantro is more pungent than what you'll get in cut bunches from herb farmers at the specialty markets. Herb farmers usually fertilize their plants for extra lush leaf growth, which dilutes the intensity of the essential oils. It's almost impossible to prevent the plant from bolting in the summer; early spring and late summer plantings are the most successful.

Cilantro de punta—or pointed cilantro (*Geringium foedidum*)—is an herb with a serrated leaf grown in many Hispanic countries and it is interchangeable in taste with cilantro. However, it is not related botanically; it is a member of the sea holly family that grows best in tropical places (though you can get it to grow in North America with special tending).

FOR NASTURTIUM EATERS • If you like to eat nasturtiums, pick the leaves and blooms early in the morning when their water content is at its peak. (The leaves are fantastic.) Wash them gently in lukewarm water and blot with paper towels. They will keep in a plastic bag in the refrigerator for 2 days, but use them the same day if possible. *Try this summer sandwich:* nasturtium leaves with cream cheese, paper-thin sliced Bermuda onion and tomatoes on fresh dark bread.

BE CAREFUL WHEN USING HORTICULTURAL OILS • Horticultural oils are an excellent option for controlling various plant ills but you must be careful when using them. Though they pose little threat to humans and have low environmental risks, they can damage certain plants under certain conditions. Always test a leaf of the plant you intend to spray the day before spraying and give it 24 hours to respond. Even if you want to spray that same plant, later in the summer, *test it again.* The conditions might have changed and those changes could adversely affect your plant.

❦ JUNE 27

A child's plastic wading pool makes a great beginner's water and rock garden. Simply set the inflated pool in the ground and line it with large flat stones, fill it with water, and plant reeds, hens-and-chicks, phlox, pansies, alyssum, and bamboo in the soil-filled crevices of the outer rocks. Find a beginner-size water pump and install it. Add some fast-growing vines to camouflage the tacky outside ring of the pool. You can add goldfish, and without any effort on your part the frogs will come.

We had a small water pond in our Key West garden a few years ago, and my husband spent literally hours at a time peacefully staring at the fish and the extraordinary plant life, which is not to say he didn't wring his hands over the filter and the algae or the stray cats who would come in for fish snacks. Water gardens really are captivating, and this baby pool might be a good opportunity to see if it's something you'd like to become obsessed with.

OKRA ON THE ROCKS • If you are sowing okra seeds mid-summer in a mild climate, follow the trick of H. S. Stevens, of the Texas Agricultural Extension Service. Freeze your seeds before planting and they'll germinate better. Fill an ice cube tray halfway with water, then drop a seed or two in each cube space and place in the freezer. Plant the little cubes the next day, sowing as usual.

MINT TEA SUGGESTION • Mint for tea should be cut when the flower heads are starting to be visible but *before* they bloom. Tie the cut mint leaves in bunches and hang them in a dark, warm, airy place. When they are dry, store the leaves in glass jars.

❦ JUNE 28

The garden is at its most pastel, and most lyrical, as June comes to its end. As a matter of fact, it's almost *impossible* to have an ugly garden right now. However, it is easy to have an ugly garden in August. Okay, not easy, but *possible*.

What you don't want in August is all of the extroverts getting into a color fight. The transition from pastels to bolder, more forthright colors must be bridged. If your garden is going from pastels to black-eyed susans, chrysanthemums, asters, coneflowers, and sedums, use annuals to cushion the color change. I always experiment with interesting annuals grown from seed in pots on the back porch and bring them out for transition duty in July and August. You can check placement before planting by trying your pots in different spots. Meanwhile, don't be afraid to pull out, throw out, or give plants to friends. You can go crazy trying to make a certain plant blend in, and going crazy is *not* gardening.

CABBAGE CLINIC • If your cabbage heart dies and the soil has a pH of at least 6.5 it's probably a symptom of boron deficiency. Mix ½ teaspoon of borax with a gallon of water and pour next to the plant.

BEET CLINIC • Poor beet germination is often caused by too warm soil temperatures, heavy rains, or lack of adequate moisture. White rings inside the beets indicate uneven soil temperatures coupled with hot weather—though sometimes the beets are intentionally bred that way. Rough-tasting beets are caused by late harvesting or lack of water. If your beets are misshapen, it's usually a result of rocky soil or the use of fresh manure.

STORING GARLIC • To store garlic for long periods of time, keep the bulbs as cold as possible—but not freezing—with good air circulation. Humidity should be about 65 percent.

❦ JUNE 29

Container plants are even more vulnerable to overfertilization than your garden plants. It is always better to underfeed your plants than to dump too much fertilizer on them. Container plants that have been overfed have weak stems, an excess of leaves, and a general flimsiness to them. If you see chalky deposits on your pots or on the surface of your soil, beware; they are overfertilized.

• Never feed your plants when the soil is dry and the leaves are wilted.

• Never feed a plant that is infested with insects or disease.

• Never feed a container plant you just purchased—it probably was well fed at the nursery.

• Never feed a plant when it is dormant—for most plants this is between October and March.

PRUNE DEAD OR DYING BRANCHES • Spring flowering shrubs and trees should have been pruned right after flowering—and before seed was set—but you can and should prune dead or dying branches no matter what point in the cycle. If you rid the plant of an insect-infested or diseased branch immediately, you will arrest its spread. The plants in their glory now can cause us to forget our trees and shrubs. Give them a once-over and check for stress or damage.

SIMPLE DRAINAGE TEST • If you suspect you have a drainage problem, perform this simple test. Dig a hole about the size you'd need for a large perennial transplant. Fill it with water. If the water has not drained in 24 hours, you have a problem.

VASES • When did vases become vaaaahses? Anyway, be sure and wash your vases with hot soapy water before adding fresh water and cut flowers. Vases tend to get a build-up of bacterial material, and in the midst of high summer it's easy to get lazy and throw our gorgeous flowers into filmy containers. Use a bottle brush to clean out all of the residue so it doesn't contaminate your new posies when they go in.

A little dirt never hurt anyone.

❦ JUNE 30

My spring crop is nearing its end and I am very glad I planted creeping flowers—verbena, nasturtium, catmint, violas, and alyssum—to quietly take over once the carrots, cabbages, cauliflowers, and head lettuces are yanked out without warning. (Don't worry, little flowers. I'd never do that to you.) If you mix your edibles and flowers, it is important to have established plants-in-waiting when a big harvest cleans out several patches of garden. Think ahead. Know what you are going to plant next. Otherwise, you'll panic and buy plants you don't want or need just to fill in. Panicking does not become the gardener or the garden.

Another thing I've learned about mixing flowers and vegetables is that it is easy to get an overly cluttered look, like a cottage garden on a very bad day. As you harvest and add a little here and there through the season, try at least to repeat your plantings in groups of threes. Vary heights, textures, and colors. Borders can be extremely helpful. An edging of santolina or chives or thyme can pull a lot of busyness together.

WHAT TO DO WITH ALL OF THOSE FANCY GREENS • By the way, if you have buckets of greens ready for harvest and haven't figured out what to do with them, have a salad bar party. Present your lettuces and other early garden crops out on platters, and have your guests bring sausages, olives, cheeses, and breads. Make some homemade croutons. Carrot cake for dessert.

AH·CHOO • Ragweed, the source of untold agony for allergy sufferers, is curiously named *Ambrosia artemisiifolia*. Ambrosia was the food of the Greek gods.

LET THEM BOLT • Don't worry if a few of your vegetables bolt and flower—they will attract beneficial insects. Beneficial insects also love mint and carrots.

Hot summer, cold winter.

❦ *July* ❦

Flower of the Month: Larkspur

❦ J U L Y 1

Gardeners' hands are unlovely, and a lot of cosmetic manufacturers have tried to come up with a way to change that. Still, the best soap I've found is Lava. After a thorough cleansing, I put petroleum jelly—yes, straight Vaseline—into my creases and etchings, and my hands are at least passable.

If they are in really bad shape, I give myself a poor man's hot cream manicure. In "better salons," the hands are slathered with lotions and oils and then put in a heated mitt for about 20 minutes for softening. I do the gardener's version. Put hand lotion or balm on your hands and then pull on a pair of clean gardening gloves (the ones you should have worn in the first place). Go out and garden for 20 minutes. Your own body heat opens the pores and allows the balm to penetrate your skin. Come in, pull the gloves inside out, and toss them in the washer. Wash and moisturize your hands. They should be clean and almost supple.

ITSY BITSY ALLIES • Don't kill the spiders in your garden. They help you keep down other insect populations.

QUEEN ANNE'S LACE • Even the most uninspired bunch of cut flowers becomes romantic when sprigs of Queen Anne's lace (*Daucus carota*) are added here and there, yet this plant is actually a wild carrot.

INSTANT BROWN MATERIAL • To really cook, your compost pile needs both green and brown material. We always have a glut of green material in the summer, from kitchen scraps to grass clippings. But brown material is much harder to come by, especially in July. So I make my own. All I do is to lay an old dropcloth on the driveway and spread out wet grass clippings to dry in the sun, along with leaves and other debris from the garden. In no time, my green material is brown material—and with a few turnings of the pitchfork, the balance to the compost pile is restored.

> *The trouble with gardening is that it does not remain an avocation.*
> *It becomes an obsession.*
> —Phyllis McGinley

❦ J U L Y 2

FLAVORED OILS • Many herbs are at their peak now, and need to be harvested and preserved. I have found that there is a limit to how many Hellmann's jars of herbs my pantry can take—and I don't have enough friends to give my surplus away (what was I thinking when I planted all of that basil?). Anyway, this year, I got in on the flavored oil bandwagon, and with good results. Flavoring oils is a wonderful way to bottle the scents of your garden. Centuries before we had refrigeration, Mediterranean gardeners preserved vegetables and herbs by drying them and storing them in locally produced oils. Now it's a big fad, but who cares? They taste sensational on vegetables or just mopped with some crusty bread.

Generally, you will use olive, canola, or sunflower oil for herbs; and canola, sunflower, or almond oil for flowers. Strip the herbs or flowers from their stems, rinse them, and allow them to dry on paper towels, blotting lightly. To measure, pack them lightly in a measuring cup. With herbs, you'll basically use 1 cup of herbs to 2 cups of oil. With flowers, use a cup of oil and a handful of blossoms, petals, or leaves. With garlic, I use 2 cups of oil with 16 large peeled cloves of garlic—but then, I really like garlic.

Just purée the herbs or flowers with the oil in a blender or food processor. Put the mixture in a broad wide-mouthed jar for 3 days (covered, of course). Shake it at least 3 times a day for the first 2 days to make sure all the flavor in the herbs or flowers is released. On the third day, let the mixture settle to the bottom of the jar. Then strain the oil through a paper coffee filter or some approximation into a clean jar that has a lid. Don't jostle the flowers or herbs—be very careful as you pour. You should now have a clear but tinted stream of oil. If your oil is cloudy, repeat the filtering process until you get the look you want. Toss out the solids left in the bottom of your original jar. Refrigerate the oil in a tightly sealed bottle and use within 2 or 3 (at the outside) weeks.

I have tried these tasty combinations: chili peppers, garlic, and basil; shallots and tarragon; and green basil oil (big hit). You can brush these oils on vegetables and meats as you grill them or use them in pastas. Yum.

MOLES AND GOPHERS AWAY • If you are plagued by gophers or moles, a property maintenance expert from San Jose, California, recommends putting chocolate-flavored Ex-Lax into the holes. The gophers love the taste, gobble it up, and then die of dehydration.

DO CERTAIN TREES ATTRACT LIGHTNING? • International studies show that elm (*Ulmus*), oak (*Quercus*), pine (*Pinus*), poplar (*Populus*), ash (*Fraxinus*), maple (*Acer*), and spruce (*Picea*) are struck by lightning more frequently than other trees; and that beech (*Fagus*), birch (*Betula*), horse chestnut (*Aesculus*), and holly (*Ilex*) are almost never struck. Decayed and rotten trees are more vulnerable to lightning than solid, healthy specimens, and deep-rooted trees are injured by lightning more often than trees with shallow, wide-spreading roots.

STRAWBERRY REPELLENTS • Taking children strawberry picking is a nice idea unless you want to take home some strawberries. The children tend to eat more than ever makes the basket. To repel children, give them a lollipop or ice cream cone *just before going berry picking*. The children will find the taste of the berries tart and unappealing, and will actually gather some berries for the table.

A garden is a thing of beauty and a job forever.
—Anonymous

Beginning today, the dog days of summer begin, lasting until August 11. The dog days were so named for their connection to the rising of the dog star, Sirius. The name originated with the Greeks, Romans, and Egyptians, who believed that the dog star actually added its heat to the Sun's and thereby caused the hot weather. The dog days are hot and crushing and not particularly advantageous to any plant or creature.

IRON CHLOROSIS • If your plants suffer from iron chlorosis, a problem common among iron-loving foundation plantings, you can use foliar applications of chelated iron and get virtually instant (2 or 3 days) results. For a preventive "time-release" program, crumble rusty clean steel wool pads at the soil surface or drive rusty nails into the soil, and iron will seep into the soil. Don't add too much iron, though. It will turn the plants' leaves black.

THAT TERRIBLE THUD • If birds keep wiping out on your glass windows, you can place plastic netting outside the glass, stretched taut (you will barely notice it) and it will alert the birds to the presence of the window. The birds can't see the glass but they can see the netting. The plastic netting used to protect fruit trees and bushes from birds will provide this protective barrier.

To own a bit of ground, to scratch it with a hoe, to plant seeds, and watch the renewal of life, this is the commonest delight of the race, the most satisfactory thing a man can do.

—Charles Dudley Warner

Squash blossoms are a romantic presence on the summer table, easy to grow and fun to prepare. When you harvest squash blossoms, you can harvest the male or the female flowers but you should pick them differently and remember that if you harvest all the females, you won't get any squash. The first flowers to appear are male. (You only need a few of them for pollination, so you can harvest them to your heart's content.) The female blossoms come about a week later, and they have a little bump behind them, on the stalk. The female flowers should be cut with the baby squash intact. Leave an inch or two of stem on the male flowers. It is tricky to grow squash organically, but you *must* if you want to eat the flowers. Chemicals stick to squash blossoms and you can't wash them off without ruining them.

I got overly involved in squash blossoms one summer and set aside a whole plot for flowers-only production. I covered them with floating row cover, which was do-able because the flowers-only plants didn't need to be pollinated. Luckily, the plants didn't overheat, and they were protected from striped and spotted cucumber beetles, among other pests and woes.

Pick your squash blossoms carefully.

STUFFED SQUASH BLOSSOMS

You can stuff squash blossoms with just about anything, but I like fresh mozzarella, prosciutto, and basil leaves in mine. (Any use for basil is a good idea to me since I am now wading in it.) I simply take a 1-inch cube of fresh mozzarella and wrap it with a fresh basil leaf and half a thin slice of excellent-quality prosciutto. Open the petals just wide enough to insert the filling. Fill the blossom just to the point where the petals divide, then twist the ends of the petals together gently.

For the batter combine 1 cup of all-purpose flour and 1 cup of beer and mix until smooth. Cover and let sit in the refrigerator for at least an hour.

Heat 2 inches of vegetable oil in a deep heavy skillet to 375 degrees. Dip the stuffed squash blossoms into the batter to coat and carefully drop them into the hot oil. Fry for 2 minutes or until lightly browned. Turn and repeat on the other side. Drain on paper towels and serve hot.

TOP YOUR PHLOX • Phlox bloom in various months of the summer (depending on the cultivar) but you can get a second bloom by topping off 10 to 20 inches from the flower-bearing stems just after the flowers appear. Within a week or so you will get miraculous new growth—and another round of flowers. The second round is not as spectacular as the first—the flowers are a bit smaller and there are fewer of them, but they're lovely just the same. With a little luck on the timing you might even get a third round from them.

❦ JULY 5

Last summer I almost broke my back pulling purslane weed out of the garden—and no wonder. One plant of purslane (*Portulaca oleracea*) can produce up to 50,000 offspring. Flowers open only 4 hours before the seed-making process begins, and seeds are mature and released in 2 weeks.

The Europeans do not engage in weed warfare with purslane. Instead, they eat it. Purslane leaves are used by Europeans in salads. The leaves have more omega-3 fatty acids (which lower cholesterol levels and reduce heart disease risks) than any other vegetable source, according to researcher Helen A. Norman from USDA's Weed Science Lab in Beltsville, Maryland. It has 10 times more linolenic acid and 6 times more vitamin E than spinach.

HARVESTING THYME • Harvest thyme in early morning when the oils are strongest. They are ideally gathered just before the flowers open by cutting the entire plant 1 or 2 inches from the ground. You'll get a second growth, but you shouldn't harvest it because it will reduce the plant's winter hardiness—particularly if the ground is bare and the temperatures rise and fall dramatically. If you are desperate for a second cutting, just snip from the top third of the plant.

Thyme is a big taker from the soil. If you transplant your thyme, make sure to replenish the soil with nutrients.

FIRST-TIME WEEDERS • Weeding isn't just about good looks. Weedy gardens generally yield about half the amount their weed-free counterparts do. Weeds are usually hardier than flowers and crops, and they will rob your plants of water and desirable nutrients. All which means you either have to mulch or get down on your knees—and weed.

Make hay while the sun shines.

❦ J U L Y 6

I have great news for those who think the marigold was not God's finest moment. Unless you have a nematode problem (or find marigolds pretty), *you no longer have to plant rows of marigolds around your vegetable garden.* Research shows that marigolds only repel certain soil-dwelling nematodes and they work in this capacity only if you plant your land solidly with them—we're talking about a dense, almost carpetlike planting, *pounds of seed,* not just a few dinky packets. For it to be effective, sow your marigold seed thickly, let it grow for about 2 months, and then chop the plants down and turn the roots and cuttings under. The cut-down-and-turn-under program does work extremely well, especially if you do a summer planting and fall turn-under. You'll get best results for nematode problems by planting Crackerjack (American), Sparky (French), or Nemakill.

STORING CUKES • Cucumbers do best in the warmest spot in the refrigerator: the crisper drawer. Don't let them get too cold. They'll get wet and mushy.

PIGEON MANURE • Pigeon manure has even a higher nitrogen content than chicken manure—but city friends, wait a minute: you can't scrap the goo off your windowsill and use it for compost. Wild pigeon manure is likely to carry diseases. It's much better to get your pigeon droppings from breeders in the country. (Yes, there actually are people who breed pigeons in the country.)

Cottonwoods turn up their leaves before a rain.

JULY 7

You don't have to know a lot about pH to have a great garden. I only just learned that the "H" in pH stands for hydrogen—and that pH is really a measurement of the concentration of hydrogen ions in a solution. . . . Of course, at that point my eyes start to glaze. Simply put, pH is a method of expressing the acidity or akalinity of soil.

Gardeners basically need to know that the pH scale ranges from 0 to 14, and any soil that measures 7 is in the neutral range. High numbers indicate an alkaline condition, and low numbers indicate the presence of acid. Most plants will accept levels between 6.0 and 7.0 without a problem. In life, most of us are not going to face pH levels any lower than 4.5 or any higher than 7.5.

The problems at extreme highs and lows are complex. When soil is too acidic or too alkaline, access to its nutrients goes awry. For instance, really low-number (acid) soils may contain so much aluminum it could kill your plants. And in very alkaline soils, iron, manganese, zinc, copper, and boron get totally locked up and are not available to plants.

The soil in the Northeast tends to be more on the acidic side; as you travel west the soil becomes increasingly neutral or alkaline.

Midsummer is a good time to do a pH check, especially after your final harvest of cold-hardy vegetables. Shepherd Ogden of The Cook's Garden, a mail-order seed company in Londonderry, Vermont (and a personal favorite), says soil that is within average pH ranges smells good and sweet, and that soil that smells sour or like vinegar is out of range and should be tested. If the soil is out of balance, make amendments gradually, ideally over a 2-year period.

PINCH YOUR HERBS • Be sure to keep pinching back your flowering herbs like basil, oregano, and mint to prevent the plant from flowering and going to seed. Seed production is very demanding on a plant. By the way, if you cut your mint to the ground in mid-summer you'll get a whole second crop.

SHOO FLY • If those little fruit flies hovering around the compost heap annoy you, just bury your food scraps about a foot into the pile and they will disappear.

MEASURING WATER • To make sure your plants are getting about an inch of water a week, dig down and check out the soil. It should be moist to the depth of about 12 inches.

❦ J U L Y 8

I have never done a cash analysis on my cost per garden tomato because to tell the truth I don't care. I assume my tomatoes are only slightly cheaper than the store-bought kind, but I also know they are impossible to value. Nothing tastes better than a home-grown tomato from my garden, except maybe one from yours.

Tomatoes are not the only fruit made magical in the home garden. A fresh-picked stalk of asparagus is a completely different creature from one that has been sitting on a refrigerated shelf at the grocer's for a week, gagged by a rubber band. And what about a garden carrot? Well, don't get me started. The difference isn't just about varieties but about harvesting and storage. All the more reason to take care with your produce in the garden now.

Pick your vegetables sooner than later. It's easy to get lax this time of year, mainly because we're burned out from all the work we did in the spring. Yet it is crucial to stay on top of the harvest. Except for obvious things like winter squash, pumpkins, tomatoes, and melons, most vegetables taste superior when picked on the early side and eaten right away. Slender zucchini and eggplants taste better than those mottled fruits you get at the market. A leaf of arugula at 3 inches is peppery and tender; the long-leafed clumps at the market are not only expensive but sometimes bitter and tough. If you sow successfully, approximately every 2 weeks throughout the planting season, you won't have to ponder whether zucchini ice cream would taste good. Harvest at the right time and store properly. If you can't eat your harvest soon enough, give it to a friend.

REUSE PLASTIC PLANT MARKERS • When you buy transplants at the nursery they are usually identified with white plastic markers, onto which have been printed the name of the cultivar, its description, and the price. They aren't much use stapled to plastic pots, so I wash mine off with some household cleaner and use them again when I plant seeds in the early spring indoors or when marking plants that are giveaways for friends. Permanent marker works best.

BERRY HARVEST • Blackberries are ready for harvest when they become soft and juicy. Thornless berries are ready to pick when they lose their glossy appearance. They will give with a simple tug.

❦ J U L Y 9

I am going to look for a quiet day in the next week or two to gear up for my fall vegetable garden. My tomatoes are still in the green marble stage, so even *thinking* about a fall vegetable garden overwhelms. Nevertheless, this is an ideal time to sit down, have a glass of lemonade, and do some preliminary thinking about fall.

First, go through your half-used seed packets. Make a pile of your tried-and-trues and then hunt for some unusual plant seeds to keep your interest level high. You really should think in terms of growing your own seedlings, because the germination rate from direct sowing is going to be uneven; a dry spell can delay germination of seeds dramatically. In addition, the choices at the nursery this time of year are pretty sad cases. (If you do go to the nursery, don't buy any of the 6-packs that have matted roots growing out of the bottom. Those poor plants are already stressed out, and transplanting in July is just too much to ask.)

Brassicas—members of the mustard family, including broccoli, Brussels sprouts, cabbage, cauliflower, kale, kohlrabi, rutabaga, and turnip—make excellent fall gardens, along with greens started a little later in the season, and numerous root vegetables like carrots and parsnips. And many of these vegetables actually taste better when they are harvested in the fall. Dropping soil temperatures have the effect of cold storage, changing the glucose composition in some vegetables, like carrots, making them sweeter, even nuttier. Besides, pulling a carrot or a turnip on a clear October day falls neatly into the category of pleasure.

Planting for fall does have its unique challenges. Sometimes the soil surface is crusty from being overworked, and seedlings have a difficult time breaking through. If this is a problem, mix some compost into the surface dirt to make a finer soil covering. One also finds that fall vegetable gardens are more susceptible to insect attack. July and August are the worst periods for many kinds of insects—aphids, leafhoppers, cabbage loopers, corn earworms all seem to peak in mid to late summer. And if you have a moist September and October, disease can spread rampantly. Just be vigilant and philosophical; this is, after all, a second helping. You can afford to lose a few.

S L U G S L I M E • If you have a handful of salted slugs to dispose of in the morning—or if you do night duty with a flashlight—you can remove that slimy slug residue on your hands with a couple of capfuls of inexpensive vinegar; then wash your hands with lukewarm water. Repeat if necessary.

> *A good garden may have some weeds.*
> —Proverb

❦ J U L Y 1 0

I am a bug squisher. I actually enjoy flattening a Japanese beetle between my gloved thumb and forefinger. I also admit to a certain thrill in hosing off aphids, watching them flow helplessly off my precious nasturtiums. But for gardeners who don't take bug warfare personally, the Dustbuster might be a solution. Dustbusters are light, hand-held vacuum cleaners that, when well charged, produce a powerful in-hale—strong enough to detach many little insects from your plants. Mostly they are good for picking up ashes around fireplaces and in hard-to-reach indoor spots, but they also work on bugs. To use a Dustbuster in the garden, just hold your plant leaf flat—gently of course—and vacuum off the bugs. The less pleasant part is emptying the vacuum, which of course will be filled with shocked but still live insects. Dump them in a pail of water with some liquid detergent in it.

CARROT CLINIC • If your carrots are coming out forked, it might be that your soil is either too rocky or otherwise coarse. You might also have mangled your carrots when you thinned them out. Fresh manure, overfertilizing, or a lack of lime can also deform carrots.

KEEPING YOUR GARDEN IN BLOOM • If you reach a point in the season where your beds or borders need more color, take the time to drive around your area to see what's in bloom, and record the date. Then make a note to put in your favorite selections at the appropriate time. Good gardeners never pass up a chance to spy.

DEER AND HUMAN HAIR • I have not been plagued with deer in any of my gardens but most reports confirm that human hair is at least somewhat effective. (You can get hair clippings from your local barber.)

In addition, a number of deer-repelling sprays for flowers and shrubs have been developed, and some of them (Ropel gets pretty good reviews) seem to work short-term. The problem with the sprays is that they wash off after a rainfall, and then the spraying must be repeated, which is both expensive and tedious.

You can sidestep the whole problem and just use plantings that deer supposedly dislike. According to Cornell Cooperative Extension/Westchester researchers, numerous perennials are not appealing to deer. Here is a partial list: *Achillea sp.* (yarrow), *Allium* (including chive, ornamental onion, and garlic chive), *Anemone sp.* (anemone), *Aquilegia canadensis* (columbine), *Artemisia sp.* (wormwood), *Astilbe sp.* (astilbe), *Bergenia sp.* (bergenia), *Buddleia davidii* (butterfly bush), *Chrysanthemum coccineum* (painted daisy), *Coreopsis* (coreopsis), *Dicentra exima* (bleeding heart), *Echinacea purpurea* (purple coneflower), *Echinops sp.* (globe thistle), *Euphorbia sp.* (spurge), *Helleborus sp.* (helleborus), *Iberis sempervirens* (candytuft), *Lavandula sp.* (lavender), *Lillum lancifolium* (tiger lily), *Lupinus sp.* (lupine), *Lythrum* (loosestrife), *Mentha sp.* (mint), Mo-

narda didyma (bee balm), *Myosotis scorpiodes* (forget-me-not), *Narcissus* (daffodil), *Nepeta sp.* (catmint), *Papaver orientale* (Oriental poppy), *Platyco-don grandiflorus* (balloon flower), *Potentilla sp.* (cinquefoil), *Primula* (primrose), *Ranunculus sp.* (buttercup), *Vinca major* (periwinkle).

❦ J U L Y 1 1

Now is the time to organize all the perennial and biennial seeds you want to sow. Don't make a face. Things haven't been all *that* hectic lately; as a matter of fact, your flower beds have asked very little of you this month. What better time to sow some flower seeds?

By sowing perennials now, you can give them an excellent start, which means good root development before the winter ahead. This is also a good time to plant biennials. Biennials are plants that go from seed to flowering in two seasons, which is why you have to get them in now if you want to enjoy their blooms next season. Your biennials will grow their leaves in the first season and flower next season. Then they die. In that sense, they are like annuals, only a little more trouble. But because they are plants like hollyhock, wallflower, and foxglove, they are well worth the effort.

Pour tea on your azaleas, rhododendrons, and camellias.

TEA LEAVES • Don't toss out that leftover tea or the bags. Pour tea and leaves on your azaleas, rhododendrons, or camellias.

LAWN STORY • According to the Lawn Institute, there are over 50 million households with lawns in the United States, representing 6 million acres of land. Americans spend $6 billion a year on feeding, weeding, and caring for their lawns.

HONEYSUCKLE BY NIGHT • The honeysuckle releases its strongest scent at day's end because it is pollinated by a nocturnal moth.

> *The heat of the beams of the sun doth take away the smell of flowers, especially those of milder odor.*
>
> —Bacon

❦ J U L Y 1 2

Wildflower gathering is big in the Northeast. Up and down the highway, cars have pulled over and people in straw hats are out with their clippers, taking armfuls of goldenrod, Queen Anne's lace, and daisies. I wonder if these people ever ask for permission. And if they do, did the owner really say take they could fill up every square inch of their vans?

Don't misread: I know where a mess of cattails are and I have been thinking of picking some for fall arrangements. But gardeners are civilized people, and we should ask first. We shouldn't take ridiculous amounts. And we shouldn't break the law. Some wildflowers are on the endangered list and must be left to themselves.

FOUND A PEANUT • George Washington Carver used to play nursemaid to his neighbor's ailing plants by singing and talking to them.

DOCTOR YOUR CORN WITH MINERAL OIL • A drop of mineral oil may be all that is needed to stop worms from infesting your corn. Once the silks have begun to turn brown, place 1 drop of oil on the tip of each ear of corn. This will effectively suffocate the worms. Do this once a week, using an eye dropper for small plots and a pump-type oil can for larger ones.

DRYING HERBS: PAPER BAG METHOD • Here's an easy way to dry herbs that usually take forever to dry, with little fuss and good result. Strip leaves and discard the stem. Put the leaves in a brown paper bag and fold closed. Refrigerate. Turn the bag a couple of times a day. In 1 to 3 weeks, the herbs will be dry and green in color. (Be forewarned: If you dry basil, it smells pretty strong when drying.) Herbs that dry well: dill, mint, oregano, rosemary, sage, thyme. Herbs that are better to freeze: chervil, cilantro, parsley, tarragon.

❦ J U L Y 1 3

Collecting seeds by drying seed heads from your herb garden is very simple and the results are quite gratifying. The time to harvest is when you see the seeds turning dark. (Don't wait for the seeds to start dropping off the plant.) Cut the stems all the way down near the base of the plant and gather a bunch, tying it with a rubber band. Put the bunch in a paper bag, seed heads nested in the bottom. Tie a piece of twine around the bag's opening and hang the bag in a cool dry place. The seeds just naturally dry and fall into the bottom of the sack. When they are all dried, your bag will contain a collection of excellent seeds. *If you are concerned with astrological principles, seed gathering should take place in a dry sign like Leo, which begins July 23.*

RACCOONS IN YOUR CORN? • Raccoons in the cornfield can be a nightmare, and I have tried everything short of a shotgun on them. Drinking champagne and throwing lit firecrackers at them at 2:00 in the morning is a very enjoyable enterprise but it only works temporarily. Hair clippings from the barbershop work sometimes but not consistently. For small plot gardeners, this works: As the corn begins to ripen, place paper bags, the size of the ears, over each ear of corn and affix with a rubber band. Check periodically. When the corn is ripe, remove it and the bag, which can be reused if you haven't had a wet month, or toss the paper bags, shredded, into the compost heap. If you have a larger plot, stringing an electric fence about 6 inches above the ground is a good solution.

One of the big breakthroughs for the home gardener was the invention of pantyhose. Melon growers have long protected their fruit by putting each melon in a "sock," which expands as the fruit grows and eliminates disease and insect problems. You can also use pantyhose on cabbages and cauliflowers and even tomatoes to the same pest-protecting end. Just cut lengths of the pantyhose (if you are one of those tall "D" types you'll get many more lengths out of a pair than most of us) and then seal off one end by sewing it or knotting it. From this point on, you need a helper. At least I do. Pull the pantyhose over the emerging fruit for a pretty snug fit. Tie the open end with some fishing line without breaking off the fruit stem. You can cover the whole garden with this stuff!

Protect your fruits and vegetables with pantyhose.

OLD METAL GARBAGE CAN • The best thing about old metal ungalvanized garbage cans is that they rust and rot. If you have one with the bottom rusted out, you are in luck—it makes an excellent compost bin. Any rough edges can be taken care of with just a few swipes of the file.

SLUG DENTALS • Slugs have somewhere in the range of 100 rows of teeth, with approximately 90 teeth per row.

Here's how to calculate fall sowing dates for different vegetables: First, determine how many frost-free days you have left. For instance, if your first frost generally happens around October 15, you have about 90 days left of frost-free weather. However, it's a good idea to subtract about 2 weeks from that figure, just because the days get shorter as we head for fall—and the days obviously also are cooler. That would leave about 75 days left to sow and grow. Check the days to maturity on the backs of your seed packets and you easily can plot a planting schedule for the rest of the season.

STOP PINCHING BACK YOUR MUMS NOW • You can stop pinching back your mums now. If you've been pinching the shoots back since spring you should get nice bushy plants this fall.

ALCOHOL SPRAY • Aphids and whitefly are all over the garden now, and I've found an excellent solution in rubbing alcohol. Fill a well-cleaned-out spray bottle with diluted alcohol, 3 parts water to 1 part alcohol. Test-spray a leaf on one of your affected plants before you start (do this, variety by variety, to make sure you don't harm any of your plants). After 24 hours, if the plant looks okay, spray the enemy. The alcohol breaks through the bugs' waxy cuticles and leaves them vulnerable to disease and dehydration.

The silver maple shows the lining of its leaves before a storm.

My mother used to tell me my arm was going to fall off because of the red rubber band "bracelets" I used to wear as a child. Classic looks never change, and I still wear rubber bands (though I now opt for blue ones, off the late edition of our home-delivered newspaper). In the summer, this peculiar habit serves me well because when I visit the garden my rubber bands are the ideal gathering device for the bunches of herbs I invariably bring back in. They are also handy for pulling up leaves around vegetables I want to blanch (see pages 203–4). If you don't want to wear them, collect rubber bands on a stake or some convenient post in the garden. You'll find a dozen uses for them over the course of the summer.

BENT PITCHFORKS • You can straighten out a bent tine on a pitchfork by sinking a piece of 1-inch galvanized pipe, about a yard long, into the ground leaving about 12 inches above the soil surface. Insert the bent tine and then bend it back as straight as you can, using the pipe as leverage.

NATURAL SOURCES OF NITROGEN

	Percentage	Release rate of nitrogen
Alfalfa meal	4	slow
Bat guano	10	medium–rapid
Blood meal	12	medium–rapid
Castor bean meal	6	slow
Compost	2	slow
Cottonseed meal	7	slow–medium
Cow manure (composted)	1	slow
Fish meal (dry)	10	slow
Grass clippings	2	medium
Soybean meal	7	slow–medium

❦ JULY 17

I had read about people growing fabulous potatoes in black plastic trash bags and concluded that trash-bag gardening was not really gardening; it was something else, a little desperate, and not for me. Then I saw in a photograph a variation on the trash-bag method—a compost bin that someone had used for growing potatoes—*and it was great looking*. Let me try to describe it. First, you take one of those waist-high lightweight circular plastic compost bins—the ones with holes poked in the sides—and set it in the garden. Then put down a layer of straw, followed by a layer of compost or aged manure, in the bottom. Scatter the seed potato pieces over the compost near the bottom holes. As the plants grow, you add dirt and compost, layer by layer, and the plant grows tubers all along the covered stems. The vines spill out of the little holes and cascade over the top. And you can harvest through the holes (if you get the potatoes young and have tiny hands) or unlatch the container and the potatoes will pour out.

PEPPER HARVEST • Don't pull your peppers off the plant. Use a pair of scissors and cut.

This used to be among my prayers—a piece of land not so very large, which would contain a garden.

—Horace

❧ J U L Y 1 8

That neon-yellow golf shirt might be a personal favorite but it is about the worst choice you could have made for garden wear today. Many insects are attracted to bright colors (think: *yellow* pest strips). Wearing bright colors is risky because you could actually *attract* unwanted insects and escort them throughout your garden. No, thank you!

GARLIC BEDS SHOULD BE KEPT NEAT AND WEED-FREE • Weed your garlic beds well and mulch with straw or leaves. If the bulbs have to compete with weeds they'll turn out disappointingly small.

MIDSUMMER VEGETABLE PLANTING CHECK-LIST • Put in some new rows of chard, spinach (though you might be advised to wait for these and other greens if it's blazing hot), curly endive, kohlrabi, parsley, radishes, turnips, and other root crops. Also sow fall-blooming annuals and transplant biennials that are self-sown.

IS YOUR LAWN THIRSTY? • Here are some ways to determine whether it is time to water the lawn: (1) Walk on it. If the grass doesn't spring back, it's time to water. (2) Look at it. If it seems bluish or grayish, it is water deprived. (3) Pick up a leaf blade. If it curls from the sides, it is definitely thirsty.

🐚 J U L Y 1 9

We had a Peter Rabbit impersonator one summer in our country garden and the little guy just loved cabbage. He did not, however, like onions. After a season of losses, we interplanted onions with our cabbages and while he was not entirely deterred by our efforts (we suspect he had friends) we were able to harvest a good number of lovely cabbages, intact. Gardening friends also advise that ashes, bloodmeal, garlic, foxgloves, and cayenne pepper keep rabbits at bay.

PULLING CARROTS • Give carrots a twist when you pull them up so the leaves don't break off. Though many grocers sell carrots with the leaves intact, they are of no special value. In fact, the leaves will pilfer moisture and nutrients from the roots, so cut them off, just above the stem, immediately.

A PRETTY IDEA • Cut zinnias look sensational in burnished copper bowls.

··

CROPS THAT CAN TAKE LIGHT FALL FROST

··

Beet	Leek
Broccoli	Lettuce
Brussels sprout	Mustard greens
Cabbage	Onion
Carrot	Potato
Cauliflower	Radish
Celery	Rutabaga
Collard greens	Spinach
Endive	Turnip
Kale	

··

WIREWORM PROBLEM • If wireworms have gone after your potatoes, onions, beets, turnips, or carrots, try this: Peel and slice some potatoes and bury them about 1½ inches down around affected crops. The larvae will opt for the skinless potato. Every week pull out the old slice and replace it with a new one.

THINK IT'S HOT? • On this day in 1913 in Death Valley, California, the temperature hit a U.S. recorded high of 134 degrees Fahrenheit.

> *But don't go into Mr. McGregor's garden.*
> —Beatrix Potter

❦ J U L Y   2 0

This is a terribly stressful time of year for lawns. The dry heat can cause serious damage, so it is important to practice good maintenance. Mow high and often with a sharp mower. Hold back on fertilizer in July and August, or you'll compound your turf problems. If you are tempted to give up the watering game, you can let your lawn go dormant and just not water at all. The grass will turn brown, but it will green up again when the temperatures fall and rainfall levels go up. On-again-off-again watering should be avoided at all cost. If you've been watering up till now, it will be a severe shock to your lawn to stop watering abruptly. Gradually taper off to minimize damage.

PLANTS AS COVER-UPS • If you have an unsightly wall or some propane tanks that jar the eye, use plants to create an attractive cover-up. A berm (which is a raised and landscaped mound of dirt) in front of the propane tank, or a trellis covered with vines, works well to disguise the area. English ivy, an evergreen, or climbing hydrangea (*Hydrangea anomala petiolaris*) or Hall's honeysuckle (*Lonicera japonica 'Halliana'*) are three plants that create excellent coverage for a trellis or fence. Designer Joe Eck of Vermont points out that many dreadfully invasive plants like Hall's honeysuckle or even hardy running bamboo can be used in this situation if a mown strip of grass borders the plants. If the invasive shoots are regularly mown, they will not take over your property.

WATERING WAND • If you keep inadvertently wetting the foliage of your plants as you water and are concerned about encouraging disease, you can create a homemade watering wand. Simply use electrical tape to attach a 3- or 4-foot length of broomstick or dowel rod along the end of your hose. It will improve your aim and also cut down on a good deal of bending and reaching.

If watercress beds steam at dusk in summer, the next day will be hot.

❧ J U L Y 2 1

Aster comes from the Greek word for star (like asterisk, or disaster—ill-starred). Swamp aster (*Aster puniceus*) likes low, marshy soil, so if your fields are filled with many of these plants, you probably have a drainage problem. Asters have a long blooming period—from June to November in some zones—and will even survive a light frost.

YOUR LETTUCE MAY BE PAST ITS PRIME • If your lettuce tastes bitter or secretes a milky white sap, it's been in the ground too long. If its juices are clear, it's still good for picking.

I SAY POTATO • When you get the first blooms on your potato plants, your potatoes are ready but small. For the bulk of your harvest, wait until 2 or 3 weeks after bloom. When the foliage starts to die back, they're pretty much full size. Let your potatoes dry out at the soil surface for an hour or so, not much more. After that, keep them out of sunlight. Don't wash your potatoes right away or they will tend to rot. And eat the ones that are bruised or chipped right away because are vulnerable to rot as well. Store your potatoes in a cool dry place until you are ready to feast.

NEW PLANTS AND TREES NEED MORE WATER THAN YOU THINK • Newly planted trees, shrubs, and perennials can take a long time to adjust to their new homes—and they need extra watering or their leaves will droop. Water them evenly and well to encourage deep root growth. Do so throughout the growing season to ensure that they winter over well.

STORING PEPPERS • Peppers will keep up to three weeks in the refrigerator, loose, in the cool—not cold—part of the fridge.

❦ J U L Y   2 2

Pressed flowers can be lovely mementos of the season, and a pretty reliable record of color—invaluable when you are sitting around in January and plotting out your garden with catalogues. To press flowers from your garden, pick the blooms and a small length of stem just before they have reached their peak and dust off the pollen with a light hand. Place them between sheets of good-quality paper towels or a fine-grade paper and weight them with a heavy book. Leave for 8 hours, then replace the paper and weight down again. The pressed flowers should stay in place for 2 or 3 weeks, after which your memento is ready. Another method is to follow the same directions but interleave the flowers in a thick edition of the Yellow Pages. Dog-ear the pages or you could easily lose your specimens.

CELERY HARVEST • Celery tastes wonderful in simple salads (try it with sliced fresh white mushrooms, shaved Parmesan, and some olive oil). In the stores, the celery is sold in its mature form—but from the garden you can take stalks when they are as wide as a fat pencil for a far more delectable taste.

CLINGY TOMATO BLOSSOMS • Pull off any tomato blossoms you see clinging to young fruit. Odd conditions called "catfacing" and "zipper streak" may result where the clingy flower pistil causes the fruit to scar at a young age.

> *God hates a quitter.*
> —Anonymous

LEO, July 23 to August 23—*A barren time; not particularly good for sowing seed*

It's high summer, the time when many of us question the sanity of this business called gardening. Some of my more experienced gardening friends are now talking about their "stupid garden" or expressing malice toward a plant or insect in particular, and then there are the threats about this being the last year for all this nonsense, and how this time one really means it. The nursery crowd seems to be thinning out; at least you can get a parking space now. The unsold annuals and perennials in their nursery pots are looking a little worse for the wear. Indeed, that gardener's sense of endless hope and perfection seems to have gotten a little brown around the edges. So take a break. There are rhythms to all of this and anyway, this is supposed to be fun, remember? Besides, the season's surprises aren't over yet.

KEEPING OUT PERENNIAL GRASSES • If perennial grasses keep invading your borders and beds, line the perimeter with a metal or plastic weed barrier sunk at least 5 inches into the ground.

CUT GRASS: A SHORT HISTORY • First there were sheep, then the scythe, and then in 1830 there was Edwin Budding's mowing machine. The first push lawn mower had a 19-inch blade, was noisy, cost about 7 guineas, and was the pride and joy of every English gentleman.

DON'T PUT IN THE FRIDGE

Potatoes
Yams
Tomatoes
Squash
Pumpkin

People get bored with green beans because they think of them as a side dish, something to put in a neat pile on each person's plate, next to the meat. But fresh-picked beans play well as an ingredient with other summer foods, especially in salads. Here are some combinations from my garden that I have enjoyed.

•••

SAVORY BEAN SALAD

½ pound of dried Great Northern beans, cooked according to
   package directions, drained (don't overcook!)
1 large tomato, seeded and diced
1 medium Bermuda onion, diced
3 tablespoons chopped chives
½ pound very young green beans, steamed to crisp-tender
½ cup your favorite vinaigrette

Combine all ingredients in a large salad bowl. Dress with vinaigrette. Delicious when served with grilled homemade sausage. Serves 6 to 8.

•••

SIMPLE GARLIC DRESSING

¼ cup extra virgin olive oil
3 tablespoons fresh lemon juice
1 large garlic clove, peeled and minced
Kosher salt
Freshly ground black pepper

Combine all ingredients and whisk well.

•••

SALAD OF GREEN BEANS, FENNEL, AND OIL-CURED OLIVES

1 fennel bulb, trimmed
1 pound green beans, cooked and chilled
¼ cup pitted oil-cured black olives
Simple Garlic Dressing to taste (see previous page)
1 lemon

Julienne raw fennel to the approximate size of your green beans, which should be nice and thin. (If the beans aren't young and thin, slice them lengthwise in half.) Pit a handful of oil-cured black olives and cut them in halves. Toss the ingredients with simple garlic dressing. Then squeeze the juice of a lemon over the whole salad and toss lightly once more.

KEEP ON PICKING • At the risk of sounding repetitious: the biggest favor you can do for your garden right now is to keep picking its fruit. A ripened fruit is like a searchlight: the fermentation attracts insects from all points. The best policy is to pick fruits the day before they are perfectly ripe. It is much better to err on the side of too early than too late.

FEEDING CARE OF PERENNIALS • Get to know the feeding habits of your perennials. Certain perennials like astilbe, bleeding heart, delphinium, and shasta daisy will benefit from regular feedings of manure tea (see page 94) or fish emulsion. On the other hand, some perennials, like yarrow or butterfly weed, thrive in less fertile ground. In many cases, a nutritious mulch like compost, grass clippings, pine needles, leaves, or straw will provide ample nutrition. If you deadhead your plants regularly they will not have to go into seed production, and therefore will require less feeding.

HOW TO AVOID MELON ROT • You can protect your melons from melon rot as they ripen by balancing them atop the open side of a large tin can. This also keeps them warmer, which hastens their maturity.

I have long experimented with cages and stakes for my tomato plants, thinking that there might be an answer to the question of which is better. There is an answer. Both. Put the seedling in a cage. If it outgrows the cage, add stakes. To tie your vines, use rags or cut up pantyhose. I have used those wire twisties and have a huge packet I'm still trying to get rid of because they're a bother to undo at the end of the season when you're taking everything down. Rags and pantyhose you can clip and toss out without a problem.

Use cages and stakes for your tomato plants.

TOMATO GROWER'S SECRET • A weekly dose of liquid seaweed foliar spray will have an amazing impact on your tomato crop. The leaves look great, diseases are kept at bay, and the yields are phenomenal.

WATER, WATER EVERYWHERE • It is already clear that I am not a fan of sprinklers for gardens, but not all sprinklers are created equal. Indeed, some are worse than others.

Rotary sprinklers are the worst. They go around so fast that the water cannot be absorbed quickly enough so it sits there and then evaporates. The **oscillating sprinklers**, which move back and forth and cover a rectangular area, deliver a slower, more easily absorbed watering. The best are **impact sprinklers**, which can be set to cover a particular area. But no matter which sprinkler you use, there is serious water loss due to evaporation. This is why other methods like furrow irrigation and drip watering (with soaker hoses or perforated plastic tubes) are vastly preferable.

THE RAINIEST DAY IN U.S. HISTORY • On July 25, 1979, it rained for 24 hours for a U.S. precipitation record of 43 inches in Alvin, Texas.

I have been a zinnia lover forever, but a loser at love, and always to powdery mildew. Every year is a story of dashed hopes. I delight in the beautiful first bloom, and then, one morning in July, I walk out and the plants are covered with mildew. Gardening is hard on the heart.

Next year will be different. I discovered recently that the Rodale Research Institute in Kutztown, Pennsylvania, studied 40 zinnia cultivars for 10 years—and determined that the series 'Ruffles' (and in particular 'Scarlet Ruffles') is the most mildew-resistant zinnia of them all. There is no doubt that next year I will be growing 'Ruffles.' The Institute also found good results with 'Chippendale,' 'State Fair,' 'Yellow Marvel,' the 'Border Beauty' series, and 'Small World Cherry.'

LONG-LASTING CUT FLOWER • I grew Lisianthus in deep purple for the first time this year and they are wonderful cut flowers; they last well over a week and since you snip stems with many buds, you get waves of single blooms—a delight. They are an annual up here in the northern zones, but a perennial in mild climates.

LAVENDER SALVE FOR SORE MUSCLES • If you have an abundance of lavender blossoms, make some lavender salve—you can use it for the sore muscles you get from tending your lavender beds. Cut lavender flowers right after they blossom and pack them loosely in a clean pint jar. Fill the jar with vegetable oil, cover tightly, and leave on a warm windowsill, shaking every day for about a month. Filter the oil through a clean cloth, then take the cloth—filled with the sediment left from the blossoms—and squeeze it back into the jar. The sediment is the salve. Discard the leftover oil. The salve will soothe various aches and pains for the rest of the gardening season.

WHY WE LOSE THE APHID WARS • One female aphid can produce up to 5 billion offspring in a single season. A female mite produces about 1 million eggs a month, a female termite about 6,000 eggs a day, the queen bee 1,000 to 2,000 eggs a day.

A morning glory at my window satisfies me more than the metaphysics of books.
—Walt Whitman

A lot of people like to serve up beer to their slugs and drown them in the night. The process goes like this: Get a tuna fish or small cat food tin, fill it with beer, and let the slugs, who are attracted by the yeast, come hither and die. The mistake is putting the pub in the middle of the garden. You can attract slugs who never even knew about your garden. Put your little dishes of beer into the ground—almost flush with the soil's surface—about 20 feet *away* from your garden. Other remedies you might try: Dissolve a package of yeast in a tin of water and serve it in a similar fashion to attract slugs at an equally satisfactory rate. Or put out some dry dog food, soaked so the pieces are spongy. Put the chow in little piles here and there in your bed or border. By morning, you'll have attracted a bounty of slugs, which you can shovel into a bucket filled with water and a splash of kerosene, where they will die.

WATER VAPOR RELEASED BY LEAVES • Leaves release water vapor, much in the way that humans perspire. An average white oak releases 150 gallons of water in one summer day.

ALLIUM FOR PAY • Members of the allium family were so valued in ancient Egypt that the builders of the pyramids were said to have been rewarded with bunches of onion, garlic, and leeks.

CUKE CLINIC • If your cucumbers aren't producing, run through this checklist: Are the plants well spaced? Did you water consistently and well? (Cukes are 95 percent water.) Did a bee population discover your patch? (If not, you can hand pollinate and get good results.) When did you plant—too early? Too late?

President George Bush may be remembered for his position on broccoli, but this is a book about gardening, not politics (though it should be okay to talk about a Bush). (Sorry.) Anyway we all know that broccoli is good for us and that it is beautiful to grow—one of the original edible flowers, along with cauliflower—but how do you get people to eat it?

First you need to examine what exactly it is about broccoli that you or your spouse or your children hate. Broccoli is actually two edibles in one: the flower and the stalk. Many people who hate the flower will happily eat the stalk with (a ton of) dip. Conversely, there are flower eaters who recoil at the stalk part, but will cheerfully munch on the broccoli head. Serve your broccoli as two different vegetables on a platter of crudités and see if that increases sales.

Another technique is to use it in stir-fries and pasta salads and let people pick it out if they don't like it. Then there is the sneaky mother method, which I employ often. Lock the kitchen door. Run the broccoli through the blender until it is chopped fine. Throw the choppings into any well-seasoned red sauce for pasta. No one has a clue that they are eating broccoli and it is delicious.

HARVESTING EGGPLANTS • The best time to harvest eggplants is when the skin is still tight and shiny. If the flesh gives just a little when pressed with your finger, it's time to pick.

TOMATO CLINIC

- Tomatoes whose leaf margins or stems are turning purplish might have phosphorus deficiency. Carefully work in some ground phosphate rock or bone meal around the plant. (Delayed fruit setting may also indicate the same problem.)

- If the plant has green-blue curled leaves and few blossoms it might need copper. Work in a small amount of manure (not fresh), sawdust, or grass clippings to remedy.

- Leaves that are yellow, brittle, and curled indicate magnesium deficiency. Epsom salts or limestone applications will remedy.

- Stems that are too woody and leaves that are yellow indicate a calcium deficiency. Wood ash or bone meal applied in small amounts should correct.

- Plants with light green leaves and few blossoms might have manganese deficiency. A moderate dressing of aged manure should help.

You may have a good remedy for that insect bite right in your garden. Costmary, lemon balm, or ribwort leaves—split open and rubbed on the affected area—will reduce the inflammation of insect bites. If you are stung, pull the stinger out before applying the leaf to the wound.

CORN EARWORM CLINIC • The best time to handpick the larva of the corn earworm off the ear is after pollination—or when the silk has begun to turn brown. Pull back the tip of the sheath slightly and simply pull off the caterpillar. You should find no more than 2 worms, as corn earworms tend to devour one another.

LOOK AROUND FOR PLANT DOLLIES • While you're out at garage sales this summer, look around for little red wagons, television stands on wheels, any small portable tables or carts. They are invaluable for moving your plants in and out, hardening, "softening," making all kinds of plant deliveries between your house, your porch, and your garden.

GARLIC HARVEST • Once the tops of your garlic have yellowed and toppled over, pull them out. I waited too long once and they all rotted.

All signs fail in dry weather.

I still have a fondness for my very first garden, though I must say the word *garish* comes to mind. I used bright reds and yellows and oranges, the colors of flowers in children's paintings. My garden was altogether too cheerful. None of my flowers was blue.

Blues bring a serenity to the summer garden, and a relief in late July and August, when there is too much brightness all around. In June, the perennials in blue are plentiful, but fewer blue perennials bloom in July and August. I rely on annuals to provide calm in the heat of summer, when the living is easy and the soul seeks rest. Imagine these blues in your garden, and make notes for next year:

Ageratum
Borago (Borage)
Browallia (x)
Cynoglossum amabile (Chinese forget-me-not)
Heliotropium (Heliotrope)
Ipomoea (Morning glory)
Delphinium (Larkspur)
Lobelia siphilitica (Great blue lobelia)
Nemophila (Baby blue-eyes)
Nigella (Love-in-a-mist)
Salvia farinacea (Mealycup sage)
Trachymene (Blue laceflower)
Verbena

RUST-RESISTANT SNAPS • If your snapdragons were slain by rust this summer, look for resistant breeds like 'Floral Carpet.' Humid summers are tough for snapdragons, but this new snap apparently holds up well.

RULE OF THUMB • Everlastings—flowers which can be used in wreaths and dried arrangements—are especially gratifying, and also easy to grow. Check your seed packs and books for specific times to harvest, but in general pick the flower at the stage you would like it to be after it's dried. Makes sense. For instance, statice, bells-of-Ireland, and immortelle should be picked when the blooms are fully open. Love-in-a-mist and celosia look best when cut after the seeds have formed.

❦ J U L Y 3 1

When I put in my *Echinacea* plants a few years ago, I had no idea that I would be spending winters downing pills of the same name. *Echinacea*, or purple coneflower, is an easy presence in the summer garden, with its daisylike appearance and prickly seedhead (the genus name *Echinacea* comes from the Greek word for hedgehog, presumably for that reason). It has a friendly appearance, and blooms well into the fall. It also is a miraculous drug. Go to any health food store now—heck, it's even in the pharmacies—and you can buy pills made from the flower that have been found effective in fighting viral infections. (I'm usually the last one on my block to try anything new, but I must say I have become a believer.) Native Americans knew this before we did and used the flower for colds and scurvy, which is why *Echinacea* is also known as Indian root.

KEEP WATER GARDEN TUBS AT EVEN TEMPS • Small water gardens cannot handle big swings in temperatures. The tubs tend to heat up fast and cool down slowly—it's best to keep the tub in a shady spot where it isn't subject to surges of heat on hot summer days. Never put the tub exposed on a patio.

FOR THE CASUAL COTTAGE GARDENER • Gardeners with a relaxed attitude can get free plants out of their own garden. Let your annuals and biennials turn brown and die. (Remember, seeds shouldn't get too dry.) Then just shake the seed heads into your garden wherever you want blooms. They won't come up in orderly drifts but will take on more of a wildflower, manic cottage-garden look, which could be wonderful.

❦ *August* ❦

Flower of the Month: Poppy

❦ AUGUST 1

Here's a simple and easy soil analysis for those who don't feel like sending their dirt to a fancy laboratory: count your worms. Howard Garrett, an organic gardener and author, offers the worm test as a quick, telling look into the nutrition of your soil. You can do it right now.

Simply dig up a 12-inch square of soil, 6 inches deep. Sift the soil into a container so you can give it a good look. Count the earthworms. For turf, you should have a minimum of 6 earthworms. For mulched beds, you should have at least 10 big ones. If you don't, Garrett says your soil is deficient, probably the victim of too many toxic pesticides or high-nitrogen fertilizers. Lay off these products and use organic techniques (compost, mulch, fertilizers, and so on) and your soil should come back in a matter of months.

IF YOU HAVE DROUGHT CONDITIONS THIS SUMMER • If the water is scarce this summer, you can forgo watering your lawn without permanently damaging it. To reduce stress on your lawn, don't mow it close to the ground or too often; it can hover at about 3 inches high if you—and the neighbors—can stand it. Less is more in drought conditions. By all means don't fertilize the lawn if your soil is extremely dry.

Meanwhile, your plants and new young trees do need water or they could suffer permanent damage. For plants, you basically want about an inch of water a week. Put coffee cans around to see how much your plants are getting from Mother Nature, then adjust accordingly.

EASY WAY TO DRY HOT PEPPERS • To dry your hot peppers without a lot of fuss, simply pull the whole plant and hang it upside down in a dry and airy spot (make sure it gets a lot of fresh air circulation). Remove the dried peppers and store in a paper bag.

Another way to dry peppers is to pick them with the stem, thread a needle with strong thread, and run the needle through the stem—not the pod. Hang them on the wall in your kitchen to dry. You can make wreaths out of excess peppers strung this way if you like; they make excellent gifts and last for about 2 years.

FOR FALL PLANTERS: FOOL THE SEEDS • When the ground temperatures are too hot for broccoli, cabbage, cauliflower, spinach, or any other fall crop to germinate, just fool the seeds by placing them in the refrigerator for a day.

If we persist, I do not doubt that by age 96 or so we will all have gardens we are pleased with, more or less.

—Henry Mitchell

❦ A U G U S T   2

If there ever was a cheap thrill, it's seeds. You can comb seed racks for marked-down packets now—there are lots of twofer sales and other bargain combinations. This is the time to find some unusual greens or other fall vegetables you might not have tried before. Go ahead. Plant a row of *Shungiku*.

I have always found fall planting tricky, especially in the middle of a drought and heat wave. To make sure my seeds don't sit on the surface, dry out, and die, I plant them deeper in late summer than I do in the spring and of course keep them consistently watered.

Another useful trick is presprouting (which is beneficial for fall crops and also when you want to get crops off to an early start in the spring). Cut white paper towels into 1½-inch squares and place a seed in the center of each square. Fold the packet in half, and then again in half, lengthwise. Moisten it but don't let it get soggy. Get some egg cartons or ice cube trays and put one paper towel packet into each little compartment. (This way your roots don't get all tangled up.) Put moist paper towels over the cartons or trays and put them in a plastic bag in a warm protected spot. Check each day, and when the shoots emerge plant the whole paper towel packet in prepared soil in the garden. Water carefully so the shoots don't topple over.

HOW TO DRY BEANS • Here's a relatively easy way to dry your pinto and kidney beans. The process should begin once the pods turn completely brown. At this point, pull up the entire plant, roots and all, and store in a dry area. When the pods are dry, pull them off and toss them into a large heavy cloth lying on the grass. Next, break the pods open by beating them with a stick. Then sweep up the beans with your hands and put them into a container (you'll get some leftover pod parts, but that's okay). Wait for a windy fall day and slowly pour the beans back out onto a large cloth so the wind will blow all of the undesirable pod parts and dust away.

By the way, don't store your beans in plastic containers with tight-fitting lids. Keep them in paper bags in a cool, dry place and they will continue to dry.

❦ A U G U S T 3

Compost that looks iffy—lots of weed seeds and possible fungi and disease—can be pasturized, but it is a big project. The late Jim Crockett, whose *Victory Garden* is well known to Public Broadcasting System viewers and readers of his books, recommended this backyard process: First, light up an old charcoal barbecue grill. Then fill the largest and worst pan you can find with compost—fill it to the top. Use a meat thermometer, and when the compost hits 180 degrees, cook it for an additional 30 minutes. Start in the morning and cook batches all day. Store the pasturized compost in a large sterile garbage can. This process is said to emit a terribly strong odor—but makes perfectly clean, superb compost.

WHAT TO DO IF YOUR PLANTS ARE WILTING • If your plants are wilted during the day but look fine after dusk, they probably—literally—can't take the heat. Impatiens, for example, often collapses in hot conditions and then perks up once the sun is down and the temperatures drop. Mulch will help keep the soil cool. Apply wood chips or some other attractive mulch to your flower beds and you will see great improvement.

RULE OF THUMB • You can time the fall-crop sowings of Chinese cabbage, beets, collards and other greens, spinach, turnips, and so on by subtracting 8 to 10 weeks from your first fall frost.

I have a rock garden. Last week three of them died.
—Richard Diran

❦ A U G U S T   4

The blueberry tide is in. Blueberries in our cereal, our muffins, our waffles, our ice cream, our cobblers, so sweet and friendly. Fresh is best, but the extras we freeze, rinsing them and drying them well, putting the berries in a single layer on a baking sheet, and freezing them individually first, then storing all of the frozen berries in a zipper-locked freezer bag for future use.

Have you ever noticed that your blueberry muffins are sometimes greenberry muffins? When the berries heat up they become juicy, and if the juice makes contact with cast iron or carbon steel (which is what many pots and pans are made of), they can turn green or yellow. It's simply a chemical reaction. If it bothers you, use cupcake liners when you bake blueberry muffins. Meanwhile, if you want purple berries, mix your blueberries with a lemony syrup. Acid causes the blueberries to turn more purple; alkalis (provided in many recipes by the presence of baking soda) will cause them to get bluer.

DRYING SUNFLOWERS • Here's an easy way to dry your sunflowers: When the flower heads sag down, cut them off, leaving enough stem to hang them upside down. Air-dry them for a month or two in a very well-ventilated area, like a pantry or dry garage or storage shed. They look great in fall arrangements or just hanging in the kitchen from a hook.

CARROT HARVESTING MADE EASIER • By now your carrot patch may be getting pretty dry. If you give it a good sprinkling before your harvest—and soften the soil—your carrots will come out much easier.

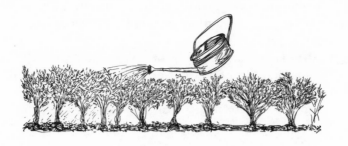

Sprinkle your carrots with water for easier harvesting.

KEEP YOUR CUTTING TOOLS CLEAN • When you take cuttings from different plants you run the risk of spreading disease. One way to prevent this is to use cotton balls soaked in alcohol each time you prune a different plant, wiping the tools off carefully. (Obviously, don't use the same cotton ball on a tool used for a number of cuttings.)

LADYBUG, LADYBUG, DON'T FLY AWAY • The ladybug was so-named in the Middle Ages for the Virgin Mary when grape farmers realized the little orange-shelled creature protected their grape harvests from infestations. The average ladybug consumes 5,400 aphids in a lifetime.

> *Nature soon takes over if the gardener is absent.*
> —Penelope Hobhouse

❧ AUGUST 5

Only a gardener could summon the mental discipline required to think about tulips at a time like this. I'm not a big tulip gardener (no doubt due to discipline problems), which is not to say I do not love tulips.

Every spring I drive around, in a serious state of envy, looking at late-blooming tulip gardens. But by August it is a forgotten passion, and another year passes, and the score is still something like *Tulipa* zero, *Narcissus*, 697. Only this year is going to be different. And what has moved me to action was a visit to a friend's early spring garden which featured an extraordinary collection of species tulips. Species tulips are wild botanical specimens that are so quietly thrilling that even garden makers with tulip inertia can be moved in late summer to order their bulbs.

Species tulips grow naturally in many places and they will naturalize easily if you find the right spot for them. They flower early in the spring—earlier than their hybrid cousins. In general they are shorter and somewhat less stagey than the hybrids. Look them up in your books if you are not a tulip person. They are wonderful! The reason we have to think about species tulips *now* is because species tulips have to be planted much earlier than regular tulips (like in September if you live in a colder zone, up to December if you live in the South). And they are trickier to find; to get a really good selection you need to use mail order catalogues. Go look them up before you check on your tomatoes.

MAKE AN HERB MIX • You can make seasoning blends very easily with dried herbs from your garden. They make wonderful holiday gifts. Any combination will do—it's mostly proportions that matter. An Italian mix, for instance, might be equal parts of dried oregano, basil, rosemary, thyme, and sage. A great herbal rub for grilling might be dried rosemary, basil, and oregano, with smaller amounts of sage, thyme, and some black pepper. Some dried red peppers would make a tasty addition for those who like it hot. You can store your mixes in attractive jars. They will keep for months in a cool, dry, dark place (don't store your dried herbs near direct sunlight).

❦ A U G U S T 6

If your compost has just been sitting there for some reason—rinds still rinds, eggshells still eggshells, clippings still clippings—and no real decomposition in sight, try spraying it with soap. In the fall, especially, it's easy to get some dud compost because the big piles of leaves you throw in there don't get enough moisture. Jim Wilson, who is a cohost on PBS's *The Victory Garden*, sprays Murphy's Oil Soap on his fall compost, which is a brilliant idea because the tackiness of the soap helps moisture to adhere, and therefore the compost to decompose.

EASY WAY TO DRY FLOWERS • You can dry any flower or leaf in tins of kitty litter—the kind that clumps. All you do is place a layer of litter in an airtight cookie tin, put the flower or foliage on top, and gently cover the plant with more kitty litter. Put the lid on tightly and put it on a shelf where it won't be disturbed for a week, and it's ready. Most dried flowers are spectacularly vivid (remember to save some for your garden journal).

FREEZE YOUR BEANS • A study at the University of Illinois at Urbana–Champaign showed that frozen green beans retain much more vitamin C content than fresh beans that are refrigerated. Beans suffer dramatic losses of vitamin C after two days of storage. Freeze them if you can't use them immediately. (And think twice before buying fresh beans in the market during the winter. Can you imagine how old those beans are?)

FIRST-TIME GARDENERS • *While preparing the dirt for fall sowing, remember that some locations may have been depleted by spring crops. For instance, you might have to add a little 10-10-10 for spinach and other nitrogen lovers—unless you have deliciously fertile soil. In any case, a little care now will pay off handsomely in a month or two.*

AND DON'T FORGET THE PEAS • Try to get in a last pea crop. The peas will mature by October and taste better than previous sowings; they're sweeter and mellower in cool weather conditions.

❧ AUGUST 7

It's too early to be suffering from tomato/corn overdose, that bewildering sensation of being sick of fresh sweet corn and home-grown tomatoes. But about this time of year, when at least two meals a day have tomatoes and corn in them, it's fun to pick up a few new tricks.

Tomatoes, sliced, *maybe* with a little salt on them, simply cannot be improved upon. But corn is another matter because it requires a cook. My sister Ginny makes the best boiled corn in the universe and it would be a terrible omission not to include it here.

GINNY'S BOILED CORN

The only time this method doesn't make perfect corn is when you have too many ears in a lobster-sized pot, because it takes so long for the water to boil that the corns gets soggy.

Pick the corn and shuck the ears immediately. Put the corn in a pot of fresh cold water to cover. Add about 1/3 cup of milk and a heaping tablespoon of sugar. Turn the flame to high and bring the uncovered pot to a boil. Let it boil for 2 minutes. Now cover and turn the flame off. Leave it there for at least 10 minutes. Enjoy.

CORN SILKS • I usually relegate corn husking and silking to the children, but after they've finished shucking and digging their little fingers into the kernels, I take a clean terry washcloth, slightly damp, and run it down the ear—it helps pull off those final reluctant threads.

OTHER CORN ADVENTURES

• To butter your corn, butter a slice of bread generously, then use the bread to smear butter all over your corn. (The corn-soggy bread tastes delicious, too.)
• You can roast corn in the oven and it will take on a nutty taste. Leave only the inner husk on and bake it at 375 degrees for 15 minutes.
• Grilling corn is really fun. Take off the outer husks but leave on the inner husks. Soak the ears in water first—for about 30 minutes. Drain very well, and grill for 10 to 15 minutes, turning the ears periodically. Try some flavored butter (like jalapeño or herb) with your grilled corn.

Cucumber lotion is excellent for a bad sunburn that you might have acquired from, say, weeding your cucumber patch. All you do is get 2 or 3 good-sized cucumbers, and peel, seed, and dice them. Boil them in just a bit of water until soft. Press them through a fine sieve or cheesecloth. You will have juice to which you add ¼ of its volume in whiskey and ⅓ of elder water. Shake well and put in a plastic container; keep it tightly covered and chilled for even more relief.

STILL GOT SLUGS? • A gardener from Oregon battling slugs had tried it all when someone suggested grapefruit rinds. Desperate, he placed about a half dozen rinds (with just a little pulp left on) all about his garden, turned over like little igloos. The slugs obediently climbed under the fruit rinds, and died. For continuous results, you simply make a periodic visits to the rinds, pick up the dead players, and return the grapefruit rinds to their igloo positions.

RULE OF THUMB • When planting cover crops consider your needs. Legumes like alfalfa, clover, peas, and beans fix nitrogen. Grasses do not.

GIVE YOUR MUMS A LITTLE BUMP • You can give your chrysanthemums a weekly drink of fish emulsion or manure tea, until color starts appearing in the buds.

WATERING GUIDELINES • Your soil type will determine how much and how often you should water. Loamy soil has moderate watering needs and requires regular, even waterings. Clay soil needs much longer waterings, and you need to take pauses between dousings because of the runoff problems. Sandy soil needs less water on average, but more frequent waterings.

Snowball bushes conjure up memories, and when the realtor first showed us the old Victorian house that was to become our home, the deal was sealed when I saw the beautiful little *Viburnum* in the yard. There is so much to admire about this woody ornamental, but what is perhaps most pleasing is the armfuls of cut branches one can bring into the house and arrange in tall vases or urns—they are simply glorious. I have the more common European snowball variety, but there are many others to chose from; I have many on my wish list for coming seasons.

Anyway, here's how to make the most of them indoors: Cut your branches at an angle ¼ inch above the bud or leaf node and watch what you are doing to the shape of the shrub as you clip away. Once you get the cut branches to your work space, make sure to strip away all the leaves you don't need and in the vase make certain no leaves are covered by water. Use some preservative crystals and warm water in the vase, and let the stems drink in this solution overnight in the basement or somewhere cool and dark. *Viburnum* are big drinkers. When you display them, make certain they are placed away from the sun and air conditioning or other drafts. You can change the water every 3 days, each time cutting the stem ends about an inch. The longer branches look fabulously dramatic in odd-numbered bunches; shorter branches make wonderful additions to casual cut flower arrangements. You can also cut *Viburnum* for its berries and foliage, but don't go too crazy—the next year's flower buds are produced on this year's growth.

Bring in lots of Viburnum *for a beautiful arrangement.*

WHERE THE HEAT IS • When you are preparing your hot chiles for cooking, remember that the heat is concentrated in the seeds and the white interior ribs. You can remove the seeds and ribs to make the pepper milder.

WATERMELON RIND PICKLES • After you've had the seed spitting contest and gnawed through the pink, juicy flesh, put your watermelon rinds to good use by pickling them. To make watermelon pickles you use the white part—no green allowed (and of course, no red). Cut the rind into half-inch cubes until you have about 2 cups. Then rub the cubes with 2 tablespoons of kosher salt and let them sit in the refrigerator for 24 hours. Rinse the salt off very well and then put the rinds in a big saucepan with just enough water to cover. Heat to boiling. Boil for 10 to 12 minutes. Drain well and allow to cool. Now combine 1 cup of sugar, ½ cup of cider vinegar, and 4 whole cloves in a saucepan and bring to a boil. Add the rinds and boil for 10 minutes. Allow the rinds and juice to cool, then transfer to 1 or 2 sterile jars and cover tightly. You need to refrigerate the rinds for about a week before you sample. They'll keep for at least a month.

AUGUST 10

If you want a good indoor afternoon project, reorganize your seeds. Turn on the AC, pour yourself a tall glass of iced tea, and spread the lot out on the kitchen table. I like to keep my seeds in glassine envelopes—the kind you might have used for your stamp collection when you were a child. I also use photographers' 35mm negative sleeves, which are long, thin glassine envelopes. You can get the envelopes at camera stores or hobby shops and they are ideal because you can write on them with a marker (dates, notes, name of the plant, etc.), seal them with tape, and then actually see how many seeds you have at a glance. I hate peering down into seed packets trying to figure out how many I've got left; the tiny seeds always get stuck in the corners.

Anyway, after I mark and seal all of my envelopes, I put the glassine packets in mason jars and seal them. Many people use silica gel in a cloth bag to keep seeds dry. Some people use dry powdered milk to absorb any moisture (put the powdered milk in 3-inch-square cheesecloth pockets sewn up on 4 sides or unused tea bags sans tea). Others use uncooked rice, on the theory that if it keeps salt shakers unclogged, it will benefit the seeds. I just make sure they are dry in the first place and then put them in their sealed jars into the freezer. I always get nice germination rates out of my second sowings so I can't complain. It feels good to get those seeds squared away, at least for the time being.

WHAT DID WE EAT BEFORE SALSA? • In our house, salsa is the new ketchup. We use it on hamburgers, in omelets, on black beans, in cheese sandwiches, on grilled eggplant—you name it. Our recipe changes depending on what's at hand, but we put together our basic concoction like this:

••

BASIC SUMMER SALSA

Combine 2 large ripe tomatoes, seeded and diced small; 1 small red onion, diced small; 2 tablespoons chopped Italian parsley; 2 tablespoons chopped cilantro; 1 large clove garlic, minced; 2 jalapeño peppers, diced small; 2 tablespoons olive oil; 1½ teaspoons sugar; salt and pepper. You also can add cucumbers, corn—almost anything to this salsa. Put in a jar with a lid. Refrigerate. This salsa lasts for 3 days, though not in our house.

••

WEED REALITY CHECK • If you are discouraged about the weeds in your garden—and have done everything by the book to prevent them or get rid of them—it's time to get some perspective. *You can't control it and you never will.* A bird flying overhead could drop a dry seedhead from 80 feet above, and thousands of plants could be sown. Weeds are carried by wind and water, from miles and miles away. Ten thousand weed seeds can lie dormant in the ground for decades and then, suddenly, right in the middle of your onion patch, decide to make their debut. Weeds are not a problem to be solved, but a condition to be accepted and dealt with. Yank, curse, pull, cultivate, and learn to live with them.

••

The kitchen looks beautiful in August. Baskets of vegetables are crammed onto the countertop, herbs and peppers hang everywhere, vases overflow with cut flowers. Sometimes I have to pinch myself. If this is a ridiculously abundant year, you can go beyond the usual recipients of your zucchini and cleome. Run a basket of veggies over to the firehouse or the police station. Senior centers have lots of people who are still gardeners in their hearts and who would take enormous pleasure in a bouquet of your flowers or a real tomato. Rabbis, priests, and ministers don't have a lot of time to garden—take a load over. You now have a bounty of perfect gifts flowing from your garden. Remember the strangers in your life.

SWISS CHARD • All of us have our trademark plants in the garden, the flowers or vegetables without which it would not be *our* garden. On the vegetable side, Ruby Red chard is my signature plant. Ruby Red chard is not only beautiful but grows quite nicely all summer, even in the furnace days of July and August. And people who have never tasted chard before are enchanted when they have it for the first time, whether it is steamed and served at room temperature with a few drops of soy sauce; or sautéed quickly in garlic-flavored olive oil; or used in lasagnes or soups.

The leaves are delicious but there is an even higher form of swiss chard: forced new small blanched buds—a major treat. And so easy! All you do is cut your chard to within an inch or so of the surface of the soil. Then hill over the plant with several inches of soil. Monitor it carefully. Within days you can poke around the hill and feel for the new buds. Just before they break the surface, harvest the buds. Delectable!

LET THE RADISHES DO IT FOR YOU • If you are still planting for fall, sow icicle radishes with your root vegetable seeds—beets, carrots, turnips, whatever. The radishes will mature before anything else, and when you harvest them you will be aerating and loosening your soil at the same time, making subterranean life more enjoyable for your other root crops.

Fair weather on St. Lawrence's Day foretells a fair autumn.

While you are paging through your bulb catalogues, remember: the bigger the bulb, the bigger the flower. That is why big bulbs are often quite expensive. If you want to create a magnificent tulip display, it makes sense to buy the biggest bulbs you can afford. Also, tulips bloom best in their first year, so you need to go in strong. Subsequent years can be somewhat disappointing.

Daffodils are a different story. In this case, you might as well save your money and buy smaller bulbs. Since daffodils multiply and bloom better year after year, especially if you maintain them and divide them from time to time, it makes sense to start out with modest-sized bulbs and let them develop gradually.

BROCCOLI HARVEST • The head of the broccoli is actually a mass of tiny flower buds. Be sure to harvest them before the hundreds of florets turn into hundreds of little yellow flowers. Harvest your broccoli often and you can get several smaller heads from the side shoots once you've cut the central one. (This may mean harvesting twice a week.) Cutting 2 to 4 inches off the stem will prevent too many side shoots.

DISEASED COMPOST • Obviously, throwing diseased plants onto your compost heap is a no-no, but if for some reason you did, you can sleep at night, albeit fitfully, if you make sure your compost heats up to at least 160 degrees. The important thing is to make sure the pile is turned every few days so that *all* of the compost reaches 160 degrees for a sustained period. Generally the outer edges of the pile are much cooler than the center.

STORING CARROTS • Store carrots in a plastic bag that is closed but perforated. Carrots need high humidity. Don't even attempt to store immature carrots—they'll go limp at once.

This is an excellent time to grab the old notebook, fancy journal, or whatever you like to keep garden notes in, and take a good hard look at the vegetable garden.

Make a note, if you haven't already, of where all your crops are located. To prevent disease and to maintain soil balance, you will want to rotate these crops next year, and there is no reason to rely on your memory about where the cabbage and tomato rows were located.

Lazy gardeners (like me) take photographs (though sometimes I am too lazy to get the film developed). My garden is modest in size, so it's easy to get a clear photographic sense of where everything was and how everything did. But it is also necessary to write down which varieties of tomatoes, for instance, tasted best, which crops seemed to be dinner for the bugs but not you, and so on. Also, if conditions were out of the ordinary or poor, note how that might have affected your plants.

And here's a great tip: videotape your garden. A detailed, witty tour of your garden in August is guaranteed to amuse and delight you in February when you are tugging at winter's bridle.

XERISCAPING FAVORITES • If you are tired of moving the soaker hose around, you might fill in your beds and borders next year with plants that are less dependent on water. Xeriscaping (from the Greek *xeros*, which means dry) originated in the Western states, and it is basically the art of landscaping with plants that do not require a lot of water. You can conserve water and still have an exquisite garden. These are good perennials to start with:

Achillea (Yarrow)

Artemisia

Asclepias (Butterfly weed)

Callirhoe (Poppy mallow)

Centaurea (Cornflower)

Chamaemelum (Chamomile)

Coreopsis

Echinops (Globe thistle)

Euphorbia (Flowering spurge, cushion spurge)

Gaillardia (Blanketflower)

Gypsophila (Baby's breath)

Heliopsis

Iberis (Candytuft)

Sedum (Stonecrop)

Sempervivum (Hens-and-chickens)

Stokesia (Stoke's aster)

Tradescantia (Spiderwort)

Yucca

DON'T LET YOUR CARROTS WORK THEIR WAY
UP • If the shoulders of your carrots are working their way out of
the soil, be sure to mound them up. If the shoulders are exposed for
too long to sunlight they'll develop chlorophyll and turn green.

Trees grow dark before a storm.

❦ AUGUST 14

Craig Cramer, editorial director of *The New Farm* magazine, makes the
point that one of the necessities of successful cover-cropping is actually having cover crop seeds on hand, which is a trick because most
garden supply stores or nurseries don't sell them. Mr. Cramer recommends birdseed—wild or pet—as an excellent and inexpensive late-
summer cover. It's easy to find: you can get it at the bulk section of
the grocery store. Bulk birdseed is mostly millet, and it will pop up
easily if you sow it thick and water it. You can get the whole thing
up and running in 4 weeks—and then it will winterkill nicely, making
it perfect for early spring crops the following year. (Make sure your
birdseed doesn't contain sunflower seed, which could affect your
plants adversely.)

SKUNKS AT THE GARDEN PARTY? • Mothballs, placed
along a fenceline or edges of the yard, helped one South Dakota gardener get rid of a serious skunk problem.

PEPPER SEED SAVERS • Seeds that come from overripe peppers germinate better than those that come from less mature fruits.

*FIRST-TIME GARDENERS • Don't fertilize or prune your woodies
(azaleas, rhododendrons, etc.) now because the new growth won't make it through
the winter. Meanwhile, if you have newly planted woodies, continue watering well
so they can "take" before the freeze sets in.*

TURNIP CLINIC • Turnips are one of my best-loved root vegetables, and for some reason I have been wholly unsuccessful in growing them. In the past three seasons of duds, this is what I learned:

The time my turnips had long and thin roots, my soil had too little potassium (so I worked in some wood ash). Next season I got a turnip harvest that was on the tough side—as in your teeth bounced off them. I was told I had too much nitrogen in the soil. My third season I had a pretty good crop but they tasted a little too strong, and I learned that I had not harvested my turnips early enough. I was also told to try a "milder variety." This year, my fingers are crossed. I remain optimistic.

> *It was as true—as turnips is.*
> —Charles Dickens

❧ AUGUST 15

If you are experiencing drought or a heat wave, it is best to leave your plants alone. Many a plant has been killed with kindness during dry spells. Don't fertilize. Don't spray for pests. Don't prune. Don't do anything but try to give your plants consistent moisture. Any kind of stimulation adds more stress to an already stressful situation. Your objective is to allow your plants to go into their own version of dormancy until the weather improves.

ONION CLINIC • If your onion bulbs split into two or more sections, it is probably the result of uneven watering, applications of fertilizers too late in the season, or because your sets were stored improperly.

FIRST-TIME GARLIC HARVESTERS • When you first pull garlic bulbs out of the soil there won't be any papery skin around the bulb. The skin forms later, after the bulbs have been set out to dry in a shady place for about a week.

STORING BERRIES • Blackberries and raspberries don't last long. Place them in a single layer on paper towels and cover loosely with plastic. Make sure you cull out the moldy ones.

I love herbal teas, and it delights me that my daughters also drink them, especially in the winter months when I hear the battle cry of our all-girl household—"C'mon, everybody, let's get cozy!"—which basically means make a cup of tea, get a book, and read with lots of quilts about you.

But not all herbs and flowers are good for you, and you really should be cautious before brewing up a pot of "whatever." Allergy-prone individuals can have serious reactions to chamomile tea, for instance. You can get coldlike symptoms as an allergic reaction to the pollen proteins and glycoproteins in chamomile and also in marigold tea. Other teas can cause more serious reactions in certain people. Some plants to avoid in blends are *Acorus calamus* (sweet flag), *Lobelia inflata* (Indian tobacco) *Mentha pulegium* (pennyroyal), *Symphytum* (comfrey), *Tanacetum* (tansy), and *Tussilago* (coltsfoot).

THE OLD VALERIAN TRICK • According to legend, the Pied Piper of Hamlin used the herb valerian (*Valeriana officinalis*) to lure the rats out of town. Valerian, like catnip, is also attractive to cats, who like to rile and frolic in its leaves, raising the possibility that the Piper used a botanical one-two punch on the rodents in town.

BRUSSELS SPROUTS MAINTENANCE • As your Brussels sprouts grow, continuously remove the lower leaves of the plant to encourage the heads to keep forming higher up the stalk. The heads will be larger, too. Do this early in the day when they will snap off easiest.

❦ AUGUST 17

Studies have shown that Vitamin C, carbohydrates, and proteins are at their highest concentration in vegetables picked late in the day. The exceptions are crisp vegetables like lettuce and cucumbers. Pick the crisp ones in the morning to retain the crunch.

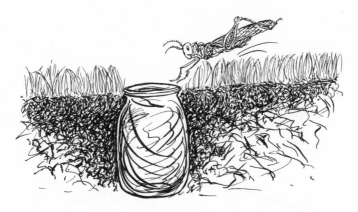

Try the old molasses trick on your grasshoppers.

GRASSHOPPER TRAP • If you are plagued with grasshoppers, this method should help. Fill a wide-mouth jar with a mixture of molasses and water. Then bury the jar flush to the ground—the grasshoppers will be attracted to the scent and will get stuck in the goo. If this doesn't affect your grasshopper population, leave the problem to your natural allies. Hawks, crows, sparrows, brown thrashers, squirrels, field mice, snakes, toads, spiders, and even cats love to eat grasshoppers.

PLANTS THAT GET US TIPSY • Corn is used in the production of gin and bourbon. Barley is used in beer and scotch. Rice is the basis of sake. Vodka is derived from fermented potatoes. Tequila comes from the agave or century plant.

❦ A U G U S T 1 8

It's tricky to grow melons in areas with short summers because part of the ripening process requires heat—not just light. One way to maximize the last weeks of summer is to take large stones, bricks, or concrete blocks and wrap them with black plastic. Place a little cradle of the wrapped stones around each of your melons. During the day, the black plastic will draw in the heat of the sun and then at night, when it's cool, the heat will be slowly be released, so that the melon continues to ripen.

ANOTHER SOIL TEST • Here's a quick way to determine whether your soil needs to be watered. Work your hand down into the soil, pick up a wad, and squeeze it hard. If it clumps together somewhat, it's okay. If it completely falls apart, you need to water.

STYROFOAM COOLERS PROTECT PLANTS • If there are big end-of-summer sales on styrofoam coolers in your area, load up—they are great protection for tender annuals or newly planted perennials in the fall. When the threat of cold or frost looms, just turn them upside down over your plants and put rocks on top of them.

HOW TO WATER A TREE • When watering trees during severe drought conditions, keep in mind that the roots from large trees may extend 50 feet or more beyond their trunks. Therefore, it's best to place the sprinkler directly under the tree's dripline and continue watering until you've slowly worked your way all around the trunk.

❦ AUGUST 19

When harvesting watermelons, researcher James Crall, Ph.D. (he developed the varieties Micklee and Minilee), advises you look for withering tendrils on the vine closest to the fruit stem, as well as a light yellow rough spot on the rind where the fruit touches the ground. The "tap the fruit" trick is unreliable, he says, though other gardeners say when a knock with your knuckle produces a hollow and dull sound—as opposed to a sharp and high sound—the melon is ripe. Watermelon harvesting is an art: watermelon pickers are paid more at harvest time than harvesters of any other crop.

FIRST-TIME HARVESTERS

• Harvest beets when they are about 2 inches in diameter. Save the greens. They're better for you than the roots.

• Pull your carrots almost any time, but don't let them get bigger than the diameter of a quarter at their shoulders. Another indicator is foliage: when it's at its greenest and darkest, the carrots are ready to come out.

- Yellow summer squash is best when it is 4 or 5 inches in length; 3 to 4 inches for the scallop varieties; and 6 to 8 inches for the zucchini. Winter squash should be hard when ripe; you shouldn't be able to cut it with your fingernail (if you can, the squash hasn't matured yet). Acorn squash does not improve with storage on or off the vine, so pick them and eat them when they are mature.

- Corn is ready about 3 weeks after the silks appear.

- Beans should be picked before the seeds are bulging and visible beneath the pods. Pick them when the weather is dry and harvest frequently to keep up production.

- Onions are ready when the tops have fallen over and begun to turn brown. When 20 percent of the tops have fallen over by themselves, knock down the rest to speed up the ripening process; a week later pull them. Leave them outside in a sunny dry location for a week or so. Cut the tops or braid them. Then store in a cool dry place that is well ventilated (use a fan if you have to). Any onions you harvest that are thick-necked should be eaten first. Thick-stalked onions store poorly over the winter.

❦ AUGUST 20

A tomato is a fruit, botanically. But however correct we might be to say so, we are speaking in direct conflict with a U.S. Supreme Court ruling. In 1893, the Court ruled that legally a tomato is a vegetable, in keeping with the dictionary definition that vegetables are included in main courses and fruits are generally served as a dessert. By strict botanical definition, however, a fruit is anything that replaces a flower on a garden plant.

FIRST-TIME GARDENERS • *Tulips are often described in catalogues as perennials, but you're lucky if you get five years out of them. The tulips in the most spectacular gardens are treated as annuals. If you want year after year of guaranteed splendor, you have to be prepared to yank out bulbs and replace them.*

HOT PEPPERS, RANKED • When the U.S. Department of Agriculture in Charleston, North Carolina, announced a new slim, 4-inch-long pepper that is 20 times hotter than the jalapeño, it got 25,000 requests for more information. This was the biggest out-pouring of interest the laboratory had received since 6 years before, when they announced the development of an insect-resistant Southern pea. The new pepper, which is a version of the old cayenne, has been named Charleston Hot. It is not clear where the Charleston Hot stands in relation to the current list of world's hot peppers, ranked at the Texas Agricultural Station by Dr. Ben Villalon. (Peppers ranked 5-plus can burn the eyes and skin.)

Bahamian, Habanero (10)
Santaka (from Japan), Choltecpin
   (from Thailand) (9)
Piquín, Cayenne, Tabasco (8)
De Árbol (7)
Yellow Wax, Serrano (6)

Jalapeño, Mirasol (5)
Sandia, Cascabel, Rocotillo (4)
Hot Ancho, Pasilla (3)
Big Jim, Anaheim (2)
R-Naky, El Paso, Cherry (1)
Bell, Pimiento, Sweet Banana (0)

❦ AUGUST 21

As you read this, one very special pumpkin in North America is grow-ing 8 to 20 pounds *per day*, well on its way to being named the World's Largest Pumpkin. What if it doesn't stop? The world's current record is held by Joel Holland of Puyallup, Washington; he grew his winning pumpkin using Dill's Atlantic Giant, acknowledged as the best giant pumpkin seed on the market. It weighed 827 pounds.

If you want to play the pumpkin game next year, you'll need to plan for it now. Pumpkins need rich soil, and by installing a fall cover crop in a 25-foot space, you'll get a head start on richly com-posted soil. Add cow manure, as well. Howard Dill, of Dill's Atlantic Giant fame (his seeds have won the World's Largest Pumpkin contest from 1980 to the present), says that the first 60 days of the giant pumpkin plant's life are the most important; at that point, select one or two fruits with good shape and remove all the others. Then give the plant lots and lots of nutrients. Protect the plant's leaves because they funnel nutrients to the stem. Hope for moderately hot weather—about 80 to 90 degrees during the growing season.

The World Pumpkin Confederation holds its annual World's Largest Pumpkin weigh-off in upstate New York every October, and you can get more information by writing WPC, 14050 Route 62, Collins, NY 14034. As a member, you will get their newsletter, *cucurBITS* (get it?), and a membership card along with information about competitions across the country. The WPC also weighs cabbages, squash, watermelon, muskmelon, and sunflower (head), and measures longest gourd and tallest cornstalk.

ROSEMARY IDEA • Throw a rosemary branch into the charcoal in your barbecue pit to give a wonderful flavor.

CARE FOR CUT FLOWERS • If you're going to be away, you can double the life of your cut flowers by placing them in a cold room or in the refrigerator at night.

STILTS FOR FLOWERS • To make cut flowers taller, insert the stems into clear plastic drinking straws before adding them to your arrangement.

❦ A U G U S T 2 2

The earlier you make your bulb selections, the better. You won't regret it if you check in with your nursery and see if their bulbs have arrived—or get a handle on when they're due. With bulbs, first pick is important, even if it's too early to plant. A lot of bulbs come in mesh bags, but if possible, buy yours individually. They're not cheap, and you should have an opportunity to look at each one. Make sure they are nice and plump, and not mushy. Check for mildew, insects, or other signs of disease. Smell them. Apply the same standards that you would to an onion that you might buy at the market. (When you are tulip shopping, in particular, don't worry if the outside papery skin—the tunic—is torn or missing. If the bulb is healthy it won't matter, and some gardeners believe that removing the tunic actually encourages rooting after the bulb is planted.) Once home, store your bulbs and corms in a cool dry place until you are ready to plant (don't let them freeze, of course). *Wait until the weather gets cooler to put them in or they might sprout prematurely.*

ONE MORE REASON TO QUIT SMOKING • If you smoke, wash your hands before working in the garden. Tomato plants are very vulnerable to tobacco mosaic disease, often spread by the hands of people who smoke. Affected plants dry up and die even when well watered.

MORE TIPS FOR FIRST-TIME HARVESTERS

- The best way to dig out potatoes is to start about a foot away from the stem and dig toward the plant with a spade. You reduce your chance of damaging the tubers this way.

- Shallots are harvested much like regular onions. Pull them out once the leaves have collapsed. Dry the bulbs outside in dry weather for a couple of days (they dry out faster than onions for obvious reasons). Then place them in mesh bags and hang them in a cool dark location.

- Summer squash is coming out in droves this month. Pick them when they are just under 6 inches long, and harvest frequently. Their growth rates are astounding just about now. And remember: Zucchini is not the Italian word for baseball bat. Unless you are growing zucchinis for a competition, smaller is better.

❦ AUGUST 23

If your carrots are looking stunted, your soil may be too warm. Carrots thrive best in soil temperatures of 65 degrees. In addition, your soil may have too much clay in it, in which case you need to add some organic matter and work it into a finer tilth. Also, carrots that have not been thinned properly deprive each other of space and nutrients; their growth will be irregular and unattractive.

COVER CROPS WARNING • Nematodes can be greatly reduced by planting certain cover crops. These roundworms tend to move on once barley or rye is tilled back into the ground. Not all cover crops work, however; chickweed, clover, and mint can actually elevate the nematode population.

DON'T REFRIGERATE BULBS • I used to hear this all the time: refrigerate your bulbs. In fact, it wasn't just refrigerate your bulbs, it was do it for 40 days at 45 degrees. In Holland, the people who know bulbs best state that refrigerator temperatures are too cold, and will cause the bulbs to bolt. The plants bloom and the blooms are short and runtlike. If you can't or shouldn't plant your bulbs now, have your nursery store them for you at the preferred 50 to 55 degrees until you are ready.

NOT FOR COMPOST ONLY • There are many vegetable leaves that actually taste good in salads or stir-fries—so sample the leaves of these vegetables before you toss them into the compost pile.

Broccoli	Kohlrabi
Rutabaga	Carrot
Radish	Cauliflower

❦ AUGUST 2 4

VIRGO, August 24 to September 23—*Good for flower blossoms but not ideal for sowing*

Chives are one of the most unappreciated plants in the garden. No other plant offers so much utility and grace, yet they are one of the least fussy plants in creation, and anyone, I mean anyone, can grow them.

Sometime over the next few weeks you should pot up some of your chives to take indoors. Dig up two or three clumps, put them in pots and leave them there—outside, on your porch or even dug back into the ground—until late November or December, depending on your zone. They need about a month to 6 weeks of dormancy to send up new growth once they get indoors.

EGGPLANTS, EGGPLANTS EVERYWHERE • They are here, in record numbers: the eggplants. Eggplants are not quite the crown jewels of the food chain, like tomatoes and sweet corn, but they are as elemental to August as the sun, and they are everywhere. This recipe is our favorite way to eat eggplant, and sometimes we make a whole meal out of it along with a salad of greens, some sliced tomatoes, and good bread. (Many people slice and salt their eggplants first to draw out the bitterness, but if you cut it and grill it right away you should be able to forgo that step.)

GRILLED EGGPLANT WITH HERBED GOAT CHEESE

2 large eggplants, cut crosswise into ¼-inch-thick slices
Olive oil
2 teaspoons minced garlic
Salt and pepper
12 ounces goat cheese, at room temperature
½ cup minced herbs from the garden; any combination of basil, thyme, chives, parsley

Brush both sides of each eggplant slice with a very thin layer of olive oil. Sprinkle with garlic, salt, and pepper to taste. Brown on both sides on a hot grill. Moving quickly, while the eggplant is still hot, spread with a thin layer of goat cheese, then sprinkle minced herbs on top. Serve warm or at room temperature.

❦ AUGUST 25

Since I am up to my ears in basil I have been forced to figure out what *else* to do with it. One of my most beloved vendors, Shepherd's Garden Seeds, recommends an easy way to make an herb-flavored vinegar, and I want to share it because it is a great use of garden herbs. All you do is pack a 1-gallon plastic or glass container *half full* with washed and air-dried basil or whatever herb you are using. You can put everything but the roots in. Then you fill up the jug with plain white or rice vinegar heated almost to a boil (the rice vinegar is considerably more expensive—use it for gifts and the plain white vinegar for everyday use). Now cover the jug and allow the herbs to steep. It takes a month or two. Give it a taste. When the flavor is fully developed, you can strain the vinegar through cheesecloth and put it in those great-looking colored glass bottles from Portugal that you can get at gourmet cookware shops. You can also remove the labels from empty wine bottles, soy sauce bottles, Worcestershire sauce bottles, or wine vinegar bottles. Label them attractively and give to friends.

FIRST-TIME GARDENERS • You don't have to peel your just-picked cucumbers, unless you really hate skin. Store-bought cukes have a thicker, unpalatable skin that is often coated with an edible wax. Not yours. Actually, the only time I peel my cucumbers is when I make my children's favorite sandwich: Spread Hellmann's mayonnaise lightly on two pieces of Pepperidge Farms "original" white bread. Cover one piece of bread with a couple of layers of thin-sliced, peeled homegrown cukes and a few grains of salt. Top with the remaining slice of bread and cut off the crusts. It's the best cucumber sandwich you'll ever eat.

❦ AUGUST 26

Tender seedlings need all the help they can get, and one way to protect them from the sun and wind is to use biodegradable coffee filters. Set out your transplants and cover each one with a coffee filter. Anchor the filter with tiny rocks and then mist the filter cover lightly. Rain and light will come right through the coffee filter. When the seedling is strong enough, slit an opening in the filter for the plant. Eventually, the filter should decompose right around the plant.

DRYING TIP • When you dry flowers with stems that secrete sap or juice (like poppies) or with hollow stems (like Mexican sunflowers and dahlias) you need to take an extra step before drying them. Cut the stems at an angle. Dip the stem ends in boiling water for ten seconds or sear them with a flame—and then plunge them into cold water to stop the flowers from bleeding. At this point you can dry the flowers using your favorite method.

MY DOG HAS CHAMOMILE • Chamomile flowers are good to put in a dog's bed to repel fleas.

My husband takes great pleasure in letting me know of an impending rain, especially when he sees I'm out in the yard watering. What he doesn't understand is that I *always* water before it rains. I do it on purpose. My thinking is that if there has been a prolonged drought, my garden will be far more receptive to rainfall if I do some preliminary watering. I try to get at least a good 30 minutes of soaking or sprinkling in to soften up the dirt before the rain comes.

Water your garden before it rains.

THE NUT TREE PROBLEM • Juglone is produced by the black walnut and, to a much lesser degree, other related trees such as pecan, hickories, and butternuts. If you have these trees on your property or if nearby neighbors grow them, they could affect the growth of numerous plants. Your best bet is to stick with plants that are not affected by the chemical. Researchers have found that snap beans, lima beans, onions, parnips, sweet corn, and dandelion are juglone tolerant; also, you can grow black raspberries, grapes, and mint. Many flowers can handle juglone, but many can't: avoid planting peonies, lilac, viburnum, autumn crocus, magnolia, and crabapple near black walnut trees.

BULBS TO PLANT IN THE FALL

Hyacinth (*Hyacinthus sp.*)
Snowdrop (*Galanthus sp.*)
Crocus (*Colchicium sp.*)
Daffodil (*Narcissus sp.*)
Lily (*Lilium sp.*)

Glory-of-the-snow (*Chionodoxa lucilae*)
Tulip (*Tulipa sp.*)
Autumn crocus (*Colchicum sp.*)
Grape hyacinth (*Muscari sp.*)

☙ AUGUST 28

If your melons were too small this year, there are a couple of possible explanations. Water, too little of it, is a classic problem. Next year water to a depth of 12 inches. Poor soil could have been the problem; add lots of organic matter next year. Too many competitors is also a reason for small fruits. Next time (ah, next time!) thin your plants out and give them lots of growing space.

KIDS WILL LIKE THIS ONE • On a hot windless day you can take a lighted match and place it near the flowers of a gas plant (*Dictamnus*) and for brief moment the volatile oils will ignite!

I can see the day looming when I shall drive a van to Sainsbury's and fill it with prime vegetables just for the pleasure of watching it rot down into food for the next generation of the same. This is the sort of madness that attacks old women, but at least it is harmless.
> —The Duchess of Devonshire on compost

☙ AUGUST 29

Cabbage is tricky to grow, but it is such a player in the fall garden you have to give it a try. The problem with late summer plantings is that the plants either fry or bolt. One way to keep your cabbages protected and cool is to make cloches for them out of the foil lining of snack boxes. Lots of snacks are overpackaged for freshness, which is bad for the earth but good for cabbages. Pull out the foil-liner bags and cut off the bottom so you can slip the whole thing over your plant. Place the bag over the transplanted seedling, foil side out, so it will reflect the hot sun. Anchor the bag with dirt and rocks. Water as you normally would.

Over the next few weeks, the foil will reflect the heat and help to keep the soil moist and cool. The reflective quality also will put off certain flying insects. The foil liners won't decompose for about a thousand years, so you can save them for future seasons.

911 EGGSHELLS • If the slugs are winning, try this one: Bake eggshells in a 250-degree oven until they turn brown and crisp. Once

they have cooled down, crush them into powder. A mortar and pestle works great for this, but you can also put the shells in a zipper-locked bag and knead them with your hands until you have a really fine substance. Make a border all around your affected plants or the whole garden. The sharp pieces of powdered shell will slice the mushy bodies of the slugs, working much like diatomaceous earth.

❦ A U G U S T 3 0
St. Fiacre's Day, Patron of Gardeners

I have in my yard a statue of an Irish monk named St. Fiacre, who from a distance looks like the monk in so many other gardens, St. Francis—but he's not. St. Fiacre is the genuine garden article, he is the official patron of gardeners, and today is his feast day. Statues of saints won't keep the leaf miners away from your columbine or help your tomatoes grow big and strong but they are reminders that miracles are the rule—not the exception—in our gardens.

In France on this day, there are petal-laden parades and floats made completely with flowers. In Ireland, devotees sing hymns written in honor of St. Fiacre. What little we know about the saint tells us he might prefer a bit more quiet and solitude in observance of his feast day. While he treated with great charity the thousands of people from all over Europe who flocked to him for food and healing and prayers, he was said to be happiest alone with God, digging in his garden. He died in 670.

START PULLING UP SPENT ANNUALS • Might as well start a gradual cleanup. Any annuals that have had it should be pulled now. Your garden will look neater and it will be easier to clean and rake out next month.

HERB CUTTINGS • Take some cuttings from your herb garden to grow indoors. Basil, hyssop, mint, and rosemary will root in water or sand for new plants.

If Farmer Jones just offered you a big load of fresh manure, thank him, and then put it in a quiet corner somewhere where it can sit undisturbed for 6 months to a year, the longer the better. It needs to age that long before you put it in your garden. (A load right now would be ideal for spring.) If you have open, unused garden space you can incorporate the manure immediately, but don't plant for at least six months.

UPPING BRUSSELS SPROUTS PRODUCTION • The goal in producing big harvests of Brussels sprouts is to increase leaf production, since the sprouts develop above each leaf on the main stalk. Cutting off the terminal bud is one method that works. Another is to wait until the plant is stable and established and then remove all the leaves from the lower 6 inches of the plant, which will increase leaf production at the top of the plant. Experiment.

TOMATO BLOSSOM ALERT • For cold-zone gardeners, it's getting toward the end of the season, and if your tomato blossoms are dropping off the plants it's probably because the night temperatures are too cold (the same thing happens when night temperatures are too hot). Most varieties prefer between 55 and 75 degrees at night. If you are suffering a serious loss, make a note to choose a variety more suited to your climate next year.

September

Flower of the Month: Aster

SEPTEMBER 1

Many perennials benefit from fall planting, even though you'd probably rather pick asters, make tomato-cheese pies, and start putting your summer clothes away. If you can rustle up the interest and the ambition, stop by the nursery and buy a plant, or two, or two hundred.

The advantage of putting perennials plants in now—as opposed to next spring—is that they have time to winter over, grow some roots, and get established. The main reason fall plantings fail is that the plants were not watered adequately, which is human error, nothing to do with the time of year.

Another point about fall planting is that many nurseries are trying to sell off their inventory now, and sometimes you can get a good deal. The selection might look doggy but usually there are a lot of perennials that are not in bloom, off in a corner somewhere. These plants have had tough lives in containers all summer but if the price is right, they're worth planting. Besides, digging in fall weather is good for you, and who couldn't use the exercise?

So make at least one last trip to the nursery, and check out their perennials. Don't get attached to any ornamental grasses, ferns, or tender species—they are better off planted in the spring. And if you have really heavy soil that tends to stay cold and wet, go back to your tomato-cheese pies. Your soil isn't right for fall planting and you're better off waiting until spring.

REMOVING MOLD AND MOSS FROM BRICKS • You can clean walkways and paths of moss and mold with a solution of ½ cup liquid laundry bleach mixed with 1 gallon of water, without seriously harming your nearby grass. Hose down thoroughly after you have scrubbed the brick surfaces with a stiff brush.

LATE POTATO HARVESTING • If you live in a northern climate with cool nights you can leave your potatoes in the ground after the foliage has died back, at least until the ground starts to freeze. Southern potato crops need to be removed once plants die down because the tubers will probably rot.

Behold congenial autumn comes,
The sabbath of the year!
—John Logan

❦ S E P T E M B E R 2

Okay. Let's talk about what you are going to do with all of those cukes and the green tomatoes you *know* will never ripen on the vine. If you are just short of feeling overwhelmed, pickles may be the answer. The first weeks of September are ideal for making pickles so why not give it a try? Hey: it's a project.

My friend John makes the best pickles in the world. *Important* pickles. Pickles out of pears. Pickles out of beets. Pickles out of green tomatoes.

His bread-and-butter pickles are crisp and flavorful and the perfect antidote to all of that beige food coming up this winter. And he has a secret: he "ices" all of his veggies before he processes them. While most pickle recipes call for soaking cucumbers in cold water for several hours or overnight, John covers his with crushed ice cubes and just enough water to cover, and then refrigerates the whole thing. His pickles are sensational. Why not give the ice-method a try?

CARROT CROPS: HOW TO STORE • If you have a particularly large carrot crop, freeze your carrots by cutting them into about ¼-inch slices and blanch in boiling water for no more than 3 minutes. Once blanched, plunge them in ice water so they do not continue cooking. Drain and dry on kitchen towels, then store them in containers in the freezer. If you are storing raw carrots in the vegetable compartment of the refrigerator, keep them whole and leave just a bit of their stem on. Take them out every now and then to air out the ethylene gas that builds up in cold storage. The presence of the gas can reduce your carrots' sweetness.

RULE OF THUMB • Fertilize roses about 6 weeks before the first expected frost date.

EARLY FALL LAWN CARE • Your lawn is pretty much in a maintenance mode for now. For fall growth you can add a balanced fertilizer, coordinating with any seeding activity you might plan.

Soon ripe, soon rotten.

❧ SEPTEMBER 3

Even if you're not a junk saver by nature, it's a good idea to save and use toilet paper rolls if you grow your own seedlings. Start saving them this fall and by February or March when you start your seedlings you'll have a whole box of them ready to go. They make excellent faux peat pots and once they're in the ground, they decompose.

Whenever you start your seedlings, line up your toilet paper rolls on an old cookie sheet or tray, sides touching. Fill with soil. Water the tray so that the bottoms of the rolls get wet and are anchored by the additional weight. Once the rolls are damp and in place, sow your seeds. You can bottom-water and also mist from the top before and after germination. When the true leaves appear and roots start growing out of the bottoms you can transplant your seedlings to the garden or to larger pots.

WATER GARDEN IN REVIEW • Was your water garden not all it should have been? Make a videotape of your garden, and send it to Van Ness Water Gardens, 2460 North Euclid Avenue, Upland, CA 91786. They will give you a full consultation for $19.95. Send along the dimensions of your water garden and its location, along with any other pertinent information, as you narrate your tape.

FIRST-TIME GARDENERS • *Don't use the ashes from your charcoal grill in your compost heap or garden. The charcoal has ingredients added to it to aid in the burning process—ingredients you don't want in your garden. Ashes from wood are okay, in moderation.*

Groundhogs will be hibernating shortly, and if you are plagued by these critters, it makes sense to intensify your efforts to kill or trap them now—before they go into hiding and breed 4 to 6 little new ones.

PERCENTAGE OF NITROGEN IN COVER CROPS

Alfalfa	3.0–4.0%	Cowpeas	2.5–3.0%
Vetch, hairy	3.0–4.0%	Rye	1.2–1.3%
Clover, crimson	3.0–3.3%	Rye grass	1.2–1.3%
Clover, red	2.8–3.2%		

❦ S E P T E M B E R 5

Many beginning gardeners have Fear of Transplant. There are legitimate worries in gardening, but this is not one of them. Do not be afraid. You will not kill a plant by moving it. If it is in the wrong spot, moving it could save its life. If you have always hated the way your *lupins* look next to your *Hemerocallis citrina* moving them will help you sleep at night.

I do all my transplanting at dusk. There's no fancy method. Just dig some compost into the hole, put the plant in, and give it a good long drink. For a few days, keep it protected by floating row cover or shelter of some kind. Baby the plant. Think how you might feel the first few weeks in a new and strange place. Keep the plant watered throughout the fall but don't let the soil get soggy.

If it still feels like August, wait awhile before moving your plants around. The heat and dryness are stressful to plants and to gardeners. Pick a nice day when there's a break in the weather to do your work.

STORING WINTER SQUASH • If you have an abundance of winter squash, rinse off each one with a very light bleach solution and then wipe the skins with a vegetable-oiled cloth. Then store them in a cool dry place whole. If you want to store them cooked, then peel, bake, and store in the freezer.

Crocus
Daffodil
Snowdrops

··

PLANT IN LATE FALL BUT BEFORE GROUND IS FROZEN

··

Tulips (plant species tulips earlier)

REMEDY FOR BULB MITES AND FLIES • Bulb flies or mites on your daffodil bulbs can be eliminated by giving them the hot water treatment. Soak bulbs in water maintained at exactly 110 degrees for 4 hours. Do this right before bulbs in your area are due to be planted.

> *When the corn wears a heavy coat, so must you.*
> —Pennsylvania saying

❦ SEPTEMBER 6

If you want to grow a winter harvest of greens in a cold frame or plastic-covered tunnel "greenhouse," plant specifically for winter—don't try to stretch fall crops into the next season. Not only are overly mature greens bitter and tough, but young fresh greens bear cold temperatures much better than their has-been counterparts. Using a cold frame or simple tunnel garden out of polyethylene plastic and wire hoop tunnels (or both), Northeastern gardeners can be assured of a harvest from Halloween through December, making adjustments for the particularities of individual zones. With protection in some zones, lucky Southerners can harvest almost all year round.

The greens will tolerate freezing temperatures but should be thoroughly thawed before harvest. Here are some plants to try: Winter Density lettuce (like romaine), Black-Seeded Simpson lettuce, Red Salad Bowl lettuce, spinach, arugula, mâche, mizuna or kyona (a mustard), and the Japanese purple mustards, among others. All of these tolerate cold well and are delicious when harvested young.

··

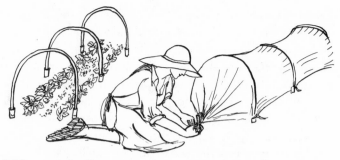

With very little effort you can have a winter harvest this year.

USE THE MICHAELMAS DAISY FOR MULCH • Once your Michaelmas daisies have flowered you can cut them back (don't take off all the leaves quite yet) and use the plants for mulch, laid down in a cross-hatch pattern. They make an excellent mulch for the garden and are a pain to compost anyway.

USE ONIONS IN THE NEMATODE WAR • Use any onion scraps from harvesting or from the kitchen to repel nematodes next year. Take the cut onion tops or peels—whatever you have— and press the juice out of them. Dig this juice into the soil at once— about 6 inches deep. Then water immediately to distribute the onion juice. (The solids can be composted.) Next year on this spot, plant to-matoes or any crop that nematodes tend to favor.

> 'Tis the last rose of summer,
> Left blooming alone;
> All her lovely companions
> Are faded and gone.
>
> —Thomas Moore

❦ SEPTEMBER 7

A cover crop (aka green manure) is good for any-size garden, and if you can get past the problem of locating seed it is totally worth your while to put one in. Basically, a cover crop is used in vegetable gardens to provide organic material for the soil. You plant it and till it under, and it enriches the soil's texture and often adds nutrients. You can put in a cover crop until 2 weeks before the soil freezes, which gives you plenty of time to order seeds unless you live in tundra country.

I recommend winter wheat or winter rye for the home gardener because you can plant it late and turn it into your soil in early spring. The blades are going to be thicker, wider, and taller than lawn grass, and since they are annuals they'll decompose once you turn them into the soil in the spring. You can plant the seed all at once or scatter it in empty rows or around plants throughout the fall until the ground freezes. The longer you let the wheat or rye grow in the spring, the more organic material it will add to your soil. I'd turn it under before it gets too high—obviously you'll want use of your garden as soon as possible—but the ground will benefit not only from the top growth but especially from the roots, which tend to clump in the soil, increasing tilth and soil pore space (also making earthworms happy to be there).

You can order seed from Johnny's Selected Seeds, Albion, MN 04910; Peaceful Valley Farm Supply, P.O. Box 2209, Grass Valley, CA 95945; Mellinger's, 2310 W. South Range Road, North Lima, OH 44452; or Pinetree Garden Seeds, Route 100, New Gloucester, MN 04260. Two and a half to three pounds of seed will cover 1,000 square feet (four ounces per 100 square feet). Cultivate the soil 2 to 3 inches deep and cover the seed lightly with soil by raking gently in. Then use the rake head to pat down the loosened, seeded ground.

FORGET THE STILL LIFE • I can't look at an eggplant without pondering the wonders of the universe. I used to pile them on my kitchen counter in baskets, gaze, and in a blink they'd start to wither. Eggplants need refrigeration, not admirers. They last for about 4 or 5 days, stored in a plastic bag in the refrigerator. Ditto for zucchini, though yellow summer squash generally lasts only 3 to 4 days.

❦ SEPTEMBER 8

Things work out. In the fall, when there is so much to do, we always seem to receive a long string of sunny, temperate days in which to complete our planting, digging, separating, moving, and pruning. For those of us lucky enough to experience a "real" fall, Indian summer— or Old Wives' Summer—provides the most stable weather of the year. Make your list of fall projects, and take your time to work in the garden. Tending to things during these weeks is especially good for the body and the soul.

BASIL UPDATE • Ah yes: basil. Not surprisingly, I have gotten pretty good at making pesto this year, and have satisfied many diners with this excellent basic recipe.

•••

PESTO

4 cups fresh basil leaves, washed and dried (all moisture should be
    blotted off)
6 large cloves of garlic, minced
⅔ cup extra virgin olive oil
1 teaspoon salt
Freshly ground black pepper to taste

Put the basil and the garlic in the bowl of a food processor. While the motor is running, drizzle in the oil through the feed tube and process until the leaves are all puréed. (You can do this in a blender the same basic way.)

Stir in the salt and pepper and then transfer to a jar or bowl. Cover and refrigerate for 2 to 3 days or freeze it.

Note: You can also add ground pine nuts and Parmesan cheese to this basic recipe.

•••

❦ S E P T E M B E R 9

The autumn crocus is not really a crocus at all, though it looks like one. *Colchicum autumnale*, also called meadow saffron, signals the beginning of early fall. It is beautiful, a deep pink, but not a color one might find in a starter fall garden. Just because the leaves are turning orange and red doesn't mean that blue and purple and pink don't have an important place in the fall garden. Many plants, some of them pink, save their best blooms for fall.

To broaden your color horizons (and link the meadow saffron to your garden picture), consider these plants which have a strong pres-

•••

ence in the fall: late-flowering roses, especially 'Mme Isaac Pereire'; Russian sage (*Perovskia atriplicifolia*); hybrid bluebeard (*Caryopteris x clandonensis*); catnip (*Nepeta nervosa* and *N. sibirica*); blue ceratostigma (*Ceratostigma plumbaginoides*); bush clover (*Lespedeza thunbergii*); Aster cordifolius and *A. lateriflorus* 'Horizontalis'—there are lots of asters to investigate; Japanese anemones (especially 'Honorine Jobert'). (See more fall perennials on page 222.)

SCRAPING CORN • Lots of recipes call for fresh corn, and using it in soufflés, fritters, salsas, and salads is part of the summer's last pleasures. Don't cut your fingers off trying to scrape corn. All you have to do is get the corn in a vertical position over a large bowl. Using a big sharp knife, slice straight down, cutting under the kernels (it takes a bit of practice not to decapitate the kernels). The juice is good to scrape off too, especially if you are making scalloped corn.

❦ SEPTEMBER 10

If you want to put in azaleas, a fall planting will give the root systems a good chance to grow and develop before summer. Azaleas like slightly acidic soil under partial shade. Use half peat moss and half sand to obtain the ideal planting medium. Most beginning gardeners make the mistake of planting azaleas too deep. The top of the root ball should be just level with the soil line or even slightly higher. Keep the soil moist.

Yellowing leaves with green veins indicate iron deficiency; you can spray iron chelate on them while making sure you're not overfertilizing with phosophorus (which would prevent the uptake of iron). Bronze-colored leaves are usually a sign of lace bug infestation; use insecticidal soap to get rid of these pests.

TAKE A GERANIUM CUTTING OR THE WHOLE POT INSIDE • Start taking cuttings from those prize plants you want to enjoy in future years. For example, if you are a geranium saver, cut off a healthy 4-inch stem and remove all but 3 leaves. Air-dry the stem for a day and then plant it in sterile potting soil and keep moist with water. By spring you should have a whole plant again—or some version of a plant. This usually works better than trying to save the whole plant.

But if you *do* want to save the whole plant, put the pots in a cool indoor sunny location (or a sunny garage window that is semiheated). When I save plants I cut them back but it is not altogether necessary. The cooler it is, the drier you should keep the plants. Don't fertilize them, of course. In the spring, trim them back, bring them out again, give them some fertilizer and a little bone meal, and you will be geranium happy.

NATURALIZING BULBS • If you have good soil and most importantly a fitting location, you can naturalize many of your bulbs with little effort. Naturalizing bulbs means letting them multiply informally on their own, under natural conditions. Sometimes bulbs will benefit from a top dressing of compost or 5-10-5 fertilizer in early spring, just when the tips show, and again in the fall, but that's about it.

The most important decision is placement. Snowdrops (*Galanthus nivalis*) for instance, will flourish and grow on the north side of a terrace or slope with little fuss, and will be there long after your children are grown. Winter aconite (*Eranthis hyemalis*) will naturalize beautifully in rock gardens or beds, but won't survive in grass. Excellent choices for naturalizing: grape hyacinths (*Muscari botryoides*), crocuses, Spanish bluebells (need a moist, shady location), daffodils (not under grass), glory-of-the-snow (*Chionodoxa luciliae*), and Siberian squill (*Scilla siberica*).

❦ S E P T E M B E R 1 1

When I first learned about tree planting, it was common wisdom to dig gigantic holes for your tree and shrub plantings, the wider and deeper the better, so the roots could wander happily where they would. Now we do it a little differently. When you get ready to put in that shrub or tree, dig your hole twice as wide, yes, but keep the depth flush with the root ball (it can even be an inch or so shallower than the root ball and mulched just to, but not touching, the trunk). Why? Because if you dig too deep the tree will sink as the soil settles, eventually becoming too deeply planted. (In the process, be sure there are no big rocks under your root ball.)

Another thing to look out for is air pockets. To eliminate air pockets when you plant a tree or a shrub, dig your hole, put in the plant, and fill in with dirt halfway up. Then rock the plant back and forth, left and right, to make sure it gets anchored properly. Fill the hole with more dirt—about three-quarters full—and water it well. Leave it for a good half hour and let the water ease down into the dirt. Tamp it down to make sure there are no air pockets, then fill it to the top.

DIVIDE YOUR DAYLILIES • Daylilies (*Hemerocallis*) can be divided about every 5 years and fall is the time to do it. You'll need to dig up the clump, then either slice it in half with a sharp spade or divide it in half with two spading forks. The first year after the division, the plants will be less prolific bloomers but the following year they will bloom profusely.

POPPING CORN IN THE MICROWAVE • If you have small popping-corn ears, experiment with your microwave. After the cobs have dried, put a whole one in a paper bag and roll it up loosely. Set the microwave on High for about 5 minutes—and pull it out when the popping sounds abate.

PEONY PROPAGATION • Peonies can last well over 50 years if you care for them properly. Early fall is a good time to propagate them. To do so, dig up the entire root system, pull it out, and locate the pink buds at the crowns. Take a knife and carefully cut through the root system so you have at least three buds on each of your new divided root balls. Plant the peony in a deep hole that has been nourished with aged manure, but make sure the plant itself stays close to the soil surface. Peonies should always be planted shallow. Cover the growth buds with just about an inch of soil, not more. Peonies like full sun in well-drained soil.

FIRST-TIME GARDENERS • *If this is your first pass at bulb arrangements, remember that planting a single variety en masse normally has a more desirable visual effect than interspersing several different kinds of bulbs.*

Are your perennials peeping "Divide me"? If such noises are emanating from your beds and borders, pick a cool morning and get the old spade out—and start dividing. This is an excellent period for taking those overcrowded perennials and giving them some badly needed space or a new home altogether.

Most perennials need to be divided and transplanted every 2 or 3 years. First dig the plant up, then take two spading forks and drive them both into the plant's center, slowly prying it apart. If it's really big, use the outer parts with the new growth for replanting and discard the center part of the old clump. You'll need leverage because many plants are really tough to separate. Add aged manure and compost to the new holes, as you go along.

Dividing plants is intimidating for beginners but it needn't be. Just practice on a plant you don't care much for; every plant after that will be easy.

PROTECT YOUR PUMPKINS • To protect your pumpkins from insect damage while still on the vine, carefully lift up the fruits and place roofing shingles under them. Salt hay works well, too.

STORING SWEET POTATOES • You'll need to get your sweet potatoes out of the ground before it gets too cold. Once you get them out, leave them on top of the soil for about 2 hours. Then take the tubers into a warm dry place—about 70 to 80 degrees—and leave them there for 2 weeks to cure. Finally, wrap each one in a newspaper and store them where they will get good air circulation and temperatures between 55 and 60 degrees (like your basement). Don't put them in the refrigerator or in a root cellar, or they'll get tough when you cook them.

RULE OF THUMB • With few exceptions, fall-blooming plants should be divided in the spring, spring bloomers should be divided just after they bloom, and summer bloomers should be divided in early fall. Share a division with a friend!

Onions' skins very thin,
Mild winter coming in.
Onions' skins thick and tough,
Coming winter cold and rough.
—Midwest saying

Brussels sprouts generally taste best when picked after the first frost, something I should have reminded you about the first week in June. Oh well. It's not a terrible thing to pick Brussels sprouts early, but if you do harvest during really hot weather they are going to be bitter. Other vegetables that taste better after a frost are carrots, kale, and parsnips.

LAWN CARE • If your lawn needs lime, you can apply it in the fall. The freezing and thawing cycles of winter allow lime to work into the soil nicely. Use pulverized limestone if you have a drop spreader; pelletized limestone if you have a rotary spreader.

To find out exactly how much you'll need, contact your local county extension service.

MASS PLANTINGS OF DAFFODILS • You can purchase smaller, No. 2 bulbs if you are doing mass plantings of daffodils. The blooms will be slightly smaller at first but in a mass situation it won't matter much.

ASPARAGUS REMINDER • In the fall, your mulched asparagus bed will benefit from some rock phosphate, greensand, and lime. Broadcast it right over the mulch and water it. If you have some good aged manure or compost, roll back the mulch, put a layer down, and pull the mulch back.

Fall insects will begin to chirp 6 weeks before a frost.

It's a little hard to believe we are already dragging plants indoors, but I find that a well-paced transition—especially for my herbs—is essential. Since you'll want to be snipping away on your herbs through the dormant winter months, the plants must be happy and well adjusted. Don't wait until the last minute, the night before the first frost forecast, to do all of your trimming, bug-inspecting, potting, and lugging.

Herbs that do pretty well indoors in a sunny window or on a light

*Bring in your herbs three weeks
before you turn on the heat.*

table include basil, chervil, marjoram, mint, oregano, parsley, rose-mary, lavender, chives, and sage. (Some herbs need to experience dor-mancy; see chives, page 193.) As a general rule, bring your herbs in about 3 weeks before you turn on the heat. Warm stuffy rooms will encourage disease and insect development; try to keep your herbs in temperatures between 55 and 70 degrees.

WHAT WAS HARDENED MUST NOW BE SOFT-ENED • Before you bring in pots of plants, place them in a pro-tected location with partial shade for a few days. Pick off any dead leaves and follow with a light rinse from a hose. If you spot disease, use an insecticidal soap. Only the healthiest plants should be brought indoors.

FIRST-TIME GARDENERS • For one of the earliest blooming flowers try planting Chionodoxa sardensis, *or glory-of-the-snow. In late winter or early spring you'll be rewarded with lavender-blue flowers perched atop a single stem often growing right next to melting snow. (Other* Chionodoxa *come in white, blue, purple, or pink.) Plant these hardy bulbs in northern zones early in the fall in well-drained soil under bright sun. They should be planted 2 or 3 inches apart and 3 inches deep. (In warm zones, glory-of-the-snow prefers a little shade and should be planted deeper.) After 3 years you may want to dig the bulbs up and separate them.*

SOFT TOMATOES SOLUTION • This is overripe tomato time, and there is an easy way to preserve them without having to wear a hairnet and work in a canning factory. Take your soft toma-toes and chop them up with cloves of garlic (according to taste). Cook covered in the microwave on High for 3 minutes, stirring twice. Pop them into plastic containers or freezer bags and use them in sauces, soups, stews.

Most of us still have some time before the first frost, but the gradual drop in temperatures is going to affect our fruits and vegetables, especially tomatoes. Tomatoes ripen most rapidly when temperatures are about 70 to 80 degrees. The rate slows when it hits 55 degrees and, below that, they suffer chilling injury. The best temperature for holding tomatoes (after they ripen) is 50 to 60 degrees. If only we all had little 55-degree storage bins in our kitchens—think what we could do!

Tomatoes don't need direct sunlight to ripen. I usually take the last green batch, wrap each fruit in a half sheet of newspaper, and leave them on shelves in a cool, dry spot in the basement. Other gardeners put their green tomatoes in plastic bags (see page 231 for a chat about stages of ripeness) and store them out of direct light in a cool place. If you store your ripening tomatoes in plastic freezer bags, make sure they are loosely packed. Open the bag after approximately 3 weeks to add more oxygen. A week or so later they should be ripe.

WHAT TO FERTILIZE NOW • For continuous blooms you can give diluted fertilizer to container plants and annuals monthly (or until they wither and die). Your spring- and summer-blooming perennials shouldn't be fertilized at this time. You can spray liquid seaweed regularly on all of your plants to help them prepare for the upcoming frosts.

MOVING CHRYSANTHEMUMS • You can move chryanthemums when they are still in bloom if you really have to. First moisten the soil lightly, then dig up the entire plant so it possesses a healthy root ball. When you transplant, firm the soil to make sure there are no air pockets. Water generously and shade with floating row cover (see page 325) for 2 days.

SOW PATCHES OF COVER CROPS • If you still have plenty of veggies in the ground but want to sow a cover crop (see pages 207–8) as soon as you can, use the "here and there" method. Sow here and there around the plants that are still growing in your garden. You can overseed now without fear of depriving your existing plants of nutritional needs. Tomatoes present a bit of a problem because they create so much shade. But most plants will allow enough light through to get your cover crops off to a good start. As you pull your plants in the weeks ahead, you can fill in empty spots with more cover crop seed.

❦ SEPTEMBER 16

You can encourage summer-season crops to keep producing by cutting off water and fertilizer. The lack of nutrients puts the plant in a final produce-and-die mode, and all of the energy will be directed to the fruit of the plant—not the foliage. With tomatoes, prune back the plant severely and cut off all flowers and tomatoes that have not reached the translucent green stage (deep green tomatoes will not mature after a hard freeze).

SHAPING UP YOUR LAWN • In September, weather conditions are optimal for seeding lawns in Northern zones. You can easily assess whatever damage was caused to your lawn during summer and seed accordingly. Also, weeds are relatively passive around this time, which makes your lawn more hospitable to new growth. In Southern zones, weeds are still pretty active, so it is better to do seeding in the spring or early summer. In either case, be sure to fertilize and lime, if required, before you seed.

If you are planning on starting a brand-new lawn, do it before serious leaf fall occurs.

CHRYSANTHEMUM CLINIC • If your chrysanthemums have no blooms and the leaves are grayish, you probably have a mildew problem. In the spring, dig up the affected plants and divide them. Good air circulation and lots of sun will lessen the chances that they get the mildew again.

RULE OF THUMB • When you are figuring out where to put broad-leafed evergreens, remember that generally speaking the bigger the leaf the more shade the plant can tolerate.

❦ SEPTEMBER 17

Part of fall gardening is about gearing up for the first frost, and no right-minded gardener would put his crops in the hands of the weatherman. In earlier days, farmers listened for the chirping patterns of katydids to predict fall frost, and did so with remarkable accuracy.

Descending temperatures numb the katydid (like so many other insects) and temporarily cut off the strength and duration of the call. You can hear it working through its stages: it becomes katie at 65 degrees, kate at 58 degrees, and then total silence when the temperature goes below 55 degrees. This year, listen for it. By the time you hear "Kate," a cool morning is in the making.

DON'T MAIL SEEDS IN ENVELOPES • Seeds from the garden, carefully saved from a favorite plant, make heartfelt gifts. If you mail some to friends be sure you put them in boxes. Even in thick padded envelopes seeds can get damaged from the weight of the mail.

BROCCOLI TALK • One cup of broccoli has twice as much vitamin C as a cup of fresh oranges, and almost as much calcium as a cup of milk. It contains 25 calories and ample amounts of vitamin A and E.

HOME CROPS HIT $18 BILLION • An estimate of the economic value of food produced in gardens in the U.S.—that's in gardens of people like you and me—is $18 billion. For perspective, that is the near equivalent of an entire U.S. corn crop.

> *Up from the meadows*
> *rich with corn*
> *Clear is the cool*
> *September Morn.*
> —John Greenleaf Whittier

❦ SEPTEMBER 18

Here in the Northeast, it takes me all season long to get an okra harvest and not without a few horticultural bribes. But it is worth it: *Abelmoschus's* blossoms are lovely to see, and the pods aren't half bad either.

Okra gets slimy when it is cooked with water, however, and it is not for all palates. Okra (and cactus, as it happens) contains sugars and acids that are linked in long mucilaginous chains. When you slice okra, it starts to ooze, and that ooze swells when you cook it in water, and then the heating process aggravates the whole situation. I admit that the slime is a definite drawback to this otherwise perfect vegetable.

There are ways to get around this: you can cook okra in butter or oil, or coat the okra in cornmeal and deep-fry it. Both methods will add serious fat to your diet, though the latter preparation is worth the health risks.

My family likes to skirt the slime and health issues altogether; they eat their okra pickled with hot red peppers. They like to eat the pickled okra when they are playing cards, and consider it good luck. I know it's strange, but we are strange people. Here's our recipe:

∙∙

LUCKY OKRA

Hot red peppers (1 for each jar)
Garlic (2 cloves for each jar)
3½ pounds of rinsed and dried small okra pods
Dill seeds (1 teaspoon for each jar)
2 cups white vinegar
4 cups water
⅓ cup salt

Place red peppers and garlic in hot sterilized jars. Remove part of the stem from each okra pod. Pack the okra into the jars. Add the dill seed. Put a metal spoon in each jar. (You will be pouring the vinegar water into the glass jars in a few minutes and the spoon will absorb the heat so the glass won't crack.) Combine vinegar, water, and salt in a saucepan; bring to a boil, and simmer for about 5 minutes. Pour over the okra. Remove the spoon. Tighten lids securely and let stand for several weeks. Refrigerate before serving.

∙∙

SOWING FALL CROPS • For tiny seeds that are difficult to sow, use an old-fashioned big-holed salt shaker and shake the little seeds into the garden. You'll get a much better distribution than you might by hand.

∙∙

GREENHOUSE FANTASY • About this time of year I ask myself what life would be like if I had a greenhouse. I am about four college educations away from a greenhouse, but for those who are a little closer, I have an address. Before you buy, send a check or money order for $1.50 to the Hobby Greenhouse Association, 8 Glen Terrace, Bedford, MA 01730. They have a list of about three dozen manufacturers with information on each company's products, along with tips on how to assess your own needs and make the best choice.

❧ S E P T E M B E R 1 9

Old friends are coming back into the house. The scented geraniums in containers have returned to my sunny dining room windows. They comprise a delightful small collection and now, back again, they take on a new, more important presence in my life.

To be honest, I forgot about them most of the summer. Their tiny blooms were easy to miss, and the more assertive flowers and vegetables and herbs in the garden competed for my interest in summer (especially the ubiquitous basil). But now they take center stage, and because they are a little leggy, I clip them often for salads of fruit, or for tea. If you have not sampled scented geranium leaves, give them a try. For a fresh fruit salad, add 1 or 2 teaspoons of rinsed, chopped scented geranium leaves for every 1 cup of sliced fruit. For a light and lovely tea, try this:

Scented Geranium Tea: In a large saucepan, combine 1 quarter of water with ½ cup rinsed, chopped scented geranium leaves and ¼ cup sugar. Bring the mixture to a boil rapidly, and then let it simmer for about 5 minutes. You might like more sugar if you like your tea well sweetened. Strain it and serve it hot, or let it cool and store it in a jar with a tight-fitting lid in the refrigerator. It will last for 2 days.

DAFFODILS AND GROUND COVER • Daffodils look beautiful springing forth from ground cover, but they do best with shallow-rooted plants like *Vinca* (periwinkle). They are not quite as successful amidst vigorous plants like ivy and pachysandra.

DON'T USE CHEAP GRASS SEED • If you are thinking of putting in some grass seed, don't go the bargain route—you'll end up with an inferior blend. Your local extension service will give you some advice on sowing times and the best blends for your area. Another source of information on your lawn is The Lawn Institute, Country Line Road, Box 108, Pleasant Hill, TN 38578.

KILLER SUNFLOWERS • All parts of the sunflower plant including the seed hulls contain an alleopathic chemical that is toxic to other plants. Some reports suggest that the seedhulls are toxic to *all* plants, which means if you have a bird feeder with sunflower seeds in the mix, you could have a problem. We have had birdseed (or should I say squirrel seed) cast all over our back garden, and from what I can assess, none of our plants suffered from sunflower alleopathy. Still, it's wise to keep the substance away from your plants and compost.

❧ SEPTEMBER 20

The fans are still whirring, but soon enough the nights will be getting longer and the temperatures will drop. If you live in a low-number zone, it's a good time to start gathering blankets, newspapers, paper bags, and burlap for the early frosts ahead. Blankets are excellent for large plants like cucumbers and tomatoes. Newspapers can be used for low-growing plants such as beans and watermelons. Grocery bags can be slipped over herbs and smaller plants and anchored with rocks. Use tarps on squash, melon, and pumpkins if a heavy frost is forecast.

GET SAMPLES FROM THE NURSERY • Make friends with the people at your favorite nursery. The trusted adviser at the nursery, along with the plumber who has no children to put through college, are two of the most valuable people one can know in life. At the nursery, I ask for "samples" and my friends are happy to comply. They allow me to "deadhead" numerous blooms from each plant I am interested in (always wear rubber bands on your wrist, they come in handy for "sample bouquets.") You take the samples home, walk around the garden, and see if they would look good here, or there, or not at all. It will stop you from making many errors in judgment about color and texture.

MORE FALL PERENNIALS • Here are a few plants to look for at your nursery right now. Some of them started blooming earlier in the summer, but they should all still be in bloom.

Aconitum (Monkshood)
Boltonia asteroides 'Snowbank'
Callirhoe (Poppy mallow)
Ceratostigma (Leadwort)
Chrysanthemum (Hardy chrysanthemum)
Cimicifuga spp. (Bugbane)
Eupatorium (Hardy ageratum)
Gelsemium rankinii (Yellow jessamine)
Helenium autumnale (Sneezeweed)
Helianthus angustifolius (Swamp sunflower)
Heliopsis
Liatris (Gayfeather)
Nepeta x faassenii (Catmint)
Physostegia (False dragonhead)
Sanguisorba (Canadian burnet)
Sedum sieboldii and S. spectabile (October plant and 'Autumn Joy')
Solidago species (Goldenrod)
Stokesia (Stokes' aster)

❦ SEPTEMBER 21

If the leaves are starting to fall, get them quickly to your compost heap. It's not good to have a lot of leaves blanketing your lawn, and your compost heap will benefit enormously. If you don't have a compost heap, this is an *ideal* time to start one. You don't need a fancy bin (although I did purchase one of those lightweight black plastic stacking contraptions and I really love it). You can just create an open-air heap if you don't want to get into buying or building one. There's so much great compost out there now: leaves, clippings, old straw, debris from your garden—don't waste it.

Leaves are your most valuable fall harvest.

FALL SOIL PREP FOR PERENNIAL BEDS • It's important to do some work in your perennial beds, and if you are dividing some of your plants, take the opportunity to pump up the soil at the same time. Perennial beds are tricky; you have to prepare the soil as best you can *around* the plants. Mix in organic material once or twice a year. One option is to spread a layer of rabbit pellets, a little bonemeal, and a little limestone (if your soil analysis calls for it) and then mulch on top of that. A great fall mulch is ground or shredded leaves, grass clippings, or compost which you can mix with coffee grounds or whatever other goodies you might be saving up. Don't pile up a lot of mulch next to the crowns of your plants.

BULBS FOR THE COTTAGE GARDEN

Muscari (Grape hyacinth)
Lilium candidum (Madonna lily) (can't plant now)
Narcissus poeticas (Poet's-eye narcissus)
Galanthus (Snowdrop)
Tulipa (Species tulips)
Lilium tigrinum (Tiger lily)
Polianthes tuberosa (Tuberose)

❧ S E P T E M B E R 2 2

If you've ever wanted to create a wildflower field, fall is the time to do it. Looking back, my one experience in trying to plant wildflowers was foolish: I followed the E-Z soil preparation directions on the fancy can, which said to till lightly, scatter seed, water, and that's it. I think three scrawny little plants made their way up the following spring.

David Baldwin, owner of Natural Gardening in California, gave me some pointers this time. Wildflowers aren't different from any other flowers; they need a good soil environment and all of the right conditions to thrive. The more you cultivate the soil, the more you weed, and the more you maintain proper moisture, the better the wildflowers will do. If you live outside the West you will need to work harder to get your wildflower gardens established. You've got to seriously prepare your soil. Weeding is key. After you broadcast the seed, Mr. Baldwin advises you work in a light layer of peat moss or potting soil or topsoil, especially if you are on a slope site. Once the seeds are moist, keep them that way. Mr. Baldwin advises Northern gardeners to wait until the soil temperature is 45 degrees to plant. Southern gardeners can plant almost any time in the fall. Also, if you are buying some of those canned mixes, check the ingredients on the label. Some of them contain filler, like clover. It is a good idea to have *some* grasses in your mix—I actually like clover—but it doesn't make sense to pay wildflower prices for grass seed filler. *If you are interested in doing more than "playing" with wildflowers, you should start with a few varieties that are known to do well in your area and develop your garden slowly, variety by variety.*

LATIN LESSON • Latin cues will help you know in an instant whether a plant is suited to your circumstance. Some of the words translate in an obvious way, but I listed them anyway, just for fun.

communis	growing in community	*nutans*	nodding
crassus	thick	*patens*	spreading
divaricata	spreading	*pendula*	hanging
elata	tall	*reptans, repens*	creeping
gigantea	giant	*robusta*	robusta
liana	climbing	*scandens*	climbing
minor	small	*suffructicosa*	shrubby
nana, pumila	dwarf	*tenua*	thin

Trees are light green
when the weather is fair;
They turn quite dark
when a storm's in the air.

Got some extra basil leaves? Small world. Frozen basil is a far cry from fresh basil, but it's better than throwing it on the compost heap. Here's a way to freeze herbs, and the results are better than satisfactory: First, pick your leaves; the morning is best. *Don't wash them.* Place them in either a plastic bag with a zipper lock or some airtight plastic containers and freeze them. They thaw out in no time but they don't look very attractive. Don't wash them while they are still frozen; wait until they are defrosted. The leaves will still be flavorful and good for cooking, especially in sauces.

GROUNDHOG DETERRENT • One gardener reports that groundhogs are put off by soiled kitty litter. If you put the freshly soiled litter down into the holes, making sure to locate all entrances and exits, the groundhogs will flee.

NICKED POTATOES • It's easy to nick and scrape potatoes in the unearthing process. If you don't want to cook all of your damaged potatoes at once, you can keep them in reasonably good shape by washing and peeling them, cutting them into chunks, and storing them covered with water in plastic containers. Put on a tight-fitting lid and store in the refrigerator for up to a week.

Amazingly, they will not turn spongy or brown. Save the water for another use, as many of the vitamins will have leached out.

CORN CAKES • Well, the corn is still coming but slowly now. We're a bit sated, if that is possible. But on Sunday afternoons in September, we find enormous pleasure in a plate of corn cakes. The children like them with syrup. I like them with grated Monterey Jack cheese and cilantro salsa. There are also wonderful next door to some pan-fried trout and sliced tomatoes.

CORN CAKES ANY WAY YOU LIKE THEM

4 eggs
½ cup milk
4 cups corn kernels, blanched
½ cup corn flour (see Note)
2 teaspoons baking powder
Salt and pepper to taste
8 tablespoons (1 stick) unsalted butter

Separate the eggs. Beat the yolks and mix in the milk and corn. Stir in the flour mixed with the baking powder, salt, and pepper. In a separate bowl, beat the egg whites until stiff. Gently fold the whites into the corn mixture.

In a small 6-inch skillet, melt a tablespoon of the butter. When the butter is hot, use a measuring cup or ladle to add about ½ cup of the mixture and swirl evenly (as you would in making an omelet). When it is golden brown on one side, flip it. Cook until golden brown on the other side and repeat for all cakes. Serve your diners as the cakes come up, one at a time. Makes 8 cakes.

Note: Corn flour (masa) is not cornmeal. You can find it at health food stores or substitute unbleached white flour.

Corn is as comfortable under snow as an old man under his fur coat.

❦ S E P T E M B E R   2 4

LIBRA, September 24 to October 23—*Good for sowing flower seeds but bad for sowing fruit*

When I first saw ornamental cabbages and kale I found them a bit ridiculous—green and purple and inedible; I just couldn't understand them. Now they are one of my favorite plants, especially as they

move into the chill of winter and become more complex and brooding. When they are frozen and dusted with snow, the cabbage ro-
settes are hauntingly beautiful and the crinkled leaves of kale lovely
even in defeat. The cabbages and kale are especially appealing in urns
and window boxes, and in spots in the garden which you will view
on winter walks.

FALL ANNUALS TO PLANT

Pansies (*Viola tricolor hortensis*)
Ornamental kale (*Brassica oleracea*)
Ornamental cabbage

ABOUT SAFFRON • It takes over 4,000 crocus blooms to make
an ounce of saffron. The saffron crocus (*Crocus sativus*) is the true crocus, and it is the stigma that is used to make saffron. It is not the
same as the autumn crocus (*Colchicum*), which is poisonous.

❦ SEPTEMBER 25

Nature magazine reports that a team of researchers from England and
New Zealand working with tomato plants discovered that when a leaf
on the plant is devoured by an insect, it sends out electrical signals
to warn the other leaves. The other leaves start producing proteinase
inhibitors, which interfere with the insects' digestive systems.

ADD VISUAL INTEREST TO FOUNDATION PLANT-
INGS • Foundation plantings can look really boring, especially the
"boxwood special" favored by many builders. One way to add some
texture and softness is to expand your bed and add interesting plants
in the front. For instance, the addition of a few feet of ground cover
in front of a boxwood adds new dimension and interest with little effort. A winding path or a bench with drifting ground cover can
soften the look. If the shrubbery is less rigid than boxwood (like azalea or abelia), you might add a new perennial border.

CAVEAT EMPTOR • Certain bulbs sold by nurseries are collected from wild habitats and are thought to be at risk for overcollection. Some of them are well known, others less known—but if you are concerned about conservation you should check carefully to see if your bulbs were collected or propagated commercially. The bulbs to be concerned about are:

Narcissus (*N. triandrus, N. asturiensis, N. cyclamineus*)
Sternbergia spp.
Erythronium
Eranthis hyemalis, E. celicica (Winter aconite)
Leucojum spp. (Snowflake)
Galanthus elwesii (Giant snowdrop)

❧ S E P T E M B E R 2 6

My first fall digging experience wasn't pleasant. I was in another world—dig, dig, hum, hum, dig, dig—when I realized that I had unearthed hundreds of earthworms. They didn't budge when I poked them with a stick. I was afraid that by exposing them to the cold, I had killed them. Covering each one with dirt seemed a bit melodramatic but I didn't know what else to do.

As it happens, they all wiggled back to a warmer place down below. If it had been freezing outside, the temperature *would* have killed the worms and their eggs. The reason the worms seemed so lifeless is that they are cold-blooded, and take on the temperature of the atmosphere around them. It was a pretty cool afternoon, and they had slowed down to a near halt.

Just remember: If it's too cold for you, it's too cold for your worms. Your worms will be fine as long as the temperature will remain above freezing for several hours after you complete your work. This gives them time to burrow home.

LET THEM EAT CORN • Not all squirrels chomp on garden produce, but once they figure out that your garden is a source, they can be almost impossible to get rid of. You can try to lure them out of the garden by setting our baskets of whole corn kernels *away* from your garden. The corn can be purchased at a farm supply center.

As the days wind down, your plants are beginning their hardening process. Woodies, especially, which have shifted from foliage and flower production will soon begin to develop their winter protection and storage systems. Don't fertilize or prune your woodies or you will confuse them. They need to slow down and prepare for the winter ahead.

Interestingly, established woodies don't take their cues to harden from temperatures but by a more reliable indicator: the changing length of the day.

SPRING HARVEST PLANTINGS • Northerners: If you have a cold frame or can thick-mulch through the winter, you can plant a number of crops for spring provided you get the plants in the ground and established before cold weather sets in. You can plant kale, garlic, chervil, spinach, parsley, and lettuce for early spring harvests. Keep them in the cold frame until the temperatures reach 40 degrees in the spring. Make sure they are watered but not soggy. Southerners can sow these crops and grow them throughout the winter, adding peas and fava beans to the list.

FISH TANK FERTILIZER • When you clean your fish tank out, pour all of the nutritious waste water into your garden.

I long for the bulbs to arrive, for early autumn chores are melancholy, but the planting of the bulbs is the work of hope and always thrilling.
                                                                    —May Sarton

My annuals were so gorgeous this summer I feel coldhearted turning them into something as anonymous as compost. I will take clippings of what I can, give away bouquets, make some potpourri, and dry some. I like to make body powder with my early autumn blossoms—it makes a great gift. Dry a bowl of petals and then—using a mortar and pestle—grind the petals into a fine powder. Add ½ cup of the ground petals to 1½ cups of household cornstarch and you have a wonderful body powder, much better than talc, and a sweet remembrance of summer. You can make your own body powder using any petal; just make certain you and your friends are not sensitive to that particular plant. Mix in a ratio of 3 to 1, cornstarch to petals. Store the powder in an attractive box or tin.

SEED STORAGE • Saving seed in the freezer increases its life expectancy tenfold, according to Kent Whealy, director of the Seed Savers Exchange in Decorah, Iowa. This is not significant for people who use their seeds in a couple of seasons, but for gardeners who are preserving an heirloom seed or seeds from an outstanding plant in the garden, this can make a serious difference. Make sure you dry your seeds completely before storing in the freezer. For large seeds, Whealy suggests smashing the seed with a hammer to see if it is dry. Dry seeds will shatter, and seeds that still contain moisture will give and bend. Jars with rubber seals are best for freezer storage.

FALL DIGGING GOOD FOR CLAY SOIL • The benefits of fall digging are especially important for heavy clay soils. If you dig now, the soil will be much easier to work with after the freezing period. The freezing and thawing action will continue to loosen up the soil structure.

IDLE LAND • Ideally, we would give our vegetable gardens a break every five years. If you can spare a plot, plant a cover crop on it during its ideal year to build up soil and nitrogen reserves, and to interrupt disease and pest cycles. Fall is an excellent time to plant.

It's time to start guessing how many paper bags of green tomatoes we're going to end up with this year. In order to make this calculation, you need to understand that all green tomatoes are not the same. Green tomatoes go through a series of stages in the ripening process, and once you become attuned to the various shades of green, you can figure out when to harvest and the best way to use or store the tomatoes.

Basically, a green tomato is either mature or immature. You can tell that a tomato on the vine is mature when it does not increase its size for 3 to 5 days. An immature green tomato is still involved in growth, and if you pick it early, it may never ripen, whereas a mature green tomato will ripen after it is picked.

A mature green tomato changes color from deep green to lime to yellow, followed by streaks of light pink. When a tomato begins to turn pink it is called a "breaker," and at this point it is able to ripen off the vine without a problem.

Breakers should ripen in about 10 days. The other green tomatoes are going to take much longer to ripen and not all of them are going to be worth the wait. This is why it is important to accept some green tomatoes for what they are. Think of them as an entirely different fruit, er, vegetable. Remember that they are better for you: green tomatoes have 30 percent more vitamin C than red ones, along with more calcium and phosphorus. Use them in salsas, stews, pickles, and whenever a recipe calls for tart apples. Try the recipe on the next page.

FRIED GREEN TOMATOES

6 medium green tomatoes, cut in ¼-inch slices
1½ cups buttermilk
1 cup yellow cornmeal
½ cup unbleached flour
1 tablespoon salt
Freshly ground pepper
2 teaspoons cayenne, or to taste
¼ cup peanut oil
¼ cup vegetable oil

Dip the sliced tomatoes in buttermilk. In a separate bowl, mix the cornmeal, flour, and seasonings together. Dredge the tomatoes in the cornmeal mixture and lay in a single layer on a platter. Heat the oils in a very large frying pan. Sauté the tomatoes over medium heat until golden on each side. Drain on paper towels and serve immediately.

If, while working in the garden your rake falls prong upwards, there will be heavy rain next day.

❧ SEPTEMBER 30

Was this your first garden? Was it extraordinary? Four-foot zinnias? Gigantic tomatoes? Not a pest or disease in sight? In fact, you are wondering what all of the hand wringing about mulch and compost and pH is for?

Well, don't get too smug, because many first-year vegetable gardens are just short of atomic. Others are complete duds—it totally depends on your soil. But there's generally not a lot in between. If you were lucky enough to have a fabulous garden, your soil this season may well be as pure and nutritious as it could be. Think about it: your garden hasn't had its nutrients depleted before—no "takers" around to throw the soil off balance. Furthermore, the cabbage loopers had no idea you were going to plant some nice leafy green heads. Next year, guaranteed, they or some other interested party will be there for lunch, every day.

If this is your first-year garden, be sure to treat your dirt like royalty this fall: make any amendments needed and build up your compost reserves. You won't be disappointed in your second-year garden if you follow the simple principles of rotation, soil pH, mulching, and compost.

ROOT PRUNING • If you have container plants that have gotten out of control, do some root pruning. Cut back no more than one-third of the tips of the roots, and then put the plant back in the same size pot with more soil. Root pruning is also a good technique for shrubs and vines in certain situations, but it's a slightly more complex operation. The only time you should *not* root prune is midsummer, when a plant is growing strong.

GARLIC RECYCLING • If you have old grocery-store garlic and it has sprouted you can separate the cloves and plant them snugly together in a pot. Snip the young shoots that come up and toss them into salads or onto baked potatoes.

Perennial: Any plant which, had it lived, would have bloomed year after year.
—Henry Beard and Roy McKie

❦ October ❦

Flower of the Month: Calendula

❦ O C T O B E R 1

Okay, so I got impatient this year and pulled out my tomato plants early. I felt guilty about the first few plants but then I really got into the joys of yanking. The green tomatoes are now wrapped and in the basement, the vines are in the compost, R.I.P., and best of all, I can see my dirt again! What a sensation it was to pull back the salt hay and *see dirt*. Then my husband gave me my birthday present: a couple of wheelbarrows piled high with his late summer compost. What a guy.

Of course, in my zealousness to see a patch of dirt again (and to get the gift-wrapped compost in) I almost forgot to test the soil—and testing is really best done in the fall, after the soil is depleted. Now is the time to test your soil so any amendments you make can kick in over the course of the winter (second best time to test it is in early spring, after the soil has had a chance to dry). Try to get a test in over the next week or so (see directions on page 235).

· ·

TREES FOR STRIKING FALL COLOR

· ·

Red maple (*Acer rubrum*)
Sugar maple (*Acer saccharum*)
White oak (*Quercus alba*)
Scarlet oak (*Quercus coccinea*)

Pin oak (*Quercus palustris*)
Sour gum (*Nyssa sinensis*)
White ash (*Fraxinus americana*)

· ·

LOUD BUZZ: BRING INDOOR PLANTS BACK IN-SIDE • For colder zones, this the final bell on the tender houseplants that need to make their way back inside. Don't move them directly indoors. Move them to a shadier spot outdoors first—so they can become acclimated to the inevitably darker, cooler environment.

Everything that slows us down and forces patience, everything that sets us back into the slow cycles of nature, is a help. Gardening is an instrument of grace.

—May Sarton

❧ OCTOBER 2

Ready for that soil test? If this is your first time, might as well do it right. The key is to make sure that your soil sample represents your soil. Divide your property up logically.

In my case, there are four general areas: my rhododendron-azalea-bulb borders, my vegetable-herb bed, my perennial borders, and the lawn. So I would need four different tests. Well, to be honest, I've never tested the lawn. Anyway, get four or five samples from a single area—like the perennial borders, digging about 6 inches down. Make sure you get nice clean dirt—no leaves or twigs. Don't dig near compost heaps or walls, obviously. Put your four or five samples in a clean bucket (tools should be clean, too). Then really mix it up well so as to have a representative sample. You'll need about a cup of dirt for a good analysis if you send it off to a lab. If you do test your lawn, you don't have to dig as deep—2 inches will do. *In autumn, test for pH, phosphate, and potash if you are planning to add slow-acting or organic fertilizers. Check out the nitrogen if you like, but it can be easily lost from the soil over the winter, so be sure to check again in the spring.*

MORE DIRT ON SOIL TESTS • You can get soil testing kits from your local agricultural extension service, or send your soil samples to a private laboratory. The extension service will give you precise directions for gathering what you need in the way of samples. Once they test your soil, they will give you a detailed briefing on the levels of your major nutrients (nitrogen, phosphorus, and potassium); secondary nutrients (magnesium, manganese, and copper); trace elements (boron, calcium, iron, molydenum, sulfur, and zinc). You will also receive an assessment of the organic matter in your garden.

SEEDS NOT WORTH SAVING • Don't save seeds from your hybrid plants. They will never bear out true. Hybrid plants are frequently labeled as F1 in catalogues. They are bred to improve flavor and disease resistance but they don't carry on to the next generation.

❦ OCTOBER 3

Here's a neat trick. Orange growers in Florida protect their orange blossoms from ruin by misting their trees the evening before a predicted frost. (Generally, they spray all night long.) Some home gardeners have applied this tactic to their own turf; a Tennessee man turned a light spray on his 30-foot pink magnolia for several hours the night before a hard frost. The next day, his blossoms were picture-perfect while the rest of the neighborhood's had turned brown. Another gardener in a Southern zone was able to keep apple, peach, and azalea blooms intact in this fashion; his roses and mums made it to Christmas.

PLANTING BARE-ROOT SHRUBS AND TREES • Fall planting of bare-root shrubs and trees can be a delicate affair. If you live in the Northeast or Midwest, you probably should arrange to plant in the spring—especially oaks, magnolias, poplars, and sour gums, among others. Other trees that might not survive a fall planting are flowering dogwoods, hawthorns, birch, and fruit trees like peach, cherry, and other stone fruits.

FIRST-TIME BULB PLANTERS • The general rule is to plant bulbs about three times as deep as they are tall (the bulbs, not the plants). This goes for most bulbs, though tulips should go about 12 inches down if you want them to come back for a second year or more. Don't plant your bulbs in singles. One tulip here or there looks foolish. Also, plant in odd sets. It is much more natural to see 5 or 7

With tiny bulbs, toss the bulbs gently and plant them where they land for a natural-looking display.

or 9 bulbs planted together than the same bulbs in even sets. With tiny bulbs you can toss the bulbs gently and plant them where they land to achieve an uncontrived appearance.

VEGETABLES TOO COMMON • Certain vegetables were considered so easy to grow that colonists in India were not permitted to eat turnips, garlic, or onions. Since peasants could grow them in their own backyards they were "not suitable" for aristocratic consumption.

❧ O C T O B E R 4
St. Francis's Day

St. Francis of Assisi is one of the best-loved saints in history, and he figures as a statue in many American gardens, granite arms open, head slightly tilted, serene. The world was a garden to Francis, intimate and full of friends, not the least of whom were the sun, the moon, and birds. He is the patron of those who love nature.

TO PROTECT YOUR BULBS FROM NIBBLERS • Bulb planting is hard, satisfying work and nothing (aside from gratitude) can bring a gardener to his knees like half-eaten flower bulbs. If your bulbs were devoured by animals last year, try planting them *without* any bonemeal. If you are doing mass plantings, you can also lay a wire screen or hardware cloth over the bulbs and remove it in early spring.

237

Another tip is to soak your bulbs in Ropel, a bitter-tasting deer repellent available in garden stores. Let the bulbs dry thoroughly (important), then plant them as usual. This brew is also being marketed as a spray to protect women against rapists, so it must be pretty disgusting. By the way, don't worry about your daffodils—they contain arsenic, and rodents will leave them alone.

KEEP PLANTS AND SHRUBS WATERED • If this has been a dry fall, make sure your shrubs are well watered before the ground freezes.

ONION HARVESTING • Don't cut off the tops of your onions after you've harvested them. They need to dry just like the bulb itself. French-braid the dried tops together, weaving a strong piece of twine throughout the braid for reinforcement. Keep in a cool, dry place.

RHUBARB REMINDER • Divide and replant rhubarb plants, sharing extra plants with your friends.

> *Where there is hatred, let me sow love....*
> —St. Francis Prayer

❦ OCTOBER 5

I am not a big fan of those leaf blower things, though I will concede they are efficient. At 8 A.M. our neighborhood is filled with blower noise, and this month is generally the worst. You or your lawn man might be neatniks, but don't get overzealous. The leaves in your beds and borders can stay. Don't rake or blow the fallen leaves from your rhododendron and azalea plantings especially. They will form a natural protective mulch and will provide a shelter for earthworms.

By the way, if your rhodie leaves are looking a bit worse for the wear, show a leaf to someone knowledgeable at your nursery to make sure the plants don't need more iron. For good-looking rhododendrons and azaleas next spring, give them a little top feeding of Hollytone or a similar product this fall; it will work its way into the plants' systems during the winter. Keep them watered, too.

COMPOST YOUR WEAK SOIL • If you have soil that is too high in clay content or too sandy, you should apply serious amounts of compost every fall until you get it in balance. About 3 to 4 inches applied at this time of year can make a world of difference. Organic fertilizer is also a good addition.

WEAR GLOVES WHEN PLANTING BULBS • Some people get "lily rash" from planting certain bulbs, particularly narcissus and hyacinths. Wear gloves.

DRAIN YOUR MOWER • Gas can become stale and break down after a while—gumming up the inside of your carburetor. You should empty your gas tank at the end of the season and fill it with fresh gas at the beginning of the season. To completely drain your mower, rider, or tractor of gas, first empty the fuel tank, according to the instructions in your owner's manual. Then run the engine until it peters out.

> *Now Autumn's fire burns slowly along the woods.*
> —William Allingham

❦ OCTOBER 6

You might want to clean up some of the mess in your perennial bed, but restraint is the better part of valor now. Besides, a host of plants are just now bursting forth. Asters light the garden anew, and chrysanthemums are having their glorious say. The garden is far from over. Your spent annuals, of course, can go, but your perennials need to be completely dormant before you begin to remove foliage to just above ground level. This may range from November to January, depending on which zone you live in.

The reason you need to leave the foliage alone is that as a general rule the leaves will continue to feed the root system throughout the fall. You can cut back the flowering stems and trim some of the most unsightly leaves, but mostly you should leave well enough alone until the leaves are frost-killed. With winter-hardy plants (like true lilies), don't even cut back the flowering stems; let the foliage brown and die on its own.

Some perennials you don't need to cut back at all. I don't touch my few *Astilbe* plants because the "feathers" look great all dried up over the winter. Some perennials with woody bases shouldn't be cut back severely until you see new growth at the base. If individual plants are in question, get some advice form your most trusted nursery person.

Anyway, it's fall. The fading leaves form an exquisite tapestry, and look best crumbling as they will, among the autumn blooms.

DAHLIA REMINDER • Wait until frost has blackened the foliage on your dahlias before digging, drying, and storing the tubers. Don't break off any of the tubers that radiate from the center when you dig up the plant. (You can divide your tubers in mid- or late spring if you want more plants.) It's best to let the tubers dry out for a few days before storing them. Sprinkle with bulb dust if you are concerned about disease. Dahlias should be stored at a temperature of between 35 and 50 degrees in a cool place like a garage or basement, and covered with damp sand or peat moss.

Sawdust also is a good storage medium. Cover the tubers with sawdust and store in cardboard boxes in a damp basement. (Leave cartons open so the sawdust doesn't dry out.)

❦ O C T O B E R 7

So what worked for you this time? October is when gardeners can pause and with the previous season fresh in mind say this worked, that I will never try again, and so on. It would be really worthwhile to take an early-morning stroll through your garden sometime in the next week and look at it squarely, soberly, without the passion of the moment, the confusion of January catalogues and rows of perennials staring at you at the nursery. Write down your impressions. Save them for January armchair gardening.

CONTAINER CLEANUP • Once your container plants are frost-killed (or whenever you tire of looking at them in their end-of-the-story state), remove them from their containers. The soil can be kept for next year; make sure it is bone dry and then simply cover it with some plastic to keep out the debris and to prevent it from getting waterlogged over the winter. Scrub empty pots and turn them up-side down; stack according to size.

DIG UP TENDER BULBS • Reminder to dig up tender bulbs before the ground freezes. Dry bulbs such as gladioli, then store them over winter in a cool area, making sure they do not freeze.

Even if everything is left undone, everyone must make time to sit still and watch the leaves turn.
—Elizabeth Lawrence

❧ OCTOBER 8

Note to the weather gods: we'd like sunny days followed by cool (below 45 degrees) nights. These are the conditions that generate the most striking fall foliage—which means vivid color on everything from the papery fading hostas in the border to blazing sugar maples in the yard. I adore watching my perennials transformed by autumn, and for many ornamental grasses, of course, this is the moment. Three factors control autumn leaf color: temperatures, the amount of sunshine, and the sugar formation in the leaves. *Rain, rain, go away.*

DON'T PICK YOUR GOURDS BEFORE THEIR TIME • Before you pick your gourds off the vine be sure they have completely matured. Gourds can be harvested when they are hard to the touch or at the first sign of frost. In addition, if the gourd is dry and the stem has withered, it is ready for picking. Cut your gourds with a sharp knife and leave at least 5 or 6 inches of stem with the gourd. Wipe off any moisture, handling very carefully. Don't wash or disinfect your gourds. You can scrape the mold off with a knife. Air-dry them on a rack until they get really hard and feel light when you pick them up. It could take anywhere from 1 month to half a year! You can shellac or varnish the small ornamentals; eventually they will rot no matter what you do.

BE ON THE ALERT FOR TEMPERATURE DIVES • If your plants experience a sudden drop in temperature before they reach their dormancy stage, both the pith inside a branch and the cambium tissue deep inside a bud will die. Each of these tissues is essential for new spring growth. Plants need a slow, gradual drop in temperature to give them enough time to reduce their moisture content and to store nutrients that will sustain them through the winter.

You're supposed to get tired planting bulbs. But it's an agreeable tiredness.
—Gail Godwin

❦ O C T O B E R 9

Most gardeners hold off on fertilizer after midsummer. Encouraging a plant to grow only to get slapped down by frost makes no sense. There is, however, a trick for fertilizing needy plants that can give a subtle, worthwhile boost without stimulating too much growth.

All you do is apply a top dressing of leaf mold or some other organic matter *after* the first frost.

Leaf mold is simple to make. Just build a bin 4 feet square with chicken wire stapled to treated 2-by-4s driven into the ground. Pile on the leaves. Get the local leaf-picker-upper guys to dump your neighbor's leaves in your yard, near your pile! Smash them down and water them periodically. If you're lucky, the leaves will decompose quickly—in time for you to apply to your garden. If they don't break down for fall use, you'll still have some wonderfully nutritious organic matter for spring.

FIRST-TIME GARDENERS • *While fall is an excellent time to transplant the majority of perennials, be careful not to transplant any marginally hardy plants. Also avoid transplanting your fall-blooming perennials if this project can wait until spring.*

FROST WARNINGS • The presence of clouds and wind lessen the chances of a hard frost. To assess cloud cover, look at the sky. To assess the wind, take a long strip of lightweight plastic and hang it on a tree. As long as it flutters about a foot in either direction, you shouldn't have to worry about frost.

October has twenty-one fair days.

❦ OCTOBER 10

If you have some extraordinary foliage this year and would like to bring it inside, you can preserve some branches for display in vases. The key is to select your branches when the leaves are at peak color—and before they start to wilt. Take a knife and peel several inches of bark off the branch beginning at the base. Make little cuts into the peeled part of the branch so it will be able to absorb lots of water. Create a well-mixed solution of boiling water and glycerine, in a 2 to 1 ratio—e.g., 4 cups of boiling water to 2 cups of glycerine. When the solution is lukewarm, put the branches in. The exposed (peeled) branch parts should be covered with the solution. Let the branches sit there, adding more solution if necessary to keep the branches covered. This process will stop the leaves from dropping. In about a week or so the branch and your leaves should be preserved.

COLD FRAME PROTECTION • Cold frames need protection, too. When it gets really cold, put old rugs or blankets on top of the cold frame to keep the plants from freezing. Also, keep your cold frame next to the south-facing side of a building, if possible.

TOADSTOOL ELIMINATOR • I like to look at toadstools, but if they seem to be taking over, rake them. Then spray with a combination of 1 rounded tablespoon of baking soda and 1 teaspoon of liquid soap or vegetable oil mixed with a gallon of water.

DOOR CLOSED ON PERENNIAL PLANTINGS • You should finish up your perennial plantings once the leaves start falling. Pretty soon it will be too late to plant safely unless you have really light, warm, well-drained soil.

The tints of autumn—a mighty flower garden blossoming under the spell of the enchanter, Frost.

—John Greenleaf Whittier

Once your pumpkins are completely orange you can harvest them. Use shears on the stem to prevent rot. If you are already full of pumpkin pie, seeds, bread, and muffins, you can delay harvesting the rest of your crop for a while. Just put a tarp over the plants if you have a frost. If a hard freeze does occur, you'll have to harvest your pumpkins or they will turn an ugly black.

Pumpkins are best stored in cool, dry conditions. After harvesting, allow them to cure in warm, dry temperatures for about two weeks. Then store at about 55 degrees, in a corner of a heated basement (away from the furnace, of course), in an enclosed porch, or even your attic, once the temperatures drop.

WINDOW BOX MAINTENANCE • Replace those spent annuals in window boxes and other containers with heaths, conifers, small broad-leafed evergreens, and dwarf winter-flowering shrubs.

CHRYSANTHEMUM REMINDER • Chrysanthemums' foliage can be cut back as close to the ground as possible after the first killing frost—or you can wait until next spring. Stems or leaves that are diseased in any way should be burned. When the soil freezes, mulch with a layer of dried leaves and follow with a cover of evergreen branches. Where I live, chrysanthemums don't have a prayer of surviving without mulch.

Your goal in putting the chrysanthemums to bed is to minimize root damage. If you notice water standing in the bed, take measures now to improve drainage (add some sand, provide a drain, raise the level of the bed). Mums that suffer severe root damage often change color or revert. Crowded plants also provoke color disturbances.

DID YOU HAVE A GRASSHOPPER PROBLEM THIS YEAR? • If you were plagued by grasshoppers, you should till your soil well after the final harvest. Egg clusters are often destroyed once they are exposed to the air.

CLEAN TOMATO STAKES AND CAGES • Used tomato stakes and cages can carry disease into the next season. Wipe off the soil and other residue. Then dip the supports into a 10 percent bleach solution. Leave the bleach on for about 5 minutes and then rinse well. Bacterial spot, bacterial canker, bacterial speck, fusarium wilt, and early blight all can come back to haunt your garden unless your supports are cleaned properly.

Of all man's works of art, a cathedral is greatest. A vast and majestic tree is greater than that.

—Henry Ward Beecher

❦ O C T O B E R   1 2
Columbus Day

Let historians argue about Columbus into the wee hours. All I know is that *before* Columbus's voyage to the New World, eating on this planet was a bland proposition. Columbus is credited with discovering plants from the genus *Capsicum*, aka hot peppers (though he thought he had discovered peppercorn plants, which in his day were so highly valued they were used as currency). The hot peppers quickly spread throughout the world, and his discovery radically changed the cuisine of India, Southeast Asia, and North Africa.

MOSS GARDEN MAINTENANCE • If you want to get fall leaves and debris out of your small moss and rock gardens, use a little whisk broom or child's broom to carefully clear out the accumulations. For larger gardens, you can use an ordinary household broom, but do so with a light touch.

NO WEEDS IN THE COMPOST, PLEASE • Unless your compost is really cooking, don't put any weeds in it right now. They'll boomerang back in the spring. But do weed energetically and get the garden looking clean and orderly.

Another no-no for compost bins is diseased plants. While a really sizzling compost heap will burn up most diseased weeds, there are a few that can survive even the hottest heap. Any branch or leaf that looks sickly should go in the trash.

PLANT YOUR GARLIC • Today is the traditional day to plant garlic in the North. Southerners plant garlic traditionally on Thanksgiving Day. For more about planting garlic, see page 255.

KEEP YOUR GARDEN WATERED • As you enter the cold season, don't let your garden dry out. Moist soil retains a lot of the sun's heat and in fact dispatches the retained heat almost on a time-release basis. Keep the top 12 inches consistently moist—not soggy, of course—for the best hedge against frost.

When you are not planting bulbs, digging up bindweed roots, rooting out poke-weed, soaking bamboo, there are still other tasks. Thousands of them. You are terri-bly behind.

—Henry Mitchell

❦ O C T O B E R   1 3

If the idea of a live Christmas tree appeals to you, now is the time to pick a spot in the yard for it. Call your nursery and discuss the kind of tree you'd like to grow, and before the ground freezes do some soil preparation.

You can prepare the hole once you estimate the size of the root ball. Put the excavated soil in plastic bags and store in the garage or some other sheltered area. Cover the hole with plywood. Forget about it until December.

Okay, it's December. (Time flies when you're planning for live Christmas trees.) When you get the tree, it should spend only 3 or 4 days indoors, decorated, and you should take pains to keep it away from radiators. Keep the ball watered (you can put it in a big galvanized steel laundry tub with good results). Important: never let the ball dry out. After the holidays, put the tree in the garage or another cool, sheltered spot for a few days to reacquaint it with the cold, keeping it in a tub with ample water. When you are ready to plant, untie the burlap and pull it away from the trunk (the burlap will eventually rot). Water the hole well, and put some of the earlier collected soil back into the hole. Plant the tree when the temperature is above freezing, and then mulch it. Water the tree every few days if the temperature continues to be above freezing.

FIRST-TIME GARDENERS • *When you plant bulbs with bone meal, make sure the bone meal comes in contact with the roots of the bulb. Put the bone meal at the bottom of the hole, and nest the bulb directly on top. Otherwise the bone meal will have no effect.*

❦ OCTOBER 14

I know you are busy transplanting, cleaning, weeding, and planting— but this is a terrific time of year to put in or move some evergreens. We are going to have a big evergreen moving day soon, and I like the fact that the evergreens will be in before winter, so I can see the changed beds in their bare form. With the exception of some junipers and a few pines, almost all evergreens require a great deal of water throughout the growing season, so monitor transplants well. If you do put in some evergreens make sure you carefully gauge their size at maturity. That charming little conifer you want to plant next to the house will grow up someday and could crack your foundation if it's planted too close.

LET EARTHWORMS DO WINTER SUBSOIL DUTY • If your dirt needs aeration, don't mulch heavily this fall. A light mulch that leaves the topsoil largely unprotected will encourage earthworms to go deeper into your soil to survive the frost, giving your subsoil an excellent workout.

DON'T MULCH YOUR ROSES TOO EARLY • It's a good idea to mulch your roses for the winter, but do so after the ground freezes. What you don't want to do is mulch too early. For roses, the purpose of the mulch is not to keep the soil warm but to keep it from thawing and heaving during the winter. When the time comes, mound soil about 8 to 10 inches deep around the base of the roses. If necessary, tie up your climbing roses against the wind.

TIME TO THINK ABOUT INDOOR FORCING • I hope you saved some bulbs for indoor forcing. Believe me, you'll be glad you did when the dregs of January and February roll around. Depending on the species, allow 10 to 12 weeks at 40 degrees to get decent rooting.

APPLES AND GREENS • I made a version of this recipe first with turnips and collards, which was superb. Then one day I had no turnips on hand but lots of apples, and substituted the apples. It was splendid with a fall supper of roast pork.

• •

SAUTÉ OF COLLARDS AND APPLES

½ pound washed collard greens, ribs and stems removed
2 tablespoons unsalted butter
½ small onion, sliced thin
1 small tart apple, peeled, halved, cored, and sliced thin lengthwise
1 tablespoon balsamic vinegar
Salt and pepper to taste

Cook collard greens in boiling water for about 5 minutes. Drain and cool, then cut into pieces about the size of large postage stamps. In a large nonreactive skillet, heat the butter and cook the onion over high heat, stirring, until the onion is soft and lightly browned (not burned). Add apple slices and cook until tender, about 2 minutes. Stir in collards. Add balsamic vinegar and cook, stirring, until the greens are coated evenly, no longer than a minute. Salt and pepper to taste. Serves 4 as a side dish.

• •

October inherits summer's hand me downs. . . .
—Rachel Peden

❦ OCTOBER 15

If your sugar maple didn't show striking color this season it might be more than a case of inhospitable atmospheric conditions. You might have too much nitrogen in your soil. Check by having your soil tested. If it shows an overabundance of nitrogen, avoid applying lawn fertilizer anywhere within 3 feet of the tree's drip line. Actually, you should avoid any fertilizers on healthy maples. If the tree has a deficiency, use a 10-6-4 blend.

HOLIDAY PLANT REMINDER • Today is a good day to prepare your Christmas cactus and poinsettia to bloom for Christmas. Place each plant in compete darkness for approximately 15 hours every night until the holidays begin.

ROASTED SEEDS • Roast the jillions of squash and pumpkin seeds you keep scooping out. Wash them, dry them well, and then lay them out on an oiled baking sheet in a single layer. Drizzle just a little more oil and some kosher salt over the seeds. Roast in a 250 degree oven until crisp and brown.

MILK RINSE • When you rinse out your milk cartons or bottles for recycling, use the milky water to give your plants a boost.

> *Listen! the wind is rising,*
> *and the air is wild with leaves.*
> *We have had our summer evenings,*
> *now for October eves!*
> —Humbert Wolfe

❦ OCTOBER 16

I have been eyeing a grassy strip at the edge of our property that would make a beautiful border of shade-loving plants. All I have to do is lift the sod. If you have a sodded area that you are thinking of converting, fall is the best time to remove the sod. (If you have a lot of sod, and want to use it in another part of your property, pull it up early in the fall so it can take root in its new location before winter comes.) Here's what you do: Cut out the squares of sod at a depth of about 3½ inches. Then simply work the spade underneath a piece and slowly pry it up. After you've removed all of the sod, shake the valuable topsoil back into the garden. Finally, prepare a bed. Dig to a depth of 8 to 12 inches, adding lime, sulfur, and organic matter as necessary.

BE CAREFUL WITH THOSE DEAD STEMS • Dead stems are notorious for carrying this year's diseases over to next year's plants. Be sure you have disposed of all vegetable vines and till under all of your vegetable patch after the last harvest. Spores plowed under die more readily than those left on the surface.

GRASS CLIPPINGS • In a single season the average half-acre lawn generates 4½ tons of grass clippings, or 334 thirty-gallon bags full.

> *I grow old, I grow old, the garden says.*
> —Robert Finch

❦ OCTOBER 17

Fall used to be a really edgy time for me. I lived in New York City, and gardened on weekends in upstate New York. I can remember driving two hours on a Friday afternoon, speeding through the mountains to get to my kitchen garden to see who won that week's game of chicken: Jack Frost or me. In the end, Jack Frost always won, of course. If you have an early frost this year and your crops were damaged there is very little you can do but pull everything out. Your peas, lettuce, carrots, dill, broccoli, parsnips, leeks, and other fall crops will be fine for quite a while, but a frost can devastate tomatoes, basil, eggplants, and squash. You'll first see soft spots. The spots eventually turn black and ugly. Believe me, I know.

If you are very sure that your plants have no disease—and you should be *very* sure—you can take all of your pulled-up summer crops, spread them on the ground, and run over them with a lawn mower (the mower should have a bag attachment to keep the plant shrapnel from trashing out your yard). The minced plants make a nice addition to your compost heap, or you can add them directly to the soil when you do your big fall soil amendment.

PEAT MOSS SUBSTITUTES • Instead of peat moss, try leaf mold, ground bark, compost, or sawdust as soil amendments.

Once it hits 55 degrees, bring in those tomatoes, ready or not.

TOMATO UPDATE • How's the tomato situation? Once you hit the 55-degree stage, you might as well bring all of them in—unless you are using covers or cold frames to keep the tomatoes ripening. Tomatoes that ripen at temperatures below 55 degrees are very mealy; those that ripen at 80 degrees and up tend to overripen.

COLD FRAME REMINDER • This is a good time to put your cold frames in good working order if you haven't already. Double-check hinges and fittings to make sure they are ready for the impending cold temperatures. If they need a paint job, do it soon.

MORE TULIP BULB REPELLENTS • Another safeguard against rodents for tulip bulbs is gravel. Toss a handful of sharp, crushed gravel into the hole when you plant. Nibblers will find the gravel a painful chew.

❧ OCTOBER 18

My mother has a black-capped Carolina chickadee who returns to her year after year. I do not have such amazing friendships with birds, but I do try to keep a small bird feeder filled through the winter months. And this is the time of year to get the little feeding apparatus operational if you haven't already. We invested in one of those squirrelproof feeders, and I don't know about your squirrels, but ours immediately did their imitation of the Flying Walendas and got right back to the business of stealing bird food and chomping on feeders. To discourage squirrels, some gardeners mount their feeders on a pole and coat the pole with a heavy application of all-purpose grease or joint linament, and apparently get good results. In any case, bird feeders should be clean and ready for customers, all of which is part of the fall ritual.

Incidentally, "Lyric" is a good brand of clean birdfood; unlike the supermarket brands, there's little waste, and lots of different birds are attracted to it. Unfortunately, so are squirrels.

PARSNIPS AGAIN TONIGHT, HONEY? • If you have a big root vegetable crop and have tried turnips every which way, try doing a mixed vegetable root roast. Cut your peeled and trimmed turnips, parsnips, beets, rutabagas, celery root, fennel—whatever—into quarter-inch slices. Drizzle some olive oil over them and toss. Lay them out in a shallow roasting pan and sprinkle with lots of pepper (and any herb you might have on hand that would combine well). Roast in a hot oven—about 450 degrees—for about 10 minutes (peek to see how they're coming). Then flip and roast 5 more minutes until crisp, brownish, tender. Salt lightly with a course salt. Fabulous.

WASH YOUR WINDOWS • Pick a sunny fall afternoon to wash your windows so your winterized container plants sitting on windowsills can get as much sunshine as possible. A significant amount of light is blocked by even a thin layer of dirt and dust.

I hope you love birds, too. It is economical. It saves going to Heaven.
—Emily Dickinson

❧ OCTOBER 19

If you are amending soil, and your soil needs a little sand to lighten it up or improve drainage, don't do what I did.

Big mistake No. 2439 for me was thinking that sand from a river bed a few feet from our cabin in the country would be a nice addition to my garden dirt. River sand (and beach sand, too) contains minuscule particles that tend to clot rather than disperse in potting mix or garden soil. It does not improve drainage; as a matter of fact, it makes drainage impossible. For a small amount of money, nice clean sharp builder's sand is your only bet.

FINAL LAWN TREATMENT • Once the last leaves have fallen, your lawn service may offer a late fall feeding which reportedly promotes rooting, improves spring greenup, and reduces leaf-spot episodes. For us, this application is made around Thanksgiving. However, the lawn services that provide this treatment commonly follow up the late fall feeding with an early spring fertilization, which is not necessary and in fact duplicates the fall effort.

GO AHEAD AND PICK THE EGGPLANTS • If frost threatens, don't hesitate to pick your smallish eggplants. You can pick them any time they have reached about a third of their mature size.

❦ OCTOBER 20

If you haven't experienced the good fun of forcing bulbs, take some time this week to see what's left at the nursery (it will probably be poor pickings but you should be able to find enough to play with). Pick the biggest bulbs you can find, clean out a pot or two, and give it a try.

I use ordinary potting soil and fill up the pots so that the tips of the smaller bulbs are about 1 inch below the soil surface; for larger bulbs like hyacinth and narcissus the tips should be just below the surface. The bulbs should be positioned so that there is ½ inch of space below the rim of the container. Hyacinths look good as singles or in groups of three. Daffodils and tulips look better in clusters. Try five, seven, or nine. In any case, leave from ½ inch to an inch of space between each bulb. Water well.

Most bulbs you'll choose need to be chilled, which means you should find a place in a cold frame or a garage that can provide consistent cool temperatures ranging from 40 to no higher than 50 degrees. *Find a spot now.* The reason many people forgo the pleasure of forcing bulbs is that they are too lazy to look around and find a place to chill them. It would take you all of 10 minutes of scouting time. Just do it.

If you live in a very cold zone and want to leave the potted bulbs outdoors, you can wrap the pots in newspapers or surround them with bags of leaves but remember to provide access; you'll need to water them from time to time.

Most bulbs need chilling: hyacinth needs 11 to 14 weeks; iris, 15; tulip, 14 to 20; crocus, 15; daffodil, 15 to 17. Poke around at the nursery; you also can get "prepared" bulbs that need fewer weeks of chilling.

SEPARATE FRUITS FROM ROOTS • If you are going to store a lot of garden produce this fall, be sure to keep the ethylene producers together and separate from the others. Carrots, parsnips, potatoes, and all of the cole veggies turn bitter when they are exposed to the ethylene gas which is emitted by ripening fruits like apples, tomatoes, peaches, plums, cantaloupes, apricots, and so on.

....

Bulbs to Force Indoors

....

Crocus (*Crocus sp.*)   Tulip (*Tulipa sp.*)
Dwarf iris (*Iris pumilla*)   Hyacinth (*Hyacinthus*)
Glory-of-the-snow (*Chionodoxa*)   Daffodils (*Narcissus*)

❦ OCTOBER 21

Those little mini-pumpkins last a long time if you keep them out of the sun and the heat. If you want to store them, dip them in a 10 percent bleach solution and keep them in a cool dry place. One year we gave them out to trick-or-treaters along with the usual sugary candies and the children loved it. The pumpkins also look great on a Thanksgiving table.

NITROGEN-FIXING TREES • Beans are famous for their nitrogen-fixing properties but there are also some trees that fix nitrogen. Be on the lookout for mimosas, alders, Russian olives, autumn olives, and black locusts because their leaves might be extra valuable as mulch or compost or leaf mold.

LEFTOVER SOD • If you carved out some new garden space this fall and decided not to till it under, you can make a sod pile in a forgotten corner of the yard. Pile up the lawn mats and let them decompose over the course of the next 12 months and then work them back into your garden. You'll have excellent-quality compost.

People who are not gardeners always say that the bare beds of winter are uninteresting; gardeners know better, and even take a certain pleasure in the neatness of newly dug, bare, brown earth.

—Vita Sackville West

....

This is peak bulb-planting weather, and most of us have visions of jonquils and tulips and hyacinths in our heads as we dig away at the soft fall earth. But this is also an excellent time to plant garlic, which after all is a bulb, too. If you put some garlic in the ground this month you will have a tremendously gratifying surprise next June. It's worth a try, especially while you have your bulb planter in hand.

This is what you do: First get some seed garlic. I have tried planting garlic from the grocery store, but I couldn't get it to sprout. On the other hand, I have friends who did get grocery-store garlic to sprout—so who knows? Maybe your nursery has some or you have an organic farmer in town who will sell you some—or you were smart and ordered some from a reputable mail-order firm months ago.

Anyway, get some garlic. Use the biggest and plumpest cloves, because what you plant is what you get. If you plant skinny cloves you'll have skinny bulbs. Make sure you plant it in a spot with excellent drainage. Put the cloves in about 3 inches deep, 4 to 6 inches apart (farther apart if you are planting elephant garlic, which is milder—closer actually to leeks than garlic and a little timid, but still good for cooking). The garlic will sprout shortly after you plant it. Mulch it. Your garlic patch should be in a sunny location, well drained, 6.5 or so pH. Sulfur in the soil is good. If you live in a cold area, you should plant your garlic deeper (about 4 inches deep) and you should also mulch deeply—at least 4 inches. In the spring you will clip off any blooms, and harvest when the foliage dies back. *By the way, if it is already freezing in your area it's too late to plant your garlic. Garlic needs some time to grow roots before the freeze, so wait until next September.*

EATING GARLIC • My love affair with garlic began in France 20 years ago, when my only friend was the elderly lady across the hall, who taught me how to cook. As a result, the only French I can read is cookbook French, but that doesn't matter. She introduced me to garlic. I like garlic every way you can prepare it, but one of my favorite ways to enjoy it is in croutons. I love these garlic croutons floating in a bowl of homemade chicken broth, with a dusting of freshly grated Parmesan cheese, while I'm listening to the opera on the radio on a Saturday afternoon . . . on a day like today.

GARLIC CROUTONS

2 tablespoons extra-virgin olive oil
2 medium garlic cloves
1 tablespoon minced fresh parsley, basil, thyme, rosemary, or
    chives—whatever you have on hand
4 slices of crusty French or Italian bread, cut on the diagonal
Kosher salt and fresh pepper to taste

Preheat oven to 350 degrees. Combine olive oil, garlic, and mixed herbs
in a small bowl. Brush the herbal mixture on one side of the bread and
then sprinkle with salt and pepper. Arrange the slices on a cookie sheet
and bake for 15 minutes, until golden.

❦ OCTOBER 23

When you are doing your post-mortem on the vegetable and flower gardens, make a note of the various diseases you had to wrestle with so
when you order seeds for next year you can get the more resistant
varieties.

Here's a list of some standard abbreviations to look for on seed packets or in catalogue descriptions.

PM	Powdery mildew
DM	Downy mildew
F	Fusarium
FY	Fusarium yellows
BR	Black rot
V	Verticillium wilt
SW	Stewart's wilt
MV	Mosaic virus (could be lettuce, maize, tobacco, bean common)
A	Alternaria (early blight)
ANTH	Anthracnose

GATHER BITTERSWEET • Now is a good time to gather bitter-sweet for holiday wreaths and arrangements—before their berries turn orange and yellow. Once you have them indoors, watch for the berries to change color. As they turn, spray clear varnish on them to stop the berries from dropping.

> *What garlic is to salad, insanity is to art.*
> —Augustus Saint-Gaudens

❦ OCTOBER 24

SCORPIO, October 24 to November 22—*The second-best time to sow*

You can combine some of the herbs you dried from summer and make an excellent, traditional mix of herbs used often in Provence, and actually throughout France, called herbes de Provence. Pick out your best dried herbs for this. Combine one part each of dried thyme, rosemary, bay leaves, summer savory, lavender, cloves, and orange zest. Store them in an opaque jar with a rubber seal. It is potent and aromatic and excellent in soups, stews, dressings, and rubbed into roasts.

ACORN SQUASH • I like acorn squash because you don't have to peel them. All you do is wash them, halve and seed them, slice the tips off for balance, and set the halves, cut side up, in a baking pan filled with about an inch of water, and you're 90 percent there. To cook, cover the pan with foil and bake at 350 degrees for about a half hour, then uncover and cook another half hour, and there, you have something wonderful.

Acorn squash can go a lot of ways. Sometimes I just put butter and brown sugar and salt and pepper in each little valley, and eat it that way. Curry and a smidgen of butter are also excellent. My all-time favorite, though, is acorn squash with little bits of hot Italian sausage. Remove the casing and fill each squash cavity with uncooked sausage. Season. Cook as directed above.

Once it gets cold enough for people to want hot food in daylight, I start making Monday Soup. First I make a broth with the usual soup bones, then I throw in every leftover from the previous week and set it to simmer early Monday morning. It allows me to start off the week without those annoying odds and ends cluttering up the fridge, and also to feel the joys of frugality and tasty food.

The soup-making really starts in the summer, though, when I grow my herbs and vegetables. Out of every good harvest, I freeze a bunch of herbs in ice cube trays. All you do is wash the herbs, mince the fresh leaves, and pack them in individual squares in the ice cube tray. Add broth to fill in and then freeze. Once frozen, I empty the cubes into a zipper-locked freezer bag, packing loosely, so I can pull out as little or as much as I need, depending on what I am making. I add the herbs in the last 5 to 10 minutes of cooking so the flavors and oils don't get cooked out. Cooking with fresh herb ice cubes, along with some thawed veggies from the summer harvest, always gives me pleasure on fall mornings, almost as though I am still gardening.

Time to give those spring-flowering bulbs a little fertilizer.

FERTILIZE YOUR BULBS • Latest research indicates that bulbs left in the ground require more nutrition than was previously thought. In addition to a complete fertilizer in the spring, hardy bulbs will benefit from a fall feeding. Bulbs produce new roots in the fall and absorb nutrients through the winter and spring, and a little boost aids them in the process.

Select a fertilizer designed for bulbs and including nitrogen and phosphorus (bonemeal is a good source). Water in well, as phosphorus does not move through the soil readily. Then add a heavy layer of compost.

In the spring, just when the foliage spears emerge from the ground, give the bulbs another feeding.

❦ OCTOBER 26

I will not try to enter the "till or no-till" fray in this modest book of days. Suffice it to say that the no-till devotees believe that disturbing the soil is not only a lot of work but harmful to the soil and all the microbes and critters who live in it. Other gardeners believe tilling is a good way to discourage weeds and get compost and manure into the soil. Actually the argument is more complicated, but I don't have room here to get into it.

I am not 100 percent sure about the garden, but tilling is good for me. I like to turn under as much as I can when I am cleaning out the garden in the fall, not only to get all of the soil amendments in place but to see with my own eyes what's happening a few inches down. I do it again in the spring just to warm the soil up a bit, but fall is my big workout. I don't do it willy nilly; I learned the hard way that you have to be really careful—especially if you've had some disease in a given season. Pull out any diseased or borderline sick plants and throw them away! Large-size annuals that won't decompose readily can go into the compost heap; no need to turn them under.

ONIONS NEXT YEAR • Onion seeds are very short-lived. If yours are over a year old, toss them. Meanwhile, if you want to get soil prepared for an onion patch, and would like onions as sweet and mild as Vidalias, you will want to create stress-free conditions—okay, low-stress conditions—and develop soil that is very low in sulfur. If you tinker now, by early spring your soil will be ready. Northern gardeners can get a jump on the season by growing their own onion sets; onion sets will mature long before those grown directly from seed.

ANOTHER WAY TO ANNOY DEER • Deer deterrent ploy No. 2649: Clip disposable sheets of scented fabric softener to plants, shrubs, fences—anywhere you'd like deer not to be. Replace after several rains. The deer find the smell unpleasant.

❦ OCTOBER 27

There are countless wonderful books on gardening, and surely part of gardening is reading about it all. To recommend every book that I have known and loved on the subject of gardening would be a small book in itself. However, if you garden by mail this book is a must. It is called *Gardening by Mail* by Barbara J. Barton and published by Houghton Mifflin Company. *Gardening by Mail* lists everything you might ever need as a gardener, sources of plants, tools, information, libraries, societies—you name it. It is well organized and truly a treasure trove for those of us who obsess or compulse or always need to know and have more on this subject. You can order a copy by phoning 1/800/225-3362 or locate it at a bookstore or your library, and I would suggest doing so now—so you will have it for the quiet, indoor times ahead.

TULIP STATS • Each year, about 3 billion—that's billion with a "b"—Dutch tulip bulbs are sold and planted. Americans buy a quarter of a billion of them. There are more than 3,500 distinct varieties of tulips available.

RULE OF THUMB • The general rule of thumb for dividing perennials is that early bloomers should be divided in the fall; late bloomers in the spring. Two exceptions to this rule are Oriental poppies and bearded irises, both of which can be divided in the summer.

❧ OCTOBER 28

My husband still reminds me about the chicken wire fence he put up around my vegetable garden in the country. We—well, he—put in this simple fence during the cold and wet spring, and I am now convinced that if he had put it in when the earth was dry and crumbly from fall digging, this fence would not be a recurring topic of conversation.

The advantage to putting a fence in now is that the weather is cool and good for a serious workout, the soil is dry and workable because you've been digging it anyway, and mainly, there's not as much to do. In the spring there is so much to do you can't see straight, let alone shovel rocks.

Okay, we had a lot of rocks. I admit that did make it a bit of a project. I felt it was important to bury a good portion of the fence so critters would be discouraged from burrowing in underground. So the rocks had to go, the posts had to be driven down deep, and the fencing buried. In any case, the fence was installed beautifully and it looked great with pea blossoms. If you have been thinking about a fence, you need a lot of determination but very little money. All that is required is 5-foot-wide chicken wire, stapled to a frame of 2-by-4 posts and rails. The hard part is this: Sink the wire at least a foot into the soil. If you can, curve it at the bottom, *into* the garden. (This isn't necessary unless you expect unwanted guests.) Some people put electric fencing on top. Once the fence is in, life in the garden is a very different and wonderful proposition.

TRY THIS ON INCOMING PLANTS • Some gardeners are finding good results dealing with spider mites and other pests by using a solution of Murphy's Oil Soap, ¼ cup per gallon of *warm* water. This is a great solution for plants you've brought in to winter over, but before you use it, experiment with a few leaves. Some plants could be too sensitive for this treatment.

❧ O C T O B E R 2 9

Well, you made it through another season *alive*. American gardeners are not quite as zealous about gardening as their British counterparts (the best-selling book in America is a sex manual, while in England it is a gardening encyclopedia) but the British do pay a price, and sometimes it is *their lives*. The Royal Society for the Prevention of Accidents reports that England loses about 30 gardeners a year, victims of gardening accidents. Last year, 30,000 British gardeners were sent to emergency rooms after falls from trees, pokes by stalks, and mishaps with garden tools.

NEVER TOP A TREE • An evergreen that has had its head lopped off is a truly pitiful sight. I know. There is a short one right outside my garage that the previous owners, for no reason known to man, decided to decapitate. Topping is ugly and also not good for your tree. The large wound resulting from topping does not heal easily, leaving itself open to fungus spores and eventual rot. I've yet to find a good reason for topping a tree. If the purpose of topping was to lessen the risk of wind damage, it doesn't work. It is much better to create a program of thinning and branch reduction than to deform your tree. Don't let a fly-by-night tree "service" sell you on the idea.

EASY COMPOST • The easiest compost heap you'll ever make: Go to your local farm or garden supply store and buy enough hay bales to make a square no smaller than 4 feet, and about 3 feet high. Start tossing your kitchen scraps, leaves, manure, and dirt into the center and before long you will be in business. The hay will eventually decompose right into your compost. Don't build it too high or it will be hard to turn.

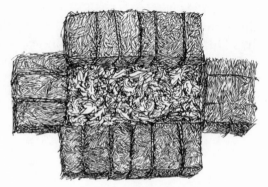

Easy compost bin.

Characteristics of a Gardening Snob: total disdain for fashionable clothes. Gardening Snobs favour very old, very baggy corduroy trousers, gumboots, and an old tweed jacket. They often only speak Latin: "I see your Viburnum Autumnalis Fragrans *is doing well."*

—Louise Guinness

❦ OCTOBER 30

Most gardeners disappear into the great abyss of November and December with a certain amount of relief. Another year, another garden—over. And we're due a break; even the Creator took a day off. But if you like to putter indoors, some quasi-greenhouse projects can satisfy the need to grow things. I use my light table in the basement to make an indoor garden of greens, and while it is not an important source of food for our family, it is a lot of fun. If you have the light and the inclination and some leftover seeds, you can grow the following greens indoors with happy results: spinach, watercress, parsley, leaf lettuce—and of course a host of herbs.

LAWN REMINDER • After your last raking, mow your lawn one last time. Cut it short, to about 2 inches. This will not only reduce chances for disease but also make debris removal easier.

RAKE UP YOUR ROSE LEAVES • If you haven't been raking up those rose leaves as they fall, be sure to do it now. A single rose leaf can carry millions of tiny spores that can winter over and plague next year's plants. Even if the petals look healthy, it's safest not to compost them.

ROMAINE LETTUCE • Romaine lettuce—or cos lettuce—has been known since 4500 B.C. and is highest of all lettuces in Vitamins A and C and potassium.

> *The stillness of October gold*
> *Went out like beauty from a face.*
> —Edwin Arlington Robinson

🍂 OCTOBER 31
All Hallows' Eve

If your St.-John's-Wort (*Hypericum perforatum*) was particularly plentiful this year, hang some in your doorway this evening to ward off evil spirits. Vampires can be repelled by onion or garlic. Witches will not visit a home with mistletoe hanging from the eaves.

JACK O' TURNIP • Before pumpkins, little Irish children hollowed out large rutabagas, potatoes, and turnips.

EAU D'PUMPKINS • For a fragrant jack-o-lantern: Make some criss-cross patterns in the lid of the pumpkin. Rub in generous amounts of cinnamon and nutmeg. When it burns it smells wonderful.

PLANTS DEER LOVE • Master gardeners at Cornell Cooperative Extension of Westchester compiled a list of plants that deer often eat. They are hollyhocks, impatiens, Mexican sunflower, crocus, daylily, hosta, cardinal flower, phlox, rhododendron, rose, tulip. Deer also apparently will dine on pansy, sunflower, wood hyacinth, cranesbill geranium, English ivy, iris, peony, coneflower, sedum, and meadow rue.

❦ *November* ❦

Flower of the Month: Chrysanthemum

❦ NOVEMBER 1
All Saints' Day

I generally wait until there's a killer blizzard to tie up my vulnerable young trees, evergreens, and mountain laurel. While everyone else is enjoying cups of cheer and singing carols, I am on a ladder, sleet burning my face, trying to tie stiff twine around branches with clumsy mittened hands. All of which is entirely unnecessary. God created November as the month of mundane preparations. What else is there to do in November except tie up your trees and study recipes for leftover turkey? If you live in really cold zones, you should have tied your trees up in October. Those of us in the moderate-to-cold zone can do it *this* month.

If you have young evergreens, tie together the upper branches that might spread and bend or break with heavy snow or ice accumulation. Take a sturdy stake slightly taller than the plant and drive it into the ground beside it. Then, starting from the bottom, begin loosely winding twine around the plant and the stake until you reach the top. Don't let the branches back out until the seasons change.

If your evergreens are exposed to strong winds or if they are close to the road and get sprayed by salt during the winter, throw some burlap over them and stake it down. It looks like the devil but it will really save your trees and shrubs. By the way, if it's been dry, make sure your evergreens and dogwoods get a drink from time to time to avoid winter stress. A wood chip mulch is also a good idea, but not until the ground is frozen.

COMPOST THAT PUMPKIN • Cut up used pumpkins and put them in your compost heap. Like all fruits and vegetables, pumpkins contain nitrogen. If you chop the pumpkin into 1-inch pieces, it will make more surface area available to microbes and it will decompose in about a week. Cover your pumpkin pieces—and all chunky pieces of kitchen waste—so that flies and rodents aren't attracted to it. If you don't have a compost heap, dig a small trench in your flower garden, put it in the pumpkin pieces, and cover with soil.

If the beech acorn is wet on All Saints' Day, the winter will be wet.

❦ N O V E M B E R 2

I promised that this year I would take good care of my tools and keep the garage nice-and-neat. Promises, promises: plastic pots are everywhere, bags and spray bottles are not where they should be, stakes with little rag ties are stacked all over the place, miles of floating row cover are unfurled, and worst of all, my tools are dirty and dull. Since November is the month of mundane preparations, tool duty is a must. Just think how good it will feel to pick up your favorite trowel, clean and sharp, in March.

To clean your gardening tools, you need the proper atmosphere. Plug in your radio and tune in your favorite station. Make yourself some hot cider. Now gather all of your worse-for-the-wear tools. Remove any clods of dirt with water and a wire brush. Dry thoroughly. Spray all exposed metal with a rust inhibitor or clean off rust with naval jelly. The wooden handles can be sanded lightly and then rubbed down with either boiled linseed oil or tung oil. Floor wax will also help shine up the handles.

PIPELINE REMINDERS • Meanwhile, it's time to get your outdoor plumbing settled in for the long winter.

• Drain and store garden hoses.

• Turn off water taps and, where necessary, drain them.

TURN YOUR COMPOST • Be sure to turn your compost after the first hard frost to discourage rodent infestation.

There is a sense of "putting the garden to bed" now, and it fits well with our own lives, as the days become shorter and darker. We are turning inward, concerned with staying warm and dry, and so we assume our plants should have the same care.

It is important to remember that the function of mulching and covering our plants is not to keep them warm throughout the winter. Our plants need protection from thawing and heaving and winter sun and wind, but presuming our plants are hardy, cold, per se, is not a threat to them. Before the ground freezes, collect and organize all of your winter protection: branches, leaves, wood chips, straw—whatever you intend to use. But don't put it down too early. Wait until the ground is frozen down to 2 inches to layer on your mulch.

FIRST-TIME MANURE HANDLERS • The best time to dump fresh manure in the garden is in the fall, so it can age over the winter and early spring before it has contact with plants. Fresh manure can burn plants—so make sure it has aged *before* you plant.

Manure is more available than you think. Both urban and suburban gardeners can get horse manure from local riding stables. Some gardeners complain that its higher nitrogen content makes horse manure risky because it burns plants too easily (to avoid, just mix it up with soil and let it age). The other concern about horse manure—and you should ask your stable owner about this—is whether pesticides or chemicals have been used to spray stalls. Fly repellents and disinfectants can pollute the soil in the garden. Make sure your horse manure is "pure."

Another good option is cow manure. It's not as potent but makes a significant contribution to the soil nonetheless.

> *Dull November brings the blast,*
> *then the leaves are whirling fast.*
> — Sara Coleridge

Biotechnologists have tinkered plenty with lettuces, and for much of their work I am grateful. There are now some slow-to-bolt varieties that extend my spring season successfully into July, and this would not have been at all possible without hybridization. And I love the new red lettuces, which are among the stars in my spring and fall garden. But where does the tinkering stop? In Salinas, California, biotechnologists at the USDA Agricultural Research Station are breeding more red lettuces, along with yellow and blue lettuces. The will-not-let-well-enough-alone crowd is also working on blue roses, carnations, and chrysanthemums.

ROOT VEGGIES REMINDER • Remember to check out the root vegetable situation. Make sure to dig them out and store them carefully unless you plan to have them winter over with the help of some mulch.

Those new to gardening should know, however, that most gardeners hate to part with dirt, clay pots, pickle jars, really good labels, stakes, tarred twine, and any kind of wooden box. They do not mind giving a plant that sells for $40 if they have an extra one, but the other stuff (which may be worth a dime) it tears the heart to part with.

—Henry Mitchell

Eighty percent of the success of any garden is the soil. If all of your crops are basically harvested or pulled out or trimmed back, you should devote yourself completely to your soil on a weekend when the weather doesn't forbid. In general, our weather is pretty cold by now but there is usually a wonderfully mild Saturday when I can get out and do final adjustments. What you want now is to aerate your soil, turn out overwinter insects, and add matter like lime or sulfur as needed to be slowly absorbed throughout the winter season. The only gardeners who shouldn't think about soil preparation in the fall are those who work with light sandy soil, which is best tended in the spring to prevent erosion.

Here is what you should do:

- Check the pH and add lime or sulfur if needed. In general, to raise the pH by one unit you add 2.6 pounds of dolomite limestone per 100 square feet. To lower the pH one unit add ½ to 2 pounds of ground sulfur per 100 square feet. The lightness or heaviness of your soil will determine the amount, and I suggest checking with a really sharp nurseryman or a county extension agent. Also, if your pH is really out of whack (2 points above or below neutral) correct the situation gradually, in two or three doses, so you don't send your soil organisms into shock.

- Add up to 3 inches of fresh horse or cow manure or any organic materials you have available—compost, peat moss, leaves. Work all of the material into the soil to the depth of 8 inches. Tillers are great for this, though shovels and elbow grease will also do the trick. It is very important to work in the manure; don't just leave it setting on the soil surface.

You can correct pH at any time of year but it is best to start in the fall and check your progress in the spring. Allow 1 month to pass between adding lime and adding fertilizer. Make up for phosphate and potash shortages, if necessary, with slow-acting fertilizers in the autumn and quicker-acting fertilizers in the spring. Add nitrogen in the spring.

ONE LAST DRINK FOR YOUR PERENNIALS • Well before they go dormant you should give your perennials, shrubs, and trees a slow, deep watering. For large trees be sure to water well beyond the base of the trunk.

> *My garden is an honest place.*
> —Ralph Waldo Emerson

❧ N O V E M B E R 6

The National Gardening Association routinely surveys gardeners, and their findings are always interesting. For one thing, I had no idea there were so many people who say they are gardeners. Apparently 72 million U.S. households—households!—are involved in lawn and garden activities. (Somehow I think their definition of "gardener"—or garden—must have been pretty loose.) By the same token, the dollars we are talking about are significant—about $23 billion, to be precise. What a lot of trowels! According to its research you are more likely to garden or to spend money on gardening purchases if you are college educated, married, living in the East, and making more than $40,000 a year. The association's research shows that we spend about $140 million on herb gardening, $1.4 billion on vegetable gardening (I would love to run numbers on cost per unit produced), $500 million on our bulbs, and a boggling $7.5 billion on lawn care.

FIRST-TIME GARDENERS • *If your garden is more than 10 by 20 feet and you don't own a rototiller, you might want to rent one. These machines eliminate the backbreaking work of turning your soil each year—and they certainly are worth experimenting with. Whenever possible, rent a rear-end tiller. When the tines are revolving in the rear, the machine's wheels do not pack down freshly tilled soil.*

THERE'S NO PLACE LIKE MEXICO • French marigolds and African marigolds both came from Mexico.

❦ N O V E M B E R 7

In gardening, there are many mysteries, and one of the greatest mysteries is how best to make compost. There are books written on composting. Gardeners argue about it on computer bulletin boards, and discuss it over coffee at the local diner. Everybody has a better way to let it rot.

I use a plastic stacking bin and it works great, while my neighbors just pile up their debris in the corner of the vegetable garden and it works great, too. I have come to believe that there are many more compost-making methods that work than don't work. I will stand by my plastic bin, but I am charmed by the Ruth Stout method, which you can read about in *How to Have a Green Thumb Without an Aching Back* and *Gardening Without Work*. Basically, it just calls for laying down a thick mulch of hay in the garden, tucking kitchen scraps under the hay, and tossing all of your other organics on top of that. I could never do that. Too casual. Too logical. Too messy. But I bet it makes great compost.

NOVEL USE OF TOMATO CAGES • If you have a deer problem and a lot of tomato cages, you can create your own barricade—sort of a poor man's electric fence. If you set the cages on their sides, stack them up high and stake them into the ground, they will form a fence that many deer will avoid so as not to get entangled.

Tomato cages make an excellent barricade for deer.

WORLD'S LARGEST TREE • The National Arbor Day Foundation has identified the world's largest tree as the 3,500-year-old Montezuma cypress (*Taxodium mucronatum*), located in a village called Tule, near Oaxaca, Mexico. One man is assigned full-time to its care. The tree of Santa Maria del Tule is 38 feet in diameter, 141 feet high, and 150 feet across its crown.

❧ N O V E M B E R 8

Hardwood cuttings can be taken at any time during dormancy, but just after the leaves have all fallen is an excellent time. Taking the cuttings from leafless shoots is advantageous because water loss due to transpiration is minimal. You can plant them at once or bury the cuttings in moist sand or peat moss; or put them in a cold frame and plant next spring.

DON'T FORGET TO TEST YOUR SOIL • Another reminder to give your soil a quick test if you haven't already. If it happens to need lime, you need to make amendments now, as ground limestone takes 3 to 6 months to be absorbed.

BRING IN STAKES AND TRELLISES • If you have removable trellising, bring it in now. Trellises that are left to winter over usually sag from exposure; it's worth it to take a minute and wipe your trellising off, then store it in the shed or garage.

❦ N O V E M B E R 9

When I need to commune with greenery, I give my wintering-over plants and houseplants the poodle treatment: a major soaking, cut, and style. Bring them all into the bath or the kitchen and run a slow trickle of water through the soil until the soil itself has been "washed." Over time, salts build up on the surface soil of your houseplants due to evaporation and it is important to their health to flush them out every 6 to 8 months. Snip a little here and there, and shape them if needed. Now they are ready for the long, dry winter ahead.

WERE YOUR PUMPKINS ON THE BITTER SIDE THIS YEAR? • If your pumpkins were on the bitter side they might have had too little nitrogen or not enough water—or perhaps you planted them too late in the season.

CUT DOWN YOUR CHIVES • I harvest my last batch of chives in late fall, trimming them down to about ground level. I don't like dried chives; they remind me too much of survival food. Instead I put the chive stems in a freezer bag and store it in the freezer, snipping off what I need throughout the winter.

❦ N O V E M B E R 1 0

Nobody who experiences cold winters expects the compost heap to simmer as usual, but there are a few steps you can take to ensure at least a little activity. Quantity is very important. Build a larger pile, because the greater mass will retain more heat. Covering the pile will also help, especially if you are experiencing a lot of rain. Too much moisture slows the rate of decomposition (not enough moisture will present the same problem). A sheet of black plastic will keep it as warm as possible over the winter months.

Also remember to give your compost a turn every now and then, before it freezes.

ROOTS • According to the Guinness Book of Records, a single winter rye plant has been shown to produce 387 miles of roots in 1.83 feet of soil.

❦ N O V E M B E R 1 1
Veteran's Day

Vegetable gardens not only feed the soul but nourish the body, and the health benefits of eating fresh and nutritious food that hasn't been sitting in refrigerated trucks for days are numerous. However, the nutritional value of vegetables varies dramatically. The magazine *Harrowsmith Country Life* assigned a numerical value to various vegetables according to their levels of vitamins A and C, folate, iron, copper, and fiber. The winner: sweet potatoes, by a long shot.

Here's how they stacked up: sweet potato, 582; carrots, 408; red pepper, 166; spinach, raw, 152; broccoli, 145; potato, baked, 114; winter squash, 110; cauliflower, 77; asparagus, 75; green pepper, 67; cabbage, raw, 39; corn, 39; green beans, 37; tomato, raw, 37; summer squash, 31; onions, 27; lettuce, iceberg, 22; celery, 14; cucumber, 11; and mushrooms, 10.

CUT DOWN YOUR HERBACEOUS PERENNI-
ALS • It's about time for the final clipping. I usually leave stems

and leaves in place, but certain disease-prone plants like peony, iris, and hollyhock should always be trimmed back to discourage contamination of next year's growth.

❦ N O V E M B E R 1 2

How's your hot pepper situation? We had a bumper crop again, and as much as I love them, there's a limit to how many of them you can eat in a sitting. I chop them up and use them in cooking whenever I can: soups, stews, casseroles, and stir-fries, but one of my favorite uses is in Texas cornbread. This cornbread is delicious with butter and a bowl of red beans. Use leftover cornbread for croutons: cut into small cubes and bake for about ½ hour in a 350-degree oven. Great in soups or salads, or as stuffing for turkey.

••

HOT PEPPER CORNBREAD

1½ cups yellow corn meal
1 cup flour
½ cup sugar
1 teaspoon salt
1 tablespoon baking powder
2 eggs
6 tablespoons butter, melted then cooled
8 tablespoons vegetable shortening, melted then cooled
1½ cups milk
¼ cup finely chopped jalapeño peppers (seeds removed)

Preheat oven to 400 degrees. Sift dry ingredients into a large bowl and set aside. In a medium bowl, beat eggs lightly. Add butter and shortening. Stir in milk and jalapeños. Add egg mixture to dry ingredients and mix until smooth. Do not overbeat. Pour into an 8 × 12-inch buttered baking pan and bake for 30 minutes or until golden brown.

••

LAST CALL FOR WEEDS • This is a crazy time to be thinking about weeds, but if you do have weeds and the ground isn't frozen solid, take an hour to examine your beds and borders and do a final cleanup. You will be well rewarded for your efforts. The weeds you miss will have extra vigor in the spring—who needs it?

COVER YOUR TARRAGON • Gardeners in colder zones should cover their tender herbs like tarragon with dry leaves or branches—or both—once the ground has frozen, to help them make it through the winter.

RULE OF THUMB • A tree's age will determine how well or poorly it can weather a severe storm. A younger tree is more likely to survive a storm than an older one (though deep roots can sometimes help a tree withstand the ravages of a flood).

In my garden, I can find solitude. I can go out there and say, "No phones, no interruptions, I am busy," and then shut myself off for a little while.
—Helen Hayes

❦ NOVEMBER 13

One of your most valuable crops is your fall leaves. Don't let any of your leaves—which can be used as leaf mold, or as a surface mulch, or in the compost pile—go to waste. "Harvest" well, and apply your leaves to the areas that need them most.

AVOIDING SALT PROBLEMS • Gardeners in colder zones may have salt to contend with when the roads and driveways get icy. Salt damage can seriously affect gardens, but there are some measures you can take to lessen the problem. After the roads are salted you should water your garden thoroughly, which, to a certain degree, will wash off the salt. Don't wait for salted snow to melt on your garden; brush it off or shovel it off. Another measure you can take is to dig ditches around your borders and beds so that the salt will run off accordingly.

Don't mulch until the ground is frozen.

MULCH REMINDER • Don't mulch in the fall until the ground is frozen. If you mulch beforehand, you will encourage mice to nest underneath and feast on your bulbs, roots, and bark. And choose your winter mulch carefully. Grass clippings, peat moss, and the leaves of poplar and maple trees tend to mat and form a water-resistant blanket over your plants, which you don't want. What you do want to use is organic matter that will not deprive the soil of the moisture it needs. I use good old salt hay—rolled back out from late summer. Pine needles, wood chips, hay, straw, leaves from deciduous trees, and compost all will work fine.

Most shrubs don't need mulch. But shallow-rooted shrubs like azaleas, camellias, and rhododendrons should be mulched, all year around actually. Most herbaceous perennials should be mulched about 3 inches deep. Don't let the mulch touch the leaves of the plant, and never place the mulch in contact with the main stem or crown. Evergreen boughs are wonderful for perennials, and you can place them directly on top of the crowns.

My hoe as it bites the ground revenges my wrongs, and I have less lust to bite my enemies. In smoothing the rough hillocks, I smoothe my temper.
—Ralph Waldo Emerson

❧ NOVEMBER 14

Topiaries have for years puzzled me; I always found it surprising that someone would take the time and effort to produce a gigantic bunny out of hedge plants. But the past couple of years I've been playing with container topiaries, heart-shaped English ivies, and some rosemary trees, and I've had good fun with it.

You can make the frames out of heavy galvanized spiral wire that comes in varying diameters and is twisted or bent to the desired shape. To brace the spirals, "ribs" are attached at right angles and secured with tape and light wire. Then you fill the frame in with sphagnum moss and plant some rooted cuttings directly in it or under the frame.

I would not recommend English ivy straight off unless you want to spend most of your free time fighting spider mites. Creeping fig is a good alternative. Rosemary is also a wonderful topiary plant. A single rosemary plant can be trained into a lollipop-like tree with very little effort.

If you are going to experiment with a form, make sure you start out simply—with an arch or a heart, or any form that can be easily identified. First-time animals all tend to end up looking like Barney.

Never allow your topiary to dry out—or get soggy. Place in a spot with indirect light and rotate it often, trimming and reforming as necessary.

Frames are available from Topiaries Unlimited, RD 2, Box 40-C, Pownal, VT 05261. You can get good topiary plants from Ivies of the World, Box 408, Weirsdale, FL 32695, catalogue $2, or Merry Gardens, Camden, ME 04843, catalogue $1.

SECOND LIFE FOR AN OLD REFRIGERATOR • If you have an old refrigerator—one that can be locked up—you have an excellent place to store herbicides and pesticides. Even the "organic" treatments like garlic-pepper oil can be dangerous to young children, and sometimes keeping them in a high place isn't altogether safe. The recycled refrigerator provides an excellent solution.

❦ N O V E M B E R 1 5

In ancient Egypt, doctors routinely prescribed walks in the garden for their disturbed patients. Today this practice is called ecopsychology, and it is being discussed earnestly as a therapeutic tool at medical schools. Researchers are testing the idea that horticultural therapy—

contact with nature and in many instances the process of gardening itself—improves self-esteem and relieves tensions and anxiety.

I like the idea, but I would posit that anyone who has tried growing *Gerbera jamesonii*, or germinating parsnips, is at risk for very *low* self-esteem. I have found that fighting losing battles with insects I can't even see and being outwitted by slugs does not exactly instill confidence. And as for relieving tensions and anxieties, running out into the night with blankets to protect the tomato plants from an unexpected frost is not my idea of decompression.

Yet millions of individuals over time would not have knelt down to stir the dirt around, and felt the same pleasure, were there so little to gardening. We'll see what happens with this "new" discipline, and we wish it well.

NEW COLUMNAR APPLE TREE • Introducing . . . the new branchless apple tree. Yes, there is a new "columnar apple tree"—a tree that grows straight up and bears apples. The apples pop out of the trunk, which is covered with an abundance of fruiting spurs. Bred at the well-known East Malling Research Station in England, the tree grows about 7 to 10 feet. At present, there are three varieties available in the U.S. Plant them 2 feet apart and they will bear in early to late September. For more information, contact Stark Brothers Nurseries in Louisiana, MO 63353, ask about the Colonade Apple Trees.

PRUNING DECIDUOUS HEDGES • Once the leaves have all fallen you can see your hedges—whoo, what a mess! I clip my formal hedges in the fall because for once I can see what I am doing, and anyway it gives me something to do on a crisp afternoon. If you are in a really cold zone, the pruning cuts may not heal properly, so don't do it now.

> *I think that I don't want to see*
> *A skinny branchless apple tree:*
> *A tree that looks at God all day*
> *And wishes it had arms to pray.*
>
> —Anonymous

In Victorian England, every respectable gardener had a bone grinder and used fresh raw bones to make fertilizer for his garden. Grind, grind, grind, voilà: bonemeal. Bonemeal formulas used to have 10 to 12 percent nitrogen content and about 20 to 25 percent phosphorus. Nowadays, you should read the label before you plunk down good money for a sack of bonemeal that may well be dehydrated pap. Many commercially available bags of bonemeal contain less than 5 percent nitrogen and 5 to 10 percent phosphorus—hardly worth the money or the time spent shoveling it into your garden.

GOOD SOURCE FOR GARLIC • Ron Engeland of Filaree Farm has the largest garlic collection in the United States—more than 350 strains—and he makes available about 100 of them by mail. If you want to try some new varieties, you can write Ron Engeland, Filaree Farm, RR 2, Box 162, Okanogan, WA 98840. Mr. Engeland also wrote an excellent book called *Growing Great Garlic*, which you will find extremely useful.

HOW TO PEEL GARLIC • To loosen up the peels on your garlic cloves, soak them for 5 minutes in very warm water.

If you have looked high and low for that pink climbing plant that was in your grandmother's garden, and just can't seem to find it, there is a unique service that will help you identify your plant and locate a nursery that sells it. All you do is send $2 to the Bailey Hortorium, 462 Mann Library, Cornell University, Ithaca, NY 14853. Sherry Vance, who spearheads this plant-locating service, will conduct a search for you, using the hortorium's 130,000-plus collection of seed and nursery catalogues to identify the plant, if necessary, and then find a source. Ms. Vance asks for a letter describing the plant and stating its botanical and common name if you know it. She will reply by mail. Checks should be made to Cornell University.

YOU, TOO, CAN GROW CAMELLIAS • Northerners have always had camellia envy, but no more. A plant from northern (brrrrr) China—*Camellia oleifera*—can now survive minus 15-degree temperatures. Spring planting is recommended, so send for information to Camellia Forest Nursery, 125 Carolina Forest Road, Chapel Hill, NC 27516 (catalogue $1) or Roslyn Nursery, 211 Burrs Lane, Dix Hills, NY 11746 (catalogue $3).

POTTED CHRYSANTHEMUMS NEED WATER • We often pick up a pot or two of store-bought mums to brighten the house at Thanksgiving. Yoder Brothers, Inc., a major chrysanthemum wholesaler, recommends that such mums be watered 2 to 3 times a week. Many consumers are advised to water when dry, but usually the plant wilts when it's dry. Wilting causes a reduction of 1 to 4 days' longevity, the wholesaler cautions.

❦ N O V E M B E R 1 8

Corn smut or fungus, aka *Ustilago maydis*, is a delicacy, and U.S. demand for it is now estimated to be 100,000 pounds a year. Though Americans are just discovering corn smut, it is not new to the culinary scene. For years, Mexicans have savored the "maize mushroom" or "Mexican truffle" as it is sometimes called (in Spanish, *huitlacoche*). Wholesalers are paying U.S. farmers up to 50 cents for a smutty ear of corn. Apparently the younger, smaller smut galls are the tastiest.

TREES THAT RESIST STORM DAMAGE • The U.S. Forest Service observed trees in the Southeast where storm intensities are high and came up with a list of trees rated according to their ability to weather storms. If your area seems to get more than its fair share of storm damage you might take note and avoid the trees named at the end of the list. Trees listed from most to least resistant include: live oak, bald cypress, black gum, sweet gum, Southern red oak, magnolia, white oak, beech, sugar maple, sycamore, ash, longleaf pine, loblolly pine, slash pine, red cedar, water oak, cherry, silver maple, dogwood, basswood, yellow poplar, red maple, hickory, box elder.

A.

Cut prunings into 6-8 inch lengths

B. Soak in water

C. Add twigs to charcoal grill

Save fruit tree prunings.

SAVE THOSE FRUIT TREE PRUNINGS • When you prune your fruit and nut trees in late winter or early summer, save the prunings. Cut them into 6- to 8-inch lengths and dry them out. An hour or so before grilling, soak the twigs in water. Light the charcoal, and add the soaked twigs once the charcoal has turned to white ash. It will impart a sweet, smoky taste to meats and poultry.

❦ NOVEMBER 19

A friend taught me how to make sprouts recently (delicious in stir-fries and winter salads when everything is so blah). After rinsing the mung beans under cold running water, she took the liquid and fed it carefully to the bay laurel in my kitchen window. Not only does she use "sprout juice" to water her garden, but all liquids reserved from cooking vegetables, as well as leftover tea, coffee, crushed-up expired vitamins made into tea—you name it. Not surprisingly, her garden sings. And those aren't the only liquids that nourish her plants. One day on a visit I came home to find her polishing my corn plant with 1 percent milk. The leaves were radiant and dust-free, and the milk removed all of those blotchy hard-water spots.

INSULATE YOUR COMPOST HEAP • One way to keep the compost heated up is to surround your pile with bales of straw. You could also use black plastic garbage bags filled with leaves to give it a bit of insulation.

USE SAGE LEAVES FOR A SORE THROAT • I have a sore throat more often than I would like, and have found the dried sage leaves from my garden a help in relieving the discomfort. Pour 1 cup of boiling water over 1 teaspoon of dried sage and let it steep for about 10 minutes. Then drink it slowly. It doesn't taste great but it seems to reduce the swelling.

❦ N O V E M B E R 2 0
St. Edmund's Day, Patron of Farmers and Garden Workers

Imagine how much easier it might have been digging out and storing your tender bulbs if each bulb were in a little mesh bag, and labeled. Someone in New Jersey had the same thought and created Bulb Savers. These are polyethylene mesh bags that are bright colored to make the whole process of digging up and sorting methodical and easy. When you plant, you spread the bag in the hole, add the bulb, and then the soil. A ring of yellow mesh with the plant's plastic ID card extends above the soil, and you can cover it with mulch so no one is the wiser. In the fall, you dig up the bulb in the bag and store it—and it's already tagged for next year. The bags last 5 years and you can get them by writing Bulb Savers, P.O. 3024, Princeton, NJ 08543. If you are ambitious I think it would be easy enough to replicate Bulb Savers with mesh bags used to store onions and garlic. Be sure the holes are wide enough for roots to develop easily.

A LIMA BY ANY OTHER NAME • Somewhere along the line I stopped turning up my nose at lima beans and became a real fan. Limas and lima-types are called different names north and south of the Mason-Dixon line. For instance, Southerners often pick their limas when they're still small and green, and cook them up in butter and milk. These small lima beans are called butter beans. Large limas are often called Fordhooks. Cranberry beans are called shell beans by Southerners. And fava beans are also called broad beans—in Great Britain. As a general rule, for every pound of limas in a pod, you'll get about 1 cup of shelled limas.

❦ N O V E M B E R   2 1

Honey, I'm home: A German study has shown that tomato plants benefit significantly from being talked to. Using its viewing audience, a German television station distributed at random tomato plants to 100 viewers who were told to speak to some of the plants each day and not to others, treating the plants equally in all other respects (lighting, food, water, fertilizer, and so on). The plants that were spoken to presented 20 percent greater yields than those that got the silent treatment. Gardeners who talk to themselves may want to redirect their conversations.

CLIP HOLLY NOW • A commercial holly grower suggests that if you would like to have your holly intact for the holidays, you can clip branches now—before birds devour all of the berries—and keep the holly in cold storage until you want to use it in December.

STORING ROOT CROPS • If you don't have a root cellar, you can keep root vegetables for about a month. Cut off the leafy tops, wrap the roots in burlap or paper towels, and keep them in a cool dark place or in the refrigerator.

❦ N O V E M B E R   2 2

In the peak of summer I sometimes wonder if the Genesis writer had it wrong, and if the serpent was really a slug. Fortunately, the cold weather gives us a little break from our preoccupation with slugs. However, a recent shipment of giant African snails, brought illegally into the United States and shipped to pet stores in Florida, California, and other states, has caused some concern. The snails which have landed on our shores are described as "voracious" herbivores which can devour numerous kinds of plants, including a head of lettuce in a single sitting. The USDA has been tracking down and destroying the snails, but they reproduce quickly and without the need of a mate.

AZALEA TREATMENT • Think back to last spring: did your azaleas bloom at the bottom but not at the top? If you remember your azaleas looking bottom-heavy, some winterizing now will correct the situation. Before the ground freezes, build a windbreak to stop prevailing winds from draining moisture from the top buds (burlap is good). If you get the same problem in the spring, you might have to consider a hardier azalea.

PUT A BARN OWL ON NIGHT DUTY • Barn owls can consume close to 250 rodents every month, and they are fairly easy to attract to your land. Barn owl boxes can be constructed by using ½-inch plywood, 24 × 24 × 24 inches, with a 6-inch square opening placed 6 inches from the top and the sides. Place the birdhouse 15 feet off the ground and somewhat away from—but overlooking—your garden. If you do attract a barn owl you should not use poisons on the rodents; they could also eventually poison your owl.

❦ N O V E M B E R 2 3

SAGITTARIUS, November 23 to December 21—*Unfavorable time to sow or plant*

Lawn mower racing has long been popular in England and is now gaining popularity in the U.S. The Lawn Mower Racing Association, sponsored by Sta-Bil, hosts an annual mower race, where competitors "put their pedals to the metal" on riding mowers without blades around a Grand Prix–style half-mile track. The "Lawn Rangers" precision power-mower drill team performs at this event, held at the Lake County Fairgrounds in Grayslake, Illinois.

"It's not like in England, where they get drunk and just go crazy," spokewoman Karin Janessa said. "Ours is very regulated. They wear helmets and everything." For more information, contact the USLMRA, 1812 Glenview Road, Glenview, IL 60025.

SHREDDED PAPER USE • Lawyers and bankers who can get their hands on shredded paper from the office have an excellent means of killing snails. Collect the paper over the winter. In the early spring, spread it in the garden as a mulch, sprinkling a little earth over it to keep it from blowing all over the place. It will deliver paper cuts to snails who are after your transplants and seedlings. In late spring, you can cover the paper with compost and soil and it will degrade.

LEAF WATCH • Fallen leaves provide a natural mulch for trees that aren't standing in grass, as well as a mulch for hedges, shrubs, and plantings. What a system! But make sure that leaves have not piled up in layers too thick for the perennials and other small plants that might be smothered underneath. *Never* allow leaves to lie for long on lawns. They will cut off light from the grass and encourage the growth of fungi.

> *A garden is something to start—but not necessarily finish.*
> —Lee Reich

❦ N O V E M B E R   2 4

Most American schoolchildren learned about fertilizing plants from Squanto, who helped the Pilgrims in the winter of 1620–21. According to William Bradford, Squanto taught the colonists how to fertilize every hillock where corn was planted with a fish. The Native Americans also furnished colonists with their first corn and bean seeds. Yet for all their efforts, the Pilgrims' survival was difficult.

The first Thanksgiving feast lasted for three days, and by all standards the first harvest was poor. The 20 acres of corn produced pretty well, but the 6 or 7 acres planted with English wheat, barley, and peas were a disaster. This did not prevent the Pilgrims from giving thanks or eating well. The first feast was not only nourishing but in modern terms stylish: besides ample meats and seafood, there were leeks, watercress, and a variety of greens. Wild plums and dried berries were served for dessert, along with a very sweet and strong wine made from wild grapes.

PLANT GARLIC IN THE SOUTH • Thanksgiving Day is the traditional day to plant garlic in the South.

PROTECT YOUR ALPINES • Alpine plants are conditioned to survive extremely cold temperatures, but they also expect a thick blanket of snow for protection from the harsh winter sun and winds. One of my most painful losses was a collection of alpine plants in upstate New York. I didn't mulch my plants because I figured they were extremely durable and accustomed to fierce conditions on a mountaintop. We had a relatively mild, almost snowless winter that year and you know what happened: they all died. Now I give artificial protection to all of my plants that are at risk, and it doesn't take much. Once the ground is frozen I put a little compost a few inches from the base of each plant, and then scatter dry leaves over them. I weight down the leaves with branches, which also protect the plants from the wind. I don't overdo it. Too much protection is just as harmful as too little.

❦ NOVEMBER 25

I recently had some dead trees felled, and while I was sad to lose the trees, I also know that I was going to get mountains of wood chips out of the deal. The tree trimmers made an 8-foot pile of the chips, and as soon as I can, I will scatter them throughout my beds and borders. If you let your wood chips just sit in a pile without being turned for long periods of time, the mulch will sour. During the winter this is less of a problem, but once the weather warms up, mulch piles, especially hardwood bark, are prone to serious souring. (Pine chips are less susceptible.) If the mulch smells like vinegar, ammonia, or sulfur, don't put it on your garden. Mulch that has turned can have a pH as low as 1.8 to 3.6 and can do serious harm to your plants.

EARTHWORM WATCH • An acre of land can contain up to 500,000 earthworms, who can move 5 tons of soil per acre per year, according to USDA research. Earthworms can move 50 times their own weight and can work as far as 12 feet below the soil surface.

The longest earthworm on record is a species from South Africa; it was 22 feet in length when discovered in 1937 in the Transvaal.

❦ N O V E M B E R 2 6

Are all your outdoor containers ready for the long winter's nap? You might need to mulch them. Top mulching is kind of a joke, since the heat loss is transmitted through the container's sides. Plants in wooden or fiberglass containers can be buried flush with the soil and then topped with mulch. Other containers that tend to crack, like terracotta or clay, need to remain above ground. These pots would do better tucked into the lee side of a porch or deck and then surrounded by some type of collar (chicken wire is an option, ugly but workable). The collar should be 6 inches larger than the diameter of the container. Fill the collar with shredded pine bark or another kind of dense mulch.

WHERE THE PROBLEM IS • Pesticides are thought primarily to be a farming problem but suburban areas consume up to 6 times the rate of pesticides as farmland.

HOUSE WINE • Garden wineries, also called microwineries, are becoming increasingly popular, and some gardeners are even marketing their wines to local restaurants. Wines can be produced from fruits, flowers, herbs, honey, tree sap, and even vegetables. Grapes are the obvious fruit of choice. French-American hybrid grapes are best grown east of the Rockies, while European *Vitis vinifera* are best suited for gardens west of the Rockies. Growing requirements are minimal— you do need full sun, good air circulation, good water drainage, and soil that is not too fertile.

Once you get the knack of growing and harvesting grapes, you can produce 10 to 20 gallons of wine, using some chemicals, a potato masher, cheesecloth, and old bottles for as little as $100. If this intrigues you, drop a note of inquiry to: American Wine Society (Attn:

Angel Nardone, executive director), 3006 Latta Road, Rochester, NY 14612 or call (716) 225-7613. This nonprofit organization offers its members literature on winemaking, and two excellent manuals on pruning and wine grape growing among numerous other materials.

LARGEST VINE • The largest grapevine in the U.S. was planted in Carpinteria, California, in 1842 and averaged 7.7 tons of grapes per year during its producing years from 1900 to 1920.

❧ N O V E M B E R 2 7

Lilies are best planted in late fall. Mail order is definitely the way to go, though a majority of the dealers don't dig out their Asiatics until late October and the Orientals don't come out until sometime in November. (Asiatic hybrids bloom around June and some later; Oriental hybrids are the last lilies to bloom, in late summer and early fall.) All of which means seriously late deliveries, especially if you live in the North.

Some northerners prepare their lily beds in advance and cover them with mulch to keep the ground from freezing. Once the bulbs arrive, they tuck them in immediately. If the bulbs arrive too late, you should pot them up in good potting soil and put the pots in a cool, frost-free shed or garage for the winter. They will begin to sprout, and in the spring you can plant them as soon as weather permits.

Of course you can forgo all of this and plant bulbs in the spring, but your first year won't be as spectacular. Last word: there is no such thing as cheap good-quality lilies. Be prepared to pay top dollar and use only the best sources available.

GET ON THOSE MAILING LISTS • Before the craziness of the holidays dominates, take an afternoon to page through old issues of magazines like *Horticulture* and *Fine Gardening* and *Organic Gardening* and send off for the catalogues you want to receive a month from now. Most mail order companies will ask for a dollar or two to send you their catalogue, but it's worth it. For seed catalogues, be sure you get copies of: Shepherd's Garden Seeds, 30 Irene Street, Torrington, CT 06790, (203) 482-3638; The Cook's Garden, P.O. Box 535, Londonderry, VT 05148, (802) 824-3400; Johnny's Selected Seeds, Foss

Hill Road, Albion, ME 04910, (207) 437-4301; and Thompson & Morgan, P.O. Box 1308, Jackson, NJ 08527, (800) 274-7222. There are many other reputable companies but these are my favorites.

❦ N O V E M B E R 2 8

After a heavy snow—especially one that threatens to turn to ice—it's a good idea to shake the boughs of your evergreens gently to dislodge the snow. The operative word here is gently. Branches are quite brittle when the temperatures drop below zero, and you run a risk of breaking them. If ice has already formed, leave the branches alone.

ROSES IN REVIEW • There are 16,000 registered varieties of roses, which makes selection difficult, especially to the newcomer. The American Rose Society surveyed its members about their most favored roses, and came up with the following list, which is presented in no particular order:

miniature 'Jean Kenneally'
hybrid tea 'Touch of Class'
shrug rose 'Sally Holmes'
miniature 'Minnie Pearl'
miniature 'Perrine'
miniature 'Snow Bride'
hybrid tea 'Pristine'
climbing miniature 'Jeanne Lajoie'
damask 'Mme. Hardy'
hybrid tea 'Olympiad'
miniature 'Rise 'n' Shine'
meilland shrub 'MEIdomonac'
kordesii 'Dortmund'

ASSESSING GARDEN SLOPES • North-facing slopes are colder than south-facing slopes because the sunlight does not hit the surface as directly. In general, throughout the United States, south-facing slopes are better protected from prevailing northwest winds.

Sometimes you could just kick yourself. My husband and I went off and installed an expensive security system when all we needed was *Poncirus trifoliata,* Chinese hardy orange. The U.S. Government uses barriers of *Poncirus* to protect nuclear and military installations. The plant has 2- to 4-inch green spines, which I suppose *would* discourage unwanted visitors. *Poncirus* is hardy to minus 15 degrees and bears white flowers and yellow fruits, which are tasty in marmalade; a security fence and jam fruit, all in one bush!

WINTER LAWN CARE • Keep debris and fallen leaves off the lawn or the grass will tend to die out under the leaves and, in the best case, discolor. An occasional snowman or angel is okay, but by and large, once it snows, stay off the lawn as much as possible.

SAVING ON ENERGY BILLS • Winter fuel bills can be reduced significantly—as much as 20 percent—by installing evergreen windbreaks on the north side of your house. Summer air conditioning bills can be reduced by planting deciduous trees on the south, west, and southwest sides of your house. If you do decide to plant a windbreak, don't make it too close to your garden as its roots will sap water and nutrients from your plants.

HYBRID CHAT • When a variety is listed with an "x," for instance *Viburnum x bodnantense,* it indicates the plant is a hybrid.

It is apparent that no lifetime is long enough in which to explore the resources of a few square yards of ground.
                                                                    —Alice M. Coats

Our village gets very romantic and brooding as we begin our slow retreat into winter, into our homes and our huddled lives. I won't see some of my neighbors for months, and when spring comes, where lived little babies, little toddlers will emerge. Every now and then smoke rises from a chimney.

The fall garden, having experienced its first light frost, is freer now from seige of insect or disease. I can put down my arms. I check on the detached garage that houses my tools, the towers of plastic pots, washed-out spray bottles, and piles of little plastic plant markers. I survey the garden. It all seems in order—for now.

THEME GARDENS • The students at Father Flanagan's Boys town, near Omaha, Nebraska, put in an 88,000-square-foot "Garden of the Bible" with 150 plant species which grew in Palestine during biblical times. Omaha is a zone 6 and Palestine is a zone 10, so some of the species had to be represented by hardier members of the same genius, but one still admires the effort. Every plant is tagged with its common name, botanical name, and the passage in the Bible in which it was mentioned.

Theme gardens are gaining in popularity, and there are many possibilities: the Shakespeare garden, Colonial garden, Victorian garden, witch's garden, Mary garden, monk's garden, scented garden, variegated garden, moonlight garden, quiet garden, and wedding garden. The biblical garden is perhaps most popular, with many gardeners establishing them at their places of worship.

GETTING ORGANICS BY MAIL • Sometimes local nurseries do not carry the organic materials that you need in the garden. If you are trying to locate matter like greensand, seaweed, or phosphate rock and can't come up with it locally, write these companies. Both of them carry organics and a host of other products: Peaceful Valley Farm Supply, P.O. Box 2209, Grass Valley, CA 95945, (916) 272-4769 or Necessary Trading Company, One Nature's Way, New Castle, VA 24127, (703) 864-5103.

Winter

❧ *December* ❧

Flower of the Month: Holly

❧ DECEMBER 1

I am ambivalent about winter, though I rather enjoy the novelty of being a human being again. The cracks in the hands are healed and the fingers are no longer stained. The knees don't ache. I can walk past my garden without even a sideways glance (most of the time). For most cold-zone gardeners, for better or worse, December is about other things. To December, then.

AN ASIDE ON SHOVELING • Instead of using your heavy metal shovel to clear out snow from paths and driveways, get a lightweight wood and plastic one; they're very inexpensive and save lots of back strain. Don't go for big loads; lots of light scoops will get you there faster and with far less pain.

ROSE MAINTENANCE • If the ground is frozen you can mulch your roses now. Any long canes should be trimmed or tied so they don't become lashes in the bitter winds.

SAVE GALLON BOTTLES • Save any glass gallon-size wine or cider jugs that you might accumulate over the holiday season. In the spring, fill the jugs with water and scatter them here and there throughout your vegetable garden. The light reflected off the bottles often scares off rabbits.

Glass gallon bottles also make great cloches (dome-shaped, protective covers for plants), but you have to be a pretty confident glass cutter to cut off the bottom without also cutting off a finger. If it appeals to you as a winter project, you can make a wonderful collection of glass cloches that you will treasure.

A diamond bandsaw is excellent for projects like this, but they are not inexpensive. Manual glass cutters from the hardware store are workable and actually pretty fun, but they take a little practice. If you don't know how to cut glass or just aren't interested, plastic jugs make excellent cloches as well.

Nature is so full of genius, full of the divinity, that not a snowflake escapes its fashioning hand.
—Henry David Thoreau, Journal 1906

❧ D E C E M B E R 2

I don't do a lot of indoor gardening but I love amaryllis plants in the dining room window and on the fireplace mantel.

You can keep your amaryllis going indefinitely with very little effort. Once the bloom dies, deadhead it, and keep it watered just enough to keep the foliage green. After the last frost, plant the bulb outside with a little bone meal, in your lily bed or somewhere that is warm, light (not full sun), and not too wet. You can leave it there all summer, where it will grow strong and healthy leaves, and may even bloom again for you. After the first light frost, pull the plant, shake off the loose dirt, and store the plant in the cellar or some other cool dry place—55 degrees or so—for 10 weeks without watering. When you want to start it again, pot the amaryllis fairly snugly in a sterile medium (it blooms best when potbound) and begin to water again. When the flower stalk emerges, set it in a light place, and begin the cycle again.

Oh yes: amaryllis is poisonous. Don't let kiddies who like to eat plants with big flowers anywhere near it. Many South American tribes use the sap from the plant to make poison arrows.

DRYING MAGNOLIA LEAVES • Dried magnolia leaves look wonderful strewn on a holiday table. Some people spray-paint them copper or gold, but they look just as well in their deep, rich green. To dry some magnolia leaves, put them in a compound of 10 parts of white cornmeal with 3 parts of borax, mixed thoroughly. You can also use 3 parts of borax to 1 part of sand. Cover the leaves with the mix and wait for 2 weeks, until they are completely dry. Once

293

dry, you can make wreaths or whatever arrangement appeals to you. If you like, you can save the mix in a tightly fitted plastic container for years, so long as you keep it dry.

BAY LEAVES AS A DETERRENT • Scatter bay leaves in your pantry to repel weevils and other bugs. Bay leaves also repel fleas (attach to Fido's collar?).

Much snow, much hay.

❦ DECEMBER 3

The stores and holiday catalogues are bulging with children's gardening products and I have mixed feelings about them (the products, not the children). For one thing, the tools can be somewhat expensive, and while it makes no sense to be chintzy when you're buying tools, buying world-class hardware for a seven-year-old is another matter. Then there's the grouchy part of me that thinks this is a children's world gone overboard—too much, too easy, too soon. Let them trip over adult-sized rakes; it's part of growing up.

Having said that, I have done everything I can to reveal for my children the pleasures of making gardens, including the purchase of little children's-sized leather gardening gloves. For children or grandchildren of any age, plants, seeds, tools, and any one of the many new gardening books for children do make excellent holiday gifts. When you select vegetable seeds, make sure they are fast-growing varieties like radishes, carrots, scarlet runner beans, tomatoes, squash, or pumpkins. Flower seeds should be showy plants, like sunflowers or zinnias. If you are planning on giving them a "plot" for Christmas—which would look great marked off with bright red ribbon and a big bow—make sure you select a spot with a bare minimum of 6 hours of sunlight a day and soil that is balanced, rich, loamy, and light. Now, that's a great gift.

HOLLY AS A PREDICTOR • If there are but a few berries on your holly, this will be a mild winter; an abundance of berries means a harsh winter.

294

The lesson I have thoroughly learnt, and wish to pass on to others, is to know the enduring happiness that the love of a garden gives. I rejoice when I see anyone, and especially children, inquiring about flowers, and wanting gardens of their own, and carefully working in them. For love of gardening is a seed that once sown never dies, but always grows and grows to an enduring and ever-increasing source of happiness.

—Gertrude Jekyll

❦ D E C E M B E R 4

If you haven't got a cold frame—or if you have a gardening friend who'd appreciate one—this is a good weekend project. Cold frames can be useful throughout the year (actually, once you have a few of them, you start seeing all sorts of uses).

To build one, get an old window sash or storm window, or construct a cover for your frame using glass, acrylic, or 10 mil. plastic. Assemble the frame by joining redwood or cedar boards 18 inches high in the back, tapering down to 12 inches in the front, reinforcing them with a 1-by-2 the precise length and width of the external dimensions of the selected cover. Use a couple of sturdy hinges (galvanized steel T-hinges would be ideal) to attach the glass cover to the frame. Install some weatherstripping between the cover and the frame. Keep some 1-by-2s handy to prop open the cold frame when you need to provide ventilation. You can also order any number of styles from catalogues.

TO SHARPEN YOUR HOE • Once you get the hang of it, it's not hard to sharpen your hoe. Be sure the hoe is clean before you start. Place it in a vise, then grasp both ends of a mill file and run it back and forth at the same angle as the beveled edge of the blade. (I tried to do it without securing the hoe in the vise first and it was impossible.) Continue sharpening. Test it on whatever is handy this time of year to make sure you've got a precision edge.

YOGURT CUPS MAKE GOOD SCORECARDS • An Ohio reader of *Fine Gardening* magazine wrote to the editors about a great use for yogurt cups. She cuts the containers into rectangles and makes "scorecards," punching a hole in each card and attaching it by a wire twist-tie to a plant. Being compulsive, I love this idea. Every time she goes to her garden, she takes a permanent marker and records on each plant the date of first harvest. She then keeps a running tally of how many tomatoes, eggplants, peppers—whatever—she harvests on each plant. At the end of the season she has a precise record of plant performance.

Yogurt cups make good scorecards.

❦ D E C E M B E R 5

Here is a gift you should give *yourself:* some paper-whites in a bowl for bloom in the gray of late winter. The blooms of *Narcissus tazetta* are so welcome in January and February, when you need a clean, aesthetic sensibility to offset the glut of the holidays. They are easy to grow in containers and need virtually no upkeep.

This is all you do: Fill a shallow bowl up to about an inch of the top with pea or aquarium gravel. The bulbs should be placed on top, side to side. Don't be stingy with the bulbs or they will look sparse and silly. Pack them in like sardines. Cover the bulbs almost completely with the gravel. Water well. For the next 2 or 3 weeks—or until green shoots appear—keep them in a cool, darkish spot. Gradually move them to a warm sunny window to grow and bloom.

Now, the problem with paper-whites is that they get leggy and collapse. I have always tied fishing line around them and used chopsticks for stakes to keep them looking good. A gardening friend shook his head when I was complaining about this one day and gave me his secret: gin. He pours a tablespoon of gin on his plants from time to time to reduce the amount of foliage. This year he showed me his indoor bulb display and indeed, the stalks were shorter, the foliage less pronounced—and his blooms proud.

SPRUCE UP YOUR WINDOW BOXES • Window boxes gain a finished, winter look when covered with evergreen boughs or pine needles. When I lived in New York City, I planted mine with small evergreens and during the holidays decorated them with little white lights.

WINTER ANNUALS FOR WARMER ZONES • In zones 8 and warmer, replant your containers with pansies, violas, calendula, stock, snapdragons, and flowering cabbage and kale.

❦ DECEMBER 6

Salt damages—no, devastates—plants. So don't throw salt down to accelerate ice thaw on your driveway or steps, particularly if the salts can seep into nearby beds and borders. Deicing salt is most damaging in late fall and late winter because feeder roots are not fully dormant during these periods. Use an alternative. I use kitty litter and it works fine. Sand also works. In the spring, you can rinse off steps and paths and your driveway with a good hosing down—both substances will make fine additions to your soil. *Do not, however, use fertilizer to thaw ice, thinking it will boost your lawn and garden. While the salts in the fertilizer will thaw the ice, they could also cause damage if applied too liberally.*

MAPLE TREE ALERT • If you have young maple trees and live in a cold climate you might have problems with your trunks splitting vertically. This happens during the winter when radical shifts in temperatures expand and contract the tree's tissues. You can avoid this effect by wrapping plastic tree wrap up to the first limb—leaving it on until the tree grows to about 5 inches in diameter.

PROTECT YOUR NONHARDY PLANTS • Plants that don't qualify as hardy can be protected by building miniwalls out of stacks of large rocks on the northwest side of the plant. The rocks not only provide protection from cold northwest winds, but supply heat absorbed from the sun during the day.

LIVING CHRISTMAS TREE • If you are going to use a living Christmas tree and live in a cold-weather zone, you should already have dug a hole for it. Sorry. (See page 246.) If you live in a warmer zone, you can still prepare a hole. When you shop for your Christmas tree, shake it to see if many needles drop (lots of falling needles is a terrible sign and means the tree was uprooted too early). Grasp 6 to 8 inches of a stem between your thumb and forefinger and pull it toward you. The needles should not fall off easily. Then evaluate shape and discuss growth habits with your nurseryman. Be sure you have room for the tree in its maturity, because they grow fast, much faster than you think.

❦ D E C E M B E R 7

On days like this, throwing scraps of orange peel and eggshells into a plastic compost container is what I call gardening. But I am a lazy gardener, which means that my trips to "the heap" in the backyard are few and far between. When it's cold like this and your in-and-out activity is at a minimum, you can take some measures to make life easier and your compost healthier. I store my scraps in plastic containers in the freezer during the winter. Freezing enables me to be a diligent composter and avoid running out into the cold and risking pneumonia every night just to make sure the banana peels get in. Once every week I'll make a deposit and that's it. During milder months, I keep a bucket with a lid on my kitchen counter. I always wondered why it didn't smell, until I read that coffee grounds absorb odors, and we are big in the coffee department. An occasional layer of sawdust or even potting soil will also absorb odors if you keep your scraps out in the open.

BEGINNER GARDENER GIFT LIST

Spade
Hoe
Rake
Spading fork
Pruning shears
Long-handled clippers
Gardening gloves

INTERMEDIATE GARDENER GIFT LIST

Bulb planter
Hand trowel
Sprayer
Wheelbarrow
Watering can
Pruning saw
Cold frame

SERIOUS GARDENER GIFT LIST

Lopping shears
Spreader
Shredder
Rototiller
Soil sifter

SOIL SIFTER • While we're on gift lists, you can easily make a soil sifter for a friend who's got a rocky garden and a contemplative nature. I recently put one together and it works great: just nail together 2-by-4s, making a frame about 2 by 3 feet, and use heavy hardware staples to attach ½-inch hardware cloth across the frame.

Come on! How often do you prune your Eugenia myrtifolia *right after it blooms, the way Martha Stewart does, in December, wearing your lipstick?*
—Anne Raver

❦ DECEMBER 8

Winter gardening is for people who are pretty far along in their horticultural journey. For the beginning winter gardener, evergreens should be the first concern. Evergreens provide texture and visual depth—and establish strong design patterns in the winter garden. Not only are evergreen trees and shrubbery important, but evergreen ground covers can make an enormous difference in the garden during this long winter season.

If you are at the point of evaluating your winter garden, this is an ideal time to do an assessment. If you live in a milder climate, you are probably running around in a sweater and planting tulips. Others of us are headed for winter in a serious way. For cold-weather gardeners, try to pick a mild day and spend some time walking around your property, looking at it from all sides. Take photographs using black-and-white film for the best sense of the architecture of your garden, its main lines and textures. Color is only subtly what winter gardening is all about, so it's best to confront your situation in its most elemental—black and white—sense, first. Then hole up in the library with some books and back issues of gardening magazines for ideas. Go have a chat with someone at your local nursery, who is probably bored to tears with all of the poinsettias in his midst, and don't be shy to ring up your favorite catalogue vendors, the best of whom are always cheery when fielding inquiries. But do it now, in the bareness of the moment, when you can really see your garden in its essence.

O TANNENBAUM • Not all evergreens make good Christmas trees. Spruces and hemlocks drop their needles too easily to make a good cut tree. Try fir, pine, or juniper for cuttings and trees.

❦ D E C E M B E R 9

If your compost heap is all fall leaves and you need some green material badly—there is a secret gold mine *right in your midst:* the local florist. You can collect all of the flower and foliage waste from the flower shop and lug it home weekly, saving the florist from having to deal with it. Offer him or her a plastic trash can or big box to toss the green compost into and empty it periodically. Everyone is a winner, but especially your garden.

WHERE THE WIND COMES RIGHT BEHIND THE RAIN • American mistletoe is the state flower of Oklahoma.

FIRST TANNENBAUM • In early Christian days, the apple tree was considered the appropriate one for Christmas celebrations, because it symbolized the fall of Adam and the reclamation of souls by the birth of the Christ child.

PROTECT YOUR STRAWBERRY BARREL • You can keep your berry barrel snug over the coming months by tying a series of evergreen branches vertically around the sides of the barrel.

POTPOURRI PICK-ME-UP • Add a few drops of brandy or port to invigorate potpourri that has gone stale.

❦ DECEMBER 10

The long lonely winter no longer has to be lonely. Now you can join Soilmates, a companion service for gardeners. For $4 you receive a 6-month membership, which includes a quarterly newsletter with gardening tips and recipes and member profiles.

Privacy is respected by this rather unusual service. You send in your own profile if you like and it will appear in the newsletter. If other gardeners decide to correspond with you, and you with them, you both pay Soilmates $1 per letter for the privilege (the organization functions as a letter forwarding service, in effect). More information can be obtained by writing: Soilmates, P.O. Box 4065, Ogden, UT 84402.

Meeting gardeners through the mail.

FOR WHAT IT'S WORTH • The American Forestry Association estimates that a species tree in good condition would have an approximate value as follows: 10-inch trunk diameter (measured 4½ feet from the ground), $1,729; a 14-inch trunk diameter, $3,388; a 26-inch trunk diameter, $11,682; and a 30-inch trunk diameter, $15,000.

BERMS AS SALT BARRIERS • In Northern zones, many people create earthen berms along the roadside of their property to act as barriers against the deicing salt that is applied in winter months. It's certainly a beautiful solution but not altogether effective, according to the Morton Aboretum in Illinois. The grassed berms actually give a lift to winds blowing off the roads so that the salt is carried even deeper into the property, completely contrary to the desired effect. To combat this, the aboretum suggests putting in a dense line of trees and shrubs on the top of the berm.

❦ D E C E M B E R 1 1

If your compost heap has turned cold and you are in a relatively warm zone, you can heat it up by adding a thin layer of "hot" chicken manure or a couple of layers of grass clippings. Some gardeners place black plastic on top of their compost to heat it up. Of course, keep turning it, and eventually it will start cooking again.

TO PROLONG AMARYLLIS BLOOM • As the flower buds of your amaryllis open, use tweezers to remove the pollen-bearing anthers before they begin to shed. This adds days to the flowering period.

RUG MULCH • The idea of using carpet rolls as mulch never appealed to me, and when a gardening acquaintance told me she got about eight giant *free* rolls from a hotel that was going out of business, I wasn't really happy for her. But the next time I saw her garden, I was amazed. The foliage in her huge vegetable garden almost completely disguised the maroon-colored diamond pattern on the carpeting—and walking up and down the rows on carpet was kind of fun. Anyway, it didn't look bad at all. My friend recommends jute-backed carpet (doesn't mold) and recommends getting it free by posting signs around town. She has found that most people will happily give you old carpeting free if you'll agree to haul it. I have also seen rag rugs and rope rugs used quite successfully as mulch—both eventually decompose right into the soil.

❦ DECEMBER 12
National Poinsettia Day

Poinsettias are not one of my favorite plants. Nevertheless, I buy them in red, each Christmas, using them for their color and then tossing them out with enormous relief on Twelfth Night. I do not play the interminable game of trying to keep them alive. This year I mixed bright red poinsettias in rustic baskets with smaller pots of the licorice plant (*Helichrysum petiolatum* 'lime light'), and its furry pale green leaves helped enormously to soften the look. I have also mixed them with scented geranium with good results. Still, though, they are poinsettias.

However blind I may be to the virtues of this plant, I like its story. According to legend, the poinsettia was heaven sent. In a tiny village in Mexico, the tradition on Christmas Eve was to place gifts before the creche at the church. A young boy, having nothing to offer, went outside and knelt in the snow to pray for a worthy gift to give the newborn king. Just where he knelt, a beautiful plant with vivid scarlet leaves appeared and the boy immediately presented his gift to the Christ Child. Thus, Mexicans call the plant *Flor de la Noche Buena* (Flower of the Holy Night), and many believe the plant resembles the Star of Bethlehem. (It's a legend, so we won't pick too much at the difficulty a poinsettia might have growing in the snow.)

It was Dr. Joel Roberts Poinsett, the first U.S. minister to Mexico, who brought the plant to this country in the 1830s, and it is for him that the plant is now named.

DECK THE TABLE • To my eye any plant looks great in a terracotta pot. But herbs, especially, in clay pots make wonderful scattered centerpieces for the holiday table. Just wrap the pots with a festive ribbon. Sprigs of artemisia can be knotted as napkin rings. Ivy sprigs can be strewn in and around plates for a cheerful, festive look.

❦ DECEMBER 13

I've spent a lot of time gardening in a serious zone 6, where winter snow and ice create astonishing beauty but also sometimes kill your plants. Or maybe it was our roof line that killed so many plants. In any case, our shrubs were constantly being damaged by avalanches of snow and ice sliding off the eaves. We'd replant only to have our shrubs wiped out again. Then someone came up with the simple idea of building a little shelter for the shrubs: a series of A-frames made of plywood on hinges. It worked. All you do is hinge big sheets of plywood together and set them out like little tents for shrubs. Sure it looked strange, but the snow pileup covered the strangeness during most of the winter. I think this would work with endangered shrubs anywhere, but if you are in a windy location, stake your A-frames for good measure.

A NEWSLETTER FOR TOMATO LOVERS • Reading about tomatoes is not as much fun as growing and eating them, but with *The Tomato Club Newsletter*, it's almost a tough call. This newsletter, written by Bob Ambrose in New Jersey, is packed with wonderful tips, lore, and horticultural information. You can get a sample copy by calling (201) 488-2231.

PRUNING REMINDER • During dry spells, prune dead or diseased branches from established deciduous trees and shrubs while they are bare.

The man who has planted a garden feels he has done something for the good of the whole world.

—Charles Dudley Warner

❦ DECEMBER 14
Halcyon Days Begin

This is the first of the fourteen days known as Halcyon Days. Halcyon Days are the seven days before and after St. Thomas's Day and/or the first day of winter. Halcyon is the name for the kingfisher bird, and it was thought the gods set aside these two weeks as a time of peace and serenity so the kingfisher might lay her eggs.

ATTENTION, SHOPPERS • Here is a wonderful gift for a gardening friend that you can make or have made for not much money. I call it a book of seasons, but really it's a blank journal in which to record firsts: first frost, first crocus, first pussy willow, first tomato.

It's a tad different from a gardening journal—not as much about successes and failures or experiments but rather a *phenological record* of the seasons. My husband started one years ago to help us gauge the rhythms of the fly fishing season. He would jot down the dates on which certain flies appeared, when the rhododendrons bloomed, and also when the ice flows broke on the river. Over time, I realized that the emergence of certain flies corresponded to the emerging life in our garden. He had created a phenological record of enormous value. We liked it so much we had some blank journals made for friends. For a few dollars, I had a calligrapher enter headings in the journals—for instance: early spring flowers and trees, birds, butterflies, spring vegetables planted and harvested, first frost, first snow, and so on. Under the headings the gardeners can list the particulars of their garden and wildlife. And over the years, these little books seem to develop their own heartbeat, an unsentimental but somehow poignant record of the passage of time.

MENORAH LEGEND • Sage (*Salvia judaica*) is thought to be the inspiration for the seven-branched menorah, according to Roberta M. Coughlin, author of *The Gardener's Companion*.

❦ DECEMBER 1 5

I use cayenne (aka ground red pepper) on my indoor plants to keep my cat, Franny, from doing her usual noshing on the ends of innocent tropical plant leaves. Nothing I have tried has ever worked better than a light sprinkling on the leaves, applied a couple of times a year. But while cats are sweet, occasionally misguided things, squirrels are mean and desperate enemies of the people. I no longer like squirrels. And I am happy to report that cayenne works as well on squirrels as it does on felines. When the squirrels got into the shed where I house the garbage (the point at which I considered investing in small firearms, *that* point) I ran to the market and bought a dozen tins of cayenne and sprinkled it everywhere. It worked. Then I had the problem of not wanting to purchase $20 worth of cayenne every time the varmints got into my hair. I am further happy to report that you can buy cayenne in big institutional tins at a great savings. And it is worth it. You can either sprinkle the cayenne on trouble spots (like the garbage area) or run it around the perimeter of your property and the squirrels will—for a time—remove themselves from your life.

PROTECT BUDS FROM FROSTS • If you are having a particularly rough winter, protect your rhododendron and azalea buds from serious frost and winds with sacks or plastic sheeting, which can be removed during mild spells.

❦ DECEMBER 16

The Christmas rose (*Helleborus niger*) is gorgeous, it is romantic, and it blooms when little else will. I am always touched when it arrives in the garden. But in the garden I must let it stay. For me, *H. niger* has never been truly happy in a vase. I have queried many individuals on the subject, and so far, the best method for keeping a cut hellebore going indoors still offers me no more than two or three good days out of them.

First, cut while about two-thirds of the blooms are open, and put them in a vase with commercial floral preservative (that stuff that comes in little packets). If you can't use them in an arrangement right away, put them, in the vase, in the 36- to 41-degree range of your refrigerator. Clip the ends before arranging. *Some people burn the tips of* H. niger *stems with a candle right after cutting, and report good results.*

PLANT PERSPECTIVE • While the majority of plants have been cultivated for at least 4,000 years, some are relative newcomers, aged 2,000 years or less. These include artichokes, coffee, currants, muskmelon, okra, parsley, parsnip, raspberry, and rhubarb. Even more recently cultivated (since Christ's birth) are the avocado, peanut, pineapple, potato, pumpkin, red pepper, rubber, squash, tomato, and vanilla.

I keep my rosemary plants in pots a few feet from the radiator during the winter, and they seem to like it. Rosemary derives its name from *ros maris* or dew of the sea, from its tendency to be covered with sea spray as it grew along its native shores of the Mediterranean. The herb craves a warm day climate with a slight need for moisture, so I spritz it from time to time. In the winter, I like to make rosemary pita toasts: brush olive oil on a thin pita bread, sprinkle it with fresh rosemary and kosher salt, and broil. Rosemary is also great with roast lamb or veal chops. Yum.

ROAD SALT • Gypsum, sold as Sof-N-Soil, is an excellent means of neutralizing salt in road spray or in water that has been processed through your water softener. It's pretty inexpensive and it stores well. If your garden borders a roadway or walkways, I would apply this religiously over the winter months.

SAVE HOLIDAY WRAP CYLINDERS • Save holiday wrap cylinders for making biodegradable collars to protect plants from cutworms. You can slice them into 3- or 4-inch pieces, and put them around transplants as soon as they go into the garden, sinking them down about an inch into the soil.

Mothballs work but they repel me just as much as they repel most moths. With some leftover dried herbs from the garden you can make a bouquet that not only repels bugs but pleases the nose and eye. Gather branches of dried wormwood, sage, southernwood, yarrow, pennyroyal, tansy, and lavender with a wire twist-tie or a rubber band. Tie a wire ribbon around the stems and slip it onto a hanger or over a nail in your closet. A bowl of potpourri of the same herbs would also work but would be somewhat less effective, depending on where you put it.

LET THEM EAT POINSETTIA LEAVES • In 1919, a two-year-old in Hawaii was reported to have died after eating a poinsettia leaf, thus giving the plant its reputation as fatally poisonous (the name "poinsettia" presumably also added to the myth). Since then, many kids have chewed poinsettia leaves—one is not sure why—but they nevertheless suffered no more than stomach pains. The leaves do not have enough poison to kill a child.

TYPES OF CHRISTMAS TREES SOLD • The most popular Christmas trees sold are the balsam fir, Douglas fir, and Scotch pine. If you want fragrance, purchase a fir tree. The longest-lasting trees are the fir and Scotch pine.

Austrian pine	Norway spruce
Balsam fir	Red pine
Black spruce	Red spruce
Blue spruce	Scotch pine
Douglas fir	Virginia pine
Eastern red cedar	White fir
Grand fir	White pine

❦ D E C E M B E R 1 9

Paper-white narcissus are the easiest bulbs to force but they are next to impossible to get through a second season in a pot. If you live in zone 8 or warmer, you can replant your paper-whites in the garden in hopes of future blooms, but if you live in colder regions, the garden is out. Containers are out. You'll just have to buy new bulbs next year.

CHECK ON YOUR NEWLY PLANTED SHRUBS • Pack the soil around the roots of newly planted shrubs and heathers if it has been dislodged by ice or snow or other dramatic changes in the weather.

On December 20, 1821, Matthew Zahm of Lancaster, Pennsylvania, mentioned the Christmas tree in his diary. It is the first American record of the Christmas tree, and no one disputes the claim that the Pennsylvania Dutch initiated it in this country. The custom originated in the fifteenth or sixteenth century near the Rhine River in Germany. The medieval German mystery plays used to feature a fir tree hung with apples to represent the expulsion of Adam and Eve from Paradise. After these mystery plays were suppressed in the churches, the "paradise tree," which had become a symbol of the plays, found its way into the homes of believers, who used it to signify the coming Saviour.

TODDLER GATES • The old-fashioned folding gates that used to keep toddlers in place (or out of place) make great trellises. You may come across one at a yard sale, and if so, grab it. All you do is extend the gate and nail stakes to either side to give it a permanent size and shape. Drive the stakes into the ground to stabilize it and it's ready to go.

SAND SPREADER • You can use your fertilizer spreader to sprinkle sand on walks and on the driveway when freezing weather requires it.

❦ D E C E M B E R 2 1
St. Thomas's Day/Winter Solstice

This is the shortest day of the year. On this day winter begins, lasting until March 21.

Rosemary Creasy, an author and landscape designer I admire greatly, has a brilliant technique for predicting the angle of the summer sun whilst in the dead of winter. All you do is go outside at midnight on the night of the full moon in, say, January. Pay attention to where the buildings and eaves and trees cast their shadows in the moonlight. The shadows you see are approximately where the sun's shadows will fall six months hence—in this case, July—at noon in your garden.

INDOOR GROWING • You can sow pots of parsley and pixie tomatoes for winter use and grow them in a bright window or under grow lights. Watercress or peppergrass is also easy to grow indoors, and adds a crisp pungent taste to salads. You can fill a large soup bowl half full with peat moss and scatter seed on top. Grow it in a bright, cool window and harvest in 10 days.

THE LARGEST ROSE IN THE UNIVERSE • The largest rosebush on record is located in Tombstone, Arizona, according to the American Rose Society. The banksia rose (*Rosa banksiae*) was planted in 1885 and it now extends over 8,000 square feet on a trellis at the Rose Tree Inn.

❧ D E C E M B E R   2 2

CAPRICORN, December 22 to January 20—*A good all-around time to sow seeds of plants that produce abundant roots and branches*

If your trees or shrubs are damaged by a winter storm and you need to build your case with the insurance company or with the IRS to take a tax deduction, contact the Council of Tree and Landscape Appraisers, 1250 I Street, NW, Suite 500, Washington, DC 20005. You should always keep all your records of landscape expenses and report damage to your insurance company immediately. In addition, a horticultural expert will probably need to be called in to make an independent assessment. There are different formulas for valuing trees and shrubs and the Council will help you to validate your case.

CHESTNUTS ROASTING IN THE OVEN • Here's an easy method for roasting chestnuts. Cut an X in the flat side of the shells. Lay chestnuts on a baking sheet in a single layer and roast in a preheated 425 degree oven for 15 to 20 minutes or until tender. The shells will peel off easily.

WINTER-DAMAGED PLANTS • When a plant is damaged by snow, ice, or wind, don't be in a hurry to start pruning. Within a few days, plants often will straighten up on their own. Broken limbs can be pruned immediately. If the plant looks lopsided after corrective pruning, prune the whole plant so its future growth will be in balance.

Uprooted trees should be straightened immediately, and staked. Damaged roots or limbs should be pruned. Keep the tree mulched and watered in the spring.

BAN ON CUT CHRISTMAS TREES • Concerned that our national forests were being depleted, President Theodore Roosevelt banned cut Christmas trees from the White House temporarily.

❦ DECEMBER 23

Americans don't like the taste of supermarket tomatoes, the U.S. Department of Agriculture concluded after surveying consumers, who ranked supermarket tomatoes as the *least* satisfying of 31 typical produce items. Yet the average American buys 18 pounds of tomatoes a year, spending $4 billion on "fresh" tomatoes. Small wonder that biotechnologists are scrambling to come up with genetically altered tomatoes with home-grown flavor.

I didn't really have an opinion on genetically altered tomatoes until I read that in an effort to get leaner pork, gene splicers had combined a human gene with a pig gene and got a peculiar-looking, wrinkle-faced pig who had really bad arthritis. The pork was leaner than usual, but I keep imagining that face, and I believe I can wait until August to have a real tomato. Of course, gardeners know how to wait. We are different from biotechnologists.

Anyway, the cherry tomatoes in the store aren't so bad, and if you marinate them in a little dressing of salt, pepper, sugar, and olive oil they can be pretty tasty. At least they won't wink back at you.

COLLECT PLASTIC NETTING • The plastic netting used to wrap Christmas trees makes an excellent protective barrier against raccoons in the summer. As tree sales wind down to a halt, ask the tree vendor if you can have some of the leftover netting. In the summer, tie the netting end to end on a fishline or cord and lay it loosely around the perimeter of the garden site. The raccoons hate getting their feet tangled up in the plastic netting.

IGNORE YOUR INDOOR HERBS FOR NOW • The best
care you can give your indoor herbs right now is no care. Hold off
on fertilizer and keep to a very light watering schedule until the days
get longer, about mid-January. At that point you can start feeding
them some liquid seaweed, diluted half strength. The potted soil
tends to get compacted from watering, so loosen it up with a fork.
By February, when the light gets brighter, you will see a pleasant
revival.

❦ D E C E M B E R 2 4

The snow came early this year, and I must say our little cold frames
have served us well, especially that day we couldn't even think about
driving to the market. I am not a "four-season gardener" à la Eliot
Coleman, who has completely reimagined what gardening for fresh
food is all about (his book *Four-Season Harvest* is pure pleasure, and
even if you aren't as ambitious as he is, I recommend it highly). We
winter-over leeks, chard, kale, and some root crops, just for the fun
of it, but there is a satisfaction in knowing that it can be done and
that we know how to do it.

For our Christmas Eve meal, we will have a feast, including Swiss
Chard with Pecans, which you also might like to try.

SWISS CHARD WITH PECANS

2 tablespoons chopped pecans
2 tablespoons butter
2 pounds Swiss chard, washed, stems removed
Salt and pepper to taste

Sauté the pecans in 1 tablespoon of butter over medium heat, until
the nuts turn golden brown. Drain on paper towels. Wilt the Swiss
chard in the water that clings to its leaves in a large fry pan, cooking
over medium heat and stirring so the leaves don't stick. Add the remaining butter and the pecans. Season with salt and pepper. Serves 4.

WHO'S WHO IN GARDENING • *Organic Gardening* magazine and National Family Opinion Research did a survey of 75,000
American gardeners just to see who's who. They divided gardeners
into four groups according to how much time each week they spent
in the garden: dabblers (4.5 hours a week during the growing season);
decorators, defined as gardeners devoted to ornamentals (7.5 hours a
week); cultivators, who focus on vegetable and fruit crops (11 hours a
week); master gardeners (15 hours minimum a week). Dabblers account for 60 percent of the gardening population, decorators and cultivators 18 percent and 19 percent respectively, and masters for 3
percent.

WOOD ASHES IN A CANISTER • Save a large tin canister
of wood ashes to use in the garden next summer for pest control.
Plants that are sprinkled with dry ashes are unpalatable to rabbits,
bean beetles, and onion and cabbage maggots. A thick layer of dry
ashes scattered on the perimeter of the soil will provide a line of de-
fense against slugs (though it will need to be replenished after a rain).
The alkalinity that is washed into the soil will discourage, even kill,
cutworms.

KEEP GLASS VASES IMMACULATE • If you want your
cut flowers to last long, your vases have got to be squeaky clean. If
you have a lot of buildup that regular soap and water won't remove,
try adding a little coarse sand or even fish gravel to dislodge the bacteria. Many globe-shaped vases are difficult to get into; using a bottle
brush helps.

Gardening makes homebodies of us all.
—Janice Emily Bowers

❦ D E C E M B E R   2 5
Christmas Day

I love the holiday revels but even gaiety can take its toll, and sometimes it is necessary to retreat from it all and walk the garden, which
is quiet, bleak, but mine, at least for now. The gardener knows a secret: that we are midwives in this life, and it could not be clearer to
me than on this cold, still Christmas Day. Blessings to all.

313

WHAT DOES THIS CHRISTMAS FORETELL • Christmas is steeped in forecast. Missourians used to believe that a mild Christmas brings a good harvest. Then there is "Green Christmas, White Easter," or "if Windy on Christmas, trees will bring much fruit." I would not take a wager on the whole lot!

FLOWER SHOWS • One of the most pleasurable ways to see flowers and to get new gardening ideas is to attend garden shows. The most celebrated show, of course, is the Chelsea Flower Show in London, which features nurseries, growers, garden centers, and landscapers' works, along with a host of other products associated with gardening.

Garden shows usually are held in February and March, when we most crave vivid color and the smell of greenery—and while we are still planning and dreaming. In this country, the Philadelphia Garden Show, held in March, is generally believed to be the best. Garden magazines regularly alert their readers to upcoming garden shows. Treat yourself!

WORLD'S TALLEST CHRISTMAS TREE • Seattle, Washington, has the distinction of being the home town of the world's largest Christmas tree, erected at Northgate Shopping Center in December 1950 and standing 221 feet tall. It was a Douglas fir (*Pseudotsuga menziesii*).

> At Christmas, I no more desire a rose
> Than wish for a snow in May's new fangled mirth.
> —William Shakespeare

❦ DECEMBER 26

You might be up to your ears in crumpled wrapping paper now, but life goes on—so let's talk about those pots of bulbs for forcing you've got hidden under the stairsteps. Have you watered them lately? If you take care of your forcing bulbs now, you will have magnificent spring flowers in late winter; just don't let them dry out. Over the next few weeks the pots will be coming out of the darkness and coolness, ready to be forced.

You can tell if your bulbs are ready by checking their roots. Once they descend through the drainage hole at the bottom of the pot they should slowly be acclimated to room temperature. Don't bring them into the dining room all at once. Start them out just below 60 degrees with very little light. Slowly bring them into brighter light and warmer temperatures (64 to 71 degrees). Daffodils and crocuses like cool temperatures; tulips and hyacinths are happy at 68 degrees. Your bulbs will flower from 12 to 16 weeks after planting (paper-whites are the happy exception; they bloom approximately 4 to 6 weeks from planting).

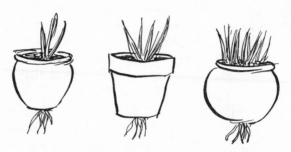

When the roots descend through the drainage hole, forced bulbs are ready to be eased in.

PEPPER ORDERS • A fabulous source for peppers is The Pepper Gal, Box 12534, Lake Park, FL 33403.

A famous philosopher said that whenever he talked to another savant, he became convinced happiness was not possible for humans; when he talked to his gardener, he was sure that it was.

❦ D E C E M B E R 2 7

I value a recycled Christmas tree as much as anyone, but I don't think, as one gardener suggested, I will strip off all the branches and carve a totem pole for the front yard. However, there are many other uses for used Christmas trees that have great appeal. Generally, we take the ax out and chop off large branches to layer on a couple of our unmulched beds and borders. The timing is great because the ground usually isn't totally frozen until about the third week in December anyway. But there are other smart things to do with your Tannenbaum. Many people anchor their tree outdoors and hang little food ornaments on the branches for hungry, winged friends. Chipper-shredder owners make an excellent wood-chip mulch out of their trees. You can also wire the widest branches over your trellised vines to protect them from drying winds. If you like to make your own potpourri, cut off the branch tips, strip the needles, and dry them for your own sachets and dried flower mixes. I have also seen shed needles strewn on winter-muddy pathways; it looks great and keeps your boots half clean.

CHECK YOUR TREES AND SHRUBS • If it hasn't been snowing or raining, your evergreens might be thirsty. As crazed as it sounds, you might need to get out there and give them a drink—because they transpire water continuously through the winter. Extremely cold and windy weather makes it worse (for you and the evergreens).

IMAGINING THAT MUCH GARLIC • Insects may be far from a worry now, but while gardeners contemplate leftover plum pudding, workers at ENVIRepel are making an organic garlic spray to be ready for gardeners' use this spring. ENVIRepel is the first EPA-approved organic product of its kind. Using a secret recipe, the company produces 25,000 gallons of the spray weekly, from the 50 tons of raw Asian garlic piled up in their factory yard.

❦ DECEMBER 28

You may have just walked in from a visit to your cold frames, with some skinny carrots in hand, feeling pretty good about yourself. Bernard Lavery of Spalding, Lincolnshire, England, also grows carrots. His biggest carrot was a record-breaking 16 feet 10 inches long.

A holder of nine world and six U.K. Guinness records for big vegetables, Mr. Lavery also has grown a 46-pound celery, 12-foot 8-inch parsnip, and a 124-pound cabbage that required a crane to be harvested. He names his vegetables (e.g., Anne the carrot, Sue the cabbage, Lucy the parsnip), and claims his secret to success is the seven-day-a-week attention he pays to his plants. To accomplish this, he left his wife and home in Wales to work and grow vegetables in England.

His seeds are available from Thompson & Morgan, P.O. Box 1308, Jackson, NJ 08527, 1/800/274-7333. A packet of 5 giant cucumber seeds is $3.

HOLIDAY SALES • Sometimes antique shops and architectural salvage stores have excellent sales after the holidays. If your favorite haunts offer a bargain or two this time of year, hunt around for a whimsical finial or iron or stone to put in the center of an island or herb garden. Or look for a bench that might work in a shady corner. If you keep the scale down, a folly or two can add much wit to your private gardens.

SAVE THOSE CATALOGUES! • As the catalogues begin to come in, save them whether you plan to order or not. When you give plants to friends you can label the containers with photos cut from catalogues to show them what the scrawny transplant will look like someday. Catalogues also make good reference materials, especially those featuring harder-to-find plants.

❦ DECEMBER 2 9

A gardener can spend a lifetime in the soil (or the ice) without knowing or using or even thinking about Latin. But a working knowledge of Latin basics can be invaluable for identifying and requesting plants, because common names commonly overlap and create confusion. The eighteenth-century Swedish botanist Carl von Linné (Carolus Linnaeus in Latin) established the two-part classification system we use today, where the first name of the organism is the genus, which is always capitalized, and the second name is the species (or a modification of the genus), written in lowercase.

The system is not overly elaborate. The genus signifies a group of closely related plants, like *Quercus* (oak) or *Rosa* (rose) or *Pelargonium* (geranium). The genus is often abbreviated after the first mention to just the first letter so that *Quercus* would be *Q., Rosa, R.,* and *Pelargonium, P.* The species defines plants within a certain genus that have even more specific similar characteristics.

Then there is the variety of the plant. If the plant has a characteristic that further particularizes it beyond the genus and species—for instance, a certain color—it will be identified with *genus, species, variety, color, name.* These characteristics can include height, growing habits, origins, and a host of other clues that can help a gardener immensely when identifying plants.

FIRST-TIME LATINIST • As a practical matter, colors are a logical starting place for those just getting into botanical names: *alba,* white; *argentea,* silver; *aurea,* gold; *autopurpurea,* purple; *azurea,* sky blue; *candida,* white; *cardinalis,* red; *coccinea,* crimson; *fuscousea* or *fuscatus,* brown; *glauca,* blue; *lutea,* yellow; *nigra,* black; *rosa,* pink; *rubra,* red; *tomentosea,* gray; *versicolor,* various colors.

❦ D E C E M B E R   3 0

You can label trees a variety of ways, but the simplest and least expensive method is to take loops of copper wire and attach aluminum strips made from frozen-food containers like TV dinner trays, potpies, and so on. Write the specimen name in pencil using a bit of pressure and the "engraving" will last indefinitely.

COLLECT FALLEN TWIGS AND BRANCHES • If storms have sent a lot of branches and twigs down to the earth, collect the straightest sticks and use them as stakes in the garden. In colonial times, gardeners would create a "pea brush" by lining up branches close together in their pea trenches, forming a natural fence for pea vines.

FOR NEW ASPARAGUS GARDENERS • While you are catalogue browsing: If you are looking for an asparagus plant, 'Jersey Giant' is an excellent choice, a male variety available from Johnny's Selected Seeds, Foss Hill Road, Albion, ME 04910, (207) 437-9294. 'Jersey Knight' is more productive than other varieties because it spends no energy on seed production. I also think it is one of the tastiest of the thicker-waisted males. For thinner asparagus, select from the varieties that produce male and female plants.

Nothing is sacred! Double-check to see if your zone is what you think it is because the United States Department of Agriculture (USDA) *changed the map.* The 1990 zone map is a redo of a map dating from the 1960s. The zone classifications are still the same (zero to minus ten is zone 6 and so on) but where the zones are have changed slightly on the map and if you are a borderline person, you might have actually changed zones.

The zone business is elusive anyway because there are many other factors that go into whether or not a plant will thrive in your climate, or in your microclimate for that matter. I have grown plants in zone 7 that gardeners in zone 8 have lost simply because no matter where you are, climactic conditions are unpredictable, and also because there are many tricks you can play to moderate the conditions of your garden in winter. And I love to play tricks.

FORECAST: GARDENING IN THE NINETIES • Charles Dunn, founder of the Garden Center Institute in Tampa, Florida, predicts that among gardeners in the 1990s, these will be the principal concerns: • Outdoor "rooms" • Intensive gardening in small areas • Privacy screens • Nighttime lighting • Aquatic gardening • Wildflowers • Ornamental grasses • Bush fruits and containerized dwarf trees • Herbs • Color as a factor in plant choice • Fragrance as a factor in plant choice • Heirloom and antique cultivars • Bird feeding • Plants that attract butterflies • Homegrown flowers for cutting • No-mow ground covers as grass substitutes • Smaller lawn areas • Environmental activism • Potted plants • Perennials emphasized, annuals deemphasized • Landscape furnishings • Plants from other countries • Aging home gardeners. Did he leave anything out?

It is unlucky to leave holly up after New Year's Day.

❦ *January* ❦

Flower of the Month: Snowdrop

❦ J A N U A R Y 1
New Year's Day

January, for gardeners, is the month of planning, aka fantasizing. In other words, the catalogues are here. Some arrived in December, but the big mail comes this week. For some reason (fear of missing out on the *one* plant in the universe that will make my garden look sensational? *That* reason?) I always feel obligated to read and to dog-ear every one. No matter that I have serious space restrictions. Forget that my perennials are so overcrowded they are gasping. And let's not even *think* about how many seeds I have left over from last season. It's time to dream. Post–New Year's Eve revelry, today is a good day to have a hot lunch—and a catalogue.

I SAY SWEET POTATO • A sweet potato is not a potato, per se. Potatoes, botanically, are tubers; sweet potatoes are roots. A sweet potato also is not a yam. While sweet potatoes are commonly grown in the United States, especially in warm-weather zones, yams are native to Africa and South America.

FIRST-TIME GARDENERS • Not that it will stop you: novice gardeners commonly purchase two to three times as many seeds as their garden can handle.

ROCKS AS PLANT MARKERS • If you like subtlety but would also like to know where the *Achillea* are, use large flat stones to mark your plants. You can write on the stones in indelible marker. Tuck the stones firmly into the ground next to the plant.

THE FORECAST • Crack a window. If there is little or no wind today, friends in the Ozarks say you will have a dry summer; a breeze foretells good summer rainfall, and if it is really windy on this New Year's Day, we'll have floods. So they say.

In any case, to all gardening friends, cheers.

The most noteworthy thing about gardeners is that they are always optimistic, always enterprising, and never satisfied. They always look forward to doing better than they have done before.

—Vita Sackville-West

❦ JANUARY 2

Big bowls of forced branches make great indoor theater. Forsythia branches are about the easiest to force. From late January to March, depending on your zone, they'll come out in just a few days. (The branches need to have experienced enough cold to ensure good indoor blooming—at least 6 weeks.) Shape your shrub as you cut but remember, this is not pruning time. Select branches with fat flower buds—the small ones are leaf buds. Once you get them inside, cut 2-inch slashes down the length of the stems so the branches can take in water faster and easier (we used to smash the ends of branches with a hammer, but it is now believed that smashing causes the stems

Mist the cut branches of your forsythia occasionally.

321

to decay faster). Soak the cut ends of the branches in a tall container or even prop them up in a bathtub overnight. After soaking, arrange the branches in jars with ample water in a cool location. Mist the branches occasionally so they think they are enjoying a nice early spring rain. Once the buds swell, you can move them into a well-lit room. Don't put them into direct sunlight but give them *some* light.

I FEEL BETTER ALREADY • The National Garden Bureau contends that gardeners live longer because gardening offers stress reduction and a connection to familiar, rhythmic chores.

THE NEW MAROON CARROT • Leonard Pike, a vegetable researcher at Texas A&M University, discovered a maroon carrot on a trip to Brazil and immediately realized its potential. Students and alumni of Texas A&M, rivals with the University of Texas (UT), had long suffered the indignity of eating UT–colored orange carrots. Texas A&M students would now be able to eat carrots of their own school color. "I thought it would be kind of a novelty to have a maroon carrot," Pike told a writer from *Texas Monthly* magazine. The maroon carrot actually may be of more nutritional value than the orange carrot, but Pike is not looking for a new product sensation. "The problem is whether people will want to eat a maroon-colored carrot," he mused. "They do look different.'

DON'T JUDGE A SHRUB BY ITS FLOWERS • While you are paging through catalogues and ooohing and ahhing at the magnificent flowering shrubs and trees, remember that most of them bloom for only a couple of weeks. Think about height and shape and leaf color and texture as well as how fabulous those pink blossoms look. Also investigate what happens in the fall and winter to the leaves and bark—it might be just as interesting as those dazzling spring blooms. It is best to study trees and shrubs firsthand—at a local nursery or arboretum—before purchasing.

❦ J A N U A R Y 3

There are big trees and there are BIG TREES. If you know of an outstanding tree in your area, bring it to the attention of the American

Forestry Association (P.O. Box 2000, Washington, DC 20013). It might be a champion! Trees to beat: a flowering dogwood with a girth of 110 inches, 33 feet high; an American elm, girth 310 inches, height 95 feet; white oak, girth 414 inches, height 107 feet; and hundreds of others.

CUT THESE BRANCHES FOR EARLIEST INDOOR FORCING

Witch hazel
Cornelian cherry
Red maple
Forsythia

AND FOR LATER SPRING FORCING

Magnolia
Flowering fruit trees
Flowering quince

PLANNING FOR ROSES • Roses should be planned for spaces far from tree roots, in a spot that gets at least 6 hours of sun a day. They like a soil pH of 6.5 to 7 and about an inch of water a week. Finding a spot for your rose bed might be easier than selecting the specimens. There are 20,000 varieties to choose from.

Never shut out the January sun.

❦ JANUARY 4

Dull January afternoons are good for washing out old pots and trays. You can actually put your clay pots in the dishwasher (rinse them well first to get rid of the salts and dirt—scrub with baking soda if you've got really caked-up pots). The dishwasher will sterilize them. Clay pots can go to the bottom rack; plastic pots should go on top to prevent melting. A good practice for clay pots: rub them with linseed oil after cleaning.

Add vegetable oil to a bucket of sand to keep tools in good shape.

STORE YOUR TOOLS IN SAND • A great place to store your hand tools year round is in a 5-gallon bucket of sand to which you have added some vegetable oil. Just thrust your shovels, spades, forks—you name it—into the bucket and they'll get an effortless cleaning and lubrication job every time you put them away. (Some people favor used motor oil to lubricate their tools in this fashion, but I don't advise it. Used motor oil contains carcinogens and should not come in contact with the skin. It is also a pain to dispose of properly, and adding sand to it makes the disposal problem even worse.)

MAIL ORDER ADVICE • Buying sight unseen from a catalogue always carries a risk, but it's not like sending for an Asian bride. For most gardeners, the selection at the local nursery is going to be limited—and catalogues offer thousands of plants you simply could not get otherwise. Actually, if plants are properly cared for and shipped, there is no reason why you shouldn't shop mail order. I buy at least 60 percent of my plants and seeds through the mail.

The key to catalogue shopping is timing. You want to order and plant your specimens at the right time, namely early spring and early fall. If you have mild summers, early spring is an excellent time to plant perennials; it gives the plant all summer to set roots and establish itself. If you live in a zone with very hot summers, plan on doing your major planting in early fall, so the plants can establish themselves without having the stress of drought and relentless sun.

JANUARY 5
George Washington Carver's Birthday (c. 1864–January 5, 1943)

Climbing vines not only look magnificent but can provide added insulation to the outside walls of your house. If you have masonry walls or trellises on your walls, deciduous leafy vines on your southern and western walls will actually keep your dwelling cooler in the summer. To keep your house warmer in the winter, evergreen vines on the north side will break the wind and help keep you warm. Boston ivy is good for summer insulation. English ivy is excellent for winter protection. *Caveat*: Don't grow climbing vines directly on the wood siding of your house or they will cause massive decay and deterioration.

FLOATING ROW COVER PROJECT • I am a major fan of floating row cover, and use it in big swathes on tender transplants in the spring, every spring. Some people use clear plastics, but I use milky white "spunbonded" fabrics, which are porous and allow the passage of water and air. You simply lay the fabric over your plants and they thrive, protected from harsh sun, wind, and even flying insects. You can get row cover from catalogues; I've never seen it at the nursery, but then I've never looked. The problem is: how do you anchor it? For the big rows, I take wood slats, line them up edge to edge, and staple them to two opposite edges of the row cover, so I have in effect a scroll. I make different sizes, according to how many rows I plan to put in and how large they are. This way, the edges rest neatly in the soil and are also easy to roll up once the seedlings are on their way.

JANUARY 6
Twelfth Night

Today is Epiphany or Twelfth Night, and from now on the days will lengthen. If you celebrate Christmas, take down the Christmas tree; you're crossing the line of serious superstition by leaving your holiday decorations up past Twelfth Night—right up there with walking under ladders and opening umbrellas indoors! Once the decorations are packed away, you might revel in the orchard. It was once the practice to gather around an old apple tree on Twelfth Night and drink too much cider, toasting the tree and the gods of the orchard.

START COLLECTING KITCHEN RECYCLA-BLES • Small tin cans from tuna or cat food make excellent cutworm collars. So do sawed-off (top and bottom) milk cartons. Start saving for yourself and for friends.

CANNING GUIDE • If you are thinking about doing some canning this year, send for an excellent guide called *The Kerr Kitchen Cookbook* by writing Kerr Glass, P.O. Box 76961, Los Angeles, CA 90076. Send them a check for $3.50 for postage and handing, along with your name and address. You can also get the guide at places that sell the Kerr jars.

> *Here's to thee, old apple tree!*
> *Whence thou may'st bud and whence thou may'st blow*
> *And whence thou may'st have apples enow!*
> —Twelfth Night Wassailing Song

❧ JANUARY 7

The California supermarket tomato is a perfect example of hybridizing gone mad. This impostor is what happens when distribution concerns like packing and shipping and shelf life take on more importance than other food product concerns, like taste. Most gardeners are satisfied with the hybrids they grow in their gardens. But real purists say heirloom seeds, which have not been hybridized at all, make for gardening (and tomatoes) at the highest level. The plants are often more resistant to insects and disease because they haven't been evolved to death, and the taste is unforgettable. If it sounds intriguing, you can join a swapping group called Seed Savers, buy a few varieties, and see what happens. Send $1 and a business-sized self-addressed stamped envelope to Seed Savers Exchange, 3076 North Winn Road, Decorah, IA 52101 and you can see what the world of nonhybrids is all about.

DECODING TOMATO SEEDS • Your seed catalogue will refer to determinate and indeterminate tomatoes. Determinate tomatoes are varieties whose vines do not grow *ad nauseam;* they're bred to ultimately take on a compact, bushy shape. Indeterminate tomatoes will continue to grow at the tips; they will grow larger fruit, later in the season.

A PLANT TO CONSIDER • Plants, like anything, go through fads, and I think one of the best deserved fads now seems to be *Sedum spectabile,* 'Autumn Joy.' I don't know about your neck of the woods, but where we live, they are everywhere. And no wonder. 'Autumn Joy' blends with almost everything. It delivers a strong presence from foliage to flower—for months. Look in the catalogues and you'll see what I mean. (If you already are a devotee, and would like to commune with other serious sedum lovers, you can join the International Sedum Society, 10502 North 135th West, Sedgwick, KS 67135.)

RULE OF THUMB • The guiding measure for most crops is that a 5-foot row will supply one person from spring to frost.

❦ JANUARY 8

Something resembling annoyance is starting to creep in as I review all the new and noteworthy flower and vegetable introductions. Don't get me wrong. I think it is splendid that four of Europe's Fleuroselect Gold Medal winners are available in many U.S. catalogues this year—and the new 'Florence White' and 'Florence Pink' cornflowers sound lovely. But "new" is relative to me. Most flowers and vegetables are "new" to me. I've never grown cornflowers (though I've always meant to), and I'm not ready to hear about a new one. And they keep creating so many more.

I know. Gardening is not about possessing or knowing it all, though it seems that the ratio of what slips through the fingers to what ends up on my little piece of land is about a jillion to one. And actually, I did order a ground cover, 'Pink Mist' dwarf scabiosa—new and noteworthy this year—at least to me. I don't *hate* new flowers. I just want them all.

GETTING BIRDS TO VISIT • If you create nesting places and make food available, the birds will come.

Shrubs they like: Japanese barberry, bayberry, rugosa rose, autumn olive. Trees they like: dogwood, pine, birch, oak, alder, crabapple, hawthorn.

ALPINE STRAWBERRY TIME • Now is the time to plant alpine strawberry seeds indoors. By May or early June you will have wonderful little perennials to use as fill-ins throughout your garden. In my experience they are not the tastiest berries you will grow but they are nonetheless a delight.

Patience is a flower that grows not in every garden.

❦ J A N U A R Y 9

One of my great failed gardening experiments was trying to grow watercress (*Nasturtium officinale*) along the banks of the Beaverkill River, which borders our front yard in upstate New York. I spent four years in waders trying to make a gentle riverbank garden, but it wasn't meant to be. I don't really garden up there anymore, but I am still fascinated with little projects matching plants and flowers to natural circumstances, whether it is a bank near a capricious river or a tiny plot near the rain downspout.

I think this year I'll opt for the plot near my downspouts. Since January is a planning month, I've got my mind working on a small marsh garden (it may turn out to be just a dream, but that's gardening too). Maybe you have a similar situation: we have a weird border where two downspouts converge. This would be a good place to put in some yellow flag or marsh marigold or cardinal flowers. Maybe even some sedges or rushes or both! Other plants that like wet places, especially with sun, would be Japanese primrose, rose mallow, dogwood violet, wood anemones, and globe flower.

Maybe you don't have your own personal rice paddy but do have rocks. This might be the year to begin that rock garden you've always thought about. If you don't have any natural circumstances but are restless for a project, what about a modest water garden? You can put together a makeshift tub and liner for much less than you think. Or if you have the place for it, how about a witty container garden with lots of unusual containers (which you can start collecting at antique and junk shops now, and flea markets when it warms up a bit)? It's January. Dream.

RULE OF THUMB • If you are contemplating new beds and borders, remember that the way to get the most sun for your plants—if sun is what you're after—is to run them east to west. Put the shortest plants in front of your garden so as not to block what's growing in back of them.

Meanwhile, if you *want* your taller plants to provide shade for adjacent plants, plant them north to south. The sun will shine east to west and as it moves over your garden, the taller crop will provide a degree of protection—at least for half the day.

❦ J A N U A R Y   1 0

No matter what size garden you have, it is essential that you rotate your crops. I know, I know, with smaller gardens it is almost impossible (and certainly a pain to figure out), but it is nonetheless *essential* for happy soil and plants. First of all, any diseases that never really died out over the winter won't have the same family of plants to torment if you put in a new family. Secondly, different plants produce different root formations which will in turn aerate the soil in different ways; why make the earthworms do all the work? Check where last year's crops were and *don't repeat any plants within these families:*

• Broccoli, cabbage, Brussels sprouts, turnips—any plant in the cabbage family

• Lettuces

• Tomatoes, potatoes, eggplant, peppers—any plant in the nightshade family

• Garlic, onions, leeks

• Carrots, celery, parsnips, parsley

• Beets, spinach, swiss chard

• Beans and peas

• Corn

LIME DISEASE • Make sure not to plant too closely to stucco, cement, or plaster walls. When your house or outer buildings were being constructed they may have released a lot of lime into the soil, and even if all of this took place long ago the effects might still harm your plants. You should test your soil, certainly, and you might also for good measure add some new earth.

SOLUTION FOR CLAY SOIL • Clay soil is a major problem for gardeners and there is no getting around the solution: you have to add mind-boggling amounts of organic matter. What qualifies as organic matter? Compost and rotted leaves are your best choices. You need to add a minimum of 2 inches and work it in to a depth of 4 to 6 inches. If it is really solid clay, you might have to add as much as a 6-inch layer. So much compost! Anyway, just add as much as you can in early spring or the fall, and over time you will get the loamy soil you dream about. (Peat moss coupled with a bit of ground limestone is also a solution. Your local extension agent or nurseryman can help you calculate ratios.)

> *That grand old poem called winter.*
> —Henry David Thoreau

❦ JANUARY 11

Have you noticed? *The days are getting longer.*

TIP FOR A BORING FACADE • If the front of your house is architecturally blah, a good solution is a terraced raised bed of shrubs and interesting interplantings. The idea is to create the depth and visual interest that the house lacks. You can use stones or lumber (depending on the design and materials of your house) to create the raised beds.

VEGETABLE PLANNING • It's helpful to know how long each vegetable takes to reach maturity. Since you will probably have three plantings—spring, summer, and fall—you should gauge how long each variety is going to reside in a certain row when planning. Here are some vegetables grouped by maturity rates:

Within 60 Days

Lettuce
Kohlrabi

Radish
Spinach

60 to 90 Days

Beet
Bush Bean
Cabbage
Carrot
Cauliflower

Corn
Lettuce
Pea
Potato
Scallion

90 Days

Beet
Brussels sprout
Carrot
Corn
Eggplant
Garlic
Melon

Parsnip
Pepper
Pole Bean
Potato
Pumpkin
Squash
Tomato

SEED STARTING • Many seeds need warm soil as well as the appropriate light—or darkness. If your seeds can germinate in a light area and need soil warmth as well, there are a lot of options even when space is limited. The top of the refrigerator can work wonders. I put a tray on top of a wide radiator shelf in the kitchen last year, and it worked beautifully—until my cat Franny discovered it. (No, Franny. That tray of seedlings is not kitty litter.) You could also put your seeds under a broad lamp, a water heater, or the top of a console television.

Start your seeds in a warm, safe place.

Much has been written and spoken on color theory in gardening, and while I find it pleasurable to read about the subject I have difficulty executing the concepts. I am too much the mother of stray plants to ever have a perfectly ordered palette. But as a rule, think of color this way: If you want your small garden to look bigger and grander, plant flowers in cool, pale colors; your garden will seem less compact. If you have a huge plot and want to make it feel cozier, warm, bold colors will bring its appearance together. Beginners usually start with bright colors—which are the hardest of all to work with. Avoid them at first.

- If you are thinking of incorporating a new color scheme, you might do a dry run and plant annuals in those colors, before you invest heavily in bulbs, perennials, and shrubs.

- If the interior of your home is done in neutral autumn colors, don't plant pale pastels in your cutting garden; coordinate your interior needs with your outdoor plantings.

- Use silver foliage to soften pinks, purples, and blues. White and very pale-colored flowers can also soften bolder colors. Think about using dark green foliage to serve as a counterpoint for bright neon colors.

FLOWERS FOR YOUR COTTAGE GARDEN

Bee balm	Lavender
Delphinium	Nicotiana
English daisy	Oriental poppy
Hollyhock	Pansy
Heliotrope	Peony
Johnny jump-up	Pink (Garden)
Lady's mantle	Scented geranium
Larkspur	Sweet pea

Half the interest of the garden is in the constant exercise of the imagination.
—Mrs. C. W. Earle

I rearrange my garden the way some people rearrange their living rooms. This year, however, one of my resolutions was to leave my garden alone. I can add plants, I can give them away or even throw them away—but I cannot move any of my plants until the fall. At least that's my resolution. Meanwhile, I need something to take up all of that fidgety moving-plants time, and I have decided to plant vine covers on ugly surfaces. Do you have ugly surfaces, like chain link fencing? Or ugly walls? Or downspouts that beg for a morning glory curling around and around? Pick out some vines that do not need little fasteners and plant them in well-worked and highly nourished soil (vines need good rich well-drained soil to thrive). You can plant Dutchman's pipe, morning glory, moonflowers, silver fleece vine, bittersweet, actinidia, akebia, honeysuckle, or wisteria and cover all sorts of visual bores.

MORE CATALOGUE USES • If you are having a hard time visualizing, for example, some *Perovskia atriplicifolia* next to *Echinacea purpurea* 'Magnus,' cut the two from a glossy, four-color flower catalogue (along with other plants that might be blooming at the same time in your border) and see if that helps. It obviously isn't precise but it will give you an impression of color and texture.

You can also use your four-color catalogues as reference books. Many of the plants I order come from catalogues with no photos, or if they do have photos, they are few and far between. The little specialty grower of scented geraniums or *Helleborus* or rare rhododendrons quite often cannot afford a splashy catalogue. Use the fancy catalogue art as a guide for plants you desire, but scout around for specialty growers and in general I think you will end up with better plants.

January wet, no wine get.

Over the years I have gotten better at eyeballing square footage, but I'm always vaguely uneasy when I do my pound-to-square-foot calculations for peat or organic fertilizers or seed. If you have a lot of garden spaces of various sizes, this is a good month to go out and measure your beds and borders, calculate square footage, and—here's an idea—*write it down*. Last week, we had a decent afternoon, and I made a crude drawing of my property with all of its variously shaped gardens, and then labeled them and noted the square footage of each. The Map of Square Footage now hangs in a plastic sleeve in my garage where I keep my gardening tools.

Another process that makes me uneasy is translating metric. I am always measuring out gardening solutions, atom by atom, and then worrying about the math. Then I stumbled onto a list of equivalents. It isn't precise to the atom, but it suffices nicely for gardening needs. The chart appeared in the letters column of *Horticulture* magazine (November 1993); it was sent in by Gilbert W. Castellan of Silver Spring, Maryland. Mr. Castellan's list is going up on the wall in the garage, next to the map.

METRIC APPROXIMATIONS

1 cup = ¼ L = 250 mL
1 pint = ½ L = 500 mL
1 quart = 1 L = 1000 mL
1 gallon = 4 L = 4000 mL

1 teaspoon = 5 mL
1 tablespoon = 15 mL
1 ounce = 30 mL

SOWING REMINDER • Subtract 10 to 12 weeks from your last spring frost date and start indoors the following: eggplant, pepper, parsley, onion, leek, perennial herbs.

A modest garden contains, for those who know how to look and to wait, more instruction than a library.

—Henri Frédéric Amiel

Dr. Martin Luther King Day

In the 1930s, Alberta Williams of 501 Auburn Avenue in Atlanta, Georgia, loved to garden, and her vegetable plot was filled with beans, collards, tomatoes, and turnip greens. Rabbits didn't bother her garden, but the grandchildren were incorrigible. After much pleading and lecturing, Mrs. Williams finally had to put in a high barbed-wire fence to keep out Martin Luther King, Jr., who could not resist the pleasures of trampling and sampling her best crops.

SELECTING COLOR FOR THE GARDEN • Color not only creates mood in our gardens but defines space and proportion. Select cool tones (blues, pink, purples) for a sense of serenity. Warm tones like reds, oranges, and yellows create a sense of good cheer. Blues will give the observer the impression that the garden is distant. Reds suggest visually that the garden is closer than it truly is.

Using a color wheel can really help you understand color relationships. Once you choose your main color, select one of four harmonies—complementary, split complementary, analogous, or monochromatic—to establish a color scheme. Complementary colors might be violet and yellow pansies, orange marigolds and blue lobelia. Split complementary colors might be yellow daylily and purple delphinium, orange Maltese cross and purple bellflower, blue ageratum and red zinnia, or blue and red salvia. Examples of analogous colors include orange and gold marigolds, yellow daylily and Oriental poppy, red and orange zinnia. A monochromatic color strategy is simply the use of a single color such as pink petunia and pink geranium.

SHORT COURSE ON MUSTARD • If you haven't planted mustard before, save a few rows for it this year. Botanical siblings of *Cruciferae*, the mustard family, include cabbage, dames rocket, shepherd's purse, radish, watercress, and turnip. The defining characteristic of the crucifers is their four-petaled flowers, which are in the shape of a rounded Maltese cross (hence the Latin *cruciferae*). Mustard comes from the Latin *must*, or unfermented wine. This is because the mustard seed has no flavor unless it is mixed with a liquid.

When rose petals fall from the stem, what is left is the urn-shaped seeds, or rose hips. The ancient Greeks ate these seeds as a staple and referred to them as the food of the gods. During World War II, the English discovered that rose hips contained 400 times more vitamin C than oranges, and suddenly everyone in England was mad for rose hips. If you want to grow your own this year, the best roses to use are rugosa roses; they'll yield large vibrant orange-red hips—the size of crabapples—by fall. Just be sure not to harvest any that had harmful chemicals applied to them (mainly, just be sure not to apply harmful chemicals!).

WHEN NOT TO PLANT PASTELS • A sunny, very bright spot in your yard should not be devoted to pastel flowers but rather to vegetables or bright, bold-colored flowers. Pastels can look washed out in bright light, unfortunately. If you are planning to put in flowers, choose reds, oranges, and/or yellows, and they will provide a vigorous, healthy appearance.

PLANTS THAT TOLERATE SANDY SOIL

Anthemis	Lamb's ear
Aster	Liatris
Baby's breath	Morning glory
Cockscomb	Phlox
California poppy	Portulaca
Coreopsis	Sage
Daylily	Spurge
Goldenrod	Yarrow
Hens-and-chickens	Yucca

DEER, DEER, EVERYWHERE • In the past 10 years, the number of white-tailed deer in the United States has tripled.

Most beginning gardeners know that crops should be rotated to thwart disease and interrupt insect cycles. Another concern for small and large gardens alike is nutritional balance. Nutritional givers and takers must be interchanged from year to year—which is important to keep in mind as you doodle with your garden plans this month.

Givers are from the nitrogen-fixing legume family: beans, peanuts, peas, and soybeans, all of which return more nitrogen to the soil than they remove. Takers can be divided into two types: heavy and light. Heavy takers are broccoli, corn, cauliflower, cucumber, lettuce, radish, spinach, and tomato. Light takers are the root crops: beet, onion, carrot, etc.

Classic rotation involves planting the heavy takers the first year, the givers the second year, and the light takers the third. I generally plant all three crops in different and succeeding locations each year.

PRIVACY HEDGE • If you want to create a privacy hedge, the Clair Martin rose is an excellent choice. This persistent bloomer yields a profusion of delicately scented pale pink flowers and rich dark green foliage that quickly forms a stately hedge. Because it's so dense, put the plant in a spot that is well ventilated and be extra vigilant about removing diseased leaves.

FIRST-TIME GARDENERS • If you are looking for the edible herb tarragon, don't be confused with the Russian type, grown from seed—it has no culinary value. You want the French variety, which you need to buy in plant form. Plant your tarragon in moist limy soil and harvest it throughout the year. A herbaceous perennial, it will die down to the ground in the fall and return in the spring.

Certain seeds require the sensation of "wintering over" in order to sprout. The process of fooling the seeds is called stratification. The back of your seed packets will indicate whether your seeds need this treatment. I use cleaned-out old salad bar containers (any container with a tight-fitting lid will do) to cool down the seeds. Put a layer of sterile, moist growing medium on the bottom of the container, scatter the seeds thickly on top, then cover with the growing medium again. Seal the container tightly and then slip a zipper-locked bag over it, taking every precaution to keep the moisture in (I had a rubber band around the whole thing for good measure). Your seed company should provide you with the ideal chilling period for each seed variety.

INDOOR LIGHT • Seedlings in flats prefer a mixture of red and blue light. A combination of warm-white and cool-white fluorescent bulbs is what works best. Avoid using incandescents; they produce only reddish light and waste energy.

SAVE THE GARDEN TOOLS • For some reason, garden tools get less respect than their counterparts in the workshop. Even the most meticulous handymen will often toss their garden tools in a pile in the garage without a care. (These are the same fellows who go ballistic when someone borrows a No. 2 wrench and doesn't put it back in exactly the right position in the wrench chorus line.)

A pegboard would change all of this. Pegboards are excellent for garden tools because suddenly there is a prescribed place for everything. I think the place-for-everything theory would help all of us have-everything-in-its-place types. Pegboards are also great because you can change the mosaic easily as you add new tools. They also look sensational, especially if painted a favorite color. Anyway, it's something to do while we wait for our seed orders to come in. Make sure you get pegboard with ¼-inch holes so they can support the heavier items.

CHICKEN WIRE FOR SEED SPACING • If you have a piece of 1-inch chicken wire around, you can lay it over the seedling flats and use it as a guide for spacing your seeds.

❦ J A N U A R Y 1 9

Cotton plants make wonderful if slightly whimsical additions to your container garden. If you can get your hands on cotton seed, start some cotton plants indoors. Cotton plants, which are members of the hibiscus family, are lovely—reminiscent of the okra plant (which I have grown in my flower garden for its looming presence and flowers alone). Cotton has a long season, 120 days, so you need to figure a way to keep your plants healthy and strong before you set them out after the last frost. Those of us who live north of Philadelphia need either a greenhouse or a good indoor setup to get the cotton off to a good start.

SOME PLANTS FOR LATE WINTER COLOR

Camellia — *Camellia japonica* 'Akebono' (Zone 7)
Lenten rose — *Helleborus orientalis* (Zone 4)
Skimmia japonica (Zone 7)
Salix melanostachys (Zone 4)
Garrya elliptica (Zone 8)
Japanese maple — *Acer palmatum* ('Sango kaku') (Zone 5)

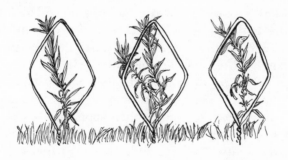

Stretched out hangers make excellent plant supports.

HANGERS MAKE EXCELLENT SUPPORTS • If you're looking for a project, gather up some of your extra wire hangers and make plant props out of them. You straighten the hook completely and then pull the bottom portion out to form a large diamond shape. The straightened hook will go into the ground and the diamond portion will help to support plants. Sometimes I will use two or three to support plants like tarragon that tend to flop all over.

TO FEED A FAMILY OF FOUR • Depending on how many members are teenage boys, a garden 20 by 40 feet will generally provide summer and fall vegetables for a family of four.

If you haven't had a great deal of experience with vines and are planning to put some in this year, you'll enjoy these pointers, which appeared in *Horticulture* magazine in an article by Charles Cresson about matching vines to their proper support. Vines have their own peculiar means of attaching themselves to available surfaces, and to grow them it is crucial to know *how* they attach.

"Clingers" attach directly to a surface. English ivy, Boston ivy, and climbing hydrangea are all clingers and would find a wooden trellis laughable. Meanwhile, they will happily climb almost any fence (and, says Mr. Cresson, they love stockade fencing).

"Grabbers" like to wrap themselves around whatever they touch. Grapes have tendrils to do this; clematis use their leaf stems to grab. Mr. Cresson grows his clematis on shrubs actually, which is lovely but requires scrupulous pruning. Grabbers will grow on fences with a wire grid.

"Twiners" twine their stems around their supports and include honeysuckle and wisteria. A twiner could grow on a fence but it also would need a wire grid. Twiners and grabbers are excellent for chain link. Twiners and clingers are suited to old posts and tree stumps provided they are fairly rot resistant and not too wide.

Finally, "sprawlers" lie on their supports and send up taller and taller shoots to curve over the highest "branches." Jasmines and roses are examples. They need to be tied to their supports.

If you want a trellis vine, choose a twiner; grabbers are not well suited. If you really wanted to force a clematis up a trellis, you should add a few strands of nonrusting wire between the crosspieces. Black plastic-coated wire is preferable. You can buy prefabricated meshwork at a good nursery or make your own.

COVER CROPS FOR WARM WEATHER ZONES • If you have a long mild spring you can spring-plant cover crops. A good choice might be crimson clover, fava beans, or oats. You can plant as soon as the soil is workable.

BUYING USED TOOLS • Used garden tools can be a good buy from garage or yard sales if the wooden parts are in good shape. If they have splits or signs of rot, pass. Replacement handles can coast as much or even more than a brand-new tool and be difficult to install. A little rust on the metal parts is okay, so long as it is not too corroded.

JANUARY 21

AQUARIUS, January 21 to February 19—*Unfavorable for seed but excellent for laying out onions*

If you have a garden in the country, ask neighbors to save those 50-pound poultry or dog food bags for you. They are great for mulching. When it's time to lay down the mulch, open a bag, cut down one side and across the bottom edge, and you have a three-foot square. You can anchor the bag with dirt or rocks. Cut holes for transplants or seeds. By the next planting season the bag will have deteriorated. They make excellent mulch and to my eye look good in a vegetable plot.

FIRST COMPOST • The first recorded use of compost in Western civilization was approximately 2,000 years ago when Marcus Cato, a Roman statesman and farmer, introduced it as a way of enhancing the fertility of the soil. He stressed the importance of composting all raw material (vegetation and manures) before adding it to the soil.

NEWSPAPER MULCHERS • If you are a newspaper mulcher, you can save up the winter papers in an orderly way by stapling editions together. Each day staple one edition to the next (length to length, not on top of each other). Just keep stapling until you have formed a length as long as your average rows. Then roll them up, storing them until you need them in the spring.

The whole year is beginning. All nature, with bud and seed and egg, looks forward with optimism.

—Edwin Way Teale

JANUARY 22

Seed purchasing for the novice can be somewhat off-putting, but once you get a handle on the jargon it's quite simple really. The first rule is to purchase seeds from a quality vendor. Cheap seeds are no bargain, a waste of good soil, water, hope, and expectation. Anyway, seeds are so inexpensive that 75 cents here or there shouldn't make a difference.

Look on the seed description for the maturity date. This is crucial, especially if you live in a place with a short growing season or if you are off to a late start. For planning, maturity dates also are important if you are growing vegetables and plan to have at least two crops.

Seed descriptions are not like real estate ads where "rustic charm" means falling apart at the seams. Gardening is a much loftier enterprise, and if a seed is described as having "heavy yields" or "outstanding flavor" the producer actually means it. Well, usually. Certain plants develop reputations for certain virtues, and a tomato labeled "juicy" will doubtless be juicier than the next one. A really important designation is "disease resistant." While you should not confine yourself only to disease-resistant plants—in fact, the heirloom seeds which yield gorgeous fruits and flowers have no innate ability to counter certain diseases—you should look for this quality, especially if you have encountered problems in the past.

Finally, look at garden space required. If your space is limited, you will want to seek out dwarf plants and determinate tomatoes (the kind that grow to a certain size and that's it) and other compact plants. Read the packets carefully, and obey spacing requirements. Cramming is the beginner's sin (and believe me I still cram), and easily avoided.

HAVE A HABANERO • A short growing season in a cold weather zone doesn't necessarily prevent you from being a pepper farmer. You can add some light and heat intensity to the equation by setting up a white reflector screen about 8 feet to the north side of your plants. It should be about 6 to 8 feet high. Another method gardeners use is to paint stockade fencing a high-gloss white (at least a couple of coats) so that the sun's rays bounce off to the north side of the plants.

WHERE TO SEED • Naturally you will want to get a jump on the growing season by seeding numerous plants indoors. Shepherd Ogden's *Step-by-Step Organic Gardening*, an updated version of his grandfather Samuel R. Ogden's invaluable classic, offers general guidelines for sowing. The lists indicate what is "normal" to sow indoors and outdoors, though there are many exceptions; for example, while it is customary to sow corn directly into the garden, you can also start corn indoors in flats.

SEED INDOORS

· ·

Eggplant	Cauliflower
Pepper	Broccoli
Basil	Tomato
Early lettuce	Cabbage
Leek	Parsley
Onion	Perennial herbs
Brussels sprout	

SEED DIRECTLY INTO THE GARDEN

Corn	Scallion
Pea	Carrot
Bean	Beet
Squash	Radish
Melon	Turnip
Pumpkin	Kohlrabi
Spinach	

❦ JANUARY 2 3

Now that I grow true oregano, my oregano plants give me and the people who eat my cooking a good deal of pleasure, but this is a new development. My first few oregano crops were a complete flop. This is because I was growing *Origanum vulgare*, which nurseries often pawn off as oregano when it is in fact wild marjoram. Wild marjoram is lovely with its pink and lavender flowers but it is relatively tasteless. So, buyer beware: make sure you get the white-flowering true oregano (*O. heracleoticum*) if you like fresh herbs on your pizza or in your sauce or brushed on grilled radicchio or maybe in a simple marinated Japanese eggplant. Greek oregano has a similar flavor but it has a rather sharp bite at the end which I am not crazy about.

STORING WOOD ASHES • Wood ashes, used sparingly, can be an excellent addition to the garden. Store your ashes from the

· ·

fireplace in metal garbage cans or buckets. Don't use cardboard boxes or store the ashes in the garage near papers for the obvious reason that an ash might still be smoldering, in which case your garage might not be far behind.

SERIOUSLY COLD • On January 23, 1971, it hit a U.S. record low of minus, yep, *minus*, 78 degrees Fahrenheit in Prospect Creek, Alaska.

❦ J A N U A R Y 2 4

I'm partial to fine-textured plants, and my flower beds often tend to be tad too wispy. A more visually intriguing flower bed will have a mixture of different textures and shapes. Always remember that coarse-textured plants will appear closer, whereas finer-textured plants appear more distant.

You're in the planning mode now, and texture is an important factor to consider. Fine-textured plants include astilbe, baby's breath, bleeding heart, columbine, golden marguerite, meadow rue, rock cress, torch lily, windflower, and yarrow. Medium-textured plants include Bee balm, bugloss, coneflower, lupine, everlasting, peony, and phlox. Coarse-textured plants can be bear's breech, leopard's bane, perennial sunflower, plume poppy, and saxifrage.

••

PLANTS THAT NEED A LOT OF WATER

••

Corn
Cucumber
Lettuce
Celery
Spinach
All root crops

BEGINNER BERRIES • Red raspberries are a good first choice for aspiring berry gardeners. Easier to grow than their black and purple relatives, the red raspberry requires a sunny, well-drained site that can be irrigated. Order fall-bearing raspberries in early spring.

••

A lot of getting your garden "right" is having graceful, intriguing drifts or swells of flowers. To make it work, an engaging mix of plant structure and height is crucial. Vertical touches are elemental to your success, whether they're in the back of your border or in the middle of an island. Here are some vertical plants to remember as you page through your catalogues. Perennials: astilbe, bear's breech, betony, delphinium, foxglove, iris, lobelia, lupine, sage, and torch lily. Biennials and annuals: hollyhock, Cleome (spider flower), sunflower, tall snapdragon, and tall zinnia.

AND SOME LOW-LYING TOUCHES • Just as important are your low-lying plants. Here are some to tuck in here and there: baby's breath, basket-of-gold, coral bells, creeping phlox, hardy pinks, lamb's ears, primrose, and saxifrage.

RULE OF THUMB • Too much of a good thing: Annual beds larger than one-third the size of the property they are placed in tend to appear overbearing.

REST IN PLANTS • Plants appropriate for cemetery plots include these easy-to-care for flowers: lily-of-the-valley, violet, hardy begonia, coral bells, and columbine. Good shrubs include Somerset daphne and the smaller leaf cotoneaster.

The great challenge for the garden designer is not to make the garden look natural, but to make the garden so the people in it will feel natural.
—Lawrence Halprin

Don't throw away that old plastic garbage can if the lid still fits tightly. It's ideal for compost. Punch out about five or six holes in the bottom of the can and set it up on a platform of bricks. You can put an old pan underneath to catch the "drippings," which will be rich with nutrients. Fill the can first with a layer of about 6 inches of sterilized soil and some leaves. Then start layering on all the other goodies (remember: no animal fats or pet manure or diseased plants). Keep the mixture moist and turn it frequently for some early spring compost.

GROWING MELONS IN SMALL SPACES • This year I'm going to try growing some muskmelons on a fence facing south. I don't have the space for lots of vine crops anymore, but using a trellis or fence provides melons with lots of sun, warmth, and air circulation—without hogging the land I *really* need for my herbs, flowers, and other vegetables. When they're about the size of softballs, I'll cradle them in pantyhose and tie them to the fence for support. The leaves quickly obscure the pantyhose, and the fruits grown this way are divine. (Other plants you can "vertical crop" are cucumbers, tomatoes, and squash.)

FEVERFEW: THE NATURAL INSECT BARRIER • Feverfew (*Chrysanthemum parthenium*) is not only attractive but makes an effective insect barrier due to its pungent odor. The self-sowing daisylike flowers grow to a height of 3 feet and tolerate poor soils. Consider them for a northern border for your garden.

BEGINNER HOTS • If you are a hot pepper neophyte you may want to start with the versatile and delectable Anaheim. It's easy to grow, excellent in salsas, and relatively mild. The plants tend to be very sensitive to cold, however, so time your transplanting carefully.

❦ JANUARY 27

Edible ornamentals work especially well in the flower and herb garden. If you are tight in space and want to "grow it all," consider planting ornamental peppers, flowering cabbage, patio tomatoes, red okra, Swiss chard, and eggplant in your flower garden.

FIRST-TIME GARDENERS • *Petunias are often seen as common, and dismissed by the gardener aiming for sophistication. Tsk. There are myriad varieties of petunias and any number of them are splendid in the garden. There are two classes of petunia:* grandiflora *and* multiflora.

Grandiflora *are for containers or any areas where they will be viewed close up. They present themselves with fewer but larger flowers.* **Multifloras** *are better viewed from a distance. They generate a profusion of smaller flowers and are more disease resistant.*

GOLDENROD VINDICATED • If you're worried about planting goldenrod because you or someone in your family has allergies, worry no more. Goldenrod has been falsely accused for years of causing sinus congestion and itchy eyes. The culprit is ragweed, which blossoms at the same time.

•••

PERENNIALS THAT TOLERATE WET CONDITIONS

•••

Astilbe	Lobelia
Bee balm	Marsh marigold
Ferns	Primrose
Forget-me-not	Purple loosestrife
Geum	Rose mallow
Globeflower	Virginia bluebell
Goatsbeard	

DON'T THROW AWAY THAT FISH TANK • If the fish are all dead and the tank's still sitting in the basement unused, put it back in business as a plant incubator. You can put little pots in the tank, cover it, and turn on the light and you'll have a nice, light, warm environment for seeds to germinate. Open the lid if it gets too hot.

❦ JANUARY 28

Growing plants from seed is a thousand times more rewarding than plucking plants out of nursery lots. If you've never done it before, try at least a few trays this spring and I'll bet you'll get hooked. Not only do you have access to an extraordinary variety of plants, but you get quite a bit of satisfaction from nurturing the wee things. I get extremely mushy about my seedlings; they seem such wondrous, helpless miracles.

Anyway, it's time to get moving on your seed orders for annuals. In general, they take longer indoors to grow. Order seeds for annuals

•••

like begonia, dianthus, geranium, impatiens, pansy, petunia, and snap-dragon immediately as they need 10 to 16 weeks of indoor growth before transplanting. Perennials can be a little trickier to grow, but there is no reason for beginning gardeners to shy away from them at all. And vegetables: ah! They will grow with almost no help at all!

TWO WAYS TO PLANT ONIONS • If you want to grow onions for summer use, grow them from sets. If you're interested in growing them for winter storage, grow directly from seed.

••

PERENNIALS THAT TOLERATE DRY CONDITIONS

••

Baby's breath (*Gypsophila*)
Basket-of-gold (*Alyssum*)
Blanketflower (*Gaillardia aristata*)
Bleeding heart (*Dicentra spectabilis*)
Butterfly weed (*Asclepias tuberosa*)
Campion (*Silene*)
Catmint (*Nepeta cataria*)
Evening primrose (*Oenothera*)
Foxglove (*Digitalis*)
Gayfeather (*Liatris*)
Golden marguerite (*Anthemis tinctoria*)
Hardy aster
Hen-and-chickens (*Sempervivum tectorum*)
Lamb's ears (*Stachys olympica*)
Lily-of-the-valley (*Convallaria majalis*)
Purple rock cress (*Aubrieta destoidea*)
Russian sage (*Perovskia atriplicifolia*)
Spurge (*Euphorbia corollata*)
Stonecrop (*Sedum*)
Sun-rose (*Helianthemum*)
Yarrow (*Achillea millefolium*)
Yucca

••

Free advice is always suspect, but there is some good free advice you can obtain through your local agent at the Cooperative Extension Services. The Cooperative Extension Service is a nationwide system linking agents, the U.S. Department of Agriculture, land-grant universities, and county government. The system was born with the 1914 passage of the Smith-Lever Act, and originally had a pointedly agricultural focus. Now it also is devoted to the needs and interests of urban and suburban gardeners.

I have had uneven experiences with County Extension agents. The good news is that when you find a smart, experienced agent, you have found gold; he or she will take you through a lifetime of challenges and difficulties. The bad news is that there are also many inexperienced "experts" offering advice. I experimented one day and called three different County Extension information services and got three different responses to a very simple question about hydrangeas. Get second and even third opinions if you're wrestling with a critical gardening issue.

Extension agents can be found by looking in the government pages of your phone book.

IF YOU CAN ONLY HAVE ONE LILAC • *Syringa vulgaris purpurea* is the most fragrant species of lilac and is ideal along pathways and near windows.

JANUARY 30

It wasn't until a few years ago that I became bold enough to try propagating from cuttings. I know, I know, there is nothing to it—but for some reason it seemed too *advanced* for me. There was no secret, of course. Rooting slips is not only simple but really satisfying and a big money saver. Why spend $3.95 on a little rosemary plant when you can make dozens from your mother plant for pennies? Here, for the still intimidated, are some simple, basic instructions you can try on your woody-stemmed plants (rosemary, oregano, thyme, scented geranium). First, find some healthy new growth on your plant. Snip off a cutting about three inches long, and clear the bottom half of its leaves. Moisten the cutting in water, then dip it into a root hormone compound (you can get it at any nursery), and plant it in a shallow pot or flat of sandy loam potting soil. Once it takes root, you simply transplant the cutting to its own pot so it can branch out.

EASIEST VEGETABLE AWARD • While you are making your wish list and checking it four hundred times, consider the Jerusalem artichoke. They are the easiest of all vegetables to grow and terribly nutritious. You can dig in just a few tubers in the corner of your vegetable garden and then forget about them. Harvest in the fall or next spring.

....

COVER CROPS TO PLANT, HARVEST, AND TURN UNDER IN SPRING
....

Snap bean
Soybean
Pea
Buckwheat
Pearl millet
Sudan grass

....

IN THE SOUTH
....

Cowpea
Hairy indigo
Lespedeza
Soybean

❦ J A N U A R Y   3 1

This year I am going to be more methodical about my vegetable plantings so my children don't end up with their usual strange nutritional imbalances (zucchini sandwiches again, Mom?)—not to mention the basil and tomato wretched-excess thing. Here are some basic guidelines for planting quantities. You will have to adjust according to your family's taste, but these guidelines make an excellent starting point and will be helpful, especially as you are planning your garden for the coming year.
....

40 crowns of asparagus
10 bulbs of garlic
30 broccoli plants (successively planted)
30 heads of cabbage (successively planted)
4 pounds of onion sets or 1 packet of seeds
1 pound of pea seeds (seems like a lot to me)
2 seed packets (each) of beets, bush beans, carrots, lettuce, radishes, and sweet corn

FIRST-TIME GARDENERS • *Orchard-making is not as simple as garden-making. Here are a few questions to ask yourself before you make your first fruit-tree purchase. It's obvious, but: What kind of fruit does your family like to eat? How much can you eat? Are you prepared to can and/or freeze the surplus? How much space do you have available? What kind of trees grow best in your zone? Make sure that your tree is a self-pollinator (also called self-fruitful) if you are buying just one. Otherwise, if the tree is self-sterile, you must buy a pollinator tree that will blossom in the same period. Also: be certain your trees are planted within 100 feet of each other so the bees can do their work.*

February

Flower of the Month: Violet

FEBRUARY 1

While you are doodling this month, consider how companion plantings might strengthen your gardening scheme. Companion gardening
has ancient roots, no pun intended, but the practice gained its mo-
mentum in the 1920s when Rudolf Steiner introduced his theories on
"biodynamics." Steiner was considered by some a fringe character in
his day, but much of what he taught is now common practice among
gardeners.

The theory behind companion gardening is that some plants form
natural alliances, though the reasons for these alliances vary. You
might couple plants to discourage pests and disease, or to encourage
growth and flavor, or to keep soil in balance. In one instance, it
might be that the plants are well suited because they make non-
competing demands on the soil's nutrients; in another, you might use
one plant to attract a certain insect away from a plant more vulnerable to that pest.

Interplanting is an extension of companion planting, really. I often
match up plants based on their root systems. For example, plants that
require only surface space for their roots—like Swiss chard—are excellent companions for plants like tomatoes, which require deep and vast
areas for root development.

While many gardeners believe strongly that the benefits of neigh-
boring certain plants are considerable, the practice is still a mix of science and way-out-there folklore. My attitude is to companion plant as
much as humanly possible and not to lose sleep if a few meaningless
or even undesirable combinations end up side by side.

DOOMED COUPLES • Some plants, like people, bring out the worst in each other. *The Moosewood Garden Book* recommends that you separate these vegetables and herbs.

VEGETABLE	INCOMPATIBLE WITH
Bean	Chive, garlic, leek, onion, shallot
Beet	Pole bean
Cabbage crops	Kohlrabi, pole bean
Carrot	Dill
Corn	Tomato
Cucumber	Potato, sage
Onion	Bean, pea, sage
Pea	Chive, garlic, leek, onion, shallot
Potato	Cucumber, squash, tomato
Tomato	Corn, dill, kohlrabi, potato

The most serious charge which can be brought against New England is not Puritanism, but February.

—Joseph Wood Krutch

❦ FEBRUARY 2
Groundhog Day

The National Geographic Society reports that in a 60-year period, Brother Groundhog's ability to predict the spring season has registered at an unimpressive 28 percent. Who invented this tradition, anyway? Actually, it was the Germans who brought the custom to Pennsylvania and substituted the groundhog for the traditional weather prognosticator in their homeland, the badger. Maybe that's the problem.

If you find groundhogs a nuisance, veterans of groundhog wars across the country suggest first and foremost shooting them. Bullet boosters say the best time to go "eliminating" is first thing in the morning or late in the evening. That seems awfully inhospitable, but then I don't have a groundhog problem. There are also battery-operated sound repellents (never tried them on groundhogs but they have worked on my mice), garlic–red pepper sprays, and Have-a-

Heart traps. For traps, the bait is important: use broccoli if it's early in the season and the garden doesn't have anything better to offer; try peanut butter smeared on celery once your garden gets up and going. Also, regular applications of fish emulsion and seaweed not only benefit your plants but reportedly offend groundhogs, usually driving them to a neighbor's garden. Happy Badger Day.

RULE OF THUMB • When you prune, don't tackle any branch that you can't reach from ground level. If you need a ladder, you need a professional.

ASPARAGUS REMINDER • In late winter or early spring, it is wise to remove the dead ferns from your asparagus plant (from last year). Add some bloodmeal or cottonseed meal for nitrogen, right through the mulch. Add traditional mulch (salt hay or straw is great) if you need to.

> *If Candlemas Day be fine and clear,*
> *Corn and fruits will then be dear.*

❦ FEBRUARY 3

Pussy willows, the darlings of early spring, can be propagated with cuttings. You can use the branches that you get at the florist's to start your plants. Make sure the cuttings are not dried out. Place the branches in a bucket of very damp vermiculite or builder's sand. Pull a plastic garbage bag up under the bucket of sand and tie it loosely at the base of the branch to keep moisture in. Keep the branches indoors in diffused light.

Pussy willows are easy to propagate.

Once roots appear, you can plant the branches in a shady spot in your yard, best of all in a low-lying area where water will fill up just a little after a good rain. The next spring, move them to a sunny spot that stays moist. The male plants are the finest (the pussies are produced only by the male) and yours will bloom after 2 or 3 years. They might even do better than bloom. A happy pussy willow can be invasive. Prune back hard after blooming.

FIRST-TIME GARDENERS • Don't prune your spring-flowering shrubs (like forsythia) or trees until they have finished blooming. Once their blooms are spent you can prune or cut back as needed.

RHUBARB SHOULD BE DIVIDED • Rhubarbs are pretty low-maintenance plants once you get them established. They are heavy feeders, and their nutritional requirements are so great that years ago it was common practice to plant them over old outhouse locations—but let's not think about that. Make sure you divide your rhubarb plants every three years or so, or the quality of the stalks will decline. In early spring and after the first buds appear, use a sharp spade to cut the root into pieces. Be sure each section has at least 2 buds on top. When you replant, position the new root so that the buds are just emerging from the soil.

❦ FEBRUARY 4

Witch hazel blooms when virtually nothing else is in flower, and we anticipate it in early winter or early spring (depending on the species) with great heart. The shrub's bark was used by American Indians for medicinal purposes, and witch hazel lotion is still manufactured in Connecticut by E. E. Dickenson. (Great label design, E. E.)

Common witch hazel (*Hamamelis virginiana*) blooms in early winter in the north. The vernal witch hazel (*H. vernalis*), which is smaller than common witch hazel, blooms in early spring and is not found so far north. It is deeply fragrant, and excellent for indoor forcing.

MEANWHILE, IN THE HIMALAYAS • The alpine flower, buried deep beneath early spring snow banks, is said to melt the snow with its own heat as it forges its way to the surface and to sunlight. *Stellaria decumbens* is found at 20,130 feet in the Himalayas.

RULE OF THUMB • Generally speaking, it is the finer seeds that require light to germinate.

SPENT BULBS FROM FORCING • With the exception of paper-whites, most bulbs that you forced indoors can be planted in the garden. You don't have to throw them away. It may take a year or two for them to get back into their cycle, but they will eventually bloom—though I've noticed they are not quite as fabulous as they were in the pot. Note, though: hyacinths, crocuses, and irises can be replanted in the garden only if they were originally forced in soil (not vases of water).

> *Gardeners, I think, dream bigger dreams than emperors.*
> —Mary Cantwell

❦ FEBRUARY 5

No flower is more reassuring than the snowdrop (*Galanthus nivalis*). Snowdrops are usually sold and planted during the fall, but I also like to plant them in the prespring weeks. When they start emerging in your area, try to find the flowering sets in the nursery, and plant them under deciduous trees in natural settings. With the awakening of the snowdrops, the first bees will emerge in search of early nectar and pollen.

SEEDLESS WONDERS • I know it's disorienting to think about *watermelons* right now, but it's seed ordering time—and there are some new seedless wonders worth adding to your list. As it happens, there are only a few seedless varieties out right now, with many more looming in research labs, but two—Honey Red (8 pounds) and Nova (10 to 13 pounds)—are worthy of your attention.

Seedless melons are not always completely seedless, so don't ask for your money back if you get a few edible white seeds in your melon next August. You should start your seeds indoors, because they need warmer soil for germination (at least 80 degrees!) than the seeded varieties, which require a minimum of about 55 degrees. Sow the seeds with the little tips pointed upward so they don't stick to the seedling. Once they've germinated, turn down the heat and drop back on your watering. In 3 to 5 weeks, you can harden them off and plant them in your garden.

When you buy seedless watermelon seeds, you'll also probably get a few seeds of a pollinating variety with your order. Just interplant the two (one pollen plant for every two fruiting plants). Start the pollen plants a few weeks after you put in the fruiting plants, because the fruiting plants are slow growers and you'll want the bloom time to coincide as much as possible.

PUT A THERMOMETER IN THE COLD FRAME • Cold frames can be employed to garden virtually year round in colder zones, but it helps if you have a thermometer tucked into each individual unit. Even in February, a cold frame on a sunny day can spike a temperature and require immediate venting.

❦ F E B R U A R Y 6

Many gardeners, anxious for any excuse to work in their gardens, use the winter months to dump wood ashes from their fireplace onto beds and borders. Applying ashes to frozen ground is mostly futile, as most of it will be blown away. The best time to apply the ashes is in the spring or the fall when they can be worked into the upper 6 inches of the soil. But don't overdo. Testers at soil clinics say the worst and most consistent problem they see is soil that has been "ashed" to death. Wood ashes contain no nitrogen, just a bit of phosphorus and a fair amount of potassium, which is why we add it to our soil (it's basically a liming material). If your soil gets too much of the ashes it will send your pH through the roof, and worse, you'll have a tricky time getting your soil back in balance. Test your soil *before* you add the ashes, and use a light hand.

INSTANT FLATS • Ask your local beverage distributor if he has any old wooden containers used to store returnable soda bottles. These handsome heavy boxes with wooden dividers, about 5 inches deep, make instant flats. You can also use cut-off milk cartons, foam or paper cups, yogurt containers, and margarine tubs—just be sure to punch holes in the bottom for drainage.

Buy All America.

BUY AMERICA • From time to time you'll see seeds labeled "All America." They're almost always worth the purchase. An All America flower or vegetable has been tested at 33 different sites across the country, each site representing a particular climate and soil composition. Only the seeds that thrive in all 33 locations are eligible for this distinction; they also must be measurably superior to the best variety in their class. The All America Selections Committee has given about 270-plus flowers and 220-plus vegetables awards. Of these, about 120 flowers and 90 vegetable varieties are currently available.

Everybody talks about the weather but nobody does anything about it.

❦ FEBRUARY 7

Sugar maple (*Acer saccharum*) sap makes the tastiest syrup, but other species can also be tapped. No matter what tree you use, it takes a lot of sap to make maple syrup—40 gallons of sap for 1 gallon of syrup—but it's not a terribly complicated process. Try it this year, when the days get warmer and the nights are still very cold. But don't wait too long. Once the buds begin to swell, the sap will develop an off flavor.

For first-timers, the Erie County Cornell Cooperative Extension in upstate New York has some good guidelines for syrup making. Standard spiles require 7/16-inch holes. Never use last year's holes. Bore holes 2 to 3 inches deep, at least 6 inches apart, and between 2 and 6 feet off the ground. They should slant upward slightly. Make sure the spiles are tapped in snugly. The number of holes per tree depends on its size at chest height: 10 to 17 inches in diameter, one hole; 17 to 24 inches, two holes; 24 to 30 inches, three holes; anything larger, four holes.

Each pail should hold 1 gallon. Covering the pails will improve the quality. Gather the sap daily, straining it through a cloth. Between runs of sap, wash the pails with diluted chlorine bleach, not detergent. Boil the sap outdoors unless you have a really good exhaust fan or don't mind a sticky kitchen. A washtub elevated on concrete blocks makes a good evaporator. Boil frequently, because the sap quality diminishes if you keep it over 48 hours without boiling. Skim off any debris on the surface as it cooks. The final boiling can be done in your kitchen using a candy thermometer, boiling to 7 degrees above your local boiling temperature (which fluctuates). Strain the syrup through orlon felt and into clean jars. Seal. Make waffles or some corn fritters! You just made a bucket of paradise.

BAMBOO SOURCE • Bamboo has an undeserved reputation. True, certain kinds of bamboo are so invasive they can turn your life into a science fiction movie (the fastest-growing bamboo grows 3 feet per day or 0.00002 mph) but there are varieties that are not invasive and that can make a beautiful addition to your garden. If you are interested in growing bamboo this year, send a self-addressed stamped envelope to Richard Haubrich, American Bamboo Society, P.O. Box 640, Springville, CA 93265 for a full list of mail order sources.

FIRST-TIME GARDENERS • *If fruit trees are calling your name, talk to your county agent or local nursery, or both, before you buy. Some trees are self-fruitful (you can plant them alone because they self-pollinate) and others, often called self-sterile, need a second tree for pollination. Be sure you have the space to plant the trees within a hundred or so feet of each other; they'll need to be close enough so the bees can travel back and forth. Unless you've got just a wisp of a tree, the smaller trees tend to establish themselves faster than the older, larger ones.*

I wanted no one lifting a finger in that garden unless he loved doing it. What if Fred had hired a man to dig those trenches and it had turned out that he didn't love to dig? Who would eat that kind of asparagus?

—Ruth Stout

One thing experience brings to the garden is a sense of frugality. In my first garden, I purchased plants willy-nilly, and used inordinate amounts of land to grow massive crops of land hogs, like corn and pumpkins. This would have been all right, but my plot was only 10 by 20 feet. Not only did they take up too much space, but I could purchase these crops for reasonable prices at the market.

I am older and wiser and more frugal now. I plant things like shallots, red peppers, and lettuces with French names, and of course all sorts of cut flowers and herbs because they not only taste and look better but save me money. Leeks are expensive in the market and so easy to grow. There are also some things you can't easily find, like sorrel or an honest tomato; these, too, obviously should have a place in your garden if you enjoy them on the table.

February is the time to plot and to think and to be mathematical— before spring and all the possibility it brings causes you to completely lose your mind. When you are planning the garden, consider the advantages of flavor, availability, and what makes sense to grow from an economical standpoint.

COMPOST WATCH • In some parts of the country, compost heaps are starting to simmer again; in others they never stopped boiling; and in some (mine) they are still frozen stiff. Once the temperature consistently rises above 45 degrees, the decomposition process will kick in again. Start turning it as soon as you can, to facilitate the process.

VITAMIN THERAPY • I've been popping antioxidants and (who knows?) they *seem* to help me, but it turns out that vitamins may also help plants from becoming stressed out. Dale Norris, a professor at the University of Wisconsin, has tested vitamins on 50 species. He applied vitamins to one leaf or to the soil in which the seed was sown and it resulted in plants better able to withstand the stress of transplanting, uneven watering, and insect infestations. (The only plants that did not seem to benefit were roses.) Interestingly, the plants grew at a slower rate than those which did not receive vitamin therapy. Very dilute solutions of the vitamins—mostly C and E— were administered in the experiment. It's too soon to know if the findings will translate into home garden practice but I think we have not heard the last about this.

Catalogue reading should not make you hungry. In general, stay away from garden catalogues that show gaudy photos of pies and cobblers and jars of jam. You are not buying baked goods, you are buying a scrawny transplant. Take your time. Move slowly. If this is your first gardening experience I would avoid most fruits, not because you can't *handle* them but because *you have your whole life to handle them* and right now your best bet is more along the lines of chives.

Mainly, don't try to start an orchard, at least not first thing. If I had some pictures of our collection of dwarf fruit trees in the country, the ones that might be mistaken for pea trellises, you would see why.

For first-time gardeners, I would suggest passing on apple, plum, cherry, pear, and apricot trees. Also pass on brambleberries, cranberries, grapes, kiwis, blueberries, and citrus fruits. You have plenty of time for all of these plants. Keep it on the simple side at first.

FIRST-TIME GERMINATORS • When you first prepare indoor seed beds, water them with warm or lukewarm water—never cold. Cold water could delay germination. If you have really slow germinators like morning glories or moonflowers, give them a boost by rubbing the seeds between two sandpaper blocks. Soak them overnight in warm water and then put in the soil.

> *If you would be happy for a week, take a wife,*
> *If you would be happy for a month, kill your pig,*
> *But if you would be happy all your life, plant a garden.*
> —Chinese saying

One of the great discoveries a home gardener can make is liquid seaweed. I was encouraged to sample it by a Californian who sang its praises sometimes mercilessly on a computer bulletin board for gardeners. A horticulture specialist, she insisted it was the panacea for most gardening ills, so I tried it. She was quite right.

To say that seaweed has magical properties would not be an exaggeration. I have conducted my own amateur experiments on plants, using seaweed on some while depriving others. The results are quite remarkable.

You can use seaweed at virtually every stage of development—early in the plant's life, when it is a seedling, you can use it at half strength to boost first growth by foliar feeding. You can spray your plants with seaweed throughout their lives. In the fall regular sprayings will extend the life of the plant well into chilling temperatures.

If your nursery does not carry seaweed you can obtain it by calling Maxicrop USA, Inc., at 1/800/535/7964. Order the smallest quantity available. A little goes a long way.

RULE OF THUMB • If you planted legumes as a cover crop for nitrogen, turn them under when the nitrogen is at its peak: about the time it flowers. If you planted a grass, take 2 to 3 weeks to plant after you turn it under.

USE IMAGINATION WITH VEGETABLE GAR-DENS • Vegetable gardens are usually a row row row affair, and doubtless there is a certain beauty and visual comfort in straight-out symmetry. But you can also add a bit of drama to the plot, and with no substantial loss of space. For instance, you can make circular arrangements of herbs or edible flowers in the corners of your garden. In the center, you also might establish a circle filled with tall or medium-sized cutting flowers. Try something new this year.

Little by little, even with other cares, the slowly but surely working poison of the garden-mania begins to stir in my long sluggish veins.

—Henry James

❦ FEBRUARY 1 1

Remember it this way: *they are all narcissus.* I still get mixed up naming varieties of that delightful family of spring-flowering bulbs. Daffodil is the common name for *Narcissus*, the Latin genus. Gardeners often refer to daffodils as the flowers with the big, trumpetlike leaves and *narcissus* as having smaller blooms, grouped in clusters—but really, they are all *Narcissus*. A jonquil is a *Narcissus*. A paper-white is a *Narcissus*. There you go.

The narcissi in the *poeticus* group are my favorites; they are fragrant and have one flower per stem which is white—indeed, when the 'Actaea' at the yard's edge burst forth I am a cheered gardener, whether it is an 'Actaea' or a *Narcissus* or just a plain old miracle. If you like fragrant narcissi (see how easy this is?), 'Cheerfulness' is a good choice. *Tazetta* narcissi—aka nonhardy paper-whites—are wildly fragrant; they have lots of flowers on a single stem, often with a tiny colored cup. The spring-blooming bulbs are of course planted in the fall or forced indoors at your pleasure.

ORGANIC GARDENING READERS CHOOSE FAVOR-ITE VEGETABLES • I enjoy reading *Organic Gardening* magazine and recommend it especially to gardeners who are attracted to a purist view of organics and loads of information. The magazine is steeped in wackiness, which you will either love or hate; but I laugh out loud when I read it and suggest you check it out at the library (it's not always available at newsstands). Anyway, OG conducted a survey of its readers to determine their favorite veggies, and the results in a good number of instances meshed with their survey of the "experts' " favorites. You might like to compare notes with your own experiences.

A capsule of the results: bush beans: Blue Lake; beets: Detroit Dark Red; broccoli: Green Comet; carrot: Danvers Half Long (among others); cucumber: Sweet Success; eggplant: Black Beauty; looseleaf lettuce: Black Seeded Simpson; okra: Clemson Spineless; watermelon: Sugar Baby; pea: Little Marvel, Wando, and Green Arrow; spinach: Melody and Tyee; potato: Yukon Gold; white corn: Silver Queen; pink tomato: Brandywine; cherry tomato: Sweet 100; paste tomato: Roma; red slicers: Celebrity and Delicious.

❦ F E B R U A R Y 1 2

Every gardener has had the joyous experience of meeting his first "volunteer"—that tomato or cosmos or Johnny-jump-up which came back the following summer without any scheming or shameless begging on your part. *Well, hello!* Self-sowers are not quite as dependable as perennials but they do come back, and if you want some annuals you can *almost* count on, experiment with these plants as you make your garden plans: cosmos, coreopsis, viola, calendula, cleome, dianthus, sweet alyssum, portulaca, cornflower, foxglove, lunaria, nicotiana. Some will reseed themselves in the same season, some will come back the next seasons, some will do both!

FIRST-TIME GARDENERS • *Garden planners should keep in mind that flowers look best in groups. A plant here or a plant there looks lonely—and has no visual impact. Sometimes you can cluster a group and then throw in a single plant for an accent, but usually clusters work best. Your design also will be more graceful if you avoid lining up plants in neat little rows—as you would for a vegetable garden. Let clusters of flowers flow into other clusters for a natural appearance.*

RULE OF THUMB • Use gloved hands when removing winter mulch, since sharp tools might easily damage emerging shoots.

DON'T OVERWATER COLD FRAMES • It is important to check on your cold frames periodically, but don't overwater them. In colder zones, they will need very little watering—if any—until late March or April. Err on the side of too little.

If a tree dies, plant another in its place.
Linnaeus

☙ FEBRUARY 13

If you can't afford to lose a single seed, try sprouting your seeds in paper towels instead of soil. Take a moist paper towel and lay down your seeds, giving each one a little space. Put a moist paper towel on top of it, and then put the "seed sandwich" into a zipper-locked plastic bag or rinsed-out salad bar container, tightly lidded. Provide the seeds with the temperature they need and when the seeds have sprouted, put them in pots. This is effective for seeds that don't need light to germinate.

SEEDS THAT NEED LIGHT TO GERMINATE

Balloon flower
Coleus
Dill
Impatiens
Lettuce
Mexican sunflower
Ornamental kale

Ornamental peppers
Petunia
Shasta daisy
Stock
Strawflower
Yarrow

SEEDS THAT GERMINATE IN THE DARK

Beet
Broccoli
Cabbage
Calendula
Carrot
Celery
Chard
Cucumber

Nasturtium
Melon
Onion
Pansy
Portulaca
Pea
Radish
Spinach

FEBRUARY 14
St. Valentine's Day

Little is known about St. Valentine—so little, in fact, that we don't know exactly who he was. There were at least two St. Valentines, both priests, and both imprisoned by the Emperor Claudius II. To build his army, Claudius launched a merciless attack on love itself, breaking up families and separating single men from women. Marriage was forbidden. At least one of the Valentines performed wedding ceremonies secretly and for this was jailed and then killed.

Pope Gelasius made the saint's day an official religious observance, but never told anyone which Valentine he was honoring. According to legend, St. Valentine would reach from his prison window and pluck violets, inscribing messages of love on the tiny leaves and sending them out to the weary populace. Birds carried his messages of hope and love. He died on February 14, 270.

READ MY EARS • In the South Seas, a female places a red hibiscus behind her left ear to say "I desire a lover." If the flower is placed behind her right ear it means "I already have a lover." Flowers placed behind both ears mean "I have a lover but would like another."

●●

ONCE BELIEVED TO BE APHRODISIACS

●●

Allium spp. (onion and leek)
Apium graveolens (celery)
Asparagus officinalis (asparagus)
Asperula odorata (sweet woodruff)
Coriandrum sativum (coriander)
Ipomoea batatus (sweet potato)
Mentha spp. (mint)
Panax spp. (ginseng)
Pastinaca sativa (parsnip)
Persea americana (avocado)
Phoenix dactylifera (date palm)
Polygonatum multiflorum (Solomon's seal)
Vanilla planifolia (vanilla orchid)
Zingiber officinale (ginger)

●●

ONCE BELIEVED TO BE ANAPHRODISIACS

●●

Angelica
Cannabis (hemp; hashish)
Coffee arabica (coffee)
Humulus lupulus (hop)
Lavandula (lavender)
Ruta graveolens (rue)
Vitex agnus-castus (chaste tree)

In one way or another, Eros operates in every garden.
—Michael Pollan

●●

Even in the most northerly zones, the oddball, balmy February day strikes, and one longs to dig in the ground. Patience is the virtue required for gardeners in the low-numbered zones. Only when the ground is dry and workable can the planting of trees and shrubs begin. For many of us, that will be a while. If it hasn't been too wet, the prespring season in warmer zones is a good time to put in broad-leafed evergreens (like rhododendron, magnolia, even some kinds of holly) because it gives the plant the whole growing season to set roots and establish itself before the fall. When you plant these evergreens, be sure to cover them with burlap bags or give them some kind of protection against drying winds—and if it is a dry early spring, make sure you water the leaves and the roots regularly. *Meanwhile, if your camellias, rhododendrons, and other shrubs that love acidic soil are growing slowly, they can get a nice boost from a nitrogen-rich time-release fertilizer as the ground thaws.*

SOIL TEST • Be sure to do an early spring soil test before putting in your plants and seeds, especially if you had to seriously amend your soil in the fall. See how your amendments "took." If they didn't, you obviously will have to make further corrections before you plant. Plan on checking again in midsummer before your fall plantings go in.

Bottom watering, for seedlings, is better than top watering. I learned this as an eight-year-old, after clumsily pouring a big glop of water on top of my bean plant. The entire contents of my paper cup—seedling, powdery dirt, and all—ran over the sides, across my desk, and onto the linoleum. Now I invest heavily in those wonderful styrofoam seed starters, the kind with the clear plastic removable lids and the gauzy underlining for bottom-watering plants. Though they are a little expensive, they amortize well. I've used mine for several seasons with great satisfaction.

If you use other systems and top-water your seeds, use a mister. Your hand will get tired of pumping but you won't dislodge the seeds or fragile seedlings. And remember not to overdo; gentle, consistent moisture, not paste, is what your seeds want.

MAKE YOUR OWN WINDOW BOX • Even the novice carpenter can construct a window box using 1-inch redwood or cedar. Use these dimensions: 8 inches wide by 8 inches deep by the length of your window, whatever it is. Drill a series of ½-inch drainage holes at the base of the box. Fill the box with 2 inches of gravel and top it off with sterile potting soil. Attach the box with screws instead of nails for added strength.

LIFE EXPECTANCIES FOR TREES • Peach trees are more ethereal than you might suspect. They live an average of only 15 years. Apple trees live 50 to 75 years. Pear trees live 35 to 50 years. Plum trees average 30 years, and sour cherry trees 30 to 40 years. Sweet cherry trees live 50 to 60 years.

SPRAY SEAWEED ON YOUR FRUIT TREES • If you spray seaweed (see pages 361–62) on your fruit trees regularly you'll protect them from a cold spell—and loss of fruit. Blossoming trees sprayed with seaweed somehow ride out the shock of a cold spell much better than those that aren't sprayed. This also applies to fall gardens. If your spray your fall garden with seaweed about once a week beginning in late August you won't lose crops as quickly to frost.

❦ FEBRUARY 17

The best tomato I ever tasted was plucked from a container on my terrace in New York City 10 years ago. Containers are excellent for vegetable gardening, and while those fantasies are in high gear, why not plan a mini-vegetable garden? Just think—no nematodes, no soil-borne diseases, no pH worries, just plain old delicious fresh food. (And, boy, will your patio or terrace look great.)

Generally, you can plant lettuce, spinach, mustard, peppers, radishes, carrots, beets, broccoli, beans, and cherry tomatoes in 1- to 2-gallon containers. For Brussels sprouts, cucumber, squash, and tomatoes, use containers 10 gallons or more. Just make sure you plan for adequate drainage—you'll need holes in the sides and bottoms. It's also smart to raise the containers off the ground with bricks or slats, to allow the water to drain freely. And since the water will be draining easily, you'll need to replenish it, often daily during the peak months of summer.

Try these varieties: beet: Little Mini Ball; broccoli: Green Valiant; cabbage: Primax; carrot: Thumbelina; cauliflower: Snow Crown; cucumber: Bush Pickle; Swiss Chard: Silverado; eggplant: Pirouette; pepper: Lipstick or Ace; pumpkin: Jack Be Little. There are countless varieties of tomatoes to choose from. Ask your nursery for recommendations or look in seed catalogues for tomatoes specifically recommended for containers. You can even put Basket King Hybrid in a hanging basket!

HOW TO PREVENT DAMPING-OFF DISEASE • Anyone who has ever brought little seeds into life and then watched them get wiped out by damping-off disease knows heartbreak firsthand. Since I began using milled sphagnum moss, I have not lost one seedling to this killer. For tiny seeds, use the moss as topsoil. For larger seeds sprinkle the moss on top of the topsoil. I am also now very careful to keep everything sterile—from pots to soil to my hands—and I thin my seedlings religiously.

NEW GARDENS FROM THE LAWN • If you've just converted your garden from lawn, you should avoid planting crops that may be subject to grubworm damage. Roots of corn, potatoes, onions, and strawberries are the grubs' favorite foods.

> *That grand old poem called winter.*
> —Henry David Thoreau

❦ FEBRUARY 1 8

One of the things that impresses me most about gardeners is their genius for invention. Germinating seeds is always tricky in late winter, when the one thing seeds need you don't commonly have: heat. One gardener, flummoxed by the problem and unwilling to shell out money for the pricey (but effective) tray heating units available in many catalogues, created a big flat wooden box out of recycled billboard and some scrap, and set the box on a pair of sawhorses. He then lined the box with an electric blanket, protected from moisture and spills by clear plastic sheeting. His seeds germinated beautifully.

Another commercial bedding plant producer grows his seedling starts in heated waterbed mattresses. He uses house gutter heating cables under the mattress instead of a conventional waterbed heater to give more uniform heat distribution. He places the trays of seedlings on the waterbed and puts clear lids on top to retain moisture. The temperature is maintained at between 70 and 72 degrees until the seeds sprout, and then is reduced. He gets about 90 percent germination. If you experiment with either of these ideas, be careful about mixing moisture and electricity.

FIRST-TIME GARDENERS • *My first few seasons as an indoor sower were a disaster because I dumped dozens of seeds into each little soil cube "just in case" nobody wanted to germinate. This is death to seedlings; there can be too much of a good thing. Don't be heavyhanded with your seeds; overcrowded seedlings are also a disaster to thin.* Sometimes mixing the fine seeds with sand before you sow helps to loosen them up. Use a lot of sand when you do this, or you'll still have crowding problems. Yet another trick is to mix fine seeds with Knox Gelatin. The gelatin is even said to be nourishing to the seeds. You can also slice a tiny piece off the corner of a regular No. 10 business envelope, put the seeds in the envelope, and tap them out of the cut corner.

MOTHER OF ALL TREE ROOTS • The biggest tree root on record belonged to Don Wismiller of Provo, Utah. In 1954, Wismiller extracted a root measuring over 114 feet long.

FORECAST: RAIN • When the flowers of the scarlet pimpernel close during daylight, rain is on its way.

The morning sun never lasts a day.

❦ FEBRUARY 19

I don't know about you, but February is a tough month for me. I've read the catalogues so many times I may have forged a new category of neurosis. And the die is cast: all my seed and plant orders have been placed. In zone 7, we still have a long wait before much happens. Ah, the wait. It's gray. I'm getting restless.

The trouble is, while I would love nothing more than a string of sunny days, that would probably be the worst thing for my garden. Wiser souls before us knew this: "a February spring is worth naething." Or: "of all the months of the year, curse a fair Februeer." Or: "One would rather see a wolf in February than a peasant in shirt sleeves." Farmers and gardeners knew that growth cycles and rhythms are fragile and that if an early spring blows in, it will also blow out—the cycle will be irreparably broken, the harvest doomed. All of which is to say that it is *supposed* to be this way: gray, dormant to the eye, buds swelling imperceptibly. We are restless, but beneath our feet there is trembling. Waiting is gardening, too.

DON'T SAVE STERILIZED SOIL • If you've already planted your seedling flats and have some sterilized soil left over, it's best just to add it to houseplants or throw it in the garden. Don't try to save it—it can develop diseases and wipe out future seedlings. Some gardeners make their own growing medium: combine 4 quarts of vermiculite, 4 quarts of peat moss, 4 tablespoons of 5-10-10, and 2 tablespoons of ground limestone for a classic homemade mixture.

IT MIGHT NOT SMELL TOO SWEET, BUT . . . • To sterilize your own soil, preheat the oven to 180 degrees and spread a gallon of soil on a shallow baking pan. Pour about 1 cup of water on top and bake for 45 minutes. Or: microwave the soil in a plastic bag with a few holes poked in it (or leave it open). Research shows that 7 minutes, 5 seconds of full power in a 625-watt microwave eliminates most nematodes and harmful fungi. Be careful, though. Sometimes the bags break if you expose them to long periods of microwaving, and it can be a real mess. *If you don't want to cook your soil, water it with room-temperature chamomile tea. Chamomile is an antiseptic which helps to kill microorganisms.*

FIRST-TIME GARDENERS • *The easiest perennials to start from seed are hardy pinks, columbine, coneflower, coral bells, coreopsis, delphinium, foxglove, lupine, and primrose.*

February sun is dearly won.

PISCES, February 20 to March 20—*Excellent time to sow*

Sometimes I need to be reminded that families with small children, like mine, do not really *need* 24 high-yield jalapeño plants, and that the rosebush tucked behind the yew has to be moved this year or it really will die. These mental jottings need to be recorded, somewhere, which is why gardening journals were invented. A journal is a tool as essential to the gardener as any hoe or trowel, and will probably improve next year's garden as much as the finest compost. A simple looseleaf notebook with dividers and pockets (I like to keep empty seed packets in them, for reference) allows you to construct a garden history. By recording experiences with plantings, insects, questionable color and texture schemes, diseases, late harvests, and so on, you can spend the winter months reviewing, reminiscing, and scheming (and in my case, eating yet another pickled jalapeño). Go to the dime store and get yourself a notebook if you haven't got one.

SAVE PAPER TOWEL HOLDERS • If you are growing leeks this year, save your paper towel tubes for "blanching." When the leeks are an inch in diameter, you can slip a tube over each one and get marvelous, pristine leeks.

PUSSY WILLOW JUICE • Pussy willows give off a chemical that encourages rooting; the water used to force pussy willows can be reserved and used with other species' branches in place of dry rooting hormones.

FIRST-TIME GARDENERS • *When you buy a bag of commercial fertilizer, it's coded in numbers, 10-10-10, 5-10-5, and so on. The numbers refer to the percentage amounts of nitrogen, phosphorus, and potassium (sometimes called potash), respectively. In a 100-pound bag, for instance, you'd be getting 5 pounds of nitrogen, 10 pounds of phosphorus, and 5 pounds of potassium. The rest is harmless filler. (If there is a fourth number, it's magnesium, which is required in some northern zones.)*

SNAIL RACING • On February 20, 1990, a garden snail named Verne achieved world record status by completing a 12-inch dash in 2 minutes, 13 seconds, at West Middle School, Plymouth, Michigan.

If in late summer you routinely find yourself with a stack of seeds that you never got around to planting, store your seed packs in an old 4-by-5 file box and use the dividers to mark off the planting season in weeks and months. This works especially well if you are sowing crops like lettuce and radishes continuously, and need a reminder every two weeks or so.

IF YOU DON'T WANT TO DEADHEAD • Deadheading (cutting off the flowers that have finished blooming) can be a chore, though some of us take a odd pleasure in it. If you don't like to be bothered, plant ageratum, begonia, impatiens, lobelia, or periwinkle. Their faded petals just fall to the ground and disappear without any gardener's assist.

BEST TEMPERATURES FOR GERMINATION • In general, potting soil should be at about 60 degrees to germinate hardy plants, and at least 70 degrees for tender ones. Once sprouted, though, most plants grow best in temperatures lower than their optimal germination temperature. For instance, a canteloupe is happiest germinating at 90 degrees but likes 68 degrees for ongoing growth.

RULE OF THUMB • If you are going to plant a less-expensive bare-rooted tree, plant it within 4 to 24 hours after purchase. When you get home, plunge the tree into a tub of water so that the roots are covered. If you have to wait to plant any longer than a day, lay the tree down horizontally and bury the roots in a shallow trench, then water generously.

Winter is a time of promise because there is so little to do—or because you can now and then permit yourself the luxury of thinking so.
                                                            —Stanley Crawford

I have a packet of tomato seeds quivering in my hand, but believe me I am not going to plant them. I made that mistake once—planting tomato seeds too early indoors—and I paid the price. What happens is this: The seeds germinate beautifully, I move them onto the light table, they thrive, I raise the lights, they grow, and too early—like the end of April—I've got beautiful tomato seedlings that can't go out. The plants become rootbound and stunted, and then—because they've been stressed out—they flower. A simple lesson, especially for those in Northern zones: hold back for at least a month to plant your tomato seeds. Other zones, adjust accordingly.

SOIL PREPARATION • If you are going to sow seed outdoors—either in a seedbed or an annual border—the soil needs to be broken down into a fine tilth. This should be done at the time of sowing, and it will be effective only on ground that has already been dug. Choose a comfortable day, preferably with a drying wind. Fork over the soil, leveling as you go, and let the surface start to dry. Break down any clumps, but go lightly. You don't want to compact the soil. Rake back and forth, in every direction, until your soil has a fine consistent grain.

A VERY BIG TOMATO • The biggest tomato of all time (at least at this writing) was 7 pounds 12 ounces—about the size of a healthy newborn. Gordon Graham of Edmond, Oklahoma, grew it, and says he used techniques learned from a 91-year-old Hopi Indian—including compost-rich soil and Miracle-Gro.

LET THERE BE LIGHT • If you are growing your seedlings using windowsill light, put your plants in a southern window if you live in colder zones and in an east-facing window if you live in the South. Seedlings do not need heat to thrive; light yes, heat no.

However, February windowsill light may not be enough for your plants even if you live in the South. As a rule, if your seedlings are getting 6 to 8 hours of natural, windowsill light they should also get 10 to 12 hours of fluorescent light. If you are using fluorescent light only, you need to provide 12 to 18 hours of light total.

Sun follows rain.
—Geoffrey Chaucer

Are those seeds still good? If you are wondering whether a packet of seeds left over from last season (or the season before that) is still good, do a little germination test. Pick out a minimum of 10 seeds and lay them down carefully on a moist paper towel. Roll up the paper towel and put it in a plastic bag, sealing tightly. Put the bag in a warm place (75 degrees would be nice) and watch for germination to take place. (Take a peek once a day.) Count the number of seeds that sprout and divide by the number of seeds you started out with. That percentage is about what you can expect from the rest of the seed packet.

Seeds you buy fresh do not germinate at 100 percent. They can germinate at rates ranging from 80 percent to as low as 50 percent and still be approved for the marketplace. All of which means that if your germination rate is below 33 percent, you'll probably want to toss the rest of the seeds.

FIRST-TIME GARDENERS • *Many first-timers get confused about compost—believing it is the same thing as fertilizer. Compost is organic material which serves a very different purpose from fertilizer in the garden soil. First, compost makes a good home for the billions of microorganisms that digest roots, leaves, and other vegetative matter; compost breaks them down into nutrients that plants can absorb easily. Second, compost stores moisture and nutrients for plants to draw from as they will. Third, it provides aeration and structure to the soil, much in the way an egg binds a cake. If you don't have compost, then peat moss, shredded leaves, and aged manure will make fine organic additions to your soil.*

PROTECT YOUR PEAS • To protect your pea seeds from mice, lay down holly clippings in the garden and they will keep their distance.

> *There seems to be so much more winter than we need this year.*
> —Kathleen Norris

My first pea patch was a disappointment because the makeshift trellising I had created for my vines started about 8 inches from the ground. Big mistake. Peas don't have much of a reach, and the vines had a terrible time making it to the trellis. When you do create supports for your pea vines, make sure it's placed no more than 2 inches from the ground. Peas grow nicely along a horizontal support (unlike their cousin the pole bean, which needs a vertical stretch to thrive).

RULE OF THUMB • As a general rule, a 5-10-5 makes a good overall fertilizer for the average vegetable garden. If the garden is primarily root crops, however, use 2-10-10.

Use plastic knives to identify your plants.

SEED MARKERS • Using permanent-ink pens, write down the names of your sown seeds on disposable plastic knives; they are excellent weatherproof markers. Be sure to jot down date planted, variety, and color.

CUTWORM TIP • Some gardeners place toothpicks right next to their vulnerable seedlings to prevent cutworms from wrapping their bodies around the stems and killing them. Or try a diluted spray of sagebrush or pineapple weed extract.

> First a howling blizzard woke us,
> Then the rain came down to soak us,
> And now before the eye can focus—
> Crocus.
> —Lilja Rogers

If it crumbles like chocolate cake, your soil is ready to be worked. Right now, mine is more like raw fudge. Working the soil too early or too late can actually damage its texture. If the ground is damp from melted snow or spring rains, it will form clods that will be terribly inhospitable to root growth. Likewise, if you wait too long, the soil may become dry and collapse—losing all of its structure. Soil is fit to be worked when you can pick up a clump, roll it in a ball, and knock it apart with your thumb. If it sticks to your shoes, it's still too wet.

FIRST-TIME GARDENERS • *Never use fresh manure in the spring.*

SOIL TESTING • It's fun to play mad scientist with those inexpensive soil testing kits, but there's a part of me that doesn't trust kits in general. If you suffer from a similar unreasoned world view or simply want more information, your county agricultural service will provide a greatly detailed assessment; you'll get the pH readings, but also nutrient content and suggestions on how to correct your soil for maximum growing efficiency. This is an especially good way to go if you live in an old house where lead paint chips might have blown into your soil or in an area where lead or arsenic pesticides might have been used.

WILD-COLLECTED PLANTS • When you order from catalogues, make certain the plants you are buying weren't stolen from wild glens in South Carolina. You want plants that were propagated in a nursery, not pilfered from the land. An excellent book provides a cross-check on the origins of plants sold for profit. Send for *The Gardener's Guide to Plant Conservation* by Nina T. Marshall (World Wildlife Fund, P.O. Box 4866, Hamden Post Office, Baltimore, MD 21211). It's $12.95. You can call (410) 516-6951 for more information. For a list of mail order nurseries that do not sell plants collected from the wild, send a self-addressed stamped envelope to Virginia Nature Plant Society, P.O. Box 844, Annandale, VA 22003.

A trellis can define a private world or transform a forgotten wall into a focal point. Most garden trelliswork in America is painted white or left natural, but in earlier times deep, vivid colors were used with tremendous effect: dark green, blue, blue-green, black, even Chinese red. I think Chinese red, in the right situation, could be absolutely stunning. Most high-quality trelliswork will last about 20 seasons, if well maintained.

PAINT THE TROWELS CHINA RED • Okay, so a Chinese red trellis would look hideous against your brick colonial. What about painting your trowel handle Chinese red? Does anyone else spend too much time hunting around the garden for the !X?*#~ trowel? The solution: paint a simple stripe in a bold color—Day-Glo, if you need extra clarity—on your tool handles.

LET THE SUN SHINE • Allow the early spring sun to warm your soil before you mulch for the summer season.

MOW YOUR GROUND COVER • To give your ground cover a spring trim, set your lawnmower blades as high as they can go (experiment with this first) and then "mow" your ground cover. Do this just before new spring growth comes in. Make sure your blades are sharp or they will tear up the leaves. Don't try this with spring-flowering ground covers—wait until after they bloom.

> *If Winter comes, can Spring be far behind?*
> —Percy Bysshe Shelley

The timing on this is tricky, but you might try it. In England, gardeners often start seed in inverted sod, cutting up the sod and planting it with the seedling. For me, getting a nice square of sod out of the ground at this point is unimaginable, but in certain climates it may well work. Certainly for plants sown later in the season it is an excellent option.

IF YOU JUST CAN'T WAIT • If you are chomping at the bit to get some seeds in the ground but the thermometer insists that it is too cold for such an enterprise, try using clear plastic to heat the ground and germinate seeds. You can heat the ground up by anchoring sheets of clear plastic with rocks or dirt. Wait until the soil temperature is about 50 degrees—at that point, a layer of clear plastic combined with sunshine can raise the temperature to 70 degrees. Lettuce is easily germinated this way. Plant it beneath the clear plastic in the warm soil. In 3 days—or when you see sprouting activity has taken place—remove the plastic. The seeds need warmer temperatures to germinate than the plant does to grow and thrive.

TIN-CAN BIRD DETERRENT • If birds pick at your seeds or pull up your seedlings for nesting material (sigh), string a clothesline of tin cans and the clatter will send the birds on their way. (You may also lose neighbors. Take down the tin can symphony once your first planting is established for use again with subsequent plantings.)

As an alternative, try laying down wet burlap over the patch and moisten it daily until the seeds germinate.

❦ F E B R U A R Y 2 8

There's no easy way to keep spinach from bolting, but it is important to get the spinach in as soon as the soil can be worked. (Not yet, cold zoners.) Thin your spinach as soon as the first true leaves appear, to prevent any delay in growth caused by overcrowding—thin plants about 3 inches apart. The faster spinach grows the better it will taste. As soon as the warm weather hits, the plant will turn to seed production. *Throw in some radish seeds when you're sowing spinach. Given the option, an insect will opt to munch on an radish leaf rather than a spinach leaf.*

RULE OF THUMB • Slope dictates the direction of your gardening rows more than compass orientation. Rows should be planted along a slope, not up and down it. Make sure tall plants don't shade shorter plants (unless you are purposely protecting them).

DESIGNING NEW BEDS AND BORDERS • Visualizing a new flower bed or border can be difficult. A common garden hose can be used to create a series of natural shapes for your flower bed. You might also use flour to trace a new border, or get a sense of spatial relationships. It's always best to move slowly and patiently in digging out new plots; the small, considered innovations tend to be more successful than the ambitious, sometimes lamentable overhaul.

Anyone beginning a journey on February 29 should be given a basket of forget-me-nots.

Index

Murphy's Oil Soap, for insect control, 261
Mushrooms, 272
Muskmelons, in small spaces, 346
Mustard, 126, 335, 368
Mustard greens, 9, 155
  preventing bolting, 77

N
Nana, meaning of, 224
Narcissus, 228, 362–63. *See also* Paper-whites
  poet's-eye, 223
Nardone, Angel, 287
Nasturtiums, 31, 34, 39, 114, 134, 365
  as companion plant for tomatoes, 73
  eating, 131
  insects and, 91
  origin and meaning of name, 50
  vining, 41
National Garden Bureau, 322
National Gardening Association, 268–69
Nematodes
  cover crops and, 192
  marigolds and, 142–43
  onions for repelling, 207
Newspaper mulch, 58
New Zealand spinach, 86
Nicotiana, 332, 364
Nighthawk, 114
Nitrogen, 14
  deficiency, 120–21
  plants that fix, 177, 337
  sources of, 28, 153
    dog fur, 31
    thunderstorms, 84
Nivalis (niveus), 110
Norman, Helen A., 142
Norris, Dale, 360
Norris, Kathleen, 375
Northeast, when to plant trees and shrubs in the,
  52
Norway spruce, 308
Notes, taking, 183
November, 264–90
Nurseries. *See also* Buying plants
  mail order, 377
  samples from, 221–22
Nutans, meaning of, 224
Nuthatch, 114

O
Oak, 138, 234, 279, 328
  varieties resistant to storms, 279
Oak leaves, 86
O'Connor, Lois, 126
October, 234–63
October plant, 222
Ogden, Shepherd, 342
Oils
  flavored, 137–38
  horticultural, 131
O'Keeffe, Georgia, 114
Okra, 2, 113, 363
  cooking tips, 218–19

lucky (recipe), 219
red, 346
sowing, 132
Old Farmer's Almanac, 24
Oliver's Nursery, 15
Onion maggots, 88, 313
Onions, 3, 86, 87, 155, 164, 196, 213, 237, 263,
    272, 329, 334, 343, 353, 365, 366, 369
  amount to plant for family of four, 351
  avoiding seed heads, 52
  as bird repellent, 33
  bulbs split into two or more sections, 185
  companion planting, 26, 73
  harvesting, 189
  hot, how to grow, 76
  as nematode repellent, 207
  ornamental, 147
  as rabbit repellent, 22, 89
  seeds, 259
  skins, as insect repellent, 71
  from sets or from seeds, 348
  soil preparation for, 259
  spring. *See* Scallions
  when to plant, 52
  worms in compost and, 73
Orange rinds, for sow bugs, 79
Orchids, 10
  origin and meaning of name, 50
Oregano, 125, 150, 215, 343, 348
Organic Gardening magazine, 363
Organic materials, mail order companies for, 290
Oriental poppy, 148, 332
Ornamental kale, 365
Ornamental peppers, 365
Ornamentals, edible, 346
Ornaments, concrete, 129
Osler, Mirabel, 88
Overfertilization of container plants, 133
Overwatering, 53
Oxeye daisy, 58

P
Painted daisy, 147
Palm, date, 366
Palustris, 110
Pansies, 11, 29, 114, 129, 227, 263, 332, 348,
    365
Paper towels
  in compost, 121–22
  sprouting seeds in, 364
Paper-whites, 308, 356, 362
  growing in containers, 296
Parsley, 3, 4, 47, 86, 125, 150, 154, 215, 229,
    262, 329, 334, 343
  as companion plant for tomatoes, 73
  growing indoors, 310
Parsnips, 3, 111, 196, 329, 331, 366
  largest, 316
Passover, bitter herbs of, 46
Pasteurizing compost, 171
Patens, meaning of, 224
Pathogenic insecticides, 65
Pathways. *See* Walkways
Patience, 11

Pole beans, 331, 353
Polk, James K., 36
Pollan, Michael, 86, 366
Poncirus trifoliata, 289
Poplar, 138
  balsam, 4
Poppy
  Alpine, 56
  plume, 344
Poppy mallow, 183, 222
Portulaca, 336, 364, 365
Potassium, 14
  deficiency, 120–21
Potatoes, 155, 157, 159, 187, 263, 272, 329, 331,
    353, 363, 369
  in black plastic trash bags, 153
  companion planting, 26
  in compost bins, 153–54
  cucumbers and, 83
  damaged, 225
  early, 86
  for French fries, 27
  harvesting, 192
    late, 203
  as incompatible with tomatoes, 73
Pot-marigolds, 52
Potpourri, 129–30, 301
  lavender for, 76
  for repelling bugs, 307
Pots. *See also* Clay pots; Containers
  of annuals and herbs as a cheating device,
    43
  experimenting with, 72
  as labor savers, 44
  for perennials, 29–30
  plastic
    for invasive herbs, 86
    washing out in dishwasher, 323
Potted plants. *See also* Container gardening
  bringing indoors, 215
Poultry manure, 15
Powdery mildew, 115, 163
Pratensis, 110
Praying mantises, 55
Premature growth, 20
Presprouting, 170–71
Pressing flowers, 126, 158
Pressure-treated wood, 8
Primrose, 32, 51, 148, 345, 347, 371
Privacy hedge, 337
Proteins, in vegetables, 186
Pruning, 354, 355. *See also* Cutting back
  dead or dying branches, 133
  deciduous hedges, 277
  flowering shrubs, 48
  roots, 233
  saving fruit tree prunings, 280
  in winter, 304
Pruning shears, 49
Pumila, meaning of, 224
Pumpkins, 3, 49–50, 58, 86, 159, 331, 343, 369
  bitter, 271
  in compost, 265
  insect control, 107
  jack-o-lanterns, 263

largest, 190–91
  planting in hills, 67
  protecting from insect damage, 213
Purple butterbur, 56
Purple coneflower, 147, 167–68
Purple loosestrife, 347
Purple rock cress, 348
Purslane, 38, 141–42
Pussy willows, 354, 372

Q
Quackgrass, 38, 126
Queen Anne's lace, 136
Quince, flowering, 323

R
Rabbits, 22
  deterring, 60, 89, 155, 292, 313
Raccoons, deterring, 95, 150, 311
Radicchio, grilled (recipe), 12
Radio, as raccoon deterrent, 95
Radishes, 3, 9, 47, 107, 154, 155, 181, 193, 331,
    343, 365, 368, 373
  amount to plant for family of four, 351
  in ancient Greece, 26
  largest, 33
Ragweed, 135, 347
Rain, 232
  on Easter Sunday, 15
  flowers before, 115, 117
  watering before, 196
Rainiest day in U.S. history, 162
Rain water
  for cut flowers, 120
  for insecticidal soap solution, 27
Raised beds, 26–27, 330
  pressure-treated wood not recommended for,
    8
Raking, 5
Rampion, 99
Rapunzel, 99
Raspberries
  black, 196
  red, 344
  storing, 185
Raver, Anne, 299
Recipes
  bean salad, savory, 160
  cold spinach with sesame and ginger, 96
  corn, Ginny's boiled, 176
  corn cakes any way you like them, 226
  dandelion country salad, warm, 80–81
  eggplant with herbed goat cheese, grilled, 194
  garlic croutons, 256
  garlic dressing, simple, 160
  green tomatoes, fried, 232
  hot pepper cornbread, 273
  lucky okra, 219
  pesto, 209
  radicchio, grilled, 11
  rhubarb crisp, 45
  salad of green beans, fennel, and oil-cured
    olives, 161

402

To order any of the
365 Ways Cookbooks

visit you local bookseller or call 1-800-331-3761

Our bestselling 365 Ways Cookbooks are wire-bound to lie flat and have colorful, wipe-clean covers.

Each 365 Ways Cookbook is $17.96 plus $3.50 per copy shipping and handling. Applicable sales tax will be billed to your account. No CODs. Please allow 4–6 weeks for delivery.

> Please have your VISA, MASTERCARD, OR AMERICAN EXPRESS card at hand when calling.

◆ 365 ◆

Days of Gardening 0-06-017032-8
Easy Italian Recipes 0-06-01630-0
Easy Low-Calorie Recipes 0-06-016309-7
Easy Mexican Recipes 0-06-016963-X
Easy One-Dish Meals 0-06-016311-9
Great Barbecue & Grilling Recipes 0-06-016224-4
Great Chocolate Desserts 0-06-016537-5
Great Cookies and Brownies 0-06-016840-4
One-Minute Golf Lessons 0-06-017087-5
Quick & Easy Microwave Recipes 0-06-016026-8
Snacks, Hors D'Oeuvres & Appetizers 0-06-016536-7
Ways to Cook Chicken 0-06-015539-6
Ways to Cook Fish and Shellfish 0-06-016841-2
Ways to Cook Hamburger & Other Ground Meats 0-06-016535-9
Ways to Cook Chinese 0-06-016961-3
Ways to Cook Pasta 0-06-015865-4
Ways to Cook Vegetarian 0-06-016958-3
Ways to Prepare for Christmas 0-06-017048-4
Ways to Wok 0-06-016643-6

FORTHCOMING TITLES

Great Cakes & Pies 0-06-016959-1
Great 20-Minute Recipes 0-06-016962-1
Soups and Stews 0-06-016960-5
Low-Fat Recipes 0-06-017137-5
Ways to Cook Eggs 0-06-017138-3
More Ways to Cook Chicken 0-06-017139-1
All-American Favorites 0-06-017294-0
Main-Dish Salads 0-06-017293-2
Jewish Recipes 0-06-017295-9
Asian Recipes 0-06-017292-4